BASS HEROES

STYLES, STORIES & SECRETS OF 30 GREAT BASS PLAYERS

FROM
THE PAGES
OF
Guitar Player Magazine

EDITED
BY
TOM MULHERN

Backbeat
Books
San Francisco

TO THE VISIONARIES WHO INTRODUCED
THE BASS TO ELECTRICITY:
LLOYD LOAR, GEORGE BEAUCHAMP,
EVERETT HULL, OLIVER JESPERSON,
AND LEO FENDER.

Published by Backbeat Books
600 Harrison Street, San Francisco, CA 94107
www.backbeatbooks.com
E-mail: books@musicplayer.com
An Imprint of the Music Player Network
United Entertainment Media, Inc.

Library of Congress Cataloging-in-Publication Data

Bass heroes : styles, stories & secrets of 30 great bass players :
    from the pages of Guitar player magazine / edited by Tom Mulhern
        p. cm.
    Discography: p.
    Includes index.
    ISBN 0-87930-274-7
    1. Bass guitarists—Interviews. I. Mulhern, Tom, 1955–
II. Guitar player
ML399.B39   1993
787.87'092'2—dc20   92-45801

Designers:
Paul Haggard, Cover
Christian Ledgerwood, Interior

Production Editor: Linda Jupiter

Cover photos: (clockwise, left to right)
Billy Sheehan © Paul Natkin/Photo Reserve Inc.
Jaco Pastorius © Tom Copi/San Francisco
Stanley Clarke © Jay Blakesberg

Printed in the United States of America

03 04 05 06   9 8 7 6

— CONTENTS —

— INTRODUCTION —

SINCE ITS FOUNDING IN 1967, *GUITAR PLAYER* magazine has been the center of the publishing universe, at least as far as many guitarists are concerned. Each issue has included something for players of all levels, musicians of all styles. And inside just about every issue has been something for bass players. Hundreds of interviews, how-to articles, tips, and even monthly columns — just for bassists — have appeared in *Guitar Player,* making the magazine a vital rallying point for the musicians who plunked, thunked, slapped, popped, and thundered an octave below the guitar.

When *Guitar Player* was founded, the electric bass guitar was only about 15 years old, and its pioneers were often glad to speak through the magazine to their peers about technique, about the instrument's role in rock, jazz, and other styles, and about their perspective on music, equipment, and what they believed the future held. As time passed, *Guitar Player* covered most of the leading bass players, providing an unequaled wealth of material for the bassist. From Motown and the British Invasion to progressive rock, fusion, and jazz, bassists from all musical walks were given a worldwide forum.

Choosing among the many, many bassists covered in *Guitar Player* and eventually settling upon 30 wasn't easy. The level of musicianship, the contribution to the instrument, and the influence upon bassists past, present, and future were all taken into account. It was no mean feat to narrow the field, but it had to be done.

Despite some hard choices, I don't think you'll find a better collection of articles on the players who defined the electric bass — some famous, others unsung, but all important. Through the profiles of these incredible musicians, one gains insight into the instrument's technique and development, its heart and soul. Sadly, some of these great musicians, such as Monk Montgomery, James Jamerson, and Jaco Pastorius, are no longer with us. To them, as well as all the others who continue to inspire us and shape this still-young instrument, we owe a collective thanks.

— Tom Mulhern

– JAZZ –

– STANLEY CLARKE –

BY TOM MULHERN – MAY 1980

EBET ROBERTS

WHENEVER A friend sneaks up behind you, puts both hands over your eyes and says, "Guess who?" you will likely have an immediate (and often correct) response identifying them. In most cases, it's not too hard: The voice, the inflections, and even the pronunciation of certain words can give the person away. The same speedy recognition of Stanley Clarke's distinctive, crisp-sounding bass comes from the clues that can only point to his style: The phrasing, the popping, and the lightning-fast runs are a dead give-away. His approach is at once aggressive and deft; the hard-charging 6'4" bassist's seemingly effortless movements belie just how much he is actually doing, and what you hear is the highly refined combination of classical, jazz, rock, and jazz-rock styles that has made him famous not only as a prominent soloist, but also as a precision sideman and band member, as well.

Stanley has won an incredible number of awards for a 29-year-old musician; since 1973 he and the group that he is most readily identified with, Return To Forever, have reaped dozens of them. Stanley's kudos include Best Bass Guitarist in *Guitar Player*'s Annual Readership Poll for the past five years. In addition, *Down Beat*, *Playboy*, *Jazz Forum*, *Billboard*, *Rolling Stone*, *Record World*, and *Melody Maker* magazines have all chosen Stanley as the best in his field, either by critical mandate or at the behest of their readers. Return To Forever has consistently been praised by many of the same polls, has been at the fore-front of jazz-rock for the past eight years, and in 1974 received a Grammy for the Best Jazz Performance By A Group for their album *No Mystery*; Stanley himself has released six solo albums, including his immensely popular *School Days* (1976), and his *Modern Man* was nominated for a Grammy (Best R&B Instrumental Performance) in 1978. His flight to the top of the jazz and jazz-rock idioms has not been simply the result of good songs or mere virtuosity Hard work and diligent study prepared him, groomed him, and pointed him in the direction of stardom in his field.

The middle child of Marvin and Blanche Clarke, Stanley was born in North Philadelphia on June 30, 1951. He grew up there with his older sister, his younger brother, his father (a machinist), and his mother, whose opera singing first stirred the young boy's interest in music. Before Stanley reached his teens, he had tried playing accordion, violin, cello, and finally string bass. He joined the All-Philadelphia Senior High School Orchestra, picked up electric bass, and attended Philadelphia Musical Academy.

In the middle of his fourth year in college, he abandoned his original plans to become a symphonic bassist and instead embarked on a trip to New York to find work as a jazz musician. Clarke made a name for himself in New York's studios almost immediately after moving there in 1970. And although much of his recorded work was for advertisements on TV and radio, he also worked as a sideman for such notable jazz pillars as tenor saxophonists Stan Getz and Dexter Gordon, drummers Art Blakey and Mel Lewis, pianists Horace Silver and Gil Evans, and trumpeter Thad Jones, as well as many others in the city's clubs. His electric and acoustic bass work on Gato Barbieri's *Under Fire* album, Pharoah Sanders' *Black Unity*, Joe Farrell's *Moon Germs,* and Flora Purim's *Butterfly Dreams* helped to further cement his association with the jazz community. Stanley was also showing his versatility by playing on jazz-rock and pop sessions with such artists as composer/pianist Eumir Deodato (on his *2001* album) and Aretha Franklin (*Let Me In Your Life*).

In 1971, while playing in his hometown of Philadelphia with saxophonist Joe Henderson, Stanley met pianist Chick Corea. The pair had worked together previously with Stan Getz, and decided to form a band which ultimately was called Return To Forever. This first incarnation included saxophonist Joe Farrell, percussionist Airto Moreira, and singer Flora Purim. Their first album, *Return To Forever,* was released in Europe and Japan in 1972, and was only available in the U.S. on import until several years later.

A second album, *Light As A Feather,* was recorded in late '72, released in '73, and distributed worldwide, but by then the group had broken up. (A second, short-lived band consisted of Stanley, Chick, guitarist Bill Connors, and drummers Steve Gadd and Mingo Lewis.) Also in late 1972, Stanley recorded his first solo album, *Children Of Forever.* On this disc were five songs; all except one were penned by Stanley (Chick Corea wrote the remaining tune), and all but one were played on string bass. Although it wasn't the landmark that 1974's *Stanley Clarke* was, it did assemble the nucleus of the next Return To Forever: Stanley, Chick, and drummer Lenny White. Pat Martino played electric guitar on the album, and Dee Dee Bridgewater added vocals.

Reforming in 1973 — this time as a quartet — Return To Forever included Bill Connors, who remained with the group just long enough to play on *Hymn Of The Seventh Galaxy* and one tour. The sound of the band began to evolve more toward electric than acoustic, although it wasn't until Al Di Meola replaced Connors in July 1974 that the band got into full electric swing, increasing the pace of many tunes and adding maniacally tight unison and harmony runs played by Al, Chick, and Stanley.

And while the group gained ever-increasing notoriety as a single unit, each member ventured forth to record solo efforts, often with success rivaling that of Return To Forever's. Stanley's *Journey To Love,* released in 1975, and *School Days* were monstrous hits. Appearing on *Journey To Love* (and, in 1978, *Modern Man*) was Jeff Beck, with whom Clarke toured Japan and Europe in late 1978. The bassist also branched into producing records by other artists: guitarist Roy Buchanan's *Loading Zone* in 1977, and Dee Dee Bridgewater's *Just Family* in 1978.

Clarke has also played on fellow Return To Forever members' solo works: Al Di Meola's *Land Of The Midnight Sun* and Chick Corea's *My Spanish Heart.* With Return To Forever, Stanley has composed for and played on *Where Have I Known You Before, The Romantic Warrior, Musicmagic,* and *Return To Forever Live* (which was released as both a single album condensation and a five-record set), while managing a healthy career as a solo artist. After completion of his double-record *I Wanna Play For You* (a 50-50 mixture of studio and live cuts) in 1979, Stanley Clarke joined forces with Rolling Stones guitarists Ron Wood and Keith Richards for a tour, billed as the New Barbarians. Currently, Stanley is putting the finishing touches on a new record, his seventh solo disc, entitled *Rocks, Pebbles And Sand,* which was released on Epic Records in May 1980.

From listening to your mother sing, were you turned on to opera, or simply music in general?

I'd say music in general. See, opera is a funny thing: I used to ask my mother what she was saying. To this day, I don't know what the hell they're talking about. Even if it's in English, I don't understand it.

You played an accordion for a while.

Oh, yeah, when I was about 10. I was really embarrassed. The first formal music lessons I had were on accordion. And it was just so weird! I didn't look right with the instrument. And the teacher was very strange: I think he was just teaching me for the money. He was like the guy down at the end of the block that made his living by having all the kids come over and charging them two bucks an hour. And a lot of times you'd be in the middle of playing a phrase and he'd say, "Okay, that's it," and shuffle you out — a real cattle type of thing. The one thing I did learn from the guy was to read some music. In all, I played accordion for about a year. I was playing a student model, but I actually got pretty good. And that inspired me with keyboard-type concepts — I just got my fingers to move really fast. I'd always noticed that my fingers were very loose and I could move them quickly with a lot of control.

What was the next instrument you played?

Violin was the first instrument that I started playing in school. I sort of liked the idea of playing violin, but it was really tiny. Mine had to be no bigger than *that* [*holds hands several inches apart*]. That thing was really little, and I always had big fingers, so I just couldn't finger the thing right.

How old were you then?

About 12. And man, I was tall at 12. It was like seeing Kareem Abdul-Jabbar playing a piccolo trumpet — it just didn't fit. I had a great teacher named Mr. Birch, who was *really* good. He was so good that when I said, "Look, man, this violin stuff is really not good for me," he said, "Well, we'll go one more up." So he gave me a cello. That wasn't happening, either, and then after about two months with that I went to the acoustic bass. I loved the sound of the cello, but the one that I had in school was simply too small. String bass was the perfect size for me — tall — so I got it. I remember my first remark about it was, "Well, the sound is a little rough, but what the hell, I guess I'll be able to work with it." I was always a melody-minded person, but I just had to find the instrument that fit best with the size of my body.

Did you play with a bow or did you pluck the strings?

I started right away using the bow. I studied from the first Simandl book [*New Method For The Double Bass*, Carl Fischer Pub.] up until the middle of high school. Then I completed the second book, and went on to the series written by Billé [*New Method For Double Bass*, Ricordi (dist. by Belwin-Mills)]. The Billé books were so hard. They really busted my chops. By the time I reached 12th grade I had gotten to the advanced stuff — the theory, thumb positions, and all that stuff. Boy, it was *very* hard. But I was real serious. I just locked myself up and practiced. It was almost sickening. It's paid off, but when I look back, I think, "Jesus Christ, how could I be that serious about something?" I don't think I take anything *that* seriously now. I was really heavy-duty, eight-hours-a-day, bleeding fingers. I also had a couple of friends like that, too. Those guys now play in symphonies. At the time that was my goal, too. I was going to join the Philadelphia Orchestra. As a matter of fact, I was going to audition for the orchestra when I met Chick Corea. I needed some money, and

"I was always a melody-minded person, but I just had to find the instrument that fit best with the size of my body."

he said, "Come on, I've got a gig," and I decided to skip the audition.

Did you have your own string bass?

When I was in high school, I used to take the bass home to practice. I started out on a half-size bass, moved to three-quarters, and then finally a five-eighths. Now I'm looking for a full-size bass.

Were you taught to use your index, middle, and little fingers (1, 2, and 4), or your index, middle, and ring fingers (1, 2, and 3) on your left hand?

I was discussing that with a bass player recently, and he was taught to use all four fingers — 1, 2, 3, 4. I was taught like 1, 2, and 4. I never used the 3rd finger down in the lower position. But as soon as I got to about the halfway point on the neck, then I used my 3rd.

Do you play the same way on your electric?

On electric, it's a totally different thing: I use every finger, even my thumbs — you know, *anything!* Now, when I was studying the Billé books, they said to use the 3rd finger. But my teacher used to always dot out that marking for the 3rd finger and write in a "4" — that was his way of doing it.

While you were practicing eight hours a day on your string bass, were you able to play in bands?

Yeah. When I was about 14, I started playing in these really, *really* avant-garde jazz bands. I mean we weren't even playing what I call music; we were just playing — like *noise* stuff. We were doing music by really strange composers, like John Cage. This was basically because we were just a bunch of guys playing orchestral instruments who also wanted to play some music that wasn't written by other people. We wanted to try playing some of our own. I had this real rich friend, a drummer, whose mother just spent all her money on his trip of being a musician. She bought him organs, drum sets, basses, guitars, saxophones, trumpets, rooms full of this, rooms full of that. We'd all just go over to his house, take our drugs, and go for it. Oh yeah, I was really a weirdo.

What kind of reaction did your parents have towards your music?

Oh, they thought I was nuts! They thought we were all from another planet. But when I was about 16, I started realizing that I had to make some money. So I tried working in a shoe store and working in a grocery store, and working here and working there. None of that stuff really felt great, so I figured,

"Well, maybe I can make some money by playing." So I got hold of a Kent hollowbody electric bass.

How was it?

Well, it was one of their $29 specials. And I didn't even have the case — I used to put it in a bag. I then started playing in a blues band. We did all Chuck Berry tunes, Freddy Stone things, Lightnin' Hopkins — everything. I actually loved that, and I had a good time. We made a lot of money playing dances and parties, in parks, for this opening and that opening. Later I was in Top 40 bands. Then I played in club-date bands, doing songs like "I Left My Heart In San Francisco." We played all the Holiday Inns. I was even in a few country and western bands. I can really play good country and western bass.

What kind of amp did you use with your Kent bass?

I had a homemade tube amp, built by a friend of mine. As a matter of fact, before going anywhere I had to take all the tubes out, put them in a bag, and then take the main meaty part of the head and stick that in a little gym bag. I also had a small cabinet with no back on it and a single 15" speaker. And did it distort.

When you first started playing electric, did you employ a lot of string bass techniques?

At first I did, but it wasn't long before I started playing it more like a guitar, because it looked like a guitar to me. I was holding it this way [*horizontally*], and I thought, "Wow, this is a guitar — well, it's a *bass* guitar, but I'll play it like a guitar." So I studied it for about six months — I spent a lot of time practicing with guitar books and everything.

Did you start to emulate any electric bass players?

Not really. Around '67 I first heard Jimi Hendrix, and by then I'd heard a lot of rock and roll, and it was great. I listened to all the stuff, and I remember listening to Jack Bruce on something that I liked. But for some reason, I was always more into *concepts* than individual players — at least until later. Kids, I believe, are more into concepts: the *whole* thing. And I remember hearing this Hendrix stuff, and I went to see him play somewhere in Philadelphia. And although Noel Redding wasn't the greatest bass player in the world, what he did in that band — maybe it was just because of Hendrix' parts — was great. It was different from what everyone else was doing, and I thought, "Yeah, that's something!" Later on I heard him in other bands, and it was terrible. But with Hendrix he was perfect; that whole unit was perfect. I loved that. And just the fact that anyone could play a guitar as well as Jimi impressed me. I

could hear a few influences in his style. I don't know whether a lot of people are that sensitive, but you could hear where he went over to England and heard people like Jeff Beck and Eric Clapton, and maybe took a few little things and put his own thing in there; his concept was definitely from somewhere else — I don't know where, but it was.

What other kinds of music did you listen to?

Well, I was like a Dr. Jekyll/Mr. Hyde. On the one hand, I'd listen to Hendrix; then I expanded and got into other groups that were trying to do something similar to that. And on the other hand, I listened to heavy classical music. I bought all the records. Wagner is one of my favorites, and I bought all kinds of Bach and Beethoven. Along with that I sort of eased the jazz stuff in between. So there were really three categories of music I was heavily into.

Were there any string bassists that you followed?

Yes. Some of my favorites were people like Paul Chambers, Scott LaFaro, and definitely Charlie Mingus. They were all into hard-core, serious, heavy-duty jazz. The thing that I liked about jazz players was that they were so technically proficient, and at the same time were able to improvise. I just found them to be highly creative. Now, the thing I liked about classical composers was that they actually wrote out all the music. I mean, to this day, Bach's music is still a bitch to play. He was smoking! These classical guys were killers. The things I liked about rock and roll players was what they were saying in their music and their concepts — the way they would present the ideas. Each category of music had its own quality that I liked, and I think it still holds true to this day. But nowadays, you have guys crossing over, and it's hard to sort out the forms.

During your exposure to the various forms of music, did you keep playing your Kent bass?

Well, I used it until I got a Gibson EB-2, a hollow-body, in 11th or 12th grade. It was the *worst* bass they ever made, but it worked for me and I loved the feeling of it. But if I wanted to turn it up to get some dB's out of it, forget it. Feedback.

Did your homemade amp finally burn out?

Man, yeah! I used to have this reputation in Philadelphia for being the loudest bass player in the world. I used to have this problem: Every time I'd borrow an amp from somebody, I'd blow it up. And to this day, there are guys that still talk about it in Philadelphia. I used to borrow Sunn amps and even blow them up. I mean, I went nuts!

So you'd play the gig just so you could afford to pay for the amp you blew up.

Sure. So in 12th grade I finally bought an amp that would hold up — a Univox with the big bass bins. God, they were terrible! Horrible! I'll never forget them, though. Those were the good old days.

Wasn't that a lot of equipment to lug around for club dates?

Yeah. But our guitarist, Steve Sikes, had a hearse. So we carried everything around in that.

Were you still playing string bass as well as electric?

Oh, yeah. Everything was going on at the same time. Plus I was in the All-Philadelphia Senior High Orchestra. Every Tuesday night there would be this rehearsal with all of the best players in Philadelphia. We'd play in a concert maybe twice a year. That's where I met my wife — she's a bass player, too.

Did you ever experience times when you would delve strictly into one style and ignore the rest?

There was a period in my late teens where I didn't get into any rock and roll at all. I even put my electric bass away because I thought that it was inferior. I got into a weird head trip — and I didn't know what was happening. To put it simply, I was just not myself. It was a period when a lot of the kids were protesting, so I protested everything! Nothing was happening — music was terrible. So I just played sort of heavy jazz and real progressive stuff for about a year or two. Then I got bored with it. There's just no warmth in that stuff, so I left it.

Did you study music or bass after high school?

Yes. I went to the Philadelphia Music Academy from 1969 till about the middle of '72. I majored in string bass, composition, and life [*laughs*]. I found that I learned a lot of good things at that school. One course that was very helpful was ear training.

Why did you quit in your fourth year?

During my last year I had been hanging around with people who had graduated the year before, and they had no jobs. All of a sudden I realized that a diploma really didn't matter unless you were going to pursue your career the way someone else would have it set up for you. For instance, if I graduated and went to the nearest elementary school and applied for a music teacher's job, it would have been perfect. But to try to become a better musician or be able to play music in front of people just because I had a diploma? You know, all the diplomas in the world aren't

"The thing that I liked about jazz players was that they were so technically proficient, and at the same time were able to improvise."

going to give you that. If I had stayed there, I'd still be there now. I would probably be either dead from the boredom or just wasted someplace. If I had to look back on my life, I'd say that the choice to leave Philadelphia was one of the major decisions that was absolutely correct.

Did it scare you at the time?

Oh yeah, because I went to New York with nothing — just the electric bass and some clothes. I first played there with [jazz pianist] Horace Silver. I went there in 1970 and lived with a friend on the Lower East Side.

Since you were basically an instrumentalist, did you find sight-reading exercises awkward?

Actually, it didn't matter to me; I always prided myself in trying to step ahead of my teachers. So, if they would say, "Do this," I'd have it together. I always had a pretty good ear.

While you were at the Philadelphia Music Academy, were you in any bands?

We had a jazz band and a small jazz ensemble. We also had an orchestra, a contemporary music ensemble, and a chamber group. And at various times I was in all the groups. We had a great jazz band that used to play at intercollegiate festivals; this gave us a chance to be judged by the stars. It's very funny — I remember going to those things and being judged by some of the guys that I know now, or have played with. Our band was kind of an outcast group. All the other bands would come in playing Duke Ellington and Count Basie, and we came in one year doing music from the Beatles' *Abbey Road*. We made a big band arrangement out of it and added electronic music — pre-recorded tapes, weird electronic sounds — and we played the tunes much as they had appeared on the record, except in a jazz style. I switched between electric and upright. You know, we were weird.

After you left the Academy for New York, did you continue playing string bass?

Well, the first time I went, I took only my electric — my Gibson EB-2. I got some work and then came back and got my upright. I had to borrow an amp, though. I found work very quickly. I just used the telephone. I couldn't afford to join the musician's union right away, though. I was just playing little jazz clubs and doing that sort of stuff. There was a lot happening in New York then. It was at the tail end of when the jazz scene was dying there. It's not really happening there anymore, but it was nice for me to actually see it. It seems like 70% of the players moved out to California: they're richer, more laid-back. I mean, back then you could see Herbie Hancock walk into a little coffeehouse, sit down and play, and be really aggressive. Those guys were poor; they were really struggling. Almost all the guys that you see in jazz today were back in New York years ago, and it was great.

Do you think that you took a lot more chances or played a little more outside in those days?

I can't really say it was that different — it was more *chancy*, but I think it was because it had a different flavor to it. When guys are hungry and striving to develop themselves and survive, they play a certain way. A musician who's 20 or 21 years old plays a certain way, and then when he gets to be 25, 28, or 30, he changes; it's natural. You just can't keep playing the same way. You have to change. And sometimes you get better. I went to see Herbie Hancock recently, and he was playing real soft stuff, and I dug it, because he's about 40 and laid-back, playing his tunes and smiling. I got a kick out of it. He went through it; he paid his dues.

Besides playing in clubs, what else did you do back then?

For a period of about eight or ten months I was doing some heavy studio work. I was playing three sessions a day — records, TV commercials, anything. I did commercials for Armour Sausage and Campbell's Soup. I did an airline commercial, too. I also did a great perfume ad with Herbie Hancock once, where I played just one note — F#. And I got called for the session at 10 o'clock in the morning. I'll never forget it. I sat around for just one note. I did loads of albums, too, that varied from doing an Aretha Franklin session to going and playing with Archie Shepp, and from Carlos Santana to Thelonious Monk.

Did any of the composers have specific lines written out for you?

No. They usually just gave me charts. I sort of had a little bit of a reputation: I was the young, fresh bass player on the scene, so a lot of times they would just give me a concept and say, "Do this." At that age, you've got a lot of ideas in your head, and they just come out every now and then — whenever someone gives you a little chance. I could go in on practically any record date, and I wouldn't even have to hear or see the music to know what was expected. I would give it to them and they were satisfied. One of the keys to being a really good studio musician is know-

ing what the game is one minute into the session. I've found that guys who don't have success in studios go in with either preconceived ideas or no ideas — either way is bad. Say that a guy goes in and says, "I don't like to play *this* because it feels contrived." Big shit! Who cares? Or someone will go into a session with someone like Paul McCartney, thinking he's going to play Beatles tunes, and finds out that McCartney wants to do polkas or something. Then what does he do? I remember one of the nicest things I did was on an Aretha Franklin album called *Let Me In Your Life*. It was slightly different from what I had been doing; it was really, really nice. Also, a song I just keep hearing on the radio came from a recording session in 1972 with a Brazilian guy named Eumir Deodato. It was a song called "2001" [Also "Sprach Zarathustra"], and for the session we had two bass players — myself and Ron Carter. He was playing upright bass and I was playing electric.

Did you expect it to be so successful?

No. With the Aretha Franklin record, and Carlos Santana record [*Borboletta*], and Donny Hathaway records — those types of things — I knew the songs would do well. You'd hear them. Great! Big deal! But with this song I had no idea. And we had recorded it early in the morning, so I was real tired, and I hated the session.

How did you come to work with Stan Getz and Art Blakey?

I played with Stan through Chick Corea. Chick was working with him and knew that he needed a bass player, so he called me. I was available at the time, so I traveled with him for about a year. It was a lot of fun. Stan is kind of an international jazz star, so he was treated very well, and therefore I was treated really well. I was scared to death of Art Blakey. God! He worked in the roughest jazz joints — guys shooting and killing and doing drugs.

How did your gig with Thad Jones and Mel Lewis come about?

I would sometimes substitute for Richard Davis on Monday nights, and go into the Village Vanguard playing with Jones and Lewis.

Davis said that other musicians accused him of selling out when he started to play electric bass after years of acoustic work. Did you encounter the same problem?

It was especially bad for him because he was an older guy. I used to get it, too, but I handled it really well. I mean, I was a younger cat, and the electric bass was part of my era. It's like a guy putting you down because you drive a Porsche instead of a Model T.

What are you going to do, man? Stop the world or something?

How did the permanent lineup of Return To Forever come about?

In 1971 I was with the Joe Henderson Quartet and I met Lenny White, Return To Forever's drummer. I only stayed with Joe for a little bit. I knew Chick Corea here and there through Joe Henderson and other people. He had just left Miles Davis and had this idea of putting a band together. So we played a few gigs together in New York, and it developed and blossomed into this whole trip — and a lot of years went by.

What kind of equipment did you have in the early days of Return To Forever?

I was still using my EB-2 and an Acoustic 136 amp with one 15 in it.

Did you use your string bass on live dates?

Sometimes. I amplified it with a microphone and a Polytone pickup. I eventually got a bigger amp — an Acoustic 140 with two dual-15" speaker cabinets.

Was the transition from upright to electric difficult?

Not really. Many acoustic bass players like playing electric, but just can't seem to make the change. I think it really lies in how you view the two instruments conceptually. You have to look at them as two totally *different* instruments. There's no way around it: You cannot play the electric bass and think in terms of an acoustic.

Do you consciously try to keep your left-hand thumb across from your second finger as you were taught on string bass?

When I was still studying acoustic bass, I used to. I think that if I grab a bass naturally, my hand is going to do that automatically because I was taught that way. And actually, it's a good habit to get into at the beginning. But sometimes I'll play a three-note chord, and use my thumb for the bass note and two other fingers to hold the notes of the chord. This works well with 7th chords — an *E*, a *D*, and a *G#*, for instance. I've had some teachers practically say that it's criminal to put your thumb over the back of the neck. It doesn't matter to me, as long as it works.

By the time you did Where Have I Known You Before, *you were playing string bass only a small part of the time.*

That's when I started becoming a serious electric bass player. I said, "Wait a minute — I think there's something to this instrument." And that's also when I

got turned on to the Alembic bass. I met Rick Turner [Alembic's co-founder and former president] when we were playing at the Boarding House in San Francisco, and in a nice way he told me, "Look, you really play well, but your sound is atrocious." He told me to try the bass he had with him; I think it was one of the first Alembic basses. So I tried it out and it was great. And I haven't changed since.

How much did the bass cost?

Oh, it was about $1,200. But by that time I was making a little bit of money, so the burden wasn't too bad. It was more of a *culture shock*, I think, because I was used to paying $400 for a bass. I looked at it, and I could see the workmanship. It had gold-plated hardware, a curly maple neck, great design, fancy pickups, and a fancy cord. I didn't know what any of it meant, but it sounded *the end*. And that night on the gig, it was like a new bass player had been born. I could suddenly play anything that I heard in my head. The problem with the Gibson bass was that I'd hear things and try to play them and my fingers would go along, but the right sound wouldn't come out. For instance, I'd want to sustain something, and it just went *thump*. The instrument simply wasn't allowing me to play, so the Alembic bass let me really play it.

Compared to later RTF albums, the second one, Light As A Feather, *wasn't too aggressive.*

It was very laid-back. It had a lot to do with the musicians in the band. There was myself, Chick, and Airto Moreira, who's not a real high-powered drummer. And we didn't have a guitar player; we had a singer, Flora Purim, and we played so that she could be heard. We did numerous tours in Europe, but we hadn't toured anywhere in the States. Europe was the only place where people would come out and hear us.

How well did Light As A Feather *sell?*

It did best in Japan — gold and platinum albums. It was very strange. It didn't do well anywhere but Japan. I still don't understand why to this day. All I remember is that when we walked off the plane in Japan, there were thousands of people waiting for us, as if we were the Beatles or something.

For the next album, Hymn Of The Seventh Galaxy, *you had Bill Connors on guitar, and the music was radically different. How did you find him?*

We were playing in San Francisco at the Keystone Korner club, and these two guitar players wanted to sit in. It really didn't matter to us — we were having a good time, and the band was really tight. So they

"You just can't keep playing the same way. You have to change."

set up on opposite sides of the stage. One of them was Billy, and he sounded so good with us that we asked him to join the band. We were getting rid of our trumpet player, so I said, "Let's get a guitarist." When Billy joined, we got bigger amps.

How long did Connors stay with Return To Forever?

Just the one album, *Hymn Of The Seventh Galaxy*. Billy also played on the *Stanley Clarke* album later. He was a great player, man. When you talk to guitar players that sort of followed the jazz-rock movement, a lot of the guys mention John McLaughlin first, and usually the second guy is Billy Connors. He wasn't really technical, but he could play the music, and he had enough technique to play the solos with a lot of feeling. He was so good. He had a great sound.

Did Al Di Meola join immediately, after Connors left?

Right away. He auditioned through a cassette tape. Some guy kept bugging Chick: "You gotta hear this guy named Al Di Meola." So Chick listened and said, "Yeah, he sounds good." So he played the tape for me and Lenny White. I didn't actually like Al in the very beginning — in fact, I thought he was terrible, and I didn't really start to like him until later, after we had played together for a while. Then I really started digging him. He's such a stylist. When his music comes on, you know it's his stuff. You either love it or hate it, but you know it's him. I have a lot of respect for people that are able to separate themselves from everyone else. And with a lot of great guitarists — Hendrix, Beck, Page, Clapton — you can hear the influences. But with Al, I don't know who his influences are!

Did you find yourself playing differently with him than with Bill Connors?

Well, Return To Forever's rhythm section was so strong that I think the guitarists that came through the band were shaped mainly by what we were into. For example, when Al Di Meola came into the band, he played nothing like he does now. He sounded like all those other guys. And from playing with us, and especially by playing Chick's music, his approach was gradually reshaped. We really had a hell of a rhythm section. It *had* to be to play that stuff. Our music was not easy.

Were all your parts written out?

All of it. The great thing about that band, and the thing that I think had the greatest hand in shaping me as a musician, was that the music was so damned hard. Even I was writing things that I couldn't play.

Return To Forever was a composer's dream. It was as if we had made this agreement that we would write whatever we wanted — we didn't give a shit what anybody said. If they play our records, great; if they don't play them, great. Fortunately, we had a lot of success with that band, which made it that much better. So we became very proud of what we were doing. On the last album that we did with that lineup, *The Romantic Warrior*, every note on there, except a few solos, was written. I still look at those scores sometimes because they're so beautiful. They're masterpieces! There's one tune that I wrote called "The Magician," which I still can just barely play. It's so difficult.

Did you use your Alembic bass on No Mystery?

Yeah, but I think it was recorded better on *Where Have I Known You Before*. I'm not sure what happened, but I remember nobody in the band liked the sound on *No Mystery*. Lenny hated it. Al hated it. There was something about the album that we simply didn't dig. But do you know what happened? We all won Grammys for it. And I listen to the album now, and it's not bad.

Your first solo album on Nemperor Records, Stanley Clarke, had a totally different feel to it than your subsequent works.

I was in a funny sort of position then. I was under a lot of pressure — it was what I considered my first solo album. I did the one before that [*Children Of Forever*], but I didn't really consider it mine — it was more the record company's and Chick's. I hated the cover, and I had no control over anything on it. So I was nervous about that first Nemperor album. It had good people on it [Bill Connors, drummer Tony Williams, and keyboardist Jan Hammer], and it was fresh. I know that when people heard it, they thought it was very fresh: They were talking about the album. On the second side, there's the "Life Suite" and "Spanish Phases For Strings & Bass" — just acoustic bass and strings. A lot of my peers listened to that and went, "Whew!" Guys started talking to me differently.

That was a difficult album to find when it first came out.

When I signed to Nemperor, they were distributed by Atlantic, who must have said, "Well, here's a bass player with an album." They would only print 3,000 copies — just 3,000 copies, man, and they had orders for over 150,000. They couldn't believe it! I remember walking around Atlantic Records, and they were all asking, "Who's this bass player? This guy's selling albums, and we don't understand it!" Then it finally clicked: None of these guys had ever heard of me — none of them knew that I'd been touring for over four years prior to that, and had been around the world 10 times. They just didn't know; they didn't do their homework.

What electric basses did you use on that album?

Just the Alembic. The Gibson was long gone. I quit using it after *Hymn Of The Seventh Galaxy*. I still have it — no head, but I have the body. I was drunk one night and put it in the car with the head sticking out, and crunch! Luckily, I had my Alembic then. When I first got it, I was using both basses — kind of growing out of one and growing into the other. With the Gibson broken, I was forced to use the Alembic, which was great.

On Journey To Love, *it seems as if you took a lot more chances and began to lean more toward the kind of sound you've had in the last few years.*

I was starting to get more energetic. And I tried to achieve a flow from song to song. See, the first album didn't have an underlying concept at all; it was just songs. I do that a lot of times. Even on the later albums I've done that. My usual approach is to write a song, get it together, and record it — boom. Next song. But every now and then I make one in which I take into consideration the *whole* album. My new album is like that — totally opposite from *I Wanna Play For You*, which is laid out like: There's this type of song and there's that type of song. It's very dispersed. But this new album has a lot more cohesiveness, like *Journey To Love* and *School Days*.

What were your biggest-selling albums?

School Days and *Journey To Love* were my two most popular, and later my bread-and-butter albums.

On Journey To Love, *you have a monstrous tone, but it's as clear as a bell. How did you do that?*

That has a lot to do with the Alembic bass I had just gotten. All the electronics were new — everything was brand-new. And the great thing about the Alembic is that you can't make it distort. Either the speakers or something else may, but it won't be the bass. I also had a great engineer, Kevin Scott. He's a true genius. You can tell a great engineer: He's a guy who has the power to make an album or destroy it. Unfortunately, some engineers are the kind that just hold a finger up, stand there, and wait: Whatever

goes on the tape goes on the tape. But Kevin can EQ the worst stuff. I've seen him take a solo that was terrible, and with EQ actually put emotion into it. He's brilliant.

To get that sound, did you go direct or use an amp?

Direct. The sound was right in there. It's direct, but there's still some depth there. You don't feel like it's right in your face, but it isn't far back, either. It lays there just right.

On "Concerto For Jazz-Rock Orchestra," did you use a bass synthesizer?

I used an old thing that Maestro made called the Universal Synthesizer System. It was a big, bulky, stupid thing. And that was the best I ever heard that thing recorded with a bass. But I didn't use a standard bass — it was a piccolo bass. It's just like a regular bass, except it's tuned an octave higher. Carl Thompson built it for me. He must have thought I was crazy, but he did it. He's brilliant with wood.

When you finally toured as a leader in 1976, you had done four solo albums. Why did it take so long?

I waited, man! And the people were waiting, too. I was literally forced to do a solo tour. When the *School Days* album came out, it just sold and sold. And everywhere I would go with Return To Forever, people in the audience would shout, "School Days! School Days! School Days!" And I was up there playing Return To Forever. It really started pissing off the guys in the band. Chick said, "Show me that tune! I'll play it! I'll do anything to shut them up!" It was very funny, very funny. I remember playing in Detroit one time, and these guys said, "Man, you're not going to leave this place until you play 'School Days.'" And they started coming up on the stage.

You don't want to mess with them in Detroit.

You're damned right! I was just playing an upright bass solo, and they didn't *even* want to hear that. They kept yelling for "School Days," so I played the opening section, and they went "Yeah!" So I just kept playing the line over and over, and they loved it.

When you compose, do you sit down with your bass, or at the piano, or do you just work the music out in your head?

It varies from song to song, but I alternate between all three ways. It also depends on whether the

> *"You cannot play the electric bass and think in terms of an acoustic. You have to look at them as two totally different instruments."*

song is for my album, in which case I'll just sit down with the bass and get it. If the tune is for somebody else — say, I'm producing it or helping somebody write a song — I'll work out the harmonies on piano.

Is the material on the new album similar in any respects to your older songs?

Well, all my earlier albums were very similar in a lot of ways, and you could view them as traveling along a road in a natural progression because each one sort of leads to the next. This one is like a jump, leaving that road and going onto another — stretching out. It's my *most different* album that I've ever done, and the bass sound is really hot — I spent a lot of time on it. We had great people on the album, too. There is a young drummer from England named Simon Phillips, a guitarist named Charles Icarus Johnson, and a keyboard player named Steve Bach. Chick Corea also played on the album, and so did Louis Johnson [bassist for the Brothers Johnson] and John Robinson, another drummer. We also had a horn section and a string section — studio players.

What other basses did you use besides your Alembics?

Well, on one track I used a Yamaha BB1200 bass, which is very similar to a Fender. And I actually did use a Fender on two of the songs; Randy Bachman let me use an old '51 Precision. I also used my piccolo basses and a bass that I designed called the Spellbinder. [*Ed. Note: The Spellbinder was made of Fiberglas and Kevlar and weighed about 6 lbs. It was never mass-produced.*]

What kind of amps did you use on the new record?

They were basically what I had on the Stanley Clarke And Friends tour, except less cabinets. I had an Alembic Input Module, an Alembic Preamp, a Biamp graphic equalizer, a Roland Space Echo, and a pair of Crown DC-300A amps. I had eight other speaker cabinets — four were JBL 4530s with one 15 in each. The other four were Cerwin-Vegas with a 15, a horn, and two piezoelectric tweeters each. [*Ed. Note: David Leonard, an independent engineer who oversaw the stage sound for the tour, mentions that Stanley's system was a combination of mono — powered by one amp — for the low end, and biamplified (with a second amp) for the higher frequencies. Stanley also used a Dean Markley Voice Box in conjunction with a Music Man amp and his piccolo bass.*] Just to get an ambience, I would put one of the cabinets in another room and distant-mike it.

Did you use any other special effects onstage besides your Space Echo?

No, just the Space Echo — just to round out some of the sounds. I operated it with a footswitch so I wouldn't have to walk over and click it on. I use it on "Lopsy Lu" [from *Stanley Clarke*] a lot, and on the new album it's all over the place. I have this one song that's called "Danger Street," which I think has the most aggressive bass sound that I've ever heard in my life. I used amps and recorded direct — I always wanted to do a song like that. The sound is really big.

Why did you want such a massive effect?

A lot of times on my albums I haven't really expressed, say, some of the more *dangerous* or evil tones that could be expressed in music — heavier things — but on this one tune it's a different story. Every city has its danger street: New York has 42nd Street, L.A. has Sunset Boulevard, and Chicago has its share. So it's about those types of streets. Therefore, I thought the bass should be very, very heavy and aggressive.

Are you more inclined toward using short-scale basses than long-scale ones?

It depends on the song I'm playing. A lot of times, if I'm playing something in which the bass line requires more of a chug-along type of feel, I use a longer-scale bass. But for solos, I prefer using a shorter-scale bass. I own just about as many short-scales as long-scales. For instance, my Yamaha is a long-scale bass. My piccolos are 32" and 34" basses — medium- and long-scale — because that makes them sound a little better. Most of my Alembics are short-scale, and the Spellbinder is long-scale.

Do you ever use your Framus electric upright for recording?

I used it on the new album, as a matter of fact. I mainly play it pizzicato [plucked], but there is some bowed stuff on there, too — just a few notes. That bass' sound is so deep that it's great for recording, whenever you want to double the bass, or just make a note sound deeper. I just throw it in with the normal bass; it's really earth-shattering.

In the photo on the sleeve of I Wanna Play For You there are a dozen basses. Can you tell what they are?

Right in the center is my string bass. Then there's the Framus electric upright laying sideways, and next to it is a Steinberger Design bass made by Ned Steinberger. It has almost no body. It doesn't have a headstock. I also have a Yamaha BB-1200. Then I have two piccolo basses made by Carl Thompson. One has a 32" scale and a big scroll on the body; the other has a 34" scale. The long-scale one is the first he made for me. It's got a black walnut body, a maple neck, and an ebony fingerboard. The other piccolo is

African walnut with a maple neck. Both of them have ebony fingerboards. [*Ed. Note: Carl Thompson says, "The first bass has a DeArmond pickup designed for use on old Harmony guitars, and the second has a Schaller 404 pickup. The electronics in both are just standard, with no active circuits. The first one has an ebony bridge, while the second one has a Leo Quan Badass bridge."*]

Three Alembics are also shown in the photo.

One has kind of a red finish, and it's the bass I've been using the most for the past year or so. Then I have another — my old main bass — with a curly maple top. The other one is a piccolo that can also be used as a regular bass by changing the strings. It has a mahogany body with Gaboon ebony on the front and back. [*Ed. Note: Susan Wickersham of Alembic says, "It has an ebony fingerboard, a graphite neck for more stability, and LEDs that act as position markers. It was built about a year and a half ago, and it is a short-scale instrument."*] It has a Bigsby vibrato bar. It's a real short bass.

Why did you have a vibrato put on it?

To get more sounds. I was talking with Pat Thrall, who plays guitar with Pat Travers, and he was asking me about a tune on *I Wanna Play For You* called "Quiet Afternoon." It sounds like a battle between two guitar players — like one guy playing a Les Paul and another playing a Stratocaster. So he asked me, "Who was the guy playing the Stratocaster?" I told him it was me playing my black Alembic piccolo, and he freaked out. I've had a lot of people ask me about that song. That thing is an amazing instrument. It can duplicate the sound of a Strat and it can get the sound of a Les Paul, plus it's got the vibrato on there, so I can get all the feedback, the growls, power chords, and whatever you like. The whole thing's there.

When you played the piccolo bass onstage, who held down the regular bass line?

I had Dave DeLeon, my roadie, who is also a bass player, come out and play the bass. Then I'd play piccolo. This allowed me and our guitar player to go out in front of the stage and have this *battle*. So it's kind of obvious why I don't use the piccolo a lot onstage; I don't always have another bass player around.

Are the basses in the photo your complete set?

No. They're just part of the collection; I also have an entire collection of Gibsons, too. There's an EB-O,

"My usual approach is to write a song, get it together, and record it — boom. Next song."

an EB-2, and an EB-3. I also have Rippers and Grabbers, and all those types of things.

When you first got your Alembics, did you use roundwound strings?

At first I had Guild flatwounds. It took me a while to finally quit using them, but I finally got into Rotosound roundwounds.

Did the windings bother your hands?

No. I was waiting for that type of string. They just had so much more life to them. They did tear up my frets a bit, but not my fingers. I had some great calluses from playing the acoustic bass. From a very young age I built up what I call "cement fingers." They're tough on the strings and can take an awful lot of wear.

How often do you change your strings?

If I'm recording, I change them every session. If I'm on the road, I replace them maybe every three or four gigs.

What kind of strings do you use on your piccolo basses?

They're specially made by D'Addario. I'm not sure what the gauges are offhand, but they're very thin. Then on some of my regular basses I use Rotosound SuperWound strings — the ones with the exposed core that goes over the bridge. I also use LaBella Deep Talking Bass Strings sometimes.

How do you like the SuperWound strings?

I like the sound better than the regular Rotosounds, but they don't really work too well on my Alembic basses, because I have to raise the bridge up so high to use them. So I mainly use the standard strings.

Do you wipe the strings to keep their windings from getting gummed up?

Yes, and I also use alcohol. Actually, what I use on a lot of my basses is Mennen's Skin Bracer, because it has the proper amount of alcohol — just enough to clean and get the stuff out — and it leaves the bass smelling alright, too. I used to use that on my upright bass all the time to clean the fingerboard. That same smut accumulates on the fingerboard, and if you rub in a little bit of alcohol or whiskey or something, it makes the instrument smell interesting.

Doesn't the alcohol hurt the wood?

I don't think so. A little moisture on wood isn't that bad, especially for such a short time. Now, if you were to soak it, I'm sure you'd have some problems. But wood comes from trees, and they seem to do okay in spite of all the storms they go through.

In the past five or six years, you've been using more double-stops, such as fifths and thirds.

When I first started playing double-stops, no one else was doing it, so there was a nice, big space for me to fill. I think a lot of bass players had thought about playing more than one note but didn't follow through because they were afraid of taking chances or something. It's great. I think the perfect fifth is one of the prettiest sounds on the bass. It definitely works better than a lot of other things, by far.

What effect does your aggressive slapping and chord strumming have on strings?

It varies. I very rarely break strings, but I take the life out of them very quickly, so I go through a lot of strings. And I wear some frets down really bad.

What tunings do you use?

On "Danger Street," for example, the bass is tuned in fifths — starting on *A* — which is something I've been working on for the last couple of months. You can really hear it, too.

What were some of the different tunings?

For instance, I tuned some of them *A, D, G, C,* from low to high. I also used *A, E, B,* and *F#.* This, of course, was in addition to the regular, standard-tuning basses, and piccolo basses.

When chording, do you use primarily upstrokes or downstrokes?

Both. I tear up and down, just opening up the fingers and hitting the chords. Then I close my hand as I'm coming up. It's rough on the cuticles, but my fingers have really gotten hard as the years go by. Sometimes it doesn't bother me, but if I'm playing every night for about two weeks or so, it's a killer.

Do you ever use your nails to pull on the strings?

No, I can't do that. I've tried, but I just don't even like the way it feels or sounds. I really keep them cut short. And I use sandpaper on my fingers — on the calluses. I think that's the best thing I've come across for saving the finger and preventing it from getting blisters. Now, when you take the skin on your finger and look at it under a microscope, you expect to see a straight line as the surface, right? But I will have little ripples — tiny things in there — and if you play a string instrument, these ripples cause friction. So when a string rubs against them, the skin keeps pulling, and that's why you get those blisters. So if you always keep the skin really smooth, the string will just brush across.

Do you use light sandpaper?

Yes. But since I've been playing so long, I can even use heavy grit now. I can even use a wall! Sometimes backstage I'll find a brick wall, rub my fingers on it, and it smooths them right out! Wash it off, and it's real smooth. Then, when I play, it's really nice.

Do your fingers become too soft if you wash them just before playing?

Oh, no. As a matter of fact, the softer my fingers are, the better. I definitely get a better sound that way — a warmer sound.

Is there a daily warmup routine that you follow?

Nothing specific like scales or arpeggios. I do warm up for a couple of minutes, though — playing lines or bits of tunes. I don't just grab the instrument and then suddenly go into virtuosity. I have to get the fingers moving — just a natural, physical kind of warmup.

Do you do any hand exercises?

Not so much anymore. I play so much these days, and I'm doing so much with my hands that they're pretty well exercised. I used to do calisthenics on the walls with my fingertips, and I also squeezed rubber balls. They really helped my strength.

How did you get into popping and slapping with your right hand?

I think some of the first guys I saw doing that stuff were in Spain. I saw these Spanish guitar players using that stuff, and I thought, "Hey, that would be kind of hip." Just getting away from this or that, and doing *anything* — using thumbs, fingers, the back of the hand, whatever I could come up with, just *using* it. That's my approach to the technique of my right hand: Get the most out of it that I possibly can.

Do you pluck with all four fingers, or just with two?

It varies. I pluck mainly with three. I have certain patterns that I can play only with four fingers. Sometimes when I get to those real fast runs that just fly, there'll be a fourth finger in there to help play it. In some cases you need as many fingers as you can get — I wish I had more!

What are some of the different ways you bend notes and harmonics?

The easiest way to bend a harmonic is if you have a bass that's set up so that the string crosses the nut and travels a fairly long distance to the actual tuning peg. If there's a space in there, you can just pull the string. But the only harmonics you can bend in that way are the stationary harmonics at the 5th, 7th, or 12th fret, such as *G, D, A,* or *E.*

Do you also bend artificial harmonics?

Yeah, but to do that with an artificial harmonic, you just bend the string up with the right-hand finger that's stopping the note. It definitely has to be done all in one flow. In other words, the finger goes down, you strike the harmonic, and then bend it.

Do you apply your string bass vibrato techniques to electric?

Definitely. I also experiment with fast and slow vibrato. It's very similar to the human voice. And it depends pretty much how a person feels emotionally. No two people naturally vibrato the same way; each person has a different approach. For instance, if a guy is an ultra-nervous type, he'll usually vibrato faster; if he's a little more laid-back, his vibrato will be a little bit more even. And if a guy feels really cocky at a particular moment, the vibrato will be wide. It's a very personal thing. I usually try not to think about how I'm doing it, and how I feel at that moment will definitely show up in the vibrato. It's easier that way, because I'll usually do the right thing for the right song. When you're doing a song, everybody wants to know how you feel, anyway. You shouldn't get into a trip where you're always thinking, "Jesus, I hope I'm vibratoing right." If you have no vibrato — if that's how you feel — fine.

Do you use any unusual vibrato techniques?

I've been really getting into one just recently: playing a note and then actually just grabbing the peghead. I haven't snapped the neck off of a bass yet, but I really get scared about it sometimes.

Do you generally anchor your right-hand thumb?

It varies. My hand moves a lot, so it all depends on what sort of position I'm using. Actually, I usually like to just have it resting against the bass somewhere, but kind of loose and open. From playing upright, I've developed so much strength in the right hand that I almost don't even need the thumb to be anchored. I could almost play electric bass without the thumb; I often just have it resting there to keep it out of the way.

You wear your instrument pretty high for a bass player.

Very high. But I don't get wrist cramps from it, surprisingly. What's really weird is that I don't know why the hell I do it. Maybe it's just so that the bass is closer to me or something. It has been getting lower through the years, though — I've got to admit that. I could show you some pictures from when it was up

by my nose, really up there! And I don't know why.

For a song such as "Rock 'N' Roll Jelly" [from Modern Man], in which you know you're going to be moving around onstage a lot, will you intentionally write it in an open-string key, such as E or A?

Definitely. I think the great keys for guitars and basses are E, A, D, and G. They're great keys because you actually get something out of open strings that you don't get with barred things, unless you've got real strong hands. You get a solid sound.

How did the 1979 tour with Jeff Beck come about?

Well, I've known Jeff for quite a long time — he played on an earlier album of mine, *Journey To Love*. When he was getting ready to go on tour, he said that he needed a bass player who could just do the gig without going through months of heavy rehearsing. So he called me up, and his music was pretty simple and I enjoyed it. He also wanted to do some of my songs. We did a great version of "School Days" together.

Wasn't your association with Jeff Beck taking a big step away from jazz towards rock?

People seem to categorize a person because of their past work, but I try not to get into that. For instance, a lot of people say Jeff Beck is a rock guitarist, but the type of music that he's playing now is actually more far-out than my music. I heard the new album that he's been working on; man, that stuff is *far* out. But he'll always be called a rock guitarist because he came on the scene as a rock guitarist. He's a *stylist*. He grew up in rock and roll and got progressive — the *Blow By Blow* album was something that might be considered rock and roll, but it's really not. It has a lot of other elements in there that I think get overlooked because people get into sensationalism of categories. It's like: Jeff Beck, the rock guitar player, or Eric Clapton or Jimi Hendrix, the blah, blah, blahs. I've even seen it done on myself, you know, although it's a little harder with me. Sometimes I get the feeling people don't know quite *what* to say about me. I actually like that better, because the real purpose for categorizing something anyway is to help businessmen.

In order to hit the right audience?

Yeah, but it wasn't always like that, nor is it a nec-

> *"There will always come another generation of bassists, and they may be even more aggressive than any of us are: guys twirling the bass in the air, biting their basses, breaking their basses."*

essary rule. I'm sure Bach didn't go around saying he played classical music. But then, later, when his stuff got on the disc, somebody in Europe said, "Dis iss classic," and that's where it went.

How did your joining the New Barbarians come about?

Well, again, I've known Ronnie Wood for a long time. I met him when he first joined the Rolling Stones. A lot of those guys in the Rolling Stones used to come to see me when I'd play in England. One night Ronnie and Mick Jagger came to the show, and afterwards I went and hung out with them. I never thought of playing with Ronnie Wood; it was the furthest thing from my mind. Then, one time I got this call from him. He said that he had gotten this band together to play a gig in Toronto with the Rolling Stones. He needed a bass player that could do old Chuck Berry tunes and all kinds of other rock and roll songs, as well as some stuff from his new album. I had been getting ready to take a four-week vacation, and this tour was done so expensively well that it was like a vacation; I had to play for a couple hours a night, and that was about it. But we had a private plane and all this and all that, so it was fun for four weeks. We had a good-sized group: me, Ronnie, Keith Richards, [keyboardist] Ian McLagen, and — whenever he showed up — Mick Jagger. Then there was Bobby Keys on saxophone, and a drummer from the Meters, Joseph Ziggy Modeliste.

How did it feel to be doing hard-core rock and roll again?

It was fun. It just reminded me of when I was 15 or 16, when I used to play all those tunes. Especially the old Chuck Berry and Freddy Stone songs. It was great. I felt really comfortable with it.

Do you think that you're becoming more of a rock bassist than a jazz player?

From one viewpoint, it might seem that I've been changing, but you couldn't say, "Well, Stanley took a course in rock and roll last year and now knows how to rock." Actually, it's just that certain parts of me that were long suppressed are coming out. I mean, I

was playing rock when I was 13 or 14. But as I grew up, I didn't play it anymore. I just kept it hushed up inside of me. There are other types of music that I'm capable of doing, and people aren't aware of it. If, say, I felt the urge or the need, I could write a full-scale classical-type symphony. But I *don't* feel a need to do it, and I don't think that there would be too much interest in listeners right now.

What would you tell a bassist who wants to be the next Stanley Clarke?

I think that everyone should have a goal. The bass player that I wanted to be as good as, or even better than, was Ron Carter — especially back when he was with Miles Davis. I think wanting to be better than the best is healthy. It's dumb to say something like, "I want to be good, but I'll never be as good as Stanley, or whoever." You have to be aggressive. And the way the music business is evolving, it seems to be getting harder. It's really difficult if you want to get into jazz or jazz-rock. But there will always come another generation of bassists, and they may be even more aggressive than any of us are: guys twirling the bass in the air, biting their basses, breaking their basses. They may be so virtuosic as to put us all to shame. But who knows? Those people are all 13 or 14 now.

How important is a positive outlook?

Well, I'm not one to dwell on the fact that it's a dog-eat-dog world, but it is. As a kid is growing up and learning, he's going to run into somebody every now and then that will make him feel like a lesser person than he actually is. A good way around that is to be aware of your own self-worth. I think it's a healthy thing to have an ego, but I don't mean you shouldn't be humble, too. It is possible to have humility while having an ego. But there's a danger if you feel that you're worth something and think that the people around you aren't. If a person can feel as if they have some value, and look at someone across a field and feel that he's worth something, too, then the net effect will be far more powerful. And you'll be able to get a lot more done in life.

– ANTHONY JACKSON –

BY JIM FERGUSON – JANUARY 1986

"ANTHONY Jackson is *the* most phenomenal electric bassist," insists Al Di Meola, who has frequently featured the 6-string specialist on tour and on record. "He's dedicated to absolute perfection, and he comes very close to achieving it. His musical ideas are incredible and his knowledge is vast." Steve Khan agrees, adding that his fellow Eyewitness member is "one of the most important and innovative electric bassists alive."

Inspired by modernist classical composers, as well as Motown bass legend James Jamerson's creative yet tasteful approach to providing support, 33-year-old Jackson has taken the instrument to new heights of technical and musical sophistication. Reluctant to solo except when it works compositionally within a tune's framework, he has an uncanny knack for spontaneous reharmonization that virtually redefines ensemble playing, elevating it to the level of improvisational accompaniment. And his expertise with both a pick and his fingers, coupled with his instrument's expanded range, affords him an uncommonly broad array of techniques and timbres.

Once a top session bassist in New York, Los Angeles, and Philadelphia, Jackson has an impressive résumé of performing and recording credits that includes the O'Jays, Chick Corea, Chaka Khan, Horace Silver, Roberta Flack, Steely Dan, and Grover Washington, Jr. However, as his highly original and creative approach solidified over the years, he found that producers more interested in trendy sounds than artistic statements ceased calling. But despite the decline in studio jobs, he remains busy, touring with artists such as Di Meola and Paul Simon, playing jingles, and working with numerous New York-based ensembles, including Eyewitness.

Since the mid '70s, Jackson has relentlessly worked toward his dream of developing a 6-string "contrabass guitar" (tuned, low to high: *B, E, A, D, G, C*), which he now plays exclusively. Over the years, he has commissioned instruments by several top luthiers — including Carl Thompson, Ken Smith, Vinnie Fodera, and Ken Parker — and he has worked closely with several companies in developing strings capable of performing to his demanding specifications. Phenomenal, important, and innovative are terms that can be honestly applied to few bass guitarists; however, Anthony Jackson is a clear exception. While most electric bassists are either supportive chameleons able to blend invisibly into their musical surroundings or supercharged extroverts out to prove who's faster and louder, Jackson stands apart in every respect — from his unique instruments to his technical prowess to his uncompromising and often controversial attitudes on soloing, artistry, and technique.

Your ensemble playing is inventive and active, yet tasteful. However, outright solos are few and far between. Do you ever decline solos?

All the time. The problem is the obligatory solo, which implies that some of the weight is taken off of the player. By that I mean, too often the attitude is: Take a great solo, take a bad solo, but just solo. Something is wrong with that for me. If I tell you up front that I'm not going to be comfortable taking a solo this set, and you want me to take one anyway, what you're really saying is that I should take it even if it's not going to be great. But my feeling is that better you should wait and hear something great. If you don't hear it tonight, you might hear it tomorrow, but it will have been worth waiting for. This is a much better attitude than, "Time for the bass solo. Oh, waitress — we'd like to order now."

When you do take a solo break, you don't tend to shoot up into the horn register right away like so many players.

It's a matter of maturity. You shoot into the horn register when it's appropriate. You don't do it to show you can do it, and you don't shoot up high or play 64th-notes to impress the other bass players in the audience. You have to be prepared to accept that if all you get to play are whole-notes in the lower middle register at low volume, you are still as much of an artist as if you get to play 64th-notes all night at loud volume. It is absolutely essential that a musician be secure enough in himself to do that. There are two conflicting schools of thought: "Make a statement as simply as you can" and "Embellish as much as possible; why have a single rose when you can have a dozen?" Neither of those make much sense to me, because you should do what is appropriate for the music.

Some bassists feel that technique isn't important.

The composer Olivier Messiaen — one of my greatest inspirations — said it very plainly: "Technique is the means by which the heart is allowed to fly freely." You cannot have at your disposal an effective musical language if every time you put it into effect, you have to reduce it to fit the limits of your technique. By the same token, to think that not to use your technique is to lose it is equally absurd. These are things that become self-evident with experience and by playing with musicians better than you. When you're working with a great musician who is absolutely intimidating you with musicianship and artistry, and yet he's not soloing, playing excessively loud, or ego-tripping in any way, there's a lesson to be learned. Most people who claim technique isn't important tend to not have a lot of technique themselves.

Has your attitude about soloing helped or hindered your relationships with members of bands you've been part of?

It all depends. When Al Di Meola discovered I could play with a pick, he wrote challenging parts expressly for me, which was very flattering. I never thought about having to take a solo, because being involved in a project like that is tantamount to soloing. In addition, when you have [keyboardist] Jan Hammer and Al Di Meola soloing and [drummer] Steve Gadd playing, you have to have a lot of balls to say, "I'm not happy; I want a solo, too." That I do not approve of. I simply do not put myself on the level of a Jan Hammer, despite the fact that I could send the chops through the roof and do all the little tricks that bass players can do to get noticed. Although I took no more than a couple of breaks on the title track of Al's *Electric Rendezvous*, it was one of the most satisfying albums I've done. And those solos were worked out; I feel they were well-considered statements. I'm also very proud of performances such as my work on the title track to Eric Gale's *Ginseng Woman*, which is more impressive than any solo I've ever done because it complements the song and helps it move along effectively. If I were a teacher, I would use that cut as an example of compositional performance using touch, dynamics, attack, and variations on themes to complement a composition. It's as effective as a solo without being as overt as one.

How would you describe what you do? You don't solo very much, yet your work goes way beyond a mere supportive capacity.

I try to bring as much intensity as I can to whatever role I'm playing. You do the very best you can, or you've no right to complain if your performance falls short of your expectations. Since the late '60s, when I felt the first real cold shoulder from the jazz world because I played a bass guitar instead of an upright, I've gotten very idealistic about labels, and I suppose I'm just a little bit touchy about being classed as simply a supportive player because there is a set of stereotypes that go along with that. When you hear someone being referred to as a supportive player, it's kind of like damning them with faint praise. It's like saying someone gave a *thoroughly competent performance*, or they're *always a pleasure to listen to*. Terms like "supportive player" and "studio musician" automatically set up a picture of someone as being okay; into music, but not floored by it; a dedicated player, but not obsessed; a good performer, but one who doesn't kick you in the ass and make you look up. Steve Gadd, who is one of the greatest musicians of the century, can play an entire night without a solo and still be at the center of attention or close to it, which shows that it's the quality of performance that counts the most, not the role of the performance. I don't make a distinction between the two.

You're known for refusing to adopt trendy bass techniques such as popping and slapping. Has this stance resulted in lost work?

You've opened a Pandora's box. There's no doubt I've experienced substantially reduced employment, but I hope I've accepted it with a certain amount of grace. I once did quite a bit of studio work, but now to call me a studio musician is a bit of a misnomer. I've always been inclined to be involved in high-quality projects — Steely Dan, Donald Fagen, Eyewitness, Paul Simon, Chaka Khan — but numerically speaking, I haven't done that much in the studio for some time, and certainly one reason is a refusal to be trendy, which is a conscious decision to stick by a set of principles. I have been extremely fortunate in finding an original musical language on this instrument. That's not to say it's a completely mature language or a very effective one in all circumstances, but it's mine. And I have absolute faith in it, and I'm going to continue developing it along lines that I dictate. I've never taken well with, "Why don't you believe in what someone else is doing?"

"When you hear someone being referred to as a supportive player, it's kind of like damning them with faint praise."

There's nothing wrong with looking at what others are doing and gaining inspiration from it, but I don't approve of taking it and making it your own. Larry Graham and Louis Johnson, and possibly Chuck Rainey, stumbled onto this approach, completely independent of each other. Within a few years, 90% of all bass players were playing that way, and you can't convince me that they all discovered it at the same time. What you have is a perfect example of people saying, "Gee, I like playing bass, but it's hard to come up with an original style. Hey, there's an original style that already exists; I think I'll make it mine." There's a problem there. You run the risk of waking up 20 years down the road saying, "What have I done? I've been ripping someone off for 20 years, and I don't have anything to say." If you're content with speaking someone else's language — Johnsonese, for example — that's okay, but my greatest inspiration has come from people who stood out on their own, had something to say, and followed it through. This posture is an inevitable result of being influenced, as far as bass players are concerned, by two of the most original minds to ever come to the instrument — James Jamerson and Jack Casady [of Jefferson Airplane].

Have you ever used slapping or popping?

I've done it on a couple of recording sessions and a soundtrack, where I was specifically asked to use it in a way that was designed to contribute, as opposed to following a producer's instructions along the lines of, "What will we have the bass play? I know, let's have him do that slap stuff they all play." It really means that they don't know what to do, so they fall back on the familiar. These techniques are so overused that I hear players slapping their asses off on *slow ballads*. I hear people using the configuration that slappers usually use — root, lowered 7th, octave — in songs where there is no dominant 7th, and it actually sounds sour. If I really wanted to slap and pop, I don't have any doubt that I could be competitive doing it, but I don't hear the instrument that way, and in most cases, I don't really care for the way it sounds.

Many players feel that they need to be fluent with a variety of techniques in order to work as much as possible.

Technical and stylistic versatility is always important, especially if you're being asked to interpret somebody else's ideas on their project. The problem is to satisfy someone else's needs while still using your own musical language — a dangerous game, but one that is essential to master if your own identity is to come through on the finished product. This is especially difficult to do when no improvisation is desired. Everyone has a different approach for keeping their self-respect as an artist. It's important for people to acknowledge that I have an approach of my own, and I'm trying my damnedest to make it grow. There is a certain hostility to this stance on the part of the musical community, and some offended people ask, "Who does he think he is?" They read off the list of bassists — many of them are great players — and ask, "If slapping, popping, or whatever is good enough for them, why isn't it good enough for you?" Sometimes they understand, if I explain that my attitude is not intended to be disrespectful of other players, but is merely an attempt to make an original statement. I don't think I'm any better; I just don't want to get swallowed up in a mass of interchangeable bassists. I've been fortunate that enough producers and musicians want something other than what current trends dictate. Things would no doubt be much more difficult if I hadn't started early and established myself as a player with something else to offer.

What are your thoughts on the impact that Jaco Pastorius has had on bassists?

Since the '60s, the technical level on the instrument has gone up considerably, yet experimentation and the quest to make a statement has been lost. Jaco was the last individual to come along who had something original to say. True to form, bass players jumped on his bandwagon, and now we're faced with the next evolution of, "Gee, it's hard to come up with a style — I think I'll just take the next one that comes along." Now there are thousands of Jaco clones; some of them are very good, but they're still clones. It's absolutely painful to hear. It's a negative trend, and I don't know what it will take to break bass players of this habit.

Why does the bass suffer in this manner?

It's still comparatively new. Lack of tradition leads to a lack of respect for study, and the instrument is very easy to play fairly well. Mastery, however, remains as difficult to achieve as on any other instrument. The guitar has the same problem, but to a lesser degree. In the orthodox jazz world, saxophone and trumpet are less affected by this syndrome. For instance, players cloned [saxophonists] Charlie Parker and John Coltrane for a while, but a number of very original voices came along — Albert Ayler, Archie Shepp, Pharoah Sanders. It's inspirational to think that Pharoah played in the same group as Coltrane yet managed to sound totally unlike him. It would be very difficult for most bassists to play alongside Jaco and not sound like him.

As a bassist who doesn't slap, pop, or tap, have you been impacted by Stanley Jordan? Do you think he'll inspire unabashed cloning like Jaco?

Stanley Jordan has been inspirational to me, but the radical nature of his approach may preclude his being copied. The man has stumbled onto something and shown himself to be a genius, and that's a word I don't throw around lightly. One of the attributes of genius is the ability to come up with an idea that is alien to what accepted authorities believe is possible or desirable, prove it workable, and then go ahead and demonstrate a maturity using it. In other words, you can stumble onto an idea for a machine but be totally incapable of building one. I had a chance to work on Jordan's second album [*Magic Touch*], the one produced by Al Di Meola, but I turned the project down because I was so stunned by his first album [*Touch Sensitive*] that I felt I would do nothing but get in his way. I haven't heard the new record yet,

and I'm not particularly interested, because it's like the case of [pianist] Art Tatum — you don't miss the fact that he didn't play with an ensemble most of the time. I also was afraid that somebody would make a conscious attempt to make him more marketable by putting him in a pop-jazz setting. I hate to say it, but I guess there's no way for Stanley Jordan to avoid the garbage that we all have to go through. For instance, his video has him playing in a store window with four girls goggling at him, and in the end he walks off with them. It has nothing whatsoever to do with him or what he's able to do. It's a $5 script and a $95 shooting.

What was it about James Jamerson's playing that impressed you?

He did tiny little things that showed a great deal of musical maturity and artistic thinking, regardless of how trite the song might be. For instance, he would wait until right before a tune repeated, and then he'd change the bass line, which would kick the hell out of things. I owe most of what I am as a musician to Jamerson.

Most bassists mention him as being innovative, but Jack Casady's work is often overlooked.

Casady was the first bass player I heard who really struck me as a bass guitarist — he had a startling, original approach to the instrument, and he did the most astounding things without soloing. I never wondered what his solos might have sounded like, because what he played was a solo statement in itself. It was Casady who got me into playing with a pick. The fact that he has been almost invisible for many years changes nothing. In commenting on statements in the press that composer Edgard Varése made great contributions to modern music but stopped in his tracks, Igor Stravinsky noted that what counts is not that he only did *one* thing. The important thing is that he *did* the one thing. You or I didn't do it; *he* did. Most people make no contribution to their field, which says a lot for people who do. If Casady comes back into the public's eye again, he will probably not be comfortable with the current bass player's Olympics — where you try to see who can stand on their head and play the fastest. But if he does come back, I think he'd knock people over again, because whether he's in or out of fashion, he remains one of the immortals.

It's surprising that you haven't mentioned Jack Bruce.

He hasn't been an influence. Bruce is a great musician, and I've always respected him, but I was never tempted to pursue his approach to the instrument.

He played a medium-scale instrument, and I've never been thrilled by that sound. I was a big Cream fan, and I went to see them in 1967 at the Cafe Au Go Go in New York, during their first American tour. It astounded me that Jack Bruce was playing with three right-hand fingers, and I went home and started working on it immediately.

Why haven't you recorded a solo album?

It simply isn't a priority. If I do one, it won't be until at least the end of the decade. At this point, my composition sounds transitional; it has to focus itself a little more, and that may or may not come with time. My writing is rather stiff and academic, so rather than record and expect people to go for it just because of my reputation, I prefer to not do it at all. I would rather get other people to write for me, which means my function is strictly as a soloist. Recently, I have commissioned several pieces, which is an idea I got from Julian Bream's album *20th Century Guitar*, where he featured works written expressly for him. A friend of mine told me that Bream sat down with some composers who apparently had never written for the guitar, and he showed them how to relate to the instrument compositionally.

Where did your interest in classical music come from?

It has been lifelong. Most of the music I've listened to consistently has been so-called classical music — mostly by modernist composers, from Stravinsky on up. I had a very early rapturous involvement with his *Le Sacre Du Printemps* [*The Rite Of Spring*], which I discovered on a recording by Leonard Bernstein and the New York Philharmonic. I listened to that album several hours a day for 10 or 12 years, and it became so worn that virtually no music was audible. From there, I discovered other composers.

Has classical music influenced your ability to reharmonize progressions, which you do so naturally?

It was probably listening to the music of Olivier Messiaen that prompted me to investigate reharmonization. Around 1972, I heard one of his organ pieces, and it had an electric effect on me and inspired me to scour New York for more of his work. His particular musical language is harmonically very angular, with an emphasis on the *tritone* [augmented fourth, or diminished fifth], which is not normally used in the Romantic, Classical, and Baroque traditions. Messiaen was able to make exquisitely warm and sweet harmony using what are thought to be

"Jaco was the last individual to come along who had something original to say."

cold and angular approaches. My solos on *Electric Rendezvous* were directly inspired by Messiaen. His compositions for the Ondes Martinot, a very expressive early electronic instrument, led me to experiment with a volume pedal and a slide. Another composer who had a great influence on me is Paul Hindemith, one of music history's greatest melodicists. He could spin a 32-bar melody without making it sound at all like he's just jumping randomly, reaching for notes. One of the most profound lessons I've learned from listening to classical music is not to get locked into a diatonic approach — all 12 tones of the chromatic scale are equally important.

Has jazz been a harmonic influence?

The tritone is important in jazz, but the bass' role is strictly supportive — playing chord changes, as opposed to melodies. However, the album *The John Coltrane Quartet Plays* did a lot to open things up for me. I was staggered that his group, which included [pianist] McCoy Tyner, could play with such energy and commitment, and make the music work without a key center. McCoy's thundering fourths were very intriguing and individualistic; he could move into a standard diatonic or chromatic context, and then flip right out of it. The first time I heard Miles Davis was on *Miles Smiles*, and I was fascinated by two things. First, on some tunes, [pianist] Herbie Hancock didn't play until it was time for him to solo — he didn't comp. That was when I realized that it's possible to say a lot even if you don't play all of the time. Second, [bassist] Ron Carter, who I've had a disagreement with for many years, didn't always play in one particular key. That was another grand inspiration, because why shouldn't the bass player step out and set the harmonic direction? Any kind of music played with absolute authority and conviction is as good as any other. Developing concepts is just a matter of listening to a lot of different music, and then fantasizing.

Why do you say you disagreed with Ron Carter?

Several years ago, he did a number of interviews where he basically said that the world was going along fine until the electric bass was invented. Being young and impressionable, I was very deeply hurt by that. For a long time, I had a chip on my shoulder, not so much from loving and listening to jazz, as from playing it. Whenever I went onstage, say with [pianist] Horace Silver, I expected someone to say, "Get that electric bullshit off, and get an upright up there." On at least one occasion, something like that did happen. I was devastated, because I wanted to be appreciated. I wondered why they couldn't at least listen to what I had to say, and then maybe they'd go away saying, "I don't like the Fender bass, but that guy's a good player." Down the road, the person might go to the next step, which is liking the Fender. After all, part of Ron Carter's beef was that he hadn't heard too many people who could play it well. He played credibly on some things, but they always sounded stiff and disinterested. If he loved the bass guitar as much as he loved the upright, he'd be one of the bass guitar's great interpreters. Steve Swallow is one player who switched from the upright to the bass guitar, and he is one of the great interpreters.

Many players approach the technique of the electric bass from the perspective of an upright. What are your thoughts on that?

When I was first starting to play, most of the older musicians I met were adamant in calling the bass guitar just "Fender" or "electric bass," and they treated it as a poor man's upright. But I consider it to be exactly what it is: a bass guitar. In the playing of the instrument, the bass guitar has more in common with the guitar than it has with the upright. True, the scale is longer than a standard guitar, but it's much shorter than an upright. And the way you hold the instrument is the same as the guitar. There's something to be gained from both areas of instruction, but the guitar has far more to offer. In 1969, I studied with Larry Lucie, who played both the guitar and the bass guitar. As far as I know, he was the first musician of his generation — he was active in the '30s and '40s — to refer to it as a bass guitar, and he really helped me cement that idea.

Many teachers who play the upright teach half positions on the bass guitar. Is that a good idea?

I don't see much point in half positions. I've found that it's possible to play with far more fluidity using a technique that leans more toward orthodox guitar than orthodox upright. There is nothing I've heard or seen done on the upright bass that cannot be played as well or better on the bass guitar with guitar technique, which is as it should be.

Besides Lucie, with whom else have you studied?

I had one very important formal lesson with Pat Martino. On three pieces of paper, he gave me enough material to last a lifetime. One aspect of the lesson was his 12-point star concept, which is a way of dividing the chromatic scale into various intervallic relationships. He also presented a system that reduces Nicholas Slonimsky's *Thesaurus Of Scales And*

Melodic Patterns [Charles Scribner & Sons, dist. by Belwin-Mills] to a series of formulas. In addition, he showed me approaches for harmonic improvisation that are difficult to reduce into simple terms. I originally went to Pat for technique, but he felt that it wasn't a priority. He was a great inspiration because he was one of the first musicians I met who was absolutely fanatical about music to the exclusion of everything else — that's the way you get results.

What did you work on to develop your facility with a pick?

Up- and downstrokes — one of the classics. I tried to play a continuous up- and downstroke without a perceptible difference from one note to the next, much in the same way that a violinist develops bow technique. For practice purposes, I often damp all the strings and use up- and downstrokes at various tempos, listening and feeling for the difference. Then, I alter my hand position, the tension, and whatever is required to make the stroke even. One of the best ways to develop facility with the pick is to play the same things you play with your fingers. The most important thing is to listen to what you're practicing.

Do you practice with your fingers and the pick equally?

In the early days, I practiced about 70% fingers, 30% pick. When I started working for Di Meola, those figures tended to be more equal. Fingerstyle is more appropriate for most musical situations I find myself in. A lot of producers and listeners find that the pick sounds a little too guitaristic. I'm an overall more superior player with the fingers — that's a gap that I am attempting to close in the next couple of years.

When using your fingers, do you basically alternate your index and middle?

It's more complex than that — you do what's required. One tends to concentrate on the first two fingers because they're stronger. Years ago, I came up with a series of exercises to strengthen the third and fourth fingers, but the easiest way is to just play with those fingers as much as possible.

So you actually use your right-hand pinky for scales and arpeggios?

I don't use it for scalar playing, but more for arpeggiation. I also use it for rasgueados [a right-hand strumming technique used in flamenco music] and five-note chords — it's handy for all instruments with six strings. Apart from using the little finger, I see no essential difference in approach between my instrument and a classical guitar. Size is the only difference.

Why did you decide upon six strings instead of five?

Because I felt limitations in range at both ends. I think I first became aware of extending the range downward when I found myself practicing to Jimmy Smith organ trio records. I really got into the sound of his bass voicings on the Hammond organ, but he often dropped below low *E*. I used to get enraged because I couldn't do that, so I tuned all four strings down. However, in doing so, I lost part of my upper register. At that point, it seemed that I could solve a lot of problems by having an extra low string. While I was thinking along those lines, it also occurred to me that guitars often have 24 frets, so why should the bass have only 19 or 20 like Fender instruments? In the late '60s and early '70s, 21-fret necks were a big advertising feature for some companies, but that still didn't make sense. Once I came to that conclusion I wondered, why not just put another string on top? From there, it was just a matter of making the commitment to look for somebody who would build the first 6-string contrabass guitar. I don't claim to be the first person to think of the idea; I just didn't get it from anybody else.

Other 6-strings have comparatively narrow fingerboards. Why do you prefer such wide ones?

It's solely to duplicate the string spacing on my Fender 4-string, which I've owned since 1972 and feel very comfortable with. It's odd, because the instrument has a Precision neck on a Jazz body, which means that it has Precision nut spacing, although mine was narrower than usual, and Jazz bridge spacing. In the beginning, I thought very carefully about the extra width that would inevitably result from the additional strings. But after seeing Renaissance music specialists playing lutes with extremely wide necks, and after seeing the great classical guitarist Narciso Yepes playing his 10-string, I thought the biggest battle would be in getting an instrument built, not in playing it.

Who built your first 6-string?

Carl Thompson; he completed it in 1975. It has a 34" scale and a mahogany and ebony body. I didn't use it very much because the string spacing at the bridge was too tight, which was an oversight on my part because I neglected to specify string spacing. Carl built one other 6-string for me — it has a 44" scale — which was one of my early attempts to elimi-

> *"Any kind of music played with absolute authority and conviction is as good as any other."*

nate dead spots on the fingerboard. We thought that by increasing the length of the scale and changing certain resonant frequencies, the dead spots would disappear, but that wasn't the case. I never played that instrument in public because at 44", it was impractical to finger, and I would have had to play it in the cello position, with the neck pointing up. I owe a lot to Carl because he was the first builder who was willing to try my ideas. Looking at those guitars years later, they are extremely fine — very simple but with an extremely high degree of fit and finish.

You're currently playing a Ken Smith contrabass guitar.

Yes; he's built two for me, both with 34" scales. My main instrument is the second one, which differs from the first in that it has slightly wider string spacing, a heavier fingerboard of high-grade ebony instead of caviuna, and a slightly more extreme fingerboard arch. Also, the body is smaller and it's primarily walnut instead of maple. The equalizer circuit was designed from scratch according to my specifications, and the pickups are Ken Smiths with ceramic magnets and adjustable polepieces. Ken also succeeded in constructing a neck that is virtually free of dead spots, and he is offering a Smith/Jackson contrabass model.

Fodera is also marketing an Anthony Jackson model contrabass guitar.

It's a nice honor. Vinnie Fodera, who used to be partners with Ken Smith, is in the process of building me a 36"-scale instrument. Although 36"-scale instruments are noticeably more difficult to play, they sound better — it's the same as going from a baby grand to a nine-foot grand piano; you have a richer sound, but the weight and size of the instrument increases enormously. In addition, I'm having another master luthier, Ken Parker, from Connecticut, construct a contrabass guitar for me. Parker is an expert arch-top builder who has stumbled onto some extremely old construction methods. For instance, he might build a guitar that uses a cable instead of a truss rod. I can't talk about most of his techniques because they're proprietary.

Have you considered approaching a large company to build you an instrument?

I've been solicited by most of the biggies, but they're not prepared to do everything I want unless I go to Japan for a month. And even then, I don't think I'd get the same cooperation that I get from using small, fanatically committed builders. It's important to note that a lot of people originally looked at me kind of strange when I told them what I really wanted, and that determined who I decided to pursue. If a particular builder honestly thinks I'm making a mistake but agrees to build an instrument anyway, it bothers me because it means he's not as dedicated to the project as I'd like. He has to be willing to take a chance and believe in what I want. The only drawback to working with small luthiers is that they can't always be expected to rush things out.

Do fretless instruments appeal to you?

They do have a certain quarter-tone expressiveness that appeals to me, but once you take the frets off the guitar — bass or otherwise — it ceases to be a guitar. The sound becomes rounded on the attack and extremely muted in the upper register. I was never willing to trade off the sharp, distinctive guitar-like quality of the bass guitar just to be able to play glides and swoops. In addition, you lose some of the harmonic possibilities.

Is it difficult to find adequate strings for your purposes?

In this bass guitar dream of mine, strings remain the largest problem area. The difficulty is in finding a string taut enough to give a good solid sound and accurate harmonic series without going to an overly long scale length. I'm probably going to go from a low *B* down to *A*, and that will compound the problem. Right now, I'm using a GHS set that reads, low to high: .128, .105, .085, .065, .045, and .028. I've arranged with at least one other company to make a heavier set. The time-consuming aspect is deciding the optimum relative diameters of the core and the winding. We haven't even touched on the ideal alloy, although I've heard some interesting theories that involve using precious metals in the winding — gold or silver — which would be recycled when the string is used up. In 1985, Neil Stubenhaus mentioned in *Guitar Player* that he's waiting until strings are perfected before he gets into the 5-string bass. I have the utmost respect for Neil; he's a great player and he's said kind things about me in the past, but if he waits, they won't be developed. Now is the time to get in. Companies are not going to develop these things unless players go to them. Another problem I've had with strings is that they lose their brilliance. In fact, in the studio, I've been known to change sets several times during the same session. For "Nite Sprite" on Chick Corea's *The Leprechaun*, I changed string sets six times. It was expensive, but it was the only way to get the sound I wanted.

How are you amplifying your contra bass guitar?

I have a quad-amped system that I've spent 11 years designing. It uses Turbosound speakers and a crossover network and power amplifiers by FM Acoustics of Switzerland. Signal processing is handled by two Eventide SP 2016 digital processors, which are software-based and updateable. Two Audio & Design peak limiters prevent signal overloading of the digital signal inputs. The 2016s are extremely powerful, and they are capable of doing a number of specialized functions using time delay, such as flanging and reverberation, which are the two basic effects I use. The system is controlled by a pedalboard and proprietary electronics designed in conjunction with Martin Audio Corporation of New York. This is the finest bass guitar system in the world, in terms of quality, and it equals or exceeds the majority of studio sound installations. Since my setup requires a lot of space, for small clubs I try to use just a portion — fewer speakers, for instance.

Since the neck of your instrument is exceedingly long, why have you dispensed with most of the usual position markers?

I'm in the process of eliminating all markers from the fingerboard. I concede that I don't have my act together as much as I'd like, because while my new Fodera will have no markers on the front of the fingerboard, it will have ones on the side at positions 9, 12, 19, and 24. Like most fretted-instrument players, I had always relied on position markers, but eventually I became annoyed with the fact that I was less comfortable when things fell between the markers — for instance, parts in the keys of *F♯, C♯* or *D*. I found myself kind of wishing that the key was up or down a half-step so I could play more with position markers under the crucial fingers. There is nothing inherently wrong with guideposts, but when the going gets rough and you tend to deal only with the markers, instead of the areas the markers are supposed to be guiding you to, then you have a problem. Frets and positions should all have equal value, and you shouldn't be guided into playing patterns based on how convenient the markers are for your fingers. It's basically a form of self-discipline. Classical guitarists, cellists, violinists, and double bassists don't get lost, because they have such a great knowledge of the fingerboard; so study is the answer. This is directly related to sight-reading and playing in position. Larry Lucie was the first to teach me about the virtues of playing in position. He said you should be able to find your way on the neck without looking at it, and the only way to do that is to know exactly what notes are under your fingers, regardless of the position your hand is in. Sight-reading is the true measure of someone's command of the fingerboard, because that's when you're most likely to see them scrambling to find a note in the only two locations they know it in. And sight-reading is especially difficult on the bass; it's hard to take the neck in at a glance because it's so long.

Have you ever taught?

Years ago, I had a few pupils, which demonstrated to me the nobility and honor of the teaching profession. Playing and teaching require fanatical commitments, and I just didn't have time to do both — I wasn't willing to be a half-assed teacher. Someday, I'd like to teach master classes where the students have worked out most of their problems and just need some polish. When it comes to teaching intermediates or beginners, you run the risk of ruining a student's technique for life, and they might have to spend months or years unlearning mistakes you've taught them. I had a couple of pupils with serious problems, and I had no luck in helping them — it was frustrating. Still, I wasn't prepared to tell them not to play bass. Suppose Segovia sat down with you and said, "Let me give you some advice — play trumpet." That might make somebody kill themselves.

"Ultimately, the responsibility for excellence is yours alone."

What's the best advice you can give an aspiring bassist?

Be honest with yourself. Honesty is an automatic self-correcting process. If people say you played great but you know that a particular tune gave you trouble or that your solo was a mishmash of ideas, then you will correct it. Unless you are a supremely arrogant, shortsighted, narrow-minded individual, your mouth should go dry when you hear yourself play and tune in to the buzzes, squeaks, and inconsistencies of all types. Ultimately, the responsibility for excellence is yours alone.

What kind of impression do you hope to make in the sands of music history?

I intend to leave this world having made some kind of contribution on my instrument. I don't intend to spend a lifetime trying to master the bass guitar only to be listed in alphabetical order behind people who made $150,000 a year for 25 straight years but had nothing else to show for it. I don't play the 4-string anymore, and I have no intention of ever doing so. Even if it kills me, I intend to do what I can to improve standards of performance on the contrabass guitar. There is nothing that is going to stop me.

– MICHAEL MANRING –

BY TOM MULHERN – DECEMBER 1989

PAUL HAGGARD

CLASSICAL GUI-tarists can stride to center stage, sit down, and begin a concert without so much as a twitch from the audience. But when Michael Manring takes the limelight alone with his bass, listeners often aren't ready. They think this guy forgot his guitar, or that the rest of the band will soon be onstage. Scarcely a few seconds pass with Manring hammering on fretless bass with both hands, and the audience is *his*.

While it's true that Annapolis-born Manring isn't following an orthodox path in his solo career, he is adamant — and good-natured — about his direction: "To me, electric bass is so special, so beautiful in any context. I really believe that someday electric bass will be looked at as a really high art form."

At 29, Manring has been playing bass ever since he entered his teens in the Washington, D.C., area, weathering the strict regimen of string bass instruction and playing in the requisite number of rock, jazz, and fusion ensembles. He was influenced by avant-gardist Harry Partch, and wrote an opera that was too "outside" for his high school drama department. He spent a brief time at Berklee, and later studied privately with Jaco Pastorius. He still practices diligently ("For a long time, I was married to my metronome!"), and today focuses almost exclusively on fretless.

In addition to working as a solo artist, he's busy with Montreux, a primarily acoustic-oriented group that

fuses elements of jazz, blue-grass, pop, and new age, and his dazzling duets with guitarist Michael Hedges often head for the outer reaches of bass/guitar blending. With two solo albums to his credit — *Unusual Weather* and *Toward The Center Of The Night* — and several more with Montreux, Hedges, Alex deGrassi, Will Ackerman, and others, Manring is reaching a lot of ears. His unorthodox approach combines standard technique with two-handed tapping, funk-style slapping, and very outside, very imaginative tunings. And even though Manring's albums are often racked alongside more sedate material, his stunning bassmanship is anything but laid-back.

You use many different tunings. How do you keep them straight?

I'm currently using some 30 or 40, in all. I don't know, actually. I just remember them. On my solo records, it's pretty much a different tuning for every piece, and I usually write one or two pieces in any one tuning. I was always fascinated with the idea of playing fretless bass as a solo instrument, but I kept finding that you always want to have the open strings as reference points. All my tunes sort of sounded the same, and retuning opened it up for new ideas. I kept getting further and further out. On "Circular Birds" [*Montreux*], for instance, it's a standard low *E* and octave *E* and *B*, and *E* again. The lowest I ever tune the low string down to is standard low *E*, and the highest I ever tune it is to *D*, a minor 7th above that — and anywhere in between. I find that I can tune all of the strings over pretty much the same sort of range.

What's your basic compositional process? Do you experiment with a new tuning to see if something clicks, and then decide whether you should continue using it?

I studied a lot of music theory and have the tendency to get scholastic, like a lot of musicians. And one thing I like about the bizarre tunings is that you don't really recognize the patterns you're playing. And that's great because it made me stop thinking, "Oh, this is not hip; I should use a major 9th chord." Instead, it became just feeling and hearing the music and deciding whether I liked it on that basis. When I was growing up, I had the tendency to overanalyze everything and try to come up with fancy chords just to do it. The new tunings helped me to get rid of that theoretical bias. When I have time, I get into a new tuning and try not to pay too much attention to what it is, and instead just listen to its sound to see what kinds of things it suggests, and then go from there.

Isn't it disquieting to approach an unfamiliar tuning with familiar licks, only to have them sound completely wrong?

That's one of the other things that really pushed me into it. I was thinking about all the things you never play on a bass with standard tuning because of some of the incredibly difficult stretches. A chord with, for instance, a ♭9, a 5th, and a major 7th sounds great, but in standard tuning it's not an easy thing to do. It's a shame to never be able to use that, and I thought alternative tunings would provide another way to expand the realm of the bass without getting into things that are absurdly difficult. When I first started working out solo pieces in standard tuning, I immediately went into the "hardest thing I can do" kind of mode, making ridiculous stretches and practicing things for months and months before I could play them at all. And I realized that I wasn't having any fun. I couldn't be expressive enough.

Fretless bass is so difficult to play in tune. Do you ever work on exercises to tame the intonation troubles?

Constantly. One way to learn to play in tune is to hang out with somebody who has a really good sense of pitch. Another way is to set up a sequence of a major scale on a synthesizer and play with that. I can

> *"I have a feeling about the fretless—the mysterious things about it, the little subtleties that happen when your finger is so close to the string."*

also play a chord on the synth and then hold down its sustain pedal and play something on bass over it. The synthesizer chord provides a strong reference. It's always a challenge, and of course changes in the weather also affect the shape of your fingerboard. Some notes' locations move slightly, and when you get into these weird tunings, the tension also affects a note's placement. So if the string is lower, you have to play the note sharper to keep it in tune. And if it's tuned higher, you have to play a note flatter, because you've got the extra tension of pushing the string down. It's madness. I've tried doing a lot of my stuff on fretted bass, but I just have a feeling about the fretless — the mysterious things about it, the little subtleties that happen when your finger is so close to the string. This keeps me on the fretless, even with all that pain of dealing with intonation problems.

How did you happen to study with Jaco Pastorius?

He lived in New York at the time, and when I met him, I very sheepishly asked if he would give me some lessons. So we got together a couple of times, and it was very, very, *very* intense, because he was just incredible. From the time I first heard him, when I was about 15, to this day, I don't think a day ever goes by when I don't spend a great bit of time thinking about what he did and how he did it. He was a big part of my life. After I studied with him, I really started to feel like I was finding my own voice.

Do you ever encounter "purists" who say you shouldn't retune your bass?

Usually, people don't even believe that it's bass. They come up to me after a show and ask, "What kind of synth were you using on that solo piece?" They're usually referring to "Thunder Tactics" [*Unusual Weather*], and I say, "It wasn't a synth — just a bass in a different tuning." Then they ask what kind of harmonizer I used. They don't believe that it's just tapping and different tuning.

A great deal of your solo material has no drums, yet bass and drums are often thought of as inseparable.

That's true. About the time I met Hedges, I was playing mostly fusion and a bit of bebop, and getting kind of tired of it. I wanted to try something really different, and playing with Hedges was a great opportunity to get into something different, and part of that was no longer thinking that bass and drums necessarily acted as a unit. Not that I have anything against it. As a matter of fact, I'm really into it, but if that's all you ever do, you're missing out on something. I spent about four years hardly ever playing with a drummer, and it enabled me to come up with different ways of looking at the bass. With Montreux, I'm back to locking with the drums, which is a good feeling. If I weren't in Montreux, I'd probably never play any regular bass [laughs]. And a lot of times, I just walk in with the drummer and go. It's great, because it's another outlet. When I play with Michael Hedges, for example, I do 90% melodic stuff, and it's not quite the same. And for the solo stuff, I use the weird tunings. But with Montreux, it's mostly just straight meat-and-potatoes bass, which is good for me. I love playing simpler, regular bass, and I usually try to cut it down to the least number of notes possible and go for a nice tone and a tight groove.

When you're doing two simultaneous taps per hand during a song such as "A Brief History Of The Wind" [Center Of The Night], you must have to pay extra close attention so you don't inadvertently cut notes off as you alternate.

This is the stuff nobody catches. A lot of people are interested in the tapping, but the hardest part is the muting — making the strings stop ringing when you're also tapping. You have to find some way to mute the ones you don't want ringing.

And you've only got 10 fingers.

Thank God, there's only four *strings*. But for that piece, the strings are tuned A♭, G♭, A♭, A♭, with the top strings in unison. On a fretless I usually try not to tap too many crazy intervals, because it's just not easy to stay in tune.

You also cross one hand over the other.

I think it's really natural to cross over a hand. Some people feel that you should always keep your hands separate, but if it feels natural to me to keep a motive going that way, then it's the right thing to do. I've got a couple of songs like that: "Geometry" [Center Of The Night] and "Circular Birds." It's really fun live.

What are your main basses?

The Paul Reed Smith [Vintage Cherry Bass IV Fretless] is my meat-and-potatoes bass, the one I use most when I play with other people. It has a mahogany body, and it's really nicely made — a very straightforward instrument. It has light-gauge strings on it, but not extraordinarily light. There are only

about eight tunes where I use my regular bass, but I wanted to get more and more weird so I got these really light-gauge strings. It's kind of like a piccolo bass, but I tune the low string all the way down to low E, so it goes as low as a regular bass. But it has a lot more spirit to it. I use a Music Man StingRay for most of the bizarre tunings. It has this weird kind of a spread-out sound, a lot of low end and a lot of top end, so it didn't really work that well as a regular fretless. However, it works great for the weird tunings. I'm going to replace it, though; that's why I'm using a Zon for some stuff. I'm working with Joe Zon to get a cleaner-sounding, more high-tech instrument. I also have a Larrivee 5-string fretless acoustic and a Riverhead fretted bass — the only thing I ever recorded on that was "Funk And Disorderly." Finding the Larrivee was like a dream come true. I almost always tune it in different ways, but right now it's F, C, G, C, D. I had been looking for an acoustic for a long time, but most are real deep and sort of funky. This one's shallow and midrangey. When I record with it, I use a Bill Lawrence transducer and two Neumann KM-84 microphones.

Do you change your strings very often?

A lot. I always practice with dead strings because I think it helps you learn to sustain longer and to work toward a better tone. But depending on what instrument I'm playing, I change them in the studio every six hours. Live, depending on the bass I use, I change them for every show. [Ed. Note: Manring uses D'Addario XL220 Nickel Round Wound strings in Super Soft Gauge.] Maybe they only have a certain amount of notes in them [laughs]. For Montreux, when I use the Paul Reed Smith most of the time, I change them for every show. It's nice to have spanking-new strings.

How do you get your sound onstage?

The trick is how do you get it on the airplane without them charging you extra! [Laughs.] It's pretty simple. I use a Rane dual-15-band graphic EQ: one channel for my Paul Reed Smith, and the other side for my Music Man StingRay. I use this old MXR graphic for the fretted Riverhead bass. Those are the three basses I take with me, because that's all I can get away with. I use the equalizers to deal with the differences in the P.A.s and the rooms. An Alesis Quadraverb is my only effect unit; it's nice and compact, and I use it for reverb and chorus. I use an Akai MB-76 MIDI-controlled mixer; it lets you program how much of what goes to where. It's like a poor man's programmable mixer. So into the mixer I plug in the PRS bass, the Music Man bass, and the

Riverhead, plus I have the Quadraverb patched in and send out to the monitor and the tuner. That way I can turn off the monitor while still routing to a tuner. I use a Meico MIDI Commander footswitch unit to select which bass is used. I never use an amp on the road. I send my bass out to the house system and into the monitor. I'd like to use an amp in a lot of cases, but with Montreux, we have so many mikes onstage that I can't play very loud.

Do you record straight into the board?

Yes, and that's what I do at home. I like doing that because amps really color the sound a lot — which is what they're supposed to do and which is a nice thing. But it can fool you if you always practice with an amp, because you can think that your bass and you are producing things that you're not, whereas if you play into a board, through the cleanest gear you can afford, then it isn't such a shock when you get into the studio.

Do you ever overdub parts to make it a little easier on yourself?

Never to make it easier on myself. I never was that smart, I guess. I usually write songs around the bass,

"You can get so much subtlety out of the electric, so much nuance, and there are so many delicate things you can do to create your own sound."

so there's usually a part like "Thunder Tactics" that works as the basis for the whole piece and gets elaborated on. Therefore, a lot of the pieces are just glorified bass solos. And they usually consist of a bass line, chords, and a melody, so it's hard to take it all apart. I record it all as one, but I might double it with a melody from another bass as a separate idea.

Is there still a lot of wide-open territory for bassists to explore?

Yes. You know what I always thought was weird? When you listen to upright bass players, everybody has a distinctive sound and approach, whereas electric bass players tend to get into a couple of different camps. I always thought that was bizarre, because on upright you have to struggle so much just to get a sound out of it, and you can get so much subtlety out of the electric, so much nuance, and there are so many delicate things you can do to create your own sound. Electric is really more suited for a very personal kind of playing. But it's often treated completely backwards. Electric bass is one of the most dynamic instruments there is. To me, electric bass is *the* most beautiful instrument.

– MARCUS MILLER –

BY TOM MULHERN & JAS OBRECHT – NOVEMBER 1983

MARCUS Miller's chameleon style defies categorization. As a session ace for such prominent jazz and pop artists as Grover Washington, Tom Scott, Earl Klugh, Stanley Turrentine, Aretha Franklin, Donald Fagen, Roberta Flack, Elton John, and George Benson, the innovative bassist with the distinctive thumb-only right-hand approach had been viewed as a bebop, rock, fusion, soul, and funk musician. It wasn't until his year-and-a-half stint with trumpet great Miles Davis that Marcus began to lose his labels: "Playing with Miles was great because he's the kind of person who just breaks those barriers down. After a while you can't say what he does. I was glad to play with him, because no one would then be able to define my bass playing."

Marcus found that in the free-form jazz context of Davis' music, the rhythm he kept on bass was as important as the notes themselves. After appearing on Miles' *The Man With The Horn* and the live *We Want Miles*, the bassist joined the house band of TV's *Saturday Night Live* in late 1981. He soon expanded his musical directions by becoming a creative partner on saxophonist David Sanborn's critically acclaimed *Voyeur* album, providing several compositions as well as playing bass, guitar, piano, sax, and drums. After the album's release, others began covering Marcus Miller compositions, notably singers Teddy Pendergrass, Aretha Franklin, and Dionne Warwick. Aretha scored a major hit with the Luther Vandross/

Marcus Miller composition "Jump To It" from the album of the same name, and Roberta Flack sang Miller's "Lovin' You" on the *Bustin' Loose* film soundtrack.

Earlier this year Marcus decided to take his music a step further by composing, co-producing, and playing most of the instruments on his first solo LP, *Suddenly*. A slick, pop-oriented production, the album displays many sides of the bassist's style and sounds: "Lovin' You" is energized by percussive funk lines with a biting, trebly tone. "Much Too Much" showcases a piccolo bass solo, and the impeccable fretless work in "Could It Be You" is tonally reminiscent of Jaco Pastorius. Even on tunes without a lot of prominent bass work, Marcus leaves a strong impression of his bass style through the lines he plays on other instruments.

Ever since his youth, Marcus has demonstrated uncommon musical abilities. He was born in Brooklyn, New York, on June 14, 1959, and moved with his family to Jamaica in the nearby Queens borough at age 10. His dad, who taught school and worked for the Transit Authority, played jazz keyboards in his spare time. Marcus' earliest musical recollections are of figuring out pop tunes on the family piano. At 10, the youth started on clarinet, and soon afterwards began singing R&B tunes with neighborhood bands. His prowess as a budding clarinetist earned him admission to New York's Performing Arts School, a division of the high school on which the movie and TV series *Fame* is based. Inspired by Kool & The Gang and Tower Of Power, Marcus began teaching himself bass at 13. By the time he finished high school, he was also proficient on piano and saxophone.

Miller scored his first professional gig on bass with Harlem River Drive, a New York club band that specialized in R&B tunes and occasional jazz numbers. As his musical influences broadened, Marcus came to appreciate the intricacies of bebop. After nearly two years with the outfit, Miller was hired to play bass for jazz saxophonist Bobbi Humphrey in 1977. During the same year, some of his compositions were covered by keyboardist Lonnie Liston Smith on his *Loveland* album. Marcus' next leader, drummer Lenny White, added several of the bassist's compositions to the band repertoire. Following a year on the road with White, Marcus entered Queens College on a clarinet scholarship. His formal studies fell by the wayside, though, as he began an intense apprenticeship in New York's record and jingle session scene, playing bass with numerous artists over the next three years. Word of the bassist's musical prowess finally spread to Miles Davis, who enlisted him for his band.

Since his stint with Davis and the release of *Suddenly,* Marcus has been finishing compositions and session projects for Aretha Franklin, David Sanborn, Dionne Warwick, and Luther Vandross. He is also busy at work on his next solo release.

"I've had enough experience where I can go for that good feeling, no matter what kind of music it is."

How does working with an instrumentalist vary from working with a vocalist?

I don't think that the difference is there as much as it is between the types of music that musicians are doing. I've done gigs with George Benson where we were playing bebop, and of course my role was that of a bebop bass player. And then on his record sessions, we did pop instrumentals, and my role changed. The bebop was more free, while the pop music was more groove-oriented. The main thing is to make it feel good. Luckily, I've had enough experience where I can go for that good feeling, no matter what kind of music it is.

How did you get into Miles' band?

I was in the studio, and people in Miles' band had heard me. He needed a bass player, and he called me to do the session for *The Man With The Horn,* and he asked me to join the band.

How many albums have you recorded with Miles?

I also did the live album and the new one. There might be more coming, because we recorded a lot of stuff. Miles has *pounds* of stuff sitting there from decades ago. I'm sure the stuff will get put out, but I'm not sure when.

Did he just call you?

Yeah. I was doing a country date, and I got a note that said to call him. I didn't think it was *the* Miles Davis. A year before that I had gotten a call from CBS, and they got together a bunch of musicians and tried to force Miles into the studio. Miles just didn't show up, and they canned that. I thought this was going to be another of those numbers. But he was there. I knew it was Miles when he walked in, and we got along great. After I left that first day, I had a real good feeling. People get so caught up in labeling me. People say *funk* bassist Marcus Miller, or some people didn't even know I played funk when I was playing the bebop clubs. There's a bebop pianist named Walter Bishop, Jr., who played with Charlie Parker when he was young. We played together, and one day he came up to me and said, "Hey, Marcus, I didn't know you played rock. I just saw you playing on TV." Everybody thought I played a different thing. Playing with Miles was great because he's the kind of person who just breaks those barriers down. After a while you can't say what he does. I was glad to play with him, because no one would then be able to define my bass playing.

Did you study bass at New York's Performing Arts School?

I stayed mostly on the clarinet, but high school is when I started on bass. I just played on the side in all the extracurricular groups like the gospel chorus and the jazz band. They offered string bass at the school, but clarinet was my major instrument. I could have probably minored in string bass, but I was minoring in electric bass, actually. I was also playing in neighborhood bands at the same time I was learning classical music.

Did you ever play string bass?

I did for a while, but I got into the electric bass and became so busy on it. You really have to put in a lot of time with it. It's not like a lot of instruments that you can automatically double on. You know the basic fingerings if you play electric, but that's where the similarity ends. It's a different instrument.

Did you have to play piano in school?

I just had a little theory. You had to know your basic chords and scales — no real piano lessons. The piano is something I've learned mostly on my own. I can't play it like I do the bass, but as far as getting the things I want to hear from it, I can do that. Same with the guitar, which I picked up on right after I started on the bass.

Did you find it hard to get into bands as a clarinetist?

Yeah. I was playing clarinet since I was 10, and in my first band I played saxophone. Then I switched to organ, because nobody else could play organ. When I moved to bass, I found that it was the instrument I really liked. I tried to get them to let me play bass, but they didn't go for it. So I had to wait a little bit to get my own band before I could play the bass in it.

At what point did bass become your main instrument?

It was half and half through high school. When I got out of high school, I had the choice of going to Mannes School of Music, which is a music college in New York, or going to a liberal arts college and trying to make it out on the streets with the bass. I thought, "Playing the clarinet is going to be kind of rough because there aren't that many offers." I'd have to read the musician's union weekly paper to see if there was an opening in something like the Phoenix Symphony Orchestra for a third clarinet player because the other guy died [*laughs*], and then go and audition with a hundred other cats who are looking for the same gig. I didn't want to go this way. And at that time, I was gaining infinite acceptance on the bass because you can gain acceptance on it with nothing but a *feel*. If that's all you've got, you can do okay. I was playing a lot, and people enjoyed what I was doing. I said, "This looks like it will give me a lot more possibilities." So I decided that I was really going to concentrate on the bass.

Were you excited by any bass players?

I was excited by all of them. The first guy, I think, was the bassist with Kool And The Gang [Robert Bell]. Then there was the bassist for Tower Of Power named [Francis] "Rocco" Prestia. He was mean. Then I got into Stanley Clarke, Alphonso Johnson, and Jaco Pastorius. I never stayed into one guy for too long, although I did listen to Jaco a lot during one period. That was good because I think he's really musical. By listening to him, you can learn a lot about more than just playing the bass. You try to figure out why he plays what he does against the chords and lines. He forces you to learn the chords, unless

you just wanted to play his solos over and over again. It just made me wonder — there just had to be some kind of method to what he was doing. Stanley also forced me to learn about music, which many bassists never do. They never learn about anything but the bass, which limits them a lot.

Did you study any books on bass?

I picked up a few, but they were kind of boring. I was trying to get my reading together. I'd read the lines, and it would be hard to figure out their rhythms. Once I figured out the rhythms and could play the music, I realized that what I was playing was so corny that I said, "Why should I take the time to learn to play this?" I learned most of my reading when I was on the clarinet in school, because we did it every day in orchestra.

Once you had established your bass chops, how did you get into playing professionally?

First of all, I was in New York, and that's a plus. Even when I was in high school, I could wander downtown to the Village. A lot of different things came together when I got into college. I played bebop with Kenny Washington, who is the drummer for [saxophonist] Johnny Griffin, and Omar Hakim, who plays drums with Weather Report. Omar and Kenny would introduce me to people. After a while, you just start planting seeds, and eventually they start coming together. Omar and I met in high school and got really tight. We had a band called the Harlem River Drive, and the guitar player was Ronnie Miller, a cousin of mine. Ronnie started playing with Bobbi Humphrey, and when Bobbi needed a bass player, Ronnie got me in the band. So I was playing with Bobbi for a while when I was 16 or 17 — we did a couple of short tours to Washington, D.C., Philadelphia, and Cleveland. When Bobbi started making records with [producer] Ralph McDonald, she did a song I wrote called "Love When I'm In Your Arms" [on *Individuals*] and let me play on it. It had a bass solo. So Ralph asked me if I could play jingles, and he got his friends to call me. I started doing R&B jingles and then moved into the more generic stuff.

After reading treble clef for so long, did bass clef reading pose a problem?

At first it was kind of weird. But with reading music, after you get past a certain point, you don't think of clefs anymore. Now, if I was playing clarinet and someone put music in bass clef in front of me, then I'd have a problem, because when you play a clarinet, you look at that note on the second line and you don't actually think *G*. It goes straight from your eyes to your fingers. You just see it and your hands go for what it is. I think everyone associates the notes with the fingering after a while, because I can't see how someone can sit there and have to figure out what every note is and then play it. I just associated the bass clef with the bass notes, and it wasn't as hard as some people might think.

Did you find the rhythms on session lead sheets to be difficult?

No. In high school orchestras we played a lot of pieces by Charles Ives and other modern American composers. Their rhythms were really intricate, and the time signatures changed every bar. I remember playing pieces where every bar went from 3/8 to 2/4 to 4/4 to 5/8 to 1/8 and so on. Every bar changed, so I got used to wild rhythms very early. The rhythms presented to the bass are actually more limited, and you see more of the same signatures recurring in the music that I played. It's the same thing with subdivisions of the beat. You don't subdivide anymore; you see a group of notes and know what the rhythm is. That seems to happen with time.

Do you ever run across proportional groupings where there will be, say, five beats in the space of three, etc.?

Sometimes, but not that often. I've gotten that stuff, but it's not that difficult. The reason they put the number up there is because they want to get from one note to the other in a certain space of time. And it just so happens that the amount of notes in between those two points isn't an even number like eight or four. So whatever number is necessary is just fit in there. They're really saying, "We just want you to squeeze the notes in." You don't have to sit there and subdivide. You just have to feel natural. I'm playing popular music now where those kinds of rhythms like fitting 5 into the space of 3 just aren't that important. You want to get a more solid groove. And if you find it, you can squeeze those notes in if you want. I've been in situations where that is important, and luckily my classical training has helped me out.

Do you think classical training would be helpful to most bass players?

It would help, but I think it depends on what you want to do. For instance, if you want to be a guy who plays a bass in his own group, doing his own kind of music — like Stanley Clarke or Jaco or some-

"Stanley Clarke forced me to learn about music, which many bassists never do. They never learn about anything but the bass, which limits them."

one like that — it doesn't matter that you can read music at all, because you're going on your feeling and the way you play — your style. But if you want to be a studio musician or go into any other situation where you have to read someone else's music, classical training — or any kind of training — would help.

What did you do after you left Bobbi Humphrey?

I was about 17 then, and I went on the road with Lenny White. I played with him for a year, which was real gratifying. He had just come out of Return To Forever, so I was playing with the drummer who had played with Stanley Clarke. I was awed, but he was just so supportive, letting me play my own way and doing what I felt. After a while, it got kind of comfortable. He really helped me in a lot of ways. Before Lenny asked me to join his band, Weldon Irvine, who was a real influential piano player in New York, asked me to do a trio bebop gig in Long Island with Lenny. I had never played with a drummer like him before. He was doing all these rhythms that I had never heard before. I just couldn't figure out where they were coming from. I was trying to hold the time for him, and I kept turning around the beat. Every time he'd play a fill, I'd end up on 1 and 3. His hi-hat would sound like it was on 1 and 3, which was *obviously* wrong, because it was actually on 2 and 4. He didn't laugh or anything; he just knew that this was something that I would just have to learn to do. After the gig I said, "Lenny, obviously I just messed up every solo you played. What should I do to get it together? Who are the drummers that you listen to?" He said that he really liked Tony Williams and Elvin Jones for that kind of stuff. So I went over to Kenny Washington's house later — he has the catalog of life of jazz records — and he gave me records of Elvin and Tony. I just sat home and snapped my fingers to the beat for hours. I listened and tried to figure out where they were coming from.

They have the uncanny ability to jump off the beat mid-measure, play outside of the beat for several bars, and come down on the 1.

Right. But I found out that it's easier to know what's going on by playing with a person rather than just listening to a record. Somehow there's a vibe that accompanies everything that he's playing, and you can latch onto it. When you're just listening to some-one like Elvin, you ask, "What is he thinking?" But if you can get into a guy's mind to see how he approaches music, it helps. That was really important for me in learning how to be a good, supportive bass player. It was especially important working with Lenny, because that's what he wanted.

Did he play a lot of drum solos?

Yeah, and he needed somebody to lay it down for him. That was my job. And working with Lenny opened up my mind to the possibilities of rhythms with drummers. It's important, because when I play with drummers, I find that they seem like they feel good about playing with me. Even if I haven't excited anybody in the audience, the drummer feels good, because I work hard to make him feel comfortable. There's two ways to look at it: Sometimes when I'm feeling my Wheaties, I want to be the one to go out and experiment, and I expect the drummer to help me by keeping it down. Then there's the situation where you and the drummer are so tight that you can both go, and know where each other is — but then no one else may know. When I play with Omar or with Buddy Williams, it's like that.

Sometimes the guitar player ends up scratching his head, trying to figure out where the bassist is heading.

The guitarist says, "Well, look . . ." When I was playing with Miles, [drummer] Al Foster and I developed that. Miles would just pull his mouth off the horn and look at us and say, "Where's the beat?" We really took it out. Al was getting into a thing where he would be playing a straight 4/4 on the ride cymbal, and on the snare drum he'd do a rhythm that was kind of like when you drop a rubber ball and each bounce gets closer together. And he'd keep that time on the cymbal. So after a while, I started to double with my bass what he was doing on the snare drum. Miles wouldn't know what we were doing, because the only thing that was holding the beat was the ride cymbal. But to do those kinds of things, you've got to know the drummer. Miles eventually got used to it. Toward the end of the year-and-a-half that I was with Miles, we really had some good stuff happening.

It seems like you couldn't really learn that kind of stuff in school.

No, I don't think you could. You can learn it conceptually, but the real thing is *doing* it. Living in New York really helps. I know a lot of players from other parts of the country who had to come to New York and find a way to pay the rent and get the experience

at the same time. Some had to take 9-to-5 jobs, and it was really hard for them. I would just go home after the day and my mother would have food waiting for me, and I had a place to stay. It really helped.

Were your parents very supportive of your musical endeavors?

Oh, yeah. I remember my mother driving me to New Jersey to do gigs. In my neighborhood — Jamaica, Queens — you could go one of two ways: You could do really, really well or you could really, really bad. A lot of guys were getting caught up in drugs. My mother was just glad that I was into *something*, and when I started making bread at it, she was really happy. I knew I was going to be a musician when I was young — I didn't know what instrument I was going to play when I was 13 or 14, but I knew. I think my mother just felt good that I had a path laid out for me.

What did you do after you left Lenny White?

I went back to New York and enrolled in Queens College to study music education. I was doing bebop gigs at night, and trying to get into the studio scene during the day. It didn't take that long, because luckily at that time there weren't that many bass players around who could read the music and play with a feel at the same time.

How did things develop once you started recording jingles for Ralph McDonald?

People liked the way I played, so by word of mouth it just snowballed. Also, people knew me from playing with Lenny White, and there were still a lot of jazz-fusion sessions going on. After a while, it all came together. I don't think I ever wanted to make being a studio musician an ultimate goal. I really wanted to do what Lenny did: have my own band and just play fusion. I've been in the studios now for about three or four years, and my values have changed. I now know that I don't want to play fusion anymore. I also calmed down a lot; the stuff with Lenny was really high-energy. Being in the studios, I learned the value of just keeping a groove for seven minutes, and the little things that make studio playing special.

You don't feel the need to solo all the time now.

Yeah. I really enjoy playing a good groove. I always did, but it just didn't seem important to the guys I was playing with when I was doing fusion. But now, all of a sudden, by playing in the studios, I could see that that was what people wanted. I also found out that just as not everyone can solo well, not everyone can play a groove well. I figured that was something I should get together, too. I'm not into studio work as much as I was, but I am still working on some projects, including my own albums and producing.

Had you ever wanted to play with Miles Davis before he asked you to join his band?

No. I didn't think it was a possibility, because he had been off the scene for about seven years, and I figured he wasn't going to play anymore. But if someone had asked me, "Do you want to play with Miles?" I would have said, "sure."

Do you have any favorite cuts that you did with Miles?

I like "Back Seat Betty." In fact I like all cuts we did with the band on *The Man With The Horn.*

Were any more difficult than others?

No. There wasn't any music written out. He just gave a downbeat and you went for what you felt. I liked some of the stuff on this last album, too, but it got more structured. It's strange. You'd think that after you'd been working together awhile, it would get looser because you knew each other. Al and I were getting looser, but the band as a whole started to sound more and more structured. I'm not saying it sounded bad, but it was getting to where you could pick out sections. I kind of liked it when it sounded more nebulous.

Who did you key off of the most?

Miles and Al. When Miles was playing, everyone keyed off of him, but when he wasn't, Al and me put it down. You key off of everybody, but since I was standing next to him, I keyed off of him the most.

Did Miles expect you to play in any particular way or use certain tones?

Not really. Every once in a while he'd ask me to add some bass or take some off, depending on the stage we were playing on. Most of the time, he'd play something on the piano, and tell me to play something like *that.*

Coming from a band background, why did you play practically everything on your solo album by yourself?

Basically, I was experimenting with different directions, and I didn't want to do an album with *everybody* on it. I'm sure I could have gotten everybody together to do an album like that, but I wanted to focus more on an individual statement.

Did you use a drum machine?

On some stuff I started with one and took it off. For "Much Too Much," I used a Roland TR-808, and on some of the other ones I used the foot from an Oberheim drum machine and played the rest of the drums myself. Basically, it was just me or whoever played the drums on the track.

In what order did you lay the tracks down?

Well, I just put the drum machine down and played the other instruments. It depended on what instrument I thought carried the main feeling of the song. Sometimes I put the bass down after the drum machine or piano tracks. Occasionally, I'd think that the bass should react more to what another instrument was doing, so I would go back and play another bass track and finally do the drums. It didn't take that long to actually record all those tracks. The hard part was finding time to do it. I was playing with Miles and David Sanborn, flying to get to their gigs. And when I had time off, I'd work on my record. Now it will be a little easier because things have calmed down and I can concentrate more on myself.

When you played the other instruments, did you find yourself thinking in terms of bass or clarinet lines?

No. I can think guitar when I play the guitar, piano when I play piano. It's like that with all the instruments I've picked up along the way. I was a real restless kid, and I've always enjoyed doing a lot of things. It's almost like a jack-of-all-trades syndrome, but if you get good enough, you can defeat it.

Is it easier for you to write songs on guitar than on bass?

Actually, most of the time I write on the piano. Or, if it's a funkier type of song, I'll use the bass and drums or the guitar. It depends, because different instruments help to give you different ideas. You can start a song from any of those instruments.

Your bass tone was much brighter on **Suddenly** *than on the albums with Miles. Was this intentional?*

I liked the tone with Miles, because it was what was needed. My role was supportive — to hold everybody down. On my album, I didn't want to lose the lows. I wanted to get the rest of that spectrum. Everything was intentional. There are so many possibilities with the bass that people don't even realize. There are a lot of available frequencies, especially if you're playing with your thumb, because it strikes off many highs that you might not get with your fingers.

Do you use your thumb most of the time?

Yeah. There are a lot of guys who have to switch back: You play the verse with your fingers, and then switch off to your thumb for the chorus where it gets a little louder. But I don't have to do that anymore because I've got a lot of control with it. So I can play the whole song with my thumb without sounding too blatant. I've been getting pretty good with it, like Wes Montgomery did. You forget how to articulate with slurs and other techniques, so by adding them back in, your sound is more interesting.

Do you ever use your nails to pluck the strings?

Oh, yeah. On "Much Too Much" I used the nail on my right-hand thumb, and it sounds like I picked up a pick and played only one line with it. I don't do anything special to take care of it — my nail just happened to be in good shape the day I recorded that.

How did you get the bass sound on "Lovin' You" to fill the whole audio spectrum?

I went direct and miked my amp also. Direct gives you a very close thing, but with the mike you get the really high highs that people often don't think a bass can produce. So I use the mike to give me the highs like up in the 10k [10,000 Hz] range, and use the direct to get the super lows, down around 60 Hz. I wanted to fill up the whole spectrum, because there was nothing but bass and drums at the beginning of the song.

What kind of amp did you use for that?

I have a rack-mounted setup with 15" Electro-Voice speakers, an Intersound IVP Voicing Preamp, and a QSC power amplifier. I also have a Lexicon PCM-42 digital delay, but I don't use it that much.

How did you do the bent harmonics in "Could It Be You"?

Let's say it's the harmonic at the 5th fret on the G string. [*Ed. Note: For this technique, rather than removing your left-hand finger immediately after sounding the harmonic, leave it in contact with the string.*] Play the harmonic, and then gently press the string against the fingerboard and slide it up or down. You'll make the harmonic note glide up or down. Most people hold the harmonic note, and after they attack the string with the right hand, they let go. You can hit a harmonic and press down. It will stay if your bass is in decent condition.

"Could It Be You" has a bass tone that's unlike anything else on Suddenly.

That's my fretless Fender Jazz Bass — it's about a '64. It has a rosewood fingerboard that was fretted, but I had the frets taken out and the slots filled. I've used that bass a lot, but mostly on jazz and bebop things. It gives a good fretless sound, but it's really *dark.*

Intonation is something that many fretless players lack, yet your notes seem clearly defined.

I worked on it for a long time, especially when I was into Jaco. Because of him, everybody started playing fretless, and it was getting nauseating. They're always sliding up and down the neck because it's fretless. It's like having a trombone, where just because you can slide notes up and down, that's all you

do. If you use it as a musical effect, fine. But I think a lot of people were sliding on the bass because they couldn't find the real note. I worked for a long time on getting my intonation together. I'm still working on it; it's a real challenge.

How do you check your accuracy?

I have a 4-track tape recorder. I'll record myself playing chords and lines on the Fender Rhodes piano, and then play a bass solo over it and listen. It's easy to tell if it's out of tune. It doesn't have to be perfectly in tune all the time. You have to look at it like a voice: Voices aren't always in tune. But the main stops — the main resting points — really have to be there. You can use vibrato, but it shouldn't be to cover up bad intonation. It should enhance your playing.

What other basses do you use often?

I have a Fender Jazz Bass that I bought around 1966 or '67. Nothing special, but I had a preamp put in by Roger Sadowsky. The pickups are stock, but the bridge has been replaced with a Badass.

Why did you want a preamp?

At first, I wasn't sure what it would do, but Roger said it was hip. I don't like when you play with your thumb and there's no bottom to it. The preamp helped me to get that bottom, so I could fill up the whole spectrum if I wanted to. A lot of the new basses sound real tinny, almost like a low guitar. That's one of the main reasons that synthesizers came into such prominence for playing bass lines. Bassists just weren't holding it down anymore. People were missing that, and the synthesizer is supplying it again. What I like about this bass is that it gives a broad spectrum of frequencies, and it's flexible. I can play in a whole lot of different settings where I would otherwise need a lot of basses. Aside from that fretless, I can get everything I need from my fretted bass. So I carry around the fretted and fretless and have everything I need.

Do you set your action high to eliminate string buzz?

Just high enough to keep them from buzzing. I don't mind some buzz, especially when I'm playing with my thumb. It's there, and I know a lot of people don't like it, but I think it's a part of my sound. On a ballad, you don't want it because it interferes, but otherwise a little buzz is okay.

What kind of strings do you use on your regular basses?

Dean Markley Super Rounds. I used the half-rounds for a long time, but I realized that with my current amplification setup I could get the same thing using roundwounds. I find roundwounds easier to play. I replace them about every two weeks. I like them when they're about a week old and lose that wiry sound.

Do you own any other basses?

I have an Aria piccolo bass. I use Carl Thompson piccolo bass strings on it, tuned an octave above the regular bass. I used it on the solo in "Much Too Much" [*Suddenly*], the one that sounds like a guitar solo with a lot of body. Stanley Clarke uses a piccolo bass, but he approaches it differently. He plays it much like a bass, but I try to approach it more like a guitar.

Do you use a pick with it?

No, just my fingers. I use a pick on the guitar. I used one on the bass for a while. I liked to use one when I'd mute the strings and get an "island" sound. I stopped using a pick for that, and now I just mute with my palm near the bridge and using my fingers.

Do you often play with your right hand over the neck?

I don't play *on* the neck. A lot of California guys play right over the neck, and there are all these harmonics in the sound because you make harmonics with your thumb in the same way as you would normally. So I mostly play right where the neck ends.

Do you use effects often?

I used to use chorus a lot, and I use my DDL [digital delay line] sometimes, mostly for slapback. When I was with Miles, I used to use it to repeat my lines a couple of beats later. It's really flexible. I sometimes pull out my old MXR Phase 90. Lately, the effects don't seem to take away from my sound. Before, I used to get invisible. I'd use a flanger and all of a sudden I sounded like Anthony Jackson. But my sound has developed to the point where I don't think the effects cover it up anymore.

What do you think makes a good bass line?

A certain amount of repetition, a good feeling, and the way it works against the drums. In many funk songs, for instance, the bass guitar is an exact rhythmic duplication of the bass drum. That's good; it works. And there's sometimes exact duplication with the exception of a few things that the bass does by itself. I like that. For me, I like to have some bass notes separate from the drum so that you can hear them. When Omar and I were playing in Japan, we used to play games where he would lift his foot off the bass drum pedal and just play the beat without the bass drum, and see if anyone would notice. Then I would

seriously use my thumb to try creating that bass drum sound. I don't think anyone noticed until they saw his white shoe on top of the tom-tom: "Hey, wait a minute!" [*Laughs.*]

Do you do any live gigs anymore?

Yeah, with a trio — some low-profile gigs in the Village, just to keep my total musical spectrum happening. It's a mix of different things, a lot of jazz. I want to get my own band together after I finish my next album.

Do you ever practice?

When I have the time, I practice bebop lines because they have scales and things that keep my fingers limber. When I play with my fingers instead of my thumb, I miss that percussiveness, so I'm trying to work it out so that I can play what I want to play and get that percussiveness. It involves using a lot of upstrokes.

When you produce other people's albums, do you usually play the bass, too?

Yes. It might be too hard on another bass player. I produced and played on Lonnie Liston Smith's last album. It's not that hard for me, except that I have to keep running back and forth from the studio into the control room. That's okay, though. I sometimes play in the control room, although I usually like to be right near the drummer. But if the drum tracks are already laid down, I'll plug in right in the control room.

What bass players do you think are vital powers on the scene?

Victor Bailey with Weather Report is going to be okay. He's bad! Anthony Jackson doesn't get the recognition he deserves, but he's really good, and he's got his own thing happening. I really like that.

Do you think the bass is up-front enough now?

Bass players have to learn to work with all the synthesizers in today's music. They have to learn to change their role, which is being pushed back in some ways. But because the bass doesn't necessarily have to hold the bottom down, its role is becoming more flexible. Whereas before you could get away with just playing a bass line, a keyboard player can do it now. So you really have to be able to do something special. This shouldn't be a problem for any of the kids coming up, though, because all the bassists they hear are doing that. They don't expect to get away with anything, and I think in the future it's going to be very good.

– MONK MONTGOMERY –

By Mike Newman – September 1977

By Mike Newman – September 1977

APPROACHING 30, with a family and a steady job in a foundry in Indianapolis, Indiana, William Howard "Monk" Montgomery decided there was something missing in his life and took up the acoustic bass. Turning to music, specifically jazz, as solace seemed the natural thing for a member of the Montgomery family to do. Brother Buddy was a gifted pianist and vibist, and, of course, Wes Montgomery went on to become one of the true innovative stylists in jazz guitar history.

Monk became an innovator in his own right when he made the switch from upright to electric bass, one of the first jazzmen to do so, as a member of vibist Lionel Hampton's band in 1951. Monk was the man responsible for introducing the bass guitar to the public and was the first in jazz (possibly in history) to record on the instrument. "Guys in other kinds of music may have beat me to the studio, though I'm not aware of any," he states. "But as far as I know, I was the first in jazz to record electric bass."

The brothers Montgomery formed two dynamic outfits, the Montgomery Brothers and the Mastersounds, which, after great success in the Midwest, became extremely influential in the wave of late '50s West Coast jazz groups. (Wes met an untimely death in 1968 of a heart attack. Another Montgomery brother, June, an aspiring drummer, had passed away at age 16 from pneumonia.)

Today, at 55, Monk is still active as a bassist, but also spends a great deal of time crusading on behalf of his music, jazz. A tireless worker and organizer,

Monk is the founder and current president of the Las Vegas Jazz Society. He was recently appointed to the Jazz, Folk, and Ethnic panel of the National Endowment for the Arts in Washington, D.C. He also has started his own jazz record label, Bean Records, and broadcasts a three-hour radio show, *The Reality Of Jazz,* over KLAV in Las Vegas.

In 1974 Monk's All-Stars with singer Lovelace Watkins toured South Africa; according to jazz historian Leonard Feather, this marked the first time a U.S. jazz band had toured that racially controversial country. Montgomery is now working with the Holiday Inn's entertainment director in South Africa to help bring qualified black musicians from the strife-ridden area to study jazz at the University of Nevada at Las Vegas.

In recent years Montgomery has actively campaigned to bring jazz to the major nightclubs and showrooms in Vegas; now such clubs as the Tender Trap feature top names in jazz, many of whom have been booked via Monk's connections in the field.

Thanks to Monk Montgomery and many of his concerned colleagues, Las Vegas, the "entertainment capital of the world," has finally allowed a truly American art form to invade its neon landscape.

What made you quit your day job and go into music at age 30?

There was something missing in me. I couldn't pinpoint it for some time, but I knew it would surface. I was a firm family man, a hard worker, and had held my foundry job for years. It wasn't enough. One night when I was hanging out at a local jazz joint where Wes had a group, I heard his bass player work and suddenly just simply said to myself, "I can do better." I beat it down to Fidd's Fiddle Shop in Indianapolis, bought an old $75 Czech upright, and began practicing. That was the beautiful beginning, and it's something I'm still saying to myself over 25 years later. I am still beginning. Life is constant growth, man.

What did your early practicing on the upright consist of?

I winged it. I'm a self-taught musician. I practiced then on the upright as I still do today on the electric. The most important thing for me was to make sure my instrument was in tune and to play it in tune. I would play scales for hours, go through all the scales, concentrate on getting the full value out of the notes. Even if it was a dumb thing like a major scale, I would try to make every note important, play each evenly and have each sustain. I spent a lot of time training my hands to play, but I also worked on getting my ears to hear. I would practice with melodies and songs like "What's New?" and "All The Things You Are" — something with changes in it. I didn't want to get into the old bass bag of just accompanying other instruments. I wanted to play with good time, good feeling, but also play melodic things; I practiced that way, breaking into my own thing, the solo instead of the sideman effect.

Can you describe the early stages of your career on the bass?

I was working one night in 1951 at Andre's; it was *the* place in Indianapolis for jazz. I had worked gigs with Wes and was becoming known as a good stand-up bass player. But when I was told that Lionel Hampton wanted me in his band, I was floored. It was absolutely impossible for me to turn it down — even though it meant going on the road for two years, here and overseas, and completely changing my lifestyle, once and for all.

Why did you switch from upright to electric bass?

Hamp handed me the Fender and told me he wanted this electric instrument sound in the band. It was like he was trying to turn me on to another chick. The electric bass was considered a bastard instrument. Conventional bass players despised it. It was new and a threat to what they knew. In fact, by

"The electric bass was considered a bastard instrument. Conventional bass players despised it."

being new, it *was* jazz. But at first I freaked out, because I was in love with my upright bass. I had no choice, though; I wanted the job. I had never been on the road before. I was playing in a band with guys like [trumpeters] Art Farmer, Quincy Jones, Clifford Brown, [alto sax player] Gigi Gryce, [tenor sax player] Benny Golson, [trombonist] Jimmy Cleveland; there were some *bad* guys in that band! It was like heaven on earth to me.

Was it a strain on you playing in such a brilliant band with an instrument you weren't used to?

Yeah, I felt bad, but it was a challenge, and I love challenges. I made up my mind to do it and did it well. The band accepted me, too. This gave me confidence. Before and after each gig I would sit in my room and play the electric. It's tuned the same way as the upright, but physically it was different — strings, size, the way you hold it, the tension. I had to do it.

What is your bass-playing technique?

When I began playing the electric bass, my approach to the instrument was to play with my thumb, because technically I was after the downstroke. I played the electric as if it were an upright, and it came out in the music.

Why the thumb?

I have never played with the fingers. There is a different effect going down than coming up. The feel is different; the attack is better. If you play with your thumb, you can't come up like you can with a pick. The downstroke came to me naturally, and I just would strike the string that way. I had no examples or influences here. I was an innovator on the electric. The stroke is used in guitar, but that's another instrument.

Would you consider the downstroke the nucleus of your bass-playing technique?

Yes, it has a lot to do with it. It doesn't make me play any faster than the next guy. He's got two or three fingers to work with; I've only got my thumb or the pick I use today. I did develop enough speed to do what I wanted to do with it. It's just that playing down, I could get more of a melodic sound.

Why do you use a pick today?

About seven years ago I was in Los Angeles and playing a "jazz for breakfast" gig with my quartet. I had always played with my thumb, but suddenly I went to work this one morning, and I had no control over it; it was like my thumb had turned deaf and dumb to any command from me whatsoever! I went to several doctors, but they could find nothing physically wrong. My thumb had simply called time out. I tried to get its use back by exercises and psyching myself out, but I finally had to just say "piss on my thumb," and get a pick. I must have tried every pick that could be bought, but none of them could give me the down-stroke "finger" sound I wanted, so I experimented with materials on my own and eventually came up with my "bionic thumb." I call it Monk's Pick.

In 1962 you gave up the electric for a couple of years. What happened?

I still loved my memory of the upright, and thought I could do it again. I was playing with [vibist] Cal Tjader at the Lighthouse in Los Angeles at the time. I was on the upright, but the transition just wasn't doing it for me. I couldn't rediscover the old feeling for the music I had originally had on the stand-up bass. Cal does a lot of Latin-type things, and I realized the electric would be more effective there. I began carrying around a Precision Bass with me to use with Cal. I found that the electric immediately gave me the strong bottom sound I wanted to elicit but couldn't from the upright. One night the Precision was stolen from the band's station wagon. I went back to the Fender company, and they gave me another electric Jazz Bass, and I've been using that steadily since. The upright is past history for me.

What kind of amplifier do you use?

When I get a bass, I stick with it. As long as the bass holds up, I stay and play. The same with amplifiers. I use a Randall amp, but I don't use it for technical reasons; I don't care about the make, as long as the sound is there. I am not an electronics specialist. I am a player.

What about your strings?

I have Esquire strings on my bass now; they were sent to me, and I have also received strings from Black Diamond.

You have a skin condition that renders your hands continually dry. What do you do for it as a player?

When I'm playing, I find I can get the feel and nat-ural slide speed I want by greasing up my fingers with Vaseline. I employ just enough to capture the touch I want and, believe it or not, the Vaseline also actually helps to keep my bass strings clean!

You really didn't have any influences with the electric bass, did you?

No. I was thrown into a pool and told to swim. But I had influences on the upright, and so those in-fluences worked on me with the electric, because I played the electric like it was an upright bass. Jimmy Blanton was my first influence. I heard him on Duke Ellington recordings that a bass player friend of mine who was really into playing had. I would watch my friend play his bass in his house, and I'd listen to Jimmy Blanton. I wasn't playing yet, but I developed an affection for the bass. If my neighbor friend had been playing the sax and given me Charlie Parker records, I might have gone a different direction. Jimmy Blanton died very young [of tuberculosis] in 1942. I never saw him play. After his influence, it was Ray Brown and Charles Mingus who knocked me out. I heard them on record first, but then I saw them play in Indianapolis. Ray Brown was the strongest in-fluence on me. He was so popular then, just like Stanley Clarke is now. I was like a kid with a hero when I met Ray. He was such a warm person — not only his playing, but as a cat. Wes had toured with him and told me about this man Ray Brown. He even-tually came to town with Jazz At The Philharmonic; they got snowbound and only a part of the band got through at first. I got called from a gig to fill in for Ray until he got there; that's how we met.

When you were hanging out in Indianapolis, did either Charles Mingus or Ray Brown sit down with you and teach you things?

Not really. I mean, I would ask them questions and they would answer them. I didn't bug guys, the players, with lots of questions. I would ask them what kind of bass they used, or strings. But mostly I would listen and watch their technique — everybody, not just the superstars. My favorite artists were Buddy and Wes. Buddy still is. This thing with my brothers is a strong statement to make, but I played with them and they were constantly creative; they both did impossible things with their instruments. Today no one person is my number-one favorite. I simply like good players, no matter if they are recog-nized or not. Charles Mingus was one of the most fascinating musicians I ever heard. I actually dig horn men the most, though. The older Trane [John Coltrane] things knocked me out. Miles Davis has had some of the most dynamite groups jazz has ever seen. You learn by listening to other instruments. Oscar Pettiford was another influence on me; he was a great bass player, but his cello playing in jazz just wiped me out. No one can equal him there. I met Oscar after I was off the upright, though.

Did you study any method books when you were learning the upright?

No. I learned in the street, in my house, in local clubs. I had no formal teacher. I would tell younger players today to go get the formal training and education, but don't forget the street experience, either. In school I felt like a misfit. I got to the sixth grade, but I just couldn't cope with the school thing. It was the tough Thirties, the Depression, and I wanted to get out in the street and start making a living. When I started working — hauling ice and coal, unloading boxcars of fruit and vegetables, earning a few quarters — I was happy. I have always worked well, whether it has been as a foundry worker or a jazz player. Work is the key, but life is the lock. Music can be theory and harmony, but jazz doesn't come from an ivory tower; it is life, living, expressing yourself. This is jazz as I know it and as I *blow* it.

What is your conception of the bass as a rhythm and solo instrument?

Today the bass has come into its own and covers all bases, so to speak. Years ago, a bass player who could just accompany other instruments in a group was good enough. Now a cat has to be doing both solo and rhythm. The bass is more dominant in music. This is good. Bass players are given more notice; we make the front cover of *Down Beat* and are written up in *Guitar Player*. We are finally making it at the level of horn players and everyone else.

What players would you name today who are giving the bass its prominence?

I can name some today who are really doing it, but it started before today. You have to go further back in order to give due credit. The modern jazz bass started with Jimmy Blanton, but do you ever think about who influenced him? Someone must have, somewhere, sometime, in some way! And the guys out front today, getting the votes in jazz polls — Ron Carter, Stanley Clarke, Richard Davis; there will be extensions from them 10 years from now. I myself must have influenced other electric bass players, but I was in turn influenced by others. Jazz is a chain reaction. Charles Mingus was a space satellite, but now they have gone to the moon and they won't stop at Mars, either.

Have your habits and attitudes in music changed a great deal as you have expanded into various projects?

I appreciate people who have some understanding about other people. When I was with Lionel Hampton's band, my peers were kind to me, enjoyed

"Music can be theory and harmony, but jazz doesn't come from an ivory tower. It is life, living, expressing yourself."

what I did, and encouraged me. It was a great period in my life. I was given a chance to be free as a musician. They just dug what I was doing, and I dug it, too. I practiced like hell. With the upright I had worked the swing shift at the factory and would then come home and maybe play my bass from midnight until the morning sun came up. I did the same with electric. Today when I don't practice or play enough, I feel guilty. I have been tied up with administrative things, but I want to stress that this is great experience, too. It's all work, and I love to work. But I want to play more. I have a company, Monel Holdings, and we book jazz weekends at the Empress Hotel in Victoria, British Columbia. But I want to do more of my own straight jazz jobs. You've got to keep growing.

Why did you come to Las Vegas?

I came here from Los Angeles in the fall of '70 to make a temporary gig with [vibist/bandleader] Red Norvo at the Tropicana. The job ended up lasting almost two years.

When you found out that jazz and Vegas were not synonymous terms, why did you begin your so-called crusade?

There was no more jazz work for me or anyone. As far back as I could remember, I or other jazz players couldn't relate to Las Vegas, the supposed "entertainment capital of the world." How could the name of its game remain the same without jazz? I refused to accept what I saw, and started knocking, drumming, on doors.

Will jazz survive in Vegas?

I couldn't imagine life without some form of this music. Jazz is a great people equalizer. Look at what Louis Armstrong did. He never met with "Yankee go home" when he came to play. Jazz is more than a universal language; it is a universal love. The Las Vegas Jazz Society, in its first two years, has staged over 17 concerts, besides publishing a monthly newsletter, *Think Jazz!*, and bringing live jazz into the local school system. Countless artists have performed here, either at our society concerts, the Tender Trap, the New Town Tavern, the University of Nevada at Las Vegas, or for Strip hotels like the Hacienda, Aladdin, Stardust, Marina, and Sahara. Many true believers have made this possible. But the fight must continue to make jazz stay; jazz can't be confined to one successful club or one successful concert. It can't be given up if one club or one concert doesn't momentarily make it, either. Jazz would have been dead long ago if it would have depended solely on its market appeal. This music is creative, spontaneous, continually changing. It is freedom of expression. When I talk, I sometimes wish I had said this and said that. When I play, I sometimes wish I had played this and played that, too. Even my fingering is free!

Are people then the heartbeat in music? Do people do it?

What else? South Africa has this black, white, and colored separation thing. A Negro is black. A Caucasian is white. An Oriental or Mexican or someone else is colored, I guess. People are one of the three, but it's changing and the universal language of jazz can help to break down the blinding barriers there. I have worked in foreign countries where the only way I could rap with another brother player was through the colorblind music, and we said it all, man, believe me! We have our own color problem right here in Las Vegas. The West Side, locally known as The Side, is Vegas' black ghetto of 40,000 people. The jazz society was involved last October in helping to throw the second annual D Street Festival there. It's a big block party. [Trumpeter] Freddie Hubbard played at the New Town Tavern on The Side after the festival; everybody pitches in and makes it happen. We have arts and crafts, street food, amateur contests, rock groups, jazz groups, gospel groups, disco groups. People come together and mix it up, wing it. We don't promise anything, but we reach out, man; we just reach out! This is what jazz is all about. This is what life is all about.

– JACO PASTORIUS –

BY BILL MILKOWSKI – AUGUST 1984

TOM COPI / SAN FRANCISCO

UTTERLY ENIG-matic, easily misunderstood, and often maligned by those who observe his unpredictable behavior from a safe distance, Jaco Pastorius is nonetheless almost universally acknowledged as the greatest electric bass player in recent years.

He is a man of many faces. There is Jaco the Rocker, a side that regularly came out in concert with Weather Report during his volatile, feedback-inflected "Purple Haze"/"Third Stone From The Sun" tribute to Jimi Hendrix. There is Jaco the Jazzman, emerging in his concert and recorded versions of sax great Charlie Parker's "Donna Lee" and John Coltrane's "Giant Steps."

There is Jaco the Big Band Leader, as evidenced by his triumphant tour and follow-up album featuring the powerhouse 20-piece Word Of Mouth aggregation. Jaco the Accompanist surfaces through his sublime and sensitive support on Joni Mitchell's *Hejira* and *Mingus* albums. And there is Jaco the Romantic, a side that emerges in his tasteful, lyrical collaborations with harmonica virtuoso Jean "Toots" Thielemans on such melodic fare as Duke Ellington's "Sophisticated Lady," Paul McCartney's "Blackbird," and Toots' own "Bluesette."

But at the heart of this very complex and extremely gifted man is Jaco the Soul Man, an essential part of John Francis Pastorius III that's rooted in his tenure on the Southern chitlin circuit with a host of funky R&B bands from Florida. The embodiment of all these faces

into one man is a statement in itself, suggesting a common thread joining seemingly divergent musical styles. Whether consciously or not, Jaco has provided a missing link between the music of Hendrix, Coltrane, Ellington, James Brown, and Johann Sebastian Bach (check out his transcription of Bach's "Chromatic Fantasy" on the *Word Of Mouth* album). Jaco the Musicologist?

Since bursting onto the scene in 1976 with his brilliant debut album, *Jaco Pastorius*, he has been at once a compelling and controversial figure. Within months of that record's release, Jaco attained near-legendary status among aspiring bassists everywhere. The sheer speed and uncanny facility he displayed on Parker's bebop classic, "Donna Lee," in a startling duo with percussionist Don Alias was enough to instantly mark Jaco as a candidate for heroic stature among instrumentalists. But beyond that, his revolutionary approach to the instrument, freely incorporating harmonics into his wide vocabulary, further amazed the steadily growing contingent of Jaco worshippers.

No less an authority than keyboardist Herbie Hancock commented on the liner notes of that landmark debut LP: "Jaco is a phenomenon. He is able to make sounds on the bass that are a total surprise to the sensibilities. Not only single notes, but chords, harmonics, and all sorts of nuances with the color of the instrument that when combined and translated through Jaco make for some of the best music that I've heard in a long time."

Hancock went on to say, "Of course, it's not the technique that makes the music; it's the sensitivity of the musician and his ability to be able to fuse his life with the rhythm of the times. This is the essence of music. On this record, Jaco captures some of that rhythm."

Bass players everywhere quickly got the message. They began thumping less and chording more, exploring more voicings and new timbres, stretching their own dexterity and experimenting with harmonics. Through his example, Jaco had liberated their way of thinking about the instrument.

Today the Jaco sound is all-pervasive. You can hardly turn on the radio without hearing some young bassist applying a portion of Jaco's technique. And it's an international phenomenon. Within the last few years there have been countless recorded examples of Pastorius-influenced bassists from practically all corners of the world. Some of this new breed are in fact shameless Jaco clones. But in spite of their ability to ape Jaco's nimble lines and lightning speed, his soul and inherent rhythm seem beyond the grasp of the imitators. That's something you just can't steal.

He has garnered several awards and is a perennial poll winner: He was named the 1981 Musician of the Year in Japan by that country's leading jazz publication, *Swing Journal,* and was recently voted number-one bassist by the readers of *Down Beat* and *Guitar Player* magazines. Yet Jaco downplays his contribution to the state of the art: "I'm not a star. I'll never be a Frank Sinatra or an Elvis Presley or a Ray Charles. I'm just an imitator myself, man. I'm just doing a very bad imitation on the bass of Jerry Jemmott, Bernard Odum, Jimmy Fielder, Jimmy Blanton, Igor Stravinsky, Fela Ransome Kuti . . . the *cats*, man. I'm just backing up the cats!"

The son of a jazz drummer, Jaco was born in Norristown, Pennsylvania, in 1952. His family moved to the Fort Lauderdale area of Florida when he was seven years old. By his teens he had become a familiar face on the South Florida nightclub circuit, having put in time with such local groups as Soul Incorporated, Tommy Strand & The Upper Hand, Uncle Wig-Out & The Solar System, the Uptown Funk All-Stars, and Las Olas Brass. His first break came at the age of 19, when he was recruited as the bassist for Wayne Cochran And The C.C. (Chitlin Circuit) Riders. His next big break came at age 22 while teaching part-time at the University of Miami, where he also conducted and played bass for the University's student jazz ensemble. An opportunity to open for Weather Report at a concert in Miami led to

a backstage encounter with the co-founders of that seminal fusion group. It was the beginning of what would become a long and fruitful relationship among Jaco, keyboardist Josef Zawinul, and saxophonist Wayne Shorter.

His first contributions to the group came on two cuts from the *Black Market* album of 1976. That was the same year he released his impressive debut album and also appeared as a sideman on albums by Joni Mitchell (*Hejira*), Pat Metheny (*Bright Size Life*), and Al Di Meola (*Land Of The Midnight Sun*). It was indeed the breakout year for Jaco Pastorius. His position in Weather Report was cemented with the band's 1977 offering, *Heavy Weather,* a punchy LP that yielded the popular radio-play tune "Birdland."

Jaco went on to become an integral part of both the sound and success of Weather Report. Besides bringing a funkier, bolder bass presence to the band, he injected new life with his rock conviction, his formidable soloing voice, and his undeniably charismatic stage presence (or antics, as some critics saw it) — part Hendrix, part samurai, wholly unpredictable, and always exciting. And, perhaps more important, he contributed several compositions and shared production credits with Zawinul on the five albums the group released since he became a full-time member: *Heavy Weather* (1977), *Mr. Gone* ('78), *8:30* ('79), *Night Passage* ('80), and *Weather Report* ('82).

Jaco left Weather Report in 1982 to put together his dynamic big band, Word Of Mouth. (Recently he performed sizzling sets with his new, scaled-down version of the Word Of Mouth band, featuring percussionist Don Alias, guitarist Mike Stern, drummer Kenwood Dennard, saxophonist Alex Foster, and trumpeter Melton Mustafa.) In retrospect, he says, "Man, when you leave a group like Weather Report, you gotta go out with a bang." But in the same breath he adds, "I never really left Weather Report. I am still promoting our music. And if those cats call me in a week or a year, if it fits, I'm back. But for now it's just the timing of what's going on that keeps us apart."

Of his former employer, Zawinul, he says, "People always say, 'Hey, you guys must hate each other, or why else would you have left the band?' That ain't true at all. I love Joe Zawinul like nobody else in the world. But he won't change. He doesn't hear anybody else but himself, and his technological overkill sucks. But I wish people would just calm down and understand that there is no friction between us. Joe Zawinul and Wayne Shorter are the greatest, and that's it. They are the two best men I know. And, of course, they are my biggest teachers to date." Earlier this year, Jaco toasted Josef Zawinul at 55 Grand, a hip, intimate jazz club in SoHo that he frequents whenever he's in New York City. A few months later, while playing a gig at 55 Grand, he honored Zawinul's recently deceased father with a stirring rendition of "Mercy, Mercy," the tune Zawinul composed as a member of the Cannonball Adderley group in the '60s. Clearly, Jaco does have great love for the man he calls his mentor. It remains to be seen, however, if they will ever play together again, given their contradictory attitudes toward the music.

Practically a trademark of your onstage appearance is a well-worn Fender Jazz Bass. Why do you continue to play the same old beat-up instrument?

Because it sounds good. My fretless, which is probably what I'm most noted for, is a '62 Jazz Bass that I got in Margate, Florida, for $90 with a case. I got it when I was 19, so I've had it for about 13 years now. My fretted bass is even older — it's a '60 Fender Jazz Bass that I got for $90 from a saxophone player in Florida named Ben Champion.

Did you buy your bass with the frets already removed, or did you take them out? [Ed. Note: Fender did not begin to market fretless basses until 1964.]

When I got the bass, the cat who had it had taken the frets out himself, and he did a really bad job of it — left all kinds of nicks and chunks taken out of the fretboard. So I really had to fix it up. I filled in all the chunks with Plastic Wood. Hell, when I was a kid, I used to make a living by fixing and dealing old, beat-up instruments. I was the first cat to use epoxy on the neck of a fretless bass so the strings wouldn't eat the neck away.

What did you use, and how did you apply it?

I used Petite's Poly-Poxy; it's boat epoxy. You can find it in any boating supply store around Florida. It's the toughest epoxy they make. You apply it with a brush, and it takes several coats. I used about six coats on my fretless, and it took about a day for each coat to dry.

Did that harm the action?

Not at all. It's *essential*. It saves the instrument from getting eaten up by the roundwound strings. When you remove those frets and use roundwound strings, there's nothing left of the neck. They eat right

> *"I know everything about these basses of mine, every bit of chicken grease and every drop of sweat that's ever been on them."*

through it. [*Ed. Note: Jaco's flawless intonation on his fretless is aided by the fret positions marked on the neck — the fret grooves that have been filled in.*]

You've been playing your fretted Fender a lot lately.

That's all I've been playing, really. See, last year, when we were in Europe, my fretless got dropped off the plane or something, and the neck got broken. So for the whole last tour, I haven't used it at all. It's back in Florida getting repaired. I'm just waiting for the glue to resettle.

What is it about the old Fenders that you like so much?

The old Fenders really have a punch, and not just a treble punch, either. More like clear lower-mids; plus, they're quick. You can play that fretless real fast. And I feel comfortable with these. I've had lots of people make basses for me, and I own different sorts of them. I've probably owned over a hundred in my life, but none of them sound like these old ones.

So you have checked out a number of instruments then, including headless ones such as the Steinberger?

Yeah, Sting turned me on to the Steinberger. The first time I ever saw one was when I went to see the Police. I tell you, Sting's a beautiful cat. We had heard about each other and talked to each other on the phone, but we had never hooked up. So when I went to see him, the first thing he said to me was, "Hey, Jaco, come on back and check out my bass." I like them. They're real good basses. I have one now, but I just haven't had enough time to even explore it. You see, one of the main reasons I use these same old basses is because I've worked so hard and so long on the road — forever — that to get another new instrument at this point, I really feel like I would have to learn how to play it from scratch. I mean, I know everything about these basses of mine, every bit of chicken grease and every drop of sweat that's ever been on them. These things are beat up, all right, but I hardly put any scars on them at all; the only ones are thumb marks. Other than that, I have not made a mark on them. Man, I used to do one-and-a-half flips off my amps and land on them — looked like I was killing them. But I really never touched them. It was just an illusion — all entertainment. That's what I am: I'm an entertainer.

Did you drop new pickups into your fretless?

Nope. Totally stock. The only things that weren't

on there originally are the potentiometers. I've re-placed them, but they're still Fender pots.

Did you go through a lot of trial and error before arriving at your choice of strings?

Nope. I just use standard Rotosound strings — the roundwound Swing Bass set.

What about your amps?

I use two Acoustic 360s, which is the same setup I've been using for the last 13 years. Same amps — old reliables. I usually put the bass setting all the way up and the treble about halfway up, depending on the condition of the strings. The older your strings are, the more treble you have to have, because the fidelity of the string really starts losing it after a while. In the studio, though, I just go direct.

What kind of effects pedals do you use?

I have an old makeshift fuzztone. There's no brand name at all. You can hear a good example of it in action on the title cut from the *Word Of Mouth* album, my last studio album. It's got a built-in delay that I can put on infinite repeat whenever I want to lay down some kind of track to play on top of in concert. [*Ed. Note: Jaco often uses this gadget for a kind of tape-loop effect on his "Purple Haze" tribute to Hendrix. He can program a few seconds of a motif that will then play on infinitely. Although he's often employed it in concert, he has never used the repeating effect on any of his recordings.*]

This effect is similar to current electronic delays.

I travel so much and play so much and I'm constantly on the road, so I never get a chance to check up on all the latest hardware. And besides, I don't really rely on effects all that much. I play an electric bass, but I deal mostly with acoustic phenomena. The sound is in my hands and in my fingers, not in some pedal.

Any other effects?

I've got an MXR Digital Delay, which I put through one amp, leaving the other amp clean, to cause a natural sort of vibrato. It's almost like an organ Leslie [rotating speaker] effect or like a flanger. A good example of that effect is the title cut from the *8:30* album, or the tune "Continuum" from my first record, or "Reza" and "Continuum" from the *Live Invitation* album. I also used that effect a lot on the Joni Mitchell records, particularly on "Coyote" and "Hejira" on *Hejira*, or "Goodbye Pork Pie Hat" and "God Must Be A Boogie Man" on *Mingus*.

How did you approach those Joni Mitchell sessions?

I approach each night — even now with my own band — totally different. I *hope*. Otherwise it wouldn't be fun. But I liked working with Joni. I really like *Hejira*.

Was there one incident in particular that got you into playing the bass?

Yeah. I started out as a drummer, but I broke my left wrist in a football game when I was 13, and I couldn't hit the snare drum anymore. My wrist would almost shatter. It was like glass. Then, when I was 17, my whole left arm from the shoulder down went completely numb. If someone would pinch me, I wouldn't feel anything. It turned out there was a calcium deposit or something, and it was just strangling it. So I had an operation to fix it when I was 17, and then the feeling came back. Well, I had always wanted to be a musician, and I tried to play every instrument. When I was 15, I was in a band called the Las Olas Brass. There was another drummer, Rich Franks, who was older than me and was a much better player, technically, at the time. The band members wanted him instead of me, so I quit playing drums. But at the same time, the bass player, David Neubauer, was leaving. He played a Hofner and was the best bass player in Florida. He was phenomenal at 13, but he couldn't stand being in the band because everybody was getting high and drunk and everything — except for me. I was always straight. So David quit, and I just sort of agreed to then go to the bass spot.

Just like that?

Yes. I can more or less pick up any instrument and play it. I mean, that's like a gift that I guess I was blessed with. Like, coming up as a kid, I just didn't repair basses, I also used to repair trumpets, saxes, drums — anything. I got to know all these instruments. And that's how I learned about harmonics. It's simply that the overtone series on a string is exactly the same principle as on a trumpet.

How many different ways do you get harmonics?

For students who want to learn the basics of harmonics, all you've got to do is get a really good violin book and read about flageolet tones [natural harmonics]. It's been done for years and years on violins, cellos, etc. All you've got to do is learn where they're at, spend a lot of time working on it, and know what they are. If you learn all the open-string harmonics on a bass — all the natural harmonics — you can play just about every note chromatically. The other way is your picking technique. Let's say on "Birdland" [*Heavy Weather*], for example, where I pick out that intro part in harmonics, I get that sound by using my thumb on my right hand to lightly touch the string at the octave and picking behind it, almost like a steel guitar player would. You can get harmonics that way; it's just a matter of subdividing the string. So I play the note with the left hand on the fingerboard, holding it down. Then with my right-hand thumb, I'll be on the note an octave higher, up around by the pickup, and pluck the string with my first and second fingers behind the thumb. That way you hear the harmonic. It's actually very simple. You just have to spend a lot of time doing it, and you've got to have really good chops because it hurts your fingers. You have to pick it very hard to get it to come out.

What techniques did you use for the harmonics on "Portrait Of Tracy" [Jaco Pastorius]?

Stretching. You hit the note with your left-hand ring finger, and then stretch your index finger to catch the harmonic. In other words, you're using your left hand as a capo the other way. So on that tune I'm hitting a B with my ring finger on my left hand and stretching my index finger all the way over to a D# harmonic. [Ed. Note: Other excellent examples of Jaco's harmonic technique include the haunting "Three Views Of A Secret" on Night Passage, his stirring unaccompanied rendition of "America" recorded live in Japan for the Invitation LP, and the Zen-like "Okonkole Y Trompa," an ongoing flow of harmonics augmented by two percussionists and French horn appearing on his debut LP, Jaco Pastorius.]

Is there any way of writing out your harmonic playing?

Yeah, I can do it. You can put it on a treble clef — way up on the telephone poles — or you can write it out on a bass clef like a cello part. They're just flageolet tones. There are legit ways of doing it: cello books, violin books. I have different ways of writing them down, though. Sometimes I indicate harmonics just by using a different-colored pen.

Is the technique of playing harmonics something you had to work on, or did you fall into it right away?

Oh, yeah, immediately. Actually, the way I did it was just from tuning up. I heard it as music right away, as opposed to just tuning. You know how you tune up to harmonics? I just heard it as something to start exploring. I was just lucky enough to get on the instrument at a time when it was still relatively new, and I just explored it, just looked at it a different way. I had never heard anybody play like that or look at the bass in that way before. So I started doing it myself.

"I play an electric bass, but I deal mostly with acoustic phenomena. The sound is in my hands and in my fingers."

Any other techniques involving your hands rather than effects?

There's a sound I get, a percussive kind of sound, almost like a conga. I get it by hitting the strings with my right palm, getting a rhythmic thing going, and then just quickly sliding my palm down the neck, from the bridge down to the nut. It adds some meat in appropriate places. I used that at the end of "John And Mary" from the *Word Of Mouth* album. And you can hear it on "The Elder" from the *Mr. Gone* album.

Do you read music?

Yeah.

Do you have a degree?

Let's say I'm formally self-taught.

What was the teaching gig you landed at the University of Miami?

Whit Sidner, who ran the jazz department, asked me to teach there. [Bassist] Will Lee's father, Dr. William Lee, was the dean of music at the time. Hiram Bullock, the guitar player, was one of my students. I gave him an "A." Curtis Lundy was also a student. Mark Egan, Frank Gravis . . .

What did you teach your students?

Most of them, just how to tune up and what the names of the strings are. For instance, there was a guy in class named Jeff Sanchez, a Cuban bass player. I gave him an "F." He could not play a single note. He didn't know anything; he was like first learning music. But right now he's probably one of the best bass players in Florida. So I guess that just goes to show how valuable school is for some players. But in general, I was mostly teaching my students how to play basic scales — nothing too advanced.

Why did you leave that teaching position?

It was driving me nuts. I was just there for one semester. I could have stayed there for as long as I wanted, but I'm a *player.*

What are your views on the music educational system today?

I suggest that the teachers should just lighten up. If a student wants to learn something, a teacher should help direct him to where he's actually already headed — just help him along. The important thing I see in any kind of teaching situation, especially music, is that teachers still have to be players. They should be staying in touch with the craft, with the music. There are certain people who might think they're great teachers, but they can't play anything. And I think students have a greater respect for teachers who are also players. I mean, that is what it's all about: playing! Also, I would suggest that in addition to studying out of books, everybody should definitely listen to some rhythm and blues, because that's what it is.

You've now worked in so many different contexts. How do you approach a gig with a big band, as opposed to a smaller ensemble?

For one thing, I like to make a big band sound like a small band, to go for the tightness that you'd find in a smaller band. The group I have now with two horns and a guitar is able to get a lot of sounds and still be very tight. With a big band, it's a little more difficult to get that same kind of swiftness. It's just basic physics: The more people, the slower the air is moving. So the main thing I try to do is just get them all to swing, to pay attention and not be talking to each other about last night's reruns of the *Mary Tyler Moore Show* when they're not playing.

Does your role as a bass player change in the different contexts?

One thing: With a big band, it's a little easier on me since I don't have to play as much, because of the roles that other people are filling. So with a big band I tend to play more fundamental bass. And with a small band I can go "out." I've been writing for big bands ever since I could write. In fact, most of the tunes you hear on my records and in concert, I actually wrote 12 or 13 years ago.

Any comments on the changing role of the bass?

Just the fact that it's more amplified now and you can hear it, which is nice.

Who are some of the bassists who you feel helped to change the role of the instrument over the years?

Jimmy Blanton, who played with the Duke Ellington band. Jerry Jemmott, Bernard Odum, Duck Dunn, and of course Monk Montgomery.

What are some of the things that young bassists ask you about?

Most young bass players ask me questions about harmonics stuff more than anything else. But that's really a very small part of my thing. Harmonics is only about a hundredth of my playing. It's really easy to play harmonics: Anybody can do it. But it's another thing to be able to swing, to make the band swing, to create a groove. Harmonics ain't everything. Being able to play harmonics certainly does not make you a good bass player. Cleverness is no substitute for true awareness.

What advice do you have for young bassists?

Learn tunes. Learn melodies. Most bass players make the mistake of just learning bass lines and nothing else. But you have to concentrate on learning a piece of music thoroughly, which includes melody and harmony and theory, as well — mainly the melody, though. All bass players should become more melody-conscious.

Are there any young bass players coming up today who you find exciting?

Charlie Haden and Steve Swallow [*laughs*]. No, seriously, I'd say Marcus Miller. He's a beautiful cat. Victor Bailey [one of Jaco's successors in Weather Report] is playing beautifully. Mark Egan is beautiful. He's a great player. I also dig Andy Gonzales.

Do you still practice?

I keep saying that I'm going to start again, but I haven't had time to practice as much as I'd like. I very rarely have practiced because I don't need to. I was on gigs every night of my life from the time I was 15 years old. When I was in Florida as the house bassist at the Bachelors III nightclub, I used to play eight shows a night. But whenever I do get a chance to practice, I play *do re mi fa sol la ti do*, and see if I can still remember how to do that — then go on from there. I try to physically keep my chops together by playing whatever pops into my head — mostly just running a major scale and working on arpeggios and triads.

How long did it take for you to acquire these chops?

I don't have 'em yet [*laughs*]. I'm still working on it. I've been playing the Fender bass since I was 15, so it's been a while now.

Do you practice piano?

I never really seriously practiced anything but the bass. I do fool around on drums a little bit just to work off tension, but the Fender Jazz Bass is the only thing I've really legitimately practiced, which is hard to say, since there are no legitimate books for bass players — at least I haven't found any. But I haven't had time to look too hard. So really, most of what I've got now has just come from my playing. I mean, I've worked so much. When I was in Wayne Cochran's band, the C.C. Riders, it got to a point where I was always on the bus or else playing in some small club somewhere. My daughter was getting old and I was never seeing her. I wasn't seeing *anybody*, and I wasn't making any bread, either, so I finally decided that it was time for me to go into another thing. So I left that band and started to woodshed it, practicing at home for about a half a year, about four hours a day. And I meditated all day. I was into some sort of a spiritual discipline thing in 1971 or '72. I don't know how to explain it. That was the only time in my life that I've actually practiced for any length of time. But I want to start up again, mainly because of Mike Stern. He's a consummate musician. He practices a lot and he's really dedicated. And he makes me stretch every night. To see somebody who really cares that much about the music is so inspiring to me and makes me reflect on my own playing.

Can you elaborate on your rapport with Mike?

I love Mike Stern. Man, I remember him from Blood, Sweat & Tears, years ago. He was so insecure then, but he's grown up to be a man now. And he's playing his butt off. Me, Mike, and Don Alias all played together in Blood, Sweat & Tears back around '76. Bobby Columby was playing drums in the band, and he ended up producing my first solo album. Don Alias and I had been playing together for a while behind Lou Rawls, doing all these show gigs. But I stopped doing that to go out on the road with Blood, Sweat & Tears. They needed a bass player because Ron McClure had just left the band. Actually, I was playing a gig in Boston with Pat Metheny when I got the call to join the band. My first gig with BS&T was at the Ed Sullivan Theater in New York City. I had to fly in on a shuttle plane from Boston, and the weather was unbelievable. We couldn't land. I was up in the air in one of those old prop planes for hours, man. We almost ran out of gas. But I made the gig, and that's how I hooked up with BS&T.

And then Mike Stern joined the band?

Yeah, within a couple of weeks, Bobby Columby got him into the band. So we played together for about six weeks. I had never really joined the band as a permanent member. I was more or less subbing for Ron McClure. But I met Stern, and we had a good time together in that band. But then I decided that I wanted to do a record of my own stuff because as a composer, I just had too much music inside of me and I was starting to get frustrated. I had to let it out. So I left the band and Bobby Columby arranged for me to do the album.

So now you've come full circle with your old buddies in this new band?

Yeah — Don Alias, Stern, and also Melton Mustafa, the trumpet player, is an old friend from Florida. Melton grew up in Liberty City in Miami, so I was playing with him way back when. It's all in the family, all coming back around now. I had a jazz

band with Melton in those days, playing exactly what I'm playing now — just a combination of jazz and rhythm and blues. And it ain't fusion music, which I think sucks. I like rhythm and blues and jazz. That's what I grew up with. I mean, jazz is rhythm and blues. So anyway, I grew up with Melton, but he got drafted and had to join the Navy, so that broke up that relationship. I was lucky enough to draw a very high number in the draft lottery, so they missed me. Melton went away and I kept playing music. I was fortunate enough to go to the service in the streets of America, which is actually worse — especially in Liberty City, man.

So you say you play jazz and R&B music. How do you react to the term "fusion"?

Just as I was learning how to say "jazz," they had to change it to "high-energy crossover fusion music." I don't like terms. I don't like being called a fusion musician. I would just like to consider myself a *musician.* But whatever they call whatever it is, it don't bug me. I would like to just be considered a decent bass player, you know? A fundamental, solid bass player. That's all.

How do you assess your own playing? Do you think you've improved?

Without a question of a doubt. Otherwise, I'd quit. I'm growing. I don't consider it *all* as growth. And there's lots of different things that come out of music due to experiences of being on the road. So in that sense, too, I'm constantly growing. Plus, I've hit on so many things that I've just touched on and never really had time to explore. But I'm starting to make time. Right now, I'm playing better than ever. My chops are there. I mean, I wouldn't want to be a bass player and have to listen to me right now, because the stuff is really starting to happen, and it must be scary. And it has nothing to do with ego or being better or this or that. It's just that I know what it is, too.

Describe your earliest musical influences.

I was influenced a great deal by my father Jack, who is a great jazz drummer. He's still playing around the Philadelphia area. In fact, I sat in with him a while back in Philly. He's the greatest. He played with me at the Savoy last year. I called him up and we did a real hip arrangement of "Watch What Happens." He's a singer, man. He's been a traveling musician all his life.

Any specific players who inspired you early on?

> *"I heard harmonics as something to start exploring. I was just lucky enough to get on the instrument at a time when it was still relatively new."*

No, not really. I just listened to whatever was on the radio — everything from the Beatles to James Brown to Frank Sinatra to Sly Stone and Jimi Hendrix. That was the real inspiration. A big influence was Cachao, the number-one Cuban bassist. I just heard a lot of different kinds of music growing up in Florida, so I was able to explore more stuff at an early age. Soul music, Cuban music, swamp music, blues, rock and roll, Caribbean music, steel pan [steel drum] music from Trinidad, all the old Stax/Volt records.

You've been working on a steel pan album. Is it available?

It's not out yet. It's almost completed. I've been working on that for about four years, on and off. It's amazing. I'm going to call it *Holiday For Pans*. We do a complete symphonic thing of David Rose's "Holiday For Strings." It's ridiculous! You've got to hear it to believe it.

Are you playing bass on the album?

Not much. Mostly bass pans. I've been playing steel pans for years. I own about a hundred different kinds of steel pans. Hell, I've got a big warehouse full of oil cans in Florida. I have supported all the steel drum players in Florida for years. Othello Molineaux and a cat named Leroy Williams, who both played on my first album, also play on this steel pan album. In fact, Othello has played on all my albums. He was a member of the Word Of Mouth big band that toured the States and Japan. [*Ed. Note: Othello's interpretation of John Coltrane's "Giant Steps" can be heard on the* Invitation *album.*] Anyway, Othello and I have designed a new harmonic way of tuning a steel drum. There are many different ways, but there was a certain thing that we were looking for, and we got it. Besides that, the album has all sorts of stuff — horns on some tracks, the L.A. Philharmonic for one piece, a children's choir.

When will it be released?

I guess it depends on the powers that be.

The record industry?

Them, too, providing there is any future in the record industry for creative music. I'm really getting tired of the whole thing, to tell you the truth — the whole game you have to play, dealing with the record industry on *its* terms instead of your terms.

Can you pick out some essential cuts that represent different landmarks in the evolution of your technique?

People always ask me, "What is your favorite album?" or, "What is your favorite tune?" or, "Who is your favorite musician?" The only answer I have is: I have four beautiful kids, and none of 'em is my favorite.

–JOHN PATITUCCI–

BY TOM MULHERN – MAY 1986

PAUL HAGGARD

ANYONE WHO has followed fusion and jazz over the past 15 years is well aware of keyboardist Chick Corea. He masterminded Return To Forever, the band that first spotlighted Al Di Meola, Bill Connors, and Stanley Clarke in the early and mid '70s, and his reputation is legendary: He only works with top-notch players. Today his bassist is 26-year-old John Patitucci, a driving, powerful performer who tears up the grooves on *The Chick Corea Elektric Band,* which also features guitarist Scott Henderson and drummer Dave Weckl (Carlos Rios added some guitar solos). Patitucci's solos move with saxophone-like fluidity, and his accompaniment is muscular yet tasteful. However, his work with Corea is only a part of the picture.

John Patitucci also plays sessions, where he has contributed to performances by the vocal ensemble Manhattan Transfer, singers Harry Nilsson and Glenn Frey, guitarists Phil Keaggy, Wayne Johnson, and Larry Carlton, pianists Victor Feldman and Clare Fischer, saxophonists Tom Scott and Stan Getz, percussionist Airto, and flutist Hubert Laws. He also performed on the soundtracks to *All Of Me* and an upcoming movie on the life of Richard Pryor, episodes of *Hart To Hart* and *Still The Beaver,* and commercials for Dodge and Subaru. In addition, he has played on gospel dates for nearly a decade.

Born in Brooklyn on December 22, 1959, John was raised with his four siblings in East Flatbush until he was 12. Then the family lived in Long Island for a year before moving to San Ramon in Northern California. John lived there until 1978, when he entered San Francisco State University. The Patitucci household was always abuzz with music; both parents sang, and the sound of opera — and especially Mario Lanza — filled the air. Older brother Tom was the first to pursue a guitar. John accompanied him on vocals, maracas, and bongos. At 11, he took up bass and picked up a Telstar short-scale for about $10. "It buzzed on every fret — which I thought was cool, because I wanted to play rock and roll," John laughs.

His earliest primary influences came from the Motown school — Stevie Wonder and Diana Ross, among others, who had the bass mixed up front — and practically anything he heard in the pop/R&B vein on the radio. By the time he was 12, John began playing in Long Island garage bands. A turning point in his listening preferences came shortly before the family moved to California: His grandfather gave the boys a few cartons of jazz albums featuring Wes Montgomery, string bassist Ron Carter, drummer Art Blakey, and organist Jimmy Smith, among others. Until then, John and Tom had been interested only in rock, but this was *different,* and they dived headlong into jazz.

A teacher named Chris Poehler gave John tapes of trumpeters Miles Davis and Quincy Jones and singer Donny Hathaway — "anything that was good," he comments. "I got really hooked and started buying records like crazy — [saxophonists] John Coltrane and Charlie Parker, as well as Stevie Wonder and rock and roll. It was funny, because Chris would bring all these Miles Davis things, and I'd tape Humble Pie or the Allman Brothers for him. At that time, my brother and I were playing in interesting bands together, doing everything from Johnny Winter to the Crusaders."

In the middle of high school, Patitucci started playing string bass and studied for a year with Charles Siani at San Francisco State, learning fingering and bowing techniques. He continued playing electric, although he was spellbound by the acoustic: "I never wanted to give up electric, but I wanted to have another sound. I heard guys like Ron Carter and thought it was amazing. Ray Brown, Eddie Gomez, Scott LaFaro, Niels-Henning Ørsted Pedersen, and George Mraz were also strong influences. George Mraz' intonation is probably the best I've ever heard, and I've even heard him play chord solos on upright. I developed a split musical personality: I had firm roots in R&B and I was heavily into jazz, and I found myself getting into classical music."

Although playing with a bow on the upright had some effect on his phrasing, Patitucci feels he was able to successfully separate the electric from the acoustic. He explains, "You sort of compartmentalize yourself when you play such different instruments. You get into a different frame of mind for each one to keep yourself from going nuts. There is *some* overlapping, so if you have an open mind and a good attitude, each can influence the other in a positive way. Like, the expressive phrasing with the bow may have inspired some of the phrasing on the fretted instrument."

During high school, John began learning theory, and his teacher incorporated such concepts as improvising over chord changes, which he reinforced by attending summer clinics on ear training by Jamey Aebersold and Jacob Baker at Diablo College. Other help came again from his brother, who was majoring in classical guitar. "He influenced my technique on electric bass a lot," John acknowledges, "as far as using the four-finger technique and practicing scales and various fingerings, hammer-ons, and pull-offs." He also built up his right-hand fingering, which he felt was at a disadvantage because he is a left-hander who plays righty.

Like many aspiring bassists of the time, the teenager took a keen interest in Stanley Clarke, hearing *Return To Forever* when he was about 13. "It had a giant bass solo with Airto playing percussion behind it," John recalls, "one of the first solos I ever learned off a record. The other thing was a Willie Weeks bass solo off a Donny Hathaway live record. I really practiced hard, trying to figure out what they were doing. And because my brother was helping me with technique, I started to get some chops together." Also like many of his peers, John went through a love affair with high-speed riffing: "I was working my tail off, because there were always 20,000 guitar players running around school, and it was important to assert yourself, like gunfighters. I'm glad I worked so hard on my technique at a young age. That's when you have the most exuberance for practicing — before you have other responsibilities. I was a hermit. I'd go to my room and practice for hours and hours. Luckily, what tempered it was playing with lots of older musicians. They told me that it's important to be musical and develop my ear and be sensitive to other players. They said, that way, you'll always get work."

College for John began with a year at San Francisco State, before his family moved to Southern California in '78. He resumed his studies for the next two years at Long Beach State, learning classical string bass. He also studied piano, an important factor in opening up his composing. While in school, he continued refining his electric bass abilities, and after his third year, he left. However, he continued studying string bass with Barry Lieberman of the Los Angeles Philharmonic. He was also working — not only in jazz clubs, but in Christian music. "When I was 17," John explains, "I really got into Christianity. So I was doing some work for gospel records in Orange County. I didn't want to teach school, and I figured the best way to learn music was to do it. There are a lot of things you can learn at college — and I don't regret going — but there comes a time when you just have to get out there and do it."

Patitucci made his first moves into big-time work in 1982, when he relocated to Los Angeles. He had been commuting to L.A. to play on some dates, and word of his performances with jazz musicians caused his workload to escalate. At age 19, he went on the road with pianist Gap Mangione, and he met bassist Abraham Laboriel, who introduced him to many other people. He landed a gig with Larry Carlton, with whom he has been playing on and off for the past few years, and another job with Victor Feldman, which later led to his joining Chick Corea.

Many of John's associates are in the jazz or fusion vein, although he is not averse to rock dates. "I suppose it depends on what you mean by rock," he says.

"There's a lot of different areas of rock. I've been interested in doing sessions, but never in going on the road with, say, a heavy metal band or something like that. It's not too exciting. I love the Police and a lot of rock groups, but that's a whole other environment and an entirely different circle of musicians. It's hard to jump through all of them. I figured if I could do some studio dates and occasionally work with rock players, I would. And if I did some jazz, R&B, classical, films, and TV here and there, I'd be happy. I've always wanted to do a little bit of everything. If you want to be entrenched in rock, you have to concentrate heavily and just do that, especially if you want to work with someone like Rod Stewart — musicians who don't cross over to other styles very much."

Recently, Manhattan Transfer received a Grammy for *Vocalese* (Best Jazz Vocal by a Duo or Group), on which John performed various bass parts. He first worked for the ensemble when regular bassist Alex Blake had to leave during a tour. "They were really gracious," he remembers, "and it was one of those exciting things where they fly you out, you go to the soundcheck, rehearse, and do the gig that night — really exciting sight-reading practice."

One of the high points of working with the Transfer was recording "Joy Spring" with trumpeter Dizzy Gillespie. For this, the bassist read from chord charts, which he encounters almost as often as fully written parts. "Last summer I worked with [saxophonist] David Sanborn," John says. "That was mostly chord charts, too; you listen to the records and you get the grooves from there. Sometimes you get a few tricky written parts, and sometimes there is no written music, and you have to listen to a tape and make up a bass line. For example, there was a session for Luis Gasca, the fluegelhorn player. He had forgotten his music, so he punched up a tape and away we went. I don't mind the pressure, because it's exciting to see if you can get through it. That's what's exciting about Chick's gig, too. Some of his music is written out, some isn't. For the album, it was really open. For instance, on "Got A Match," it was a melody line and chords, and he wasn't sure what he wanted for a bass part. I saw the melody, and it was really challenging. I said I'd like to play the melody with him, and it turned out to be very effective. I like to keep trying to advance. It's natural, I know."

"Saxophonists always sound so free. I don't know if I'm succeeding at it, but I want that kind of musicality."

Everybody always wants to get better. But I like to *force* myself."

John met Chick Corea a few years ago while playing at an educators' convention in Albuquerque. Later, he met some of Corea's musicians and told them how much he would enjoy working with the keyboardist. In early 1985, he played with Victor Feldman's trio and became reacquainted with Corea. Soon after, when Chick was working on some Mozart arrangements, John played string bass with him. John recalls, "Afterwards, he said that he was putting together an electric band and asked if I played electric. I said sure, that's my first instrument." In April, Patitucci sent a tape to Corea, and a week later he was formally asked to join the band. Soon after, the group did a three-week minitour of California, took some time off, and in the fall of '85 did a two-month tour followed by recording throughout December.

Also during the fall, John became accustomed to a new instrument: a Ken Smith BT Custom 6 6-string bass. He calls it one of those "shock treatments" that jar him out of complacency. "I wanted to see if I could expand and grow a little bit," he says. "I had heard Anthony Jackson play 6-string and always thought about what it would be like to have some more strings, because I was always running out. I have some old Fenders, and before the 6-string I started getting Ibanezes with 24 frets. I thought the extra range was great, but I still ran out of room every once in a while during solos. Anthony came on the scene years back with these 6-string basses, and I said, 'Wow, that's something that appeals to me.' I was looking for those low notes, and for soloing I wanted a hornlike looseness, more range. With the 6-string, I could work across the neck, and go to low *B* and other notes I couldn't otherwise get. I got that bass a week before I went out on the road, so I was forced to learn it very quickly, because for our first major tour I couldn't go onstage and sound terrible. Chick was excited about the bass, and he encouraged me."

John says that part of the reason he was able to acclimate himself to the Ken Smith was that it was so well made, although he encountered a little difficulty in sight-reading because the added strings slightly disoriented him. For the week of pre-tour rehearsal, Chick brought in several new tunes, requiring intensive sight-reading. "It was really hard," Patitucci says. "I was laughing at myself because I hit the wrong strings, and I couldn't believe how different it felt. Sight-reading on a 4-string for Chick's music is difficult enough. But I hung in there, and the guys in the band thought it was all right. If I made a mistake, they didn't mind, because they liked the sound so much." [*Ed. Note: According to Ken Smith, the bass' front and back are figured walnut with a maple center, and the 5-piece maple-and-caviuna neck passes through the body. The instrument also has an ebony fingerboard, two truss rods, and active circuitry.*]

Onstage, John uses a Hafler 500 power amp and a 500-watt Yamaha power amp, both driven by a Mark Levinson preamp and an RSL preamp (with a built-in 10-band graphic equalizer). He also uses an Ashly crossover. For the highs, he employs a Bag End birch cabinet with two Electro-Voice 12" speakers; another Bag End cabinet with a Gauss 18 fills in the bottom end. His effects include an Ibanez HD-1000 Harmonics/Delay, an Ibanez analog delay, and a Boss Octaver, which is on a pedalboard with a tuner.

Among his other instruments are a Fender Jazz Bass with a Novatone interchangeable fretboard system (he has fretted and fretless boards). When playing fretless, John prefers an instrument with markers that correspond to frets. "All the best bassists I've ever heard use lines," he states. "Jaco has lines, and he's the foremost, as far as I'm concerned." He is acutely aware of how bad a fretless can sound if the player has poor intonation, and believes that his training on string bass has helped him: "Even though the spacing of the notes on the upright is different from the electric, my ear was attuned to adjusting to notes without frets. You get used to it, but you must constantly monitor your intonation."

John gets to solo quite a bit on the Corea album, and on "Got A Match" he plays at his best. "I guess Chick enjoyed a different concept," he shrugs. "I don't know how different I am, but I try as hard as I can to be different. I try to get a flexibility like John Coltrane, Mike Brecker, or Joe Henderson. They have that flowing way they play through changes — it doesn't sound like they're hobbling through the changes. Saxophonists always sound so free. I don't know if I'm succeeding at it, but I want that kind of musicality. I've spent a lot of time studying the masters of improvisation. Just listen to them and how they approach things. I realize how flexible, loose, and lucid you have to be. You must have lots of concentration; at the same time, you have to be loose enough to let things happen. You can't be pre-programmed."

Part of John's grasp of soloing comes from tran-scribing the improvisations of other musicians. He's fascinated by the works of Corea and Michael Brecker, and a few years ago he worked through some of John Scofield's solos on *Rough House*, as well as some of keyboardist Herbie Hancock's lines. "But never bass players," he insists. "I love to listen to other bassists, but I try to avoid playing like someone who plays the same instrument as I do. It's too close to home. That's why I avoided fretless for several years: Too many people were trying to emulate Jaco. I loved the way Jaco played so much, but I knew that because I was a different person, I could never play just like him. I could come *close*, but why do somebody else's stuff when they do it so beautifully? A lot of people tried, and the difference is obvious."

Patitucci admires specific attributes of various bass players, among them Marcus Miller ("he's a good all-around player who can write and play well in all the styles"), Stanley Clarke, and Jaco Pastorius. "Anyone who is serious about electric bass has listened to them," John states. "Stanley's first album [*Stanley Clarke*] and Jaco's first [*Jaco Pastorius*] were strong statements. I also love Abe Laboriel and Chuck Rainey. Willie Weeks, James Jamerson, and Jerry Jemmott — they were some of my first influences. Anthony Jackson is one of my all-time favorites. He kills me. He's got such conviction, and he has some intense views on music, and I respect that. More than anybody else, when you hear something he's done on record, you say it's *perfect*. You couldn't find anything wrong with it if you tried. On that Chaka Khan album, *What Cha Gonna Do For Me*, he plays some of the most unbelievable stuff for a pop record. And it fits. It's creative, and it's still a pop record. He takes a lot of chances. When I talk to bassists, they all seem to agree that Anthony has the most awesome time ideas on the instrument."

Patitucci laments that there is so little actual exchange of information among bassists. Part of the problem is that they seldom play together on sessions, although John gets together with Abe Laboriel occasionally and talks shop. "I was talking with Neil Stubenhaus," he says, "and we both agreed that sometimes we'd like to see more exchange. Guys get so busy, and you never find out how someone got a great sound on a record. There are so many different players with so many totally different touches."

For John, getting a consistent sound in the studios is sometimes elusive. The variables of the studio, the engineer, and the music itself have a profound effect: "I've walked out of one studio excited about the sound I got, went to another session that day with the same bass and couldn't get anything happening." On Chick Corea's album he uses a variety of electrics (and string bass on a few parts), including a Fender Jazz Bass with a bright funk tone for "Elektric City" and the Ken Smith 6-string for "Silver Temple" and all of the bass solos.

John believes that versatility is the key to a bassist's success, particularly in the studio. He occasionally gives seminars (he's done one at the Bass Institute of Technology, or B.I.T.), and he encourages players to be open-minded rather than obsessed with current fads. "Many kids focus on two-handed tapping and thumb-popping," he reports, "but I try to encourage overall bassmanship. Everybody is excited when they start out, and they want a lot of technique. I'm a firm advocate of being technically able, because if you don't have a broad range of technique, how can you express yourself? It's like a painter who doesn't have a good selection of paints. But you have to be practical. I was fortunate to have guys tell me that when I was young."

Aside from the seminars, Patitucci has all but abandoned private lessons, due to his busy schedule. Teaching steadily since he was 16, he often focused on left-hand exercises and classical technique builders that his brother Tom showed him. John firmly believes that his abilities derive from spiritual sources and that it's his duty to develop them as much as possible. "Bach said something I hold close to me all the

"There are a lot of things you can learn at college, but there comes a time when you just have to get out there and do it."

time," he explains. "He said that he dedicated every note to the glory of God. Pretty interesting. If you do that and you're really conscious of where your gift comes from, it will keep things in perspective, keep you humble. You have to know you weren't the cause of it. I mean, you can practice all you want, but unless you have that God-given gift in the first place, I'm sorry, it doesn't really make it. I don't believe there's no such thing as God-given talent. Some people say that anybody who works hard enough can be a great musician, but I'm not sure. It's got to be there, and you have to work your tail off and develop it. That's just the way it is. I'm not so foolish and presumptuous to think that if I work hard at it, I can become a great architect. Appreciating God-given talent teaches you to have perspective."

Besides his regular studio work and playing with Chick Corea, John also works on gospel sessions. He approaches all gigs with the same zest, saying, "I try to give 1,000% on every project — TV, film, gospel, rock, or jazz. Sometimes you get on a jingle that's a lot of fun, and other times it just seems silly. But I'm also practical. I'm not going to say that I'll only do a certain kind of work. Maybe some people will accuse me of selling out, but it's my life, it's my love, it's my art — but it's also my job. I feel really fortunate that I've been able to do so much creative music, where the emphasis is on the collective expression of the players."

– STEVE RODBY –

BY JIM ROBERTS – DECEMBER 1987

PAUL NATKIN/PHOTO RESERVE. INC.

STEVE RODBY lays down the foundation for the improvisational flights of the Pat Metheny Group. While he's one of the most thoroughly trained bassists working anywhere today — he began studying classical technique at the age of 10 and has been playing pop music and jazz since he was a teenager — he's also one of the least flamboyant.

Rodby is a student of what he calls "bass function." He's always looking for ways to edit and simplify his parts, to reduce each one to its most essential elements. The perfect bass line, to him, is one that supports all the other musical lines without drawing attention to itself.

Pat Metheny, who has known Rodby since they were both teenagers, is amazed by his dedication to the details of bass playing. "Steve's style is deeply rooted in the tradition of bass," says Metheny. "It's a quality that's becoming more and more rare in young bassists. With the influence of Jaco Pastorius and Stanley Clarke, it's almost like the bass has become some sort of tenor guitar. Steve has no interest in that. He really has a relationship to what happens at the low end of the sonic spectrum. It's incredibly deep and profound. He wants to hear a certain thing happen down at the bottom. It's very specific, and it's more than just the right notes. He'll sit there and think about whether he should go bum-*ba*-bum or bum-ba-*bum*. He'll think about it for two hours, really worry about it. It's refreshing to run across a musician like that, let alone have him in the band."

Rodby plays both acoustic and electric bass with the Pat Metheny Group, and he says that each instrument has made a different contribution to his musical understanding. "Playing jazz on the acoustic bass taught me how to be loose and improvise," he explains. "And it taught me how to accompany a soloist. Playing pop music on electric bass taught me about economy and editing, about taking responsibility for every detail of every note, which I really try to do. So now I combine them, and I try to apply what I've learned on each instrument to the other one."

Steve was born in Joliet, Illinois, in 1954. He says there was always music in the house (his father was a high school choir director), but he traces his fascination with the bass to an episode of the Captain Kangaroo show. "I remember watching TV when I was about three years old," recalls Rodby. "I saw this guy with a string bass, and my heart skipped a beat Then he started to play it, and I heard the sound of bass. I couldn't get over it. I became completely convinced that this was the instrument for me."

Steve had to wait seven years before he was big enough to tackle the string bass. "I started playing classical music when I was 10," he says. "As soon as I could play a little, my father bought a guitar and we started playing songs together. He would write out the root notes and bar lines, and I had to make up the bass lines. I'm lucky, because I've been improvising from the very beginning. There I was, 10 years old and improvising with a guitar player — and I'm still doing the same thing today. I'm still playing these simple bass parts, trying to pare them down and just play the good notes. It seems it was my destiny somehow."

While in high school, Rodby began to play jazz with some friends. "Then I walked into a record store one day," he says, "and they were playing the Ramsey Lewis Trio. It sounded great to me. They were doing these kind of semi-rock, semi-soul tunes — the bassist was Cleve Eaton and the drummer was Maurice White, soon to be with Earth, Wind & Fire — and that music made a big impression on me. I feel that a lot of what I'm doing now comes from those early days."

Soon after that, Steve attended one of the National Stage Band Camps. "I went after my junior year in high school," he says. "I didn't know anything, but I was fortunate to be put in a group with a very talented piano player named Lyle Mays [now with the Pat Metheny Group]. The next year, just before I went to college, I went again and was put in a group with Danny Gottlieb [the original Pat Metheny Group drummer] and Pat Metheny. Pat had been a teacher, but he was just hanging around and playing that week. So Pat and Danny and I had a chance to play together that summer. It was a wonderful experience."

Rodby was unconvinced that he could make a living as a jazz musician, though, so he enrolled at Northwestern University, where he studied bass performance with Warren Benfield of the Chicago Symphony Orchestra. He also took some lessons from jazz bassist Rufus Reid and started to do studio work, where he began to explore the possibilities of the electric bass. "I taught myself electric bass," says Rodby, "and there's a lot of the string bass in my electric bass work. I play with the 1-2-4 acoustic bass fingering, which is a non-guitar concept. I like it because the outside of my hand can get I, IV, V, ♭VII — all the good notes for the kind of bass function playing that I dig.

"I want to have some kind of continuity in the relationship between the acoustic bass and the electric bass. And one thing that's really fascinating to me is the powerful effect that all this electric bass playing has had on my acoustic approach. I've spent the most time working on trying to develop a certain kind of

"Playing pop music on electric bass taught me about economy and editing, about taking responsibility for every detail of every note."

straight eighth-note acoustic bass playing that has an awful lot to do with what I've learned from listening to electric bassists in pop music, especially soul: Aretha Franklin, the Four Tops, the Spinners, Earth, Wind & Fire. That music is still completely satisfying to me. The bass function in that music has got so many lessons.

"The better I've learned how to listen, the better I've learned how to play. And in learning how to hear what's in this great music that I love, I've taught myself. I pay close attention to note duration. To me, the end of a note sounds like a backbeat. When I cut off a note, I hear this *whack* that's like a percussion instrument. There's also the lift you get from short notes or ghosted notes. They're all over the music that I play, and they're details that give the music a lot of vitality. They give that slight upward movement of the groove.

"The bass players on many of those soul tunes were able to take just a few notes — I, V, and VI — and work them to death. Many of my bass lines will use only those notes. My approach isn't scale-oriented at all. I know the chord scales, and I can even play fast, but I just don't hear those things."

After graduating from college in 1977, Rodby spent many of his days playing electric bass in Chicago recording studios, and picked up his acoustic bass for jazz gigs at night. For several years he was the bassist in the house rhythm section at the Jazz Showcase, where he got a chance to work with many excellent soloists. He also toured with pianist Monty Alexander and singer/songwriter Michael Franks, and began his still-active association with the Contemporary Chamber Players, a classical new music group.

His call from Pat Metheny came in 1981. "I'd decided I wanted to change the band a little bit," recalls Metheny, "and I wanted somebody who could play both acoustic and electric bass. Steve was the first guy who came to mind. We had him come to New York for an audition, and we knew instantly that he was the guy. We asked him right on the spot, and he joined the band."

In the Pat Metheny Group, Steve has been able to fully explore his ideas about bass function. "I feel a real continuity between the first time I played with Pat and playing with the band now," says Rodby.

"Back then, he would put the tunes in front of me, and I could play what I heard and it just clicked. It's still like that; I can rely on my first intuition and just play it how I hear it."

Most of the time, Rodby says, he develops his own bass lines for the tunes written by Metheny and/or Lyle Mays. "Sometimes they're collaborations," he says. "One of my favorite bass parts is on the song we did with David Bowie, "This Is Not America" [*The Falcon And The Snowman* soundtrack]. Pat had a demo of that with a bass part, and I just moved the octaves around and put some things in. Other times, the demos will just have the bass pedaling the chords, and I'll write the bass parts. The more elaborate bass parts, like 'Yolanda' or 'First Circle' [both on *First Circle*], are all my patterns. But it's easy to do because it's such great music. The music will always strongly suggest something to me. There's so much information on the top, it's clear to me what should be on the bottom."

In creating his bass lines, Rodby tries to combine the tight, disciplined style he learned from studio work with the responsiveness he acquired on jazz gigs. "I always think of 'Are You Going With Me' as one of the really good examples of my approach. [*Ed. Note: The original studio recording of the song is on* Offramp; *a longer live version appears on* Travels.] It's a very simple part on electric bass, but it's very hard to play. There are so many little decisions to be made in every single measure. I have to decide: Of the 40 different variations I have of that little pattern I'm playing, which one is going to make it groove the most? It's a different one every night, and it's a different one for each part of that little story that we're telling you."

Rodby's basic pattern has a simple samba beat. He can vary that pattern by different note choices, or he can vary it by changing note durations. The pattern can be altered in many other ways, too, including attack articulation, dynamics, and tempo (rushing or dragging the beat). There is an almost infinite number of possible variations, notes Rodby, many more than can be shown with conventional notation.

As he "reinvents" his bass parts in concert, Steve has to be aware of both human and mechanical factors. "We're playing with a lot of sequences now," he notes, "which is like playing with a click track. I've had years of experience playing with a click doing studio work, but it's a whole other thing, playing this music with sequencers. Both Paul [Wertico, the drummer] and I aspire to making it feel very loose. You can't really cheat — you can't speed up a whole lot and slow down at the cadences — but we push and pull enough on it that we give it that jazz factor. We're in there jamming, even though we're playing with these robots."

In addition to recording all the bass lines on *Still Life (Talking)*, the band's latest album, Rodby was also credited as an associate producer. The music is richly textured, with many small details that only emerge after repeated listening. Getting it right, says Steve, took a long time. "We worked very hard and learned a lot of lessons the hard way," he explains, "but it was really great to get in there and put my stamp on thousands of those little details that we put into the music. We tried to max out the production and also keep a real jazz thing happening. We tried to arrange all the tunes so that not only does the melody tell a story and each solo tell a story, but the entire form of the arrangement, from beginning to end, tells a story. It's the most ambitious thing we've ever tried to do."

Although recording and playing with the Pat Metheny Group fills up most of Rodby's schedule, he found time recently to complete a duo album with an old friend, guitarist Ross Traut. (Several years ago, Rodby was the bassist on Traut's eponymous debut album.) He hopes to find more time to do other drummerless projects, he says, because they fit in perfectly with his concept of bass function: "Once again, it's that idea of getting it all happening from the bass."

– STEVE SWALLOW –

BY JIM ROBERTS – NOVEMBER 1987

STEVE SWALLOW feels that now is the time to come forward with his own music. Although he has made two previous albums as a leader, the 47-year-old bassist sees his new release *Carla* as a milestone, the first in a series of projects that will expand his role as one of the leading instrumentalists, composers, and producers in modern music.

For some Swallow fans, *Carla* will come as a shock. He has deliberately taken a step toward reaching a larger audience, basing his new tunes on solid R&B grooves that have a smooth, sensuous feel. If that sounds like easy-listening pop-jazz, don't be fooled; some of his intricate jazz solos and harmonies have the sophistication of a classical piece. The rhythm section work is also incredibly subtle, with more and more details emerging under close listenings.

Throughout his career, Steve Swallow has been unafraid to be different. Trained in classical piano as a child, he soon switched to playing trumpet and then acoustic bass. Midway through college at Yale, he dropped out to become a full-time jazz musician. In 1968, after establishing himself as an up-and-coming star with such leaders as guitarist Jim Hall and saxophonist Stan Getz, he suddenly dropped the acoustic bass cold and switched to electric bass.

As an electric bassist, Swallow has followed a singular path that's been largely unaffected by musical trends. His first electric was a Gibson EB-2, a short-scale, semi-hollowbody that he felt retained some of

the warmth of an acoustic bass. He later switched to Fender and then began experimenting with instruments. In his search for the right combination of playability and clear sound, he has tried dozens of different bodies, necks, bridges, and pickups. His current bass looks like a Fender, but it's actually a custom semi-hollowbody outfitted with Zeta Systems piezo transducer pickups. Swallow always plays with a pick, drawing forth a unique sound that has been widely praised by both critics and his fellow musicians.

Half a dozen years ago, Swallow was working in groups led by vibraphonist Gary Burton, guitarist John Scofield, and keyboardist/composer Carla Bley. Swallow no longer plays regularly with Burton or Scofield, although he produced Scofield's last three albums. These days, he's focusing his attention on his emerging career as a leader, as well as his role in the Carla Bley Sextet, where he is often the featured soloist. *Carla* completes a trilogy of albums co-produced by Swallow and Carla Bley. Taken together, the records form an illuminating portrait of Swallow's musical personality. The series began with Carla's *Night-Glo*, released in 1985. Written by Bley, its five tunes put the spotlight on Swallow's bass, which plays most of the melodies and solos. Bley's next album, *Sextet*, features her current working band. Swallow solos several times on the album, but his primary task is anchoring the rhythm. *Carla* is the reverse of *Night-Glo:* This time Swallow wrote the music to feature Bley's organ playing. His bass parts are critically important throughout, though, and the album has one bass showcase, "Hold It Against Me." Steve's string and synthesizer arrangements give the music a warm, full sound.

Now that the album is done, Swallow is taking an active role in promoting and distributing it through Watt/XtraWatt Records, the independent label operated by Carla Bley and her husband, trumpeter Michael Mantler. "I want to see this project through all of those steps that lead to its arrival in the stores and over the airwaves," says Swallow. "I'm hopeful that it'll be able to extend the control over my music much further than I have in the past."

Does your new music aim beyond jazz circles?

Very definitely. I'm hoping to reach a broader audience than I have in the past. The jazz audience is wonderfully staunch and loyal, and they've tried much harder than could be expected to sustain me. But I'm going to need a little help from across the fence. I'm also not as grateful as I used to be to be seen as a "musician's musician." It's flattering to be well regarded by your peers, but I'm more interested now in reaching people who are not at all concerned with the technical or craft aspects of what I do.

Where do you hope to place your music?

I've been speculating on that, and where I'd like to put it, I think, is in the bedroom. I've noticed that a lot of my friends have record players in their bedrooms, and that's a point worth paying attention to. Music on record is private music, and lately I've come to think that the record offers you the possibility of making an intimate statement. You're able to talk to somebody alone, or two people alone, in their room and there's a vast difference in the way you speak, the way you modulate your voice, even the content of what you're saying. Some of the music I admire most is on a grand scale, but I must say I'm disinclined to listen to that music very often in my room. I'm more likely to listen to João Gilberto or somebody of that sort.

When did you decide you wanted to do an album of your music?

Its inception was in September 1985. When Carla asked me to write her an album. I wanted to right away. We were already in the process of doing *Night-Glo*, which was essentially an album for me, and she politely suggested that I return the favor. It took me about a year, with time I could borrow and steal, to write the record's eight tunes. But I knew I'd be writing for the members of her sextet [organist Bley,

Swallow, guitarist Hiram Bullock, pianist Larry Willis, drummer Victor Lewis, and percussionist Don Alias], plus Ida Kavafian on violin, Ik-huan Bae on viola, and Fred Sherry on cello. The string players are that recent breed of classical musicians from New York who love to play music with a groove. The strings give the music more texture and gloss. Both Carla and I played synthesizers, too. She actually dislikes synthesizers intensely and avoids them, but I love them. I've been fascinated with them for some time, and there are quite a few of them lurking in my album. They're not always obvious.

How long did it take to record the album?

We rehearsed three times, then did the tracks in a couple of days in September of last year. It was done at the studio in Carla's basement, Grog Kill Studio, in Willow, New York. Then Carla and I spent some time operating the machines ourselves and adding synthesizer, organ, and bass parts. It's a blessing indeed that we used Carla's studio, because we were able to spend a lot more time than is generally spent on a jazz record. Then in May, the strings were added. After that, over a period of about a week or 10 days, we mixed the thing.

Are you considering taking your own group on the road?

I'd like to tour, to take a crack at the entire process of leading a band. I feel that I'm prepared to do that. I've been scurrying around more behind the scenes, and in the course of doing that I've learned what I need to know to do this work for myself. I hope also to continue playing with Carla and to do all the other projects that have been sitting on the shelf for years, but I'd like to present myself and my own music more often than I have. I love the role of the bass in the band, which is not usually the leadership role, and the social aspects of playing the bass have always appealed to me. So I've been reluctant in the past to stride to the fore. But now I have some urgent matters to express, and I see this album as a first step in exposing my point of view. It's the first of a series of records.

Are there aspects of your musical point of view that haven't come out in other people's music?

Probably, although I must say I've had ample opportunity, in one context or another, to express myself. More to the point is that I've *come* to a point of view. I see myself as a late bloomer. Of late, I've felt some certainty about some things, and also the sense that I'm obliged to make my feelings known. There are different ways of doing that. Live performance is one way of exposing music to folks, but it's not really very efficient — although there's no greater feeling than a good night in a hot, small room. But I'm more interested in recordings as a means of disseminating my music. I'm fascinated by the technical aspects of making records, and I'm finally becoming comfortable in the studio. I see it as a sympathetic playing environment. For many years, my attitude toward it was adversary.

There's a lot going on with musical technology. So many people are scared of it, and others are fascinated by it.

I see it as an ally. I'm one old dog who's learned a couple of new tricks recently. The die was probably cast when I switched from acoustic bass to electric bass, which was about 18 years ago.

And that was a revolutionary thing to do.

It was considered downright rude at the time. I lost some good friends, but I made some others. And I think that once I faced up to the fact that I wanted to play an electric instrument more than I wanted to play an acoustic one, I began to pay attention to music I had ignored. At first it was a matter of searching out electric bassists. I knew very little about what the instrument could do and who had played it in the past. So, through an interest in players like James Jamerson and Duck Dunn, I also found an interest in the music they were playing. As a teenager I had been an adamant bebopper. And if I hadn't discovered the electric bass, I probably would have lagged behind even longer before discovering singers like Marvin Gaye and Otis Redding. Over the last decade, that music has had a tremendous, abiding effect on my taste, and all of that is just beginning to surface strongly in the music that I'm doing now. Apparently, it takes a great deal of time to assimilate music. It took quite a while for me to feel free to express myself in that vernacular. For some considerable time, I was embarrassed to do so.

You were embarrassed to be a middle-class white boy playing rhythm and blues?

Exactly. Should I do this at all? I had come to terms with playing jazz already, so it would have been a fairly easy transition. But it was difficult to leave the climate of approval that exists for playing jazz. There's the sense, in many people's perception, that it's almost as good as classical music. If you play jazz, you're a kind of real musician. But again, it's like when I switched to electric bass and immediately

> *"I feel as comfortable with digital delays as with the fingerboard of my bass — and as strongly connected to them."*

experienced the prejudice against that instrument from my peers. That didn't sit well with me, so dealing with my own prejudices about rhythm and blues and related forms was a lot easier to take.

The electric bass isn't considered such a bastard instrument anymore. Now synthesizers, sequencers, and drum machines are seen as even more threatening.

That's right. The electric bass is seen as downright human at this point. It's an interesting irony. And I'm interested in sequences myself, so I'm prepared to lose even more friends, if necessary.

One argument against many of the electronic devices is that you can create music without being able to play at all — or barely.

That argument doesn't wash too well with me. I've always thought that the means are fair game. You use whatever is necessary to make music that has value.

Don't you think that the really difficult part is mental, not physical — that you have to be able to conceive great music? The computer won't write it for you.

No, it won't. Although if it could, I'd be happy to consign music writing to computers — if they get better than we folks are. We shouldn't resist the possibility of being outwritten by computers. It reminds me of when I bought my first tuning machine many years ago. For a long time, I always told folks that I was using the machine to get roughly in tune, and that the ear was the final arbiter, far better than the machine. But at this point I'm willing to admit without shame that the machine tunes the instrument better than I do. I've come to realize that it's unwise for me to fiddle with those pegs, although there is a way in which pitch is a subjective issue. I'm inclined to play sharp when I'm anxious, and flat when I'm tired. That's an element of expression, and playing is an expressive act.

You get to be very expressive with the Carla Bley Sextet, since you're often the featured soloist. How long have you been working with her?

I first met her in 1960, when she was still married to [pianist] Paul Bley. She'd been writing since the mid '50s, and Paul was already playing a repertoire that consisted substantially of her tunes. I actually joined her band around '78, and I've been playing in it ever since. I'm the only survivor from her bands of the late '70s, so I've been there through most of her time as a bandleader. And, prior to that time, I'd taken her music with me wherever I went and caused my various bandleaders to play her music. There's a need for tunes out there. I'm convinced that tunes and rhythm sections are most important to the course of the sort of music that I play.

To advance what's going on?

I think so, and most often the perspective is not that. Critics and the public tend to see soloists as major figures. The classic instance of that is the underappreciation of James Jamerson and [drummer] Ben Benjamin. They were given no credit on the Motown records — and precious little bread. I've been studying Motown carefully of late, with great respect and admiration. The sense that it's the songs and the rhythm section that are most important springs from this research. It's just miraculous how many good songs and good grooves were generated by a small group of people for a period of about 10 years in the '60s. It's just breathtaking. And it's my intention that XtraWatt be the Motown of the '90s.

Does your vision of XtraWatt include more work for yourself as a producer?

Yes, it does. I recently produced a big band recording of Steve Weisberg's music, *I Can't Stand Another Night Alone (In Bed With You)*. There are some great players on the album, and I have a few other things planned for the future. I hope to do as much producing as possible — I love that work, and it's a valuable service occupation. Most of the producers I've worked with tended not to see production as a service occupation, but as a kind of imperial function. That can hurt rather than help. I've been abused by enough producers to be wary of them in general. But I'm convinced there's a lot a producer can do to improve a record. At this point, I'm fairly well along in learning how to engineer. I can actually plug microphones in and cause tape machines to work. And I've begun to understand the mysteries of the outboard equipment that enhances the sound of a record. The more I see of it, the more I want to know about it. I've come to find that my relationships with machines are very complex and highly emotional at times. The idea that humanness has gone out of the world because of machines makes no sense at all to me.

How did you learn to be comfortable with machines?

It was a kind of slow unraveling of my prejudices. Initially, I was able to play the electric bass fearlessly, but I was still wary of my amplifier. I saw it as the thing across the room. At some point — probably when I was listening a lot to Jimi Hendrix — I realized that the amplifier was as much a part of the in-

strument as what I was touching. Several years later, I was willing to accept that other pieces of equipment were similarly musical instruments. At this point, I feel as comfortable with digital delays as with the fingerboard of my bass — and as strongly connected to them.

Are you using more electronics onstage?

Yes. Presently — and it changes every now and then — I'm carrying a Yamaha REV7 digital reverb, an Aphex Aural Exciter Type C, a Yamaha PB-1 preamp, and a Carver 1.5 power amp. Occasionally, I use a T.C. Electronic 1140 parametric EQ/preamp instead of the Yamaha, and I also have a Korg SDD-2000 digital delay. And I still find occasion to use my Walter Woods amplifier, which is a 300-watt, one-channel MI225-8 that I've had for years. I recently used it at a concert with the Lincoln Center Chamber Music Society for a piece of Carla's, since the sound of the fan in my Carver would have been distressing. I also have a Mesa/Boogie D180 bass head that I still use.

Have you tried any bass synthesizers?

Not the ones with fingerboards, because I keep hearing about all the problems they have with tracking. But I've used some keyboard bass synthesizers. There's a synthesized bass sound on the Korg 6000 that I like. And I've had occasion to use the bass sound on the Minimoog, as well, which is a very nice one. In the studio I occasionally double a part that I've already played on electric bass. And I sometimes elect to use a synthesizer bass rather than a stringed instrument. I'm not bound in any way to using any particular mechanism to achieve a sound. Whatever works is fine with me — I don't see moral issues in this area. I'll rephrase that: The morality of it is to make the music sound as good as possible.

What speakers do you use?

I used to use a couple of 12s, but now I prefer 15s. I generally use Electro-Voice 15s. When I'm out on the road, I often use whatever speaker cabinets are available, but when I bring my own speaker, it's a Mesa/Boogie bass-ported cabinet with one E-V 15. And I still have an old Fender Dual Showman cabinet with two E-V 12s.

You have an instrument that looks like a shrunken cello with a fretted fingerboard. What is it?

Its an entirely hollow instrument with a maple back and a spruce top. It's called a cello bass. A guy at Gibson made about 20 of these things, but never finished them before he died. I have no idea when, but perhaps it was in the '50s. I would love to know more about this instrument. I'd been imagining an instrument exactly like this for years, and I'm very excited to see what comes of this. I'm going to take it to an excellent cello repairman and have it set up to play as well as it can acoustically, and at that point confront what to do about amplifying it. I'll speak to Keith McMillen of Zeta Systems, Larry Fishman in Boston, or one of the other transducer people, and see what comes of it. I have high hopes for this instrument. It's so lovely, such a beautifully made and strange instrument. There are about 20 of them, all without any bridge or tailpiece, never been strung up. A friend found this in a Chicago music store, called me up and told me about it, and I bought it sight unseen.

You've done a lot of experimenting with setting up an electric bass, trying different pickups, bodies, and bridges. You once theorized that you could "buy" a better sound. Do you still feel that way?

I do, and I'm still showing up with my bucks whenever I can. The bass I'm using most of the time now is one I've had for five years or so, a hollowbody instrument with a spruce top. It was made by Froc Fillipetti. It's got Schaller tuning machines and Zeta Systems transducer pickups, rather than magnetic ones. It has one pickup for each string, built into a bridge I designed myself. There's also a preamp for each transducer.

Why do you play with a pick?

I get closer to the sound that I want with a pick. I use a copper pick made by a company called Hot Licks, the thickest one they make [.010]. It turns my hand green, but it's a price I'm willing to pay. I'm trying to create the illusion that there is no pick, but I need the pick to get sufficient clarity, and I like the possibilities for articulation. There are lots of ways to strike the string with it, lots of angles that achieve different sounds. But it's best if the listener is unaware of the physical agency that produces sounds. So in a sense I'm working to make all of that stuff — the instrument, the amplifier, the pick — disappear when I'm playing.

What do you want in an electric bass?

What I want runs contrary to the direction that's being taken by most instrument makers who are concerned with making as stable an instrument as possible, an instrument as free of errant vibrations as possible. Because of my days as an acoustic bass player, I love anomalies in the response of an instrument. I see that as an aspect of its character. It's been difficult for

"The trick with fretted instruments is to make them sound as flexible and expressive as fretless instruments."

me to persuade instrument makers to move in the other direction, to come to terms with the wonderfully eccentric things that wood can do. And the transducers have moved me further along in this direction, because they receive information that the magnetic pickups ignore. This creates problems, but has its rewards. I'm still looking for a more richly colored sound than I have, and I'm confident that I can buy it.

On recent recordings, your tone sounds sharper — not only at the top end, but in the middle and lower registers, as well.

My sound has changed recently. I tend to use a much treblier EQ than I have in the past. Also, I've been experimenting with the flange-reverb setting on the Yamaha REV7. I've modified it to my own purposes; I tweaked the parameters of the program that combines reverb and flanging. The effect is set at a very low level, and it seems to color the sound a bit.

Some of your recent solo work is high-pitched beyond the range of a regular bass. What causes that?

For the last couple of years, to increase my range on the top and be able to play higher, I've carted two Fillipetti basses around. One of them is tuned up a fourth — from the bottom to the top, it's *A, D, G, C.* On some tunes with Carla's sextet, she plays the bass parts on the synthesizer and I use the solo-tuned instrument. On "Hold It Against Me," that's this instrument playing the melody. It really gets up there. Right now, I'm having a 5-string bass built, and I hope I'll like it very much, so I won't have to carry two basses around with me. I'm going with the high fifth string, not a low one. If I'm able to deal with five strings, I'll consider six — but first things first. There's a point at which physics will tell me to stop. Anthony Jackson, for instance, has taken the bass about as low as it can reasonably go. I'll occasionally detune the instrument to get a low *D* or a low *C* on the bottom string, but not often.

Is your solo-tuned bass similar to the other one?

It's a little different. It has a 1959 Fender Precision "C" neck that I've had for a number of years. The other one has a neck through the body. Froc and I collaborated on the design of both basses. As an acoustic player, I learned a great deal from my repairman in New York City, Jules Callman. He had been making violins and repairing basses all his life. I spent hours in this guy's workroom, which was a fascinating place. I listened to him very carefully when he talked about the physics of the instrument and sound in general. Over the years I've made my fingers do what was necessary to extract tone from a wooden instrument in a direction that this man pointed out to me. He was not a player at all, but he had a great sense of what happens when a piece of wood vibrates. And I really want that in my playing with the electric bass. I don't see why an electric bass has to be an absolutely stable and efficient plank of wood. There's no reason why it can't be a construction of wood that has its own eccentricities and anomalies.

Since there are so many percussive electric bass players now, many of whom use their thumb, there seems to be a tendency toward building stable, incredibly twangy instruments.

Yes, and it may be a mixed blessing. On the one hand, I want to exploit the virtues of acoustically produced sound in my music. That's always been important. And, on the other hand, I want to use the technology that's exploded in the last decade. I don't see those as contradictory impulses at all. They're just parallel.

So your music tries to strike a balance between acoustic and electric elements.

On a personal level, it's a matter of a balance between your history and what you are at the present moment. The technology of the '80s provides us with better means than we've had in the past to understand the nature of acoustic sound. It's possible to be more analytical about what the sound of an acoustic instrument is. On the other hand, it's wise to bring an understanding of the properties of acoustic sound to dealing with the technology. It strikes me that the people who play synthesizers best have had considerable experience in acoustic music and are sensitive to the beauty of the sound of an unamplified acoustic piano. Their imagination is enriched by that experience.

When you switched from acoustic to electric bass, you changed from the classical 1-2-4 left-hand fingering to 1-2-3-4, using one finger per fret. How did that affect your playing?

The fingering was one disadvantage that I had to overcome. I had habits, especially left-hand habits, that were inappropriate to the fingerboard of the fretted electric bass. The use of the 3rd finger was the primary issue, and it took me several years to use it without being conscious of doing it. Studying the piano and playing it quite a bit over the years has had an effect on the vocabulary I use as a bassist. I'm not as concerned with what's possible on the fingerboard as I am with hearing bass parts and realizing

them by whatever means are necessary. I tend to learn away from the instrument and then confront the instrument and try to realize what I've thought. I've always enjoyed the resistance I've gotten from the bass. I enjoy being told by the instrument that something can't be done, then wrestling with it for some time. You win some, you lose some, but it's always fun. And very often you end up with something that you hadn't anticipated.

The electric is more difficult than some people think, especially playing things cleanly.

Yes, very difficult, and I'm more concerned with articulating clearly and expressively than I am with playing fast. Manipulating the strings is a dodgy business itself. I use roundwound LaBellas, a package of standard soft-gauge 760RSs. On the solo-tuned bass, I use 760RXs, which are even thinner, and a .027 string for the high C. I use whatever .027 I can find; lately it's been a GHS. I've progressed from a fatter string to a thin string over the years as my touch has become more sensitive. There's a point at which the instrument just begins to look back at you. If you play with as much force as you can on the electric bass, you don't get as much sound out of it as you do if you play with controlled force, with a sense of where the line is you shouldn't cross. There's a point at which the flap of the string actually works against your tone production. I spent years working on a vibrato for the fretted fingerboard, and the kind of vibrato I use is more like a string player's than an electric guitarist's. That's a purely technical issue, and it's necessary to spend hours and hours watching your hand execute vibrato. But it's also a deeply personal matter. How you choose to vibrate the string really makes a statement about the sort of fellow you are.

You also do quite a bit of string bending.

On electric bass, that's harder than on guitar. The strings are thicker and harder to manipulate. The trick with fretted instruments is to make them sound as flexible and expressive as fretless instruments. Conversely, the fretless demands that you pay particular attention to accuracy of intonation and other things that are not quite as difficult on the fretted fingerboard. There's a trade-off there.

You seem to be doing more bending now than in the past. Have you been working on it?

A while ago I did several concerts opposite B.B. King, and I was really impressed at how much his playing sounded like the human voice. I watched the extensive physical maneuvering he went through to achieve his beautiful offhand vocal quality to his sound; then I scurried back to my hotel after the concert and worked on bends for hours on end. I practiced them very slowly. That's another thing I've come to lately — practicing slowly. Almost everybody, when he or she is young, tends to practice for velocity. I received strong hints early on that I ought to slow down. Jim Hall was the first person who made me strongly aware of the virtues of playing slowly, thinking slowly, talking slowly. But it's taken me all these years to really take that to heart — to spend extensive amounts of time playing whole-notes instead of eighth-notes.

You play several tunes on Sextet *using whole- and half-notes. On "The Girl Who Cried Champagne," for instance, you play half-notes that are tremendously anticipated. Their placement gives the song an exceptional amount of momentum.*

I owe that approach to the influence of Latin music, which has been strong on me the last few years. Andy Gonzales has been incredibly patient and generous in teaching me aspects of Latin bass playing. If there's any bass playing that epitomizes this kind of thing, it's Latin bass: With an absolutely stringent economy of means, the bass does so much.

In various polls over the years, your name has been right at the top of electric bassists. You're up there with Jaco Pastorius and Stanley Clarke, who both have many imitators, but there aren't a lot of bassists who sound like Steve Swallow. Why is that?

I don't know — just lucky, I guess. I also think I've been slower in coming into my voice than many people have, although there may be something to be said for proceeding cautiously in this terrain. I've won some hard-fought battles in the course of arriving at a voice of my own, and there's some value to that. At this point, I feel that I'm on firm ground, and that gives me the confidence to play exactly what I want to play. I'm aware that the direction I'm taking is likely to alienate some of the people who've been faithful to me for a number of years, but there's nothing I can do but throw myself at their mercy. They'll just have to understand that this is something I have to do. They'll have to accept on faith, I suppose, that I'm serious — like a heart attack.

> *"Almost everybody, when he or she is young, tends to practice for velocity. I received strong hints early on that I ought to slow down."*

– ROCK –

— JEFF BERLIN —

BY TOM MULHERN – JUNE 1981

OST MUSI-cians try to protect their hands — sometimes to the extent of constantly wearing gloves or shunning handshakes. Quite the opposite is true of Jeff Berlin, who likes to use his hands *a lot*: Not only does he play bass whenever and wherever possible, but in recent years his love for the sport of boxing has lured him into the ring, where his hands are subjected to nonstop assaults. Nevertheless, Berlin's fingers move with remarkable dexterity, providing a distinctively intricate but powerful bass that stands out on heavyweight performances by jazz giants like George Benson, Lenny White, Herbie Mann, Bill Evans, Dave Liebman, Sonny Fortune, Joe Farrell, and Al Di Meola. Jeff has performed in Atlantic Records' house band at the 1977 Montreux Festival, added punch to many TV and radio commercials, and has sat in with everyone from Toots Thielemans to Larry Coryell. Even as a sideman Jeff receives a great deal of attention, often becoming the focus of glowing reviews of concerts and albums.

In 1977, Berlin teamed with guitarist Allan Holdsworth, keyboardist Dave Stewart, and the eclectic British drummer Bill Bruford in a progressive rock quartet called Bruford, to record the first of three studio albums and one live LP. Their association as a touring band lasted until 1980, when they decided to take a year off for individual pursuits. This hiatus has afforded Jeff the opportunity to perform throughout Boston with a number of jazz bands, as well as with guitarist Mick Goodrick.

Berlin is also composing music for his own band, and further developing his already sophisticated, driving sound.

Jeff Berlin has always been aggressive in his pursuits. Born in Queens, New York, on January 17, 1953, he acquired a love of classical music fostered by his opera singer father and pianist mother. "I heard all the great pieces," he says, "and by the time I was three I was singing operatic lieder." At five, Jeff began almost a decade of violin lessons, and by the time he was 11, he had advanced to violin concerti by Brahms, Mendelssohn, and Beethoven. So engrossed was he in the classical idiom that the young Berlin had no interest in rock and roll, jazz, and other styles. An adoring fan of Beethoven, Jeff couldn't get enough of the composer's music, and even carried a small statue of him at all times. At 13, Jeff was chosen as one of the top five violinists at the Long Island String Festival. But while still in his early teens, he began to doubt his abilities on the violin and turned to the bass guitar. He continued playing the violin, but soon lost all interest. He quit playing it, and since his mid teens hasn't picked it up again.

Wasn't your family disappointed when you quit playing violin?

At first. I had to stop, it just became too technical. I couldn't achieve feeling anymore, and I didn't think I could play that well.

When did you quit playing violin?

When I was about 12 or 13. I saw the Beatles on *Ed Sullivan* and didn't give a darn about them. But later on, I began to like them and started to dislike violin. And the more that I listened to the Beatles, the more I really began to understand that there was something more to rock and roll than just the I-IV-V progression. I didn't know anything about other kinds of music then; it was just classical or rock and roll, so I really had a lot of growing to do.

Did you go right to playing bass?

I was playing bass while I was still playing violin. I wanted to be a drummer, but my mother said, "No! Too much noise! That's not a musical instrument!" I thought I'd never be able to play guitar; I didn't understand how it works. And I couldn't play drums, so I took up bass.

Was string bass your next step?

No, I played electric right off — I used to practice by myself on a yardstick before I got an instrument. I realized the bass is a totally different thing. With violin, your fingers are at a much closer proximity, while on the bass there are huge half-steps.

Did the new fingerings cross you up?

At first they did, but I got to the point where it didn't really matter. I figured that anybody who knows a little about music can easily assimilate another instrument. When I first picked up the bass, I couldn't do anything. But I immediately tried to play fast. If I wasn't playing Beatles songs, it was classical melodies. In fact, I attempted on bass the third movement from a Mendelssohn violin concerto. It's really a nuts thing on the violin, so I never could do it. But I was an adventurous guy even back then.

Are you formally trained on electric?

One or two guys locally tried to teach me the bass clef, but I'm mostly self-taught. I got slick on it pretty quick when everyone was playing *boom-chick-boom*. I said, "Yeah, but what about *teddity-teddity-toodelly-toodelly*?" I always heard something else, regardless of the instrument. I mean, if I were a drummer, I might have approached it the same way. I didn't want to play root-5th-root-5th all the time.

Did you use any method books to guide you?

No. I could already read treble clef, and bass clef is only slightly different. I had friends in the school orchestra, and I used to go and read the string bass parts. At first, I had to get used to bass clef. I just read the lines and spaces. It's really a matter of being used to the symbols, so I just read slowly till I got it.

What was your first bass guitar?

A Hagstrom solidbody. I didn't know anything about basses. A guy in Great Neck, Long Island, was supposed to be a great bass player, and he had a Hagstrom. So I thought, "If he plays one, I'd better play one."

Were you in bands during your teens?

Yeah, pretty adventurous ones, at that. We did more or less the standard repertoire of Steppenwolf and Jefferson Airplane. But I fell in love head-over-heels with Jack Bruce, and tried to get all these guys to play Cream tunes; unfortunately, they weren't really into Cream. Even back then, people would say, "Hey, Jeff, would you kindly quit playing in the higher registers? Would you please play some *bass* for us?"

Were you playing lines like Jack Bruce in "Crossroads" [from Wheels Of Fire]?

"Crossroads!" Did you hear how nuts he went on that tune? That's some of the most musical rock and roll bass that guy played, man. He was like the innovator for everybody, the first guy that I know of to not play *boom-chick-boom* bass. I've always liked the atypical approach, and his certainly was. He sang his heart out, wrote fantastic music, and was the best bass player of that age — of that idiom. So I went absolutely wild for him.

Did you get a Gibson bass and a Marshall stack?

I couldn't afford the Marshall stack, but I got the EB-0. I put a Gibson treble pickup on it, and more or less had a homemade EB-3. One of the guys in our band made a speaker cabinet with two JBL D-140s, without grille cloth. I accidentally damaged it and bought it from him, and that became my speaker stack, which I used with an Acoustic 150 power head. I just cranked it, and it spat that lovely midrange — that lovely distortion — and boy, I was Jack Bruce.

Did you reach a point where you got tired of rock?

I graduated from high school in 1972, barely — I was never a good student — and loafed for several months. I didn't know what to do. So I said, "I have to go into the Army." I didn't tell my parents; I didn't tell anybody. I got down to the induction office just as they were closing. They said they'd be glad to have me, but I'd have to come back the next day. Lord! I don't know who was looking over me, but that night I got a phone call to do a Broadway show, *The Me Nobody Knows*. That was my first professional gig, and they were going out on the road for six weeks. I don't know how they heard about me, but I auditioned and that was it!

Were you nervous?

No. I knew I could do it. As a matter of fact, I was

so sure that I was great that I really let loose. In one section, the band played an *F7* kind of rock and roll vamp, and I went absolutely nuts on it — like 365 notes per bar! I syncopated that thing to death! I thought what I did was really slick. Afterwards, they asked me to stop because the dancers couldn't find the beat.

Besides gaining experience reading charts, what else did you encounter?

There was a jazz guitarist on that gig who played unusual chord voicings, and I had never heard anything quite like that — melodies with lovely chords underneath, and tension in the voicings. He told me that there's a school called Berklee that I ought to check out. After the show closed, I hopped the bus to Boston and spent two years at the Berklee College of Music.

What was your aim in going there?

I can't really say. I just knew that there were many things I didn't know, things I'd better check out. You know: Maybe there is something to jazz, and more than just Jack Bruce, etc. At the time, there was a dearth of really good musicians around Long Island, so I felt that I had to find a more active musical environment. Berklee was it, and I *studied* — the best thing I ever did. I worked really hard and learned a lot. For instance, I met [vibraphonist] Gary Burton, who was a big influence on me. Apparently I could play jazz back then — I didn't think so, but some people thought I could. I was in the hippest ensembles and sight-reading classes. Gary taught a modern composition class, and he needed an electric bassist to play the parts, so he asked me. I was flattered. I used to get all kinds of gigs at the school. If someone needed an electric bass player, they'd inevitably call me.

What kind of curriculum did you follow?

They had a bass curriculum, but I imagine the people who taught me quickly saw that they couldn't really show me anything as far as the *electric* bass went. I'm not being egotistical; it's just that most of the teachers were string bass players. The school began to get an influx of electric bassists, and what were they supposed to do — turn them away? They *had* to teach.

What did you learn, then?

Not much in terms of electric music, but a lot in terms of the logistics of harmony, theory, melody, and writing. I played all the time, constantly making up

"By using other types of instrumental literature, you can't do anything but help your bass playing."

ensembles. I was in Michael Gibbs' ensemble. You might remember Mike — he was the orchestrator of John McLaughlin's *Apocalypse*. I heard that album, and I fell down! I didn't understand how anybody could write so beautifully. When he came to the school, I walked up and said, "Hello, Mike? My name is Jeff. I've *got* to play with you." He said, "Okay," and I was in his ensemble.

Did you study any other instruments at Berklee?
No.

Didn't you even play string bass?

Only for a while. I went through a lot of hard times there, because I didn't really know what I was studying for. They kept telling me things like, "Man, you've got to play like Ron Carter and do walking 4/4." It's true, when I think about it today, but I didn't really dig that stuff. They said it would help me, so I got an upright that I played for six or eight weeks. Afterwards, I said, "What am I — crazy? How did these people talk me into this? I don't hear it, I don't like it; I don't want to play it." So I sold it, and I've never regretted it. I didn't learn anything off the upright to benefit my electric playing.

What was the most stimulating subject matter?

Improvisation, chord voicings. I never knew about different chord spellings and substitutions. When I finally noticed how melodies and harmonies link up in a certain fashion, I began to think, "If guys play all that stuff on other instruments, why can't I?"

Did you transpose, say, horn music for the bass?

Constantly. I found it especially helpful to adapt trombone literature, because rarely are there ledger lines that go out of the electric bass' range. And the stuff is just so melodic; it was written for an instrument that can play in a way that the electric bass was never designed to. By using other types of instrumental literature, you can't do anything but help your bass playing.

Can you recommend any books that you found particularly helpful?

Probably the greatest book that I've seen for the bass is *Chord Studies For Trombone* by Joe Viola and Phil Wilson [Berklee Press Pub.]. It's chock-full of stuff for the electric bassist. I think it's so informative because a lot of teachers advise bass guitarists to study upright bass books, which offer very little for electric, really, except for beginning reading. Too often they go into different clefs, such as tenor clef, which you may never have to read. Also, they deal too much with bowing techniques.

Being immersed in music every day, did you tend to be less enthusiastic about it?

No. When I saw my improvement, I got more enthusiastic. If you're dedicated to something, you've got to put in your all. In order to pay tuition and rent, I played seven nights a week for about a year and a half in the house band at Flick's. And although it was a nightclub, for some reason it had the cream of the Boston jazz players there all the time. A lot of veterans from Woody Herman's band played there, as did John Scofield, the guitar player.

Did you just quit Berklee after two years?

Yeah. Around 1975 I felt like I had to go out and play. I'd hear records back then and say, "Man, these guys are great, but they don't have any really smoking bass players!" I wanted to get out there, so I quit school, returned to Long Island, and immediately landed a job with [drummer] Carmine Appice, Ray Gomez on guitar, and Steve Hill on keyboards. We stayed together for several months. That was at the height of the jazz-rock thing, and I felt right at home. It really didn't bother me when the band fell apart, because I wanted to do something else.

What did you do then?

I got heavily involved in soul music. I began to check out those rhythm bass players on songs by James Brown, Wilson Pickett, Jackie Wilson, Aretha Franklin — all of them. I began to play a lot of R&B. Around then I played with [drummer] Tony Williams for a very short time. It was a good trio: Allan Holdsworth on guitar, Tony, and myself — but after a while I realized I didn't want to work in a trio. I wanted a four-piece. Also, Tony wanted to be phenomenally loud, like a real rock trio. It was a great idea, and I should have stuck with it, but I didn't. I quit.

When was that?

That was still in '75. I was pretty busy. Then I did a record in Geneva with [keyboardist] Patrick Moraz, called *i*. It was excellent when we did it, but probably one of the poorest mixes in the history of recording. We did the first side as a trio — [drummer] Alphonse Mouzon, Patrick, and me — and it had some of the smokingest trio work you ever heard. The rough mixes sounded great, but when the final mix came out I was nearly in tears. It was 650,000 synthesized keyboards and an itty-bitty Alphonse Mouzon and a teeny-weeny Jeff Berlin.

Did you head back to the States right away?

Yes. I joined a quintet with [guitarist] Pat Martino

and [pianist] Gil Goldstein, which was a great gig. We toured quite a bit. I'd only been out of school for about eight months and really wanted to play my ass off. I still meet people who remember me from that gig.

Didn't you also work with Al Di Meola?

Yes, for a short time in '76. We did one really big gig in France. It was a great band, and I was the only unknown in it. There was Al and [drummer] Lenny White, the [horn players] Brecker Brothers, [conga player] Ray Barretto, and [keyboardist] Brian Auger. Tony Williams even sat in with us. That same year I played on and off with [pianist] Gil Evans, and we toured Japan, Hong Kong, Bangkok, and Manila.

Did you try to make that a permanent working relationship?

No. I didn't know whether I could be satisfied with one band for a long time. I felt that if I played in many different musical situations, it would help my playing all around. And it did.

Did your aggressive style land you in hot water with band leaders?

Oh, sure — all the time. But I wasn't oblivious to the fact that I was part of a group. I just wanted to do it my way, regardless of who the leader was. The leader has the right to say, "Please perform it this way." And if it isn't so completely obnoxious to my being, I'll do it — and I'll see if I can do it my way, too.

After you left Gil Evans, you played with Ray Barretto.

Yeah, he paid me a great compliment: He said that I was the only white bass player that he knew who could play legitimate Latin music. And he taught me. We did a record called *Eye Of The Beholder*, and although I wasn't on every cut, I was able to do it my way.

Did you feel restrained otherwise?

Well, we did vamp-like things, and New York vamp bass playing is pretty stagnant, unmoving. Because the Crusaders were producing the record, they didn't want me to play the kind of bass I wanted to; they wanted the kind of New York *dunk-dunk dunk-ti-dunk*. So I said, "Sure." And when I went back into the studio, I did what I wanted anyway. What were they going to do — turn off the tape machine because the bassist got a little bit snazzy? As it turned out, I set the groove for many of the songs, and although I was mixed a little low for my taste, it was a good album for me. Right after that I started working with [flutist] Herbie Mann, and I went to the '77 Montreux festival in Switzerland as a member of Atlantic Records' house band.

That must have afforded you the opportunity to

work with a broad group of music fans.

Well, I must have played with a zillion bands — Herbie, [saxophonist] Sonny Fortune, John McLaughlin, and Larry Coryell. We'd play until two or three in the morning, and right down the corridor from the main stage was a bar where we'd hang out and jam all night long. I can't remember all the people I played with, but it was terrific. Also that year I sat in with [saxophonist] Dave Liebman and [composer/keyboardist Eumir] Deodato. With Liebman I played on *Lighten Up, Please*, although I'm sure it's nowhere near my better stuff. I was only allowed a certain amount of freedom.

Have you recorded any jingles?

For a while I did loads of them. I haven't done any in a while, but I did "America Is Drinking 7-Up" and "You're Gonna Like Us — TWA." I also did the Chevy Citation commercials and some for Lee Jeans and K-Mart. A lot of real studio heavies work on commercials, but I have no desire to do any now, although they are very lucrative.

The money didn't outweigh the disadvantages?

No, I just couldn't take it after a while. I thought I was starting to play some really good stuff, but then I couldn't cop a gig because I was doing jingles. Regardless of the other gigs I had done, I still couldn't manage to land anything that I wanted.

How did you connect with Bill Bruford?

I'd known him since '75. He was doing his first record, *Feels Good To Me*, in 1977, and asked me to play on it. All the parts were written, and I had to learn them really fast. We went in and recorded it in about four days.

Wasn't Allan Holdsworth on that album?

Yes. Dave Stewart played keyboards, and Annette Peacock sang. Kenny Wheeler added fluegelhorn at my suggestion. For the most part, Bill, Allan, Dave, and I recorded our tracks, and the others were overdubbed.

Did Bruford have any stylistic quirks that you had to get used to?

Loads of them, at first. His strange kind of drumming is in a way his trademark. But I'm more accustomed to a real time-oriented drummer — somebody with a strong pulse in their playing, like Tony Williams or Alphonse Mouzon. Bill, on the other hand, has a very English approach, which to me is really angular — remember how Yes didn't swing? On the other hand, certain rock groups do swing —

especially those in the '60s. Even the Beatles swung.

What did you say to Bill?

"Don't change your style, don't change your sound. Just get way into it." We went over that for a long time. Bill told me, "Look. You're playing in front of so many thousands of people. Why don't you play to them — it's a show, you know." So we were good for each other.

Did you ultimately develop an inherent feel for each other's musical nuances?

Definitely. We did something that I hadn't ever done before: We would watch each other at certain times like hawks, just zero in on each other. He would drop these bombs — suddenly lay accents down — and no matter where he put an accent, I was there with him. It was uncanny. That's part of what I developed by working with so many people. I really checked out their styles. With Bill it got to the point where he could just lay down a heavily accented thing, and I'd play every note with him, as if it were an arranged piece.

"Hear your own point of view, and try to realize it. That takes time and determination."

How much of Bruford's music was written out for you?

Parts here and there. You can feel where most parts were written out. I occasionally wrote them for myself, too. On all three albums, Bill, Dave, and Allan — and later, John Clark — rehearsed together. Then they'd put the chart in front of me. I would learn the piece and comment on the parts and make suggestions. After several days the music would really change, because it had my approach in it — an American approach. You can hear a metamorphosis in the three albums: Each subsequent one has more of a lilt or swing to it.

Your live material, particularly songs like "Beelzebub" on The Bruford Tapes, *seems to have even more life.*

Well, that's a funny album. We recorded the second day of our 1979 American tour, and to me it sounds like it because I always play funny on the first four or five gigs. After that, I kind of settle in. We're a lively group, no doubt about that. The live stuff did have a little bit of zip-a-dee-doo-dah because of my influence. I even used to get the other guys mad, but what are you going to do? After a while we did get a bit of swing going. Why shouldn't they dance to it? — if you know what I mean.

Much of your best work on One Of A Kind *seems to be mixed too low.*

Yeah. They used to overdub after I left, and I ended up buried. It really infuriated me — I thought some of my work on there was pretty slick. I mean, listen to "Hell's Bells." Can you hear any bass on that? It's stuff I should be proud of, but you can only catch glimpses of it.

It's more like a synthesizer extravaganza with a guitar solo.

And it shouldn't be! It shouldn't be a bass show-case, either. It should be the band's extravaganza. But there's this roar of a *Cm* chord or something coming from the synthesizers, and the bass is practically obliterated. I can't really blame those cats, but it's still the way I feel about it.

Were you there for the mixing?

Not on the first two albums. But on the *Gradually Going Tornado* mix I was there. It turned out better — at least I'm audible — but the mixes always seemed to end up strange. Everyone says that bass is a hard instrument to mix, but I don't really believe so. If I were behind the board, I don't think it would be so difficult.

What would you do — put everybody else down at one level and crank up the bass?

I wouldn't do that to anybody. I know how to balance. I figure if someone plays strong, and they're doing something that's going to sound good on record, then it should be heard. I mean, if a guy's burning on a solo, stand back. Don't jump on him. That's why I get so many calls as a sideman — because I can do stuff on the bass that almost nobody else can do. I can also play the strong, simple things, too — right to the point. I recently did a week or two with [keyboardist] Bob James and [guitarist] Earl Klugh, because their regular bass player had another call. He normally plays New York-style bass: simple and strong. That seems to be all that most of those guys do. I came into the gig with Harvey Mason on drums — he's an amazing drummer — and I just started to pump on the bass. As soon as I got it going, everyone else started to pump, too.

With Bruford, did you ever spontaneously work things out in the studio?

Sure. Sometimes we would just put the machine on and play, and see what transpired, using the studio it-self as a composing tool, like on "Q.E.D." [*Gradually Going Tornado*]. In fact, the piano part is actually Dave's overdub of my original piano line. In the beginning, I played some fuzz bass and then set the bass down. If you listen to the record at the point where they start tinkering on electric piano, drums, and guitar, you won't hear any bass. That's because I walked across the studio to the acoustic piano to tap out the line. Afterwards I went back and picked up my bass, and then we burned into the rest of the tune.

Have you received any calls to play in other bands during your hiatus from Bruford?

Earlier this year I got a call from Frank Zappa while I was in London working with [guitarist] Robert Fripp and Bill Bruford. The audition was great, even though his music has possibly the most difficult bass parts I've ever seen. His music in general is phenomenally difficult, but played properly it's absolutely fantastic. We planned a European tour, but unfortunately it was canceled.

Do you do any teaching?

Once a month, gigs permitting, I teach at B.I.T. It's a very good bass school.

What kinds of things are vital to a bassist's development?

Probably the most important thing is one's own ideas about what you want to do. For me, that required a lot of playing with a lot of different people. Even now, when I'm not working steadily on something, I try to work with many musicians. So, when I'm not on the road, I'm here in Boston, playing and trying to develop my feelings about my music. That's what everybody should do: Hear your own point of view, and try to realize it. That takes time and determination.

Do you think running through scales and exercises is worthwhile?

Nothing can hurt; they're more tools for you to use. But I don't sit around and say, "Now I'm going to do the *B♭* minor-major 7th scale." It all becomes part of the overall picture. Some people work on scales constantly, and they're terribly disappointed when they can't seem to use them in their playing. It doesn't work like that. It takes a lot of time, a lot of investigating, and a lot of playing with different people — or even with one guy all the time; you can develop something unique that way too.

Can you suggest anything for maintaining sight-reading chops?

Read out of those trombone books, or just brand-new music. And transpose a lot. Transcribing solos from other instruments is fantastic. Recently, I did a 14-page transcription of a song called "The Eternal Triangle" [from *The Champ*], by Sonny Stitt. It features Stitt and Sonny Rollins on alto and tenor saxes, respectively. It took me five or six days to do both solos.

That's a lot of work.

Well, how else does one get better? I'm really

pleased that many people seem to like my playing, but it didn't happen in three days — it didn't happen in three years! I'm not a genius who suddenly became a good bass player. I play a lot with different people to keep my hand in. I do some jamming with [guitarist] Pat Metheny once in a while. He lives here in Boston. I think it's as good for him as it is for me, a different point of view. I also play with Mick Goodrick, probably one of the greatest guitarists I've ever worked with. He's a very heavy influence on Pat, too. I also jam with a lot of tremendous drummers, such as Mike Clark, who was featured on Herbie Hancock's *Thrust* album. When I'm in Los Angeles, I play with guys like Vinnie Colaiuta, who's in Frank Zappa's band. He's the greatest invention for a set of drums there ever was. What he can do with sticks is unbelievable.

If the drummer is weak, how does it affect your performance?

Terribly! If you're driving on the highway and one of your wheels is out of alignment, it's got to screw up the rest of the car's motion. That's how music is for me. I mean, if everybody's listening and playing great — and I'm not just talking about chops, but playing strong and to the point — then it makes a statement. If the drummer's weak, it's terrible. It *has* to hurt. As a matter of fact, when I went to Japan with Gil Evans, the gig was terrible for that reason. The drummer just wasn't that good. His timing was bad, and it made the whole band feel uncomfortable.

So you hate to devote your energy to covering for his weakness.

Right. How could it make me sound good? I'm a dangerous bass player to work with. If the music isn't cohesive, I sound precarious and untogether. On the other hand, I can be a very staid, solid bassist. In a soul group, I make an anchor that you wouldn't believe. I don't mind playing simple, chug-a-lug bass, but if the drummer isn't happening, I can't take it.

What do you think are your strong and weak technical points?

Without trying to sound like an egomaniac, I don't think there's anything I can't do. Reading-wise, I haven't been stumped by anything, except for that Zappa music. And then I took it home, and in a few days I really began to get it down. I'm not trying to be a wise guy. The only weak points I would guess are the things that I don't know yet, or would like to develop.

> *"A bass player should find a great instrument with either a good sound or a good body — probably the good body. Afterwards, augment that."*

Don't you even find that rapid octave changes pose problems?

No. I have no trouble getting around my instrument — it's my home. I know where all the furniture is; I know where the chicken salad is. There's no place I can be on it and not feel like I belong.

Your bass has a very bright sound. Do you ever use a pick?

No. I don't like the feeling of a pick. Don't forget, I came from violin, where even though you use a bow, there are times when you pluck with your right hand. I can think of only three smoking pickstyle bass players: Anthony Jackson, Steve Swallow, and Bobby Vega.

Which right-hand fingers do you use? Do you have a predetermined plucking order?

I use just my thumb, my index, and my middle fingers, and I don't believe that there's a set pattern for any musician in the world. The attacking of strings varies with the music and what's most natural physically. After a while, it's instinctive. If a particular ostinato line requires a specific fingering, then I'll learn a good one in order to make it sound right. I'll almost always fall into a natural execution pattern, though.

Do you always include your thumb in your attack, or is it reserved for snapping?

I use my thumb a lot, because I play many chords. I often mix my bass lines with harmonies or melodies, and then my thumb is indispensable. I also use it for snapping.

How do you position your right hand?

It just floats most of the time. Occasionally, I rest it on the body of the bass. I also tend to pick toward the bridge; it's a nice place to be. In fact, I pluck a lot right over the bridge pickup, and for more legato things I sometimes move closer to the neck.

Do you try to keep your left hand in the traditional form — with the thumb in the center of the neck?

Yeah. I play with my hand in the "C" shape. You know — like if I'm going to scratch your eyes out, with the fingers and thumb curled.

Did your positioning come from your violin technique?

In a way, yes. Because on violin, you use the tips of your fingers, and even though I may not be consciously aware of it — it's been a lot of years — you just can't ignore 10 years of study on an instrument.

Do you experiment with moving riffs from one set of strings to another for a more suitable tone?

Certainly. Sometimes I'll move a line to a place where it's harder to play but sounds better. After all, I want the best sound I can get.

Do you play a fretless bass?

Well, around '78 or '79 I tried one for a few months. But I realized I can do an awful lot with frets. And I didn't really like the instrument, because *everyone* was playing the damn thing.

Most fretless players tend to slide in and out of notes rather than landing squarely on them.

Sliding up and down is okay sometimes, but everybody began playing fretless, and claimed that they invented it. It's like everybody saying that they invented jumping harmonics. Bullshit! Nobody invented it. If one guy is going to get credit for the development of the popular fretless style, it should be Jaco Pastorius.

Did you use a fretless on "Palewell Park" [from Gradually Going Tornado]?

No. I just played legato as cleanly and as purely as I could, without any real fret sound and interference. A lot of people think I play fretless because I play very smooth. Also, the bass' treble was wide open. I don't often use effects, but I used a Boss Chorus to give it a lovely, ambient sound. If you listen carefully, you can hear my bass was sharp. Somehow the Chorus made me ever so slightly sharper than the piano.

What kind of bass do you use?

I play two Fenders. One is a '66 or '67 Precision with a natural finish; the other is a black 1962 Jazz Bass. The Precision's neck was too wide, so I had it cut down to more like Jazz Bass dimensions. Both have rosewood fingerboards, brass nuts, and Leo Quan Badass bridges. The pickups were made for me by [Leo Quan co-founder] Glen Quan. When I was with Pat Martino, my Precision was terrible. Glen came down to a gig and said, "Well, let me fix it up for you." And he was a nice cat: He even lent me a bass to finish up the tour. What he returned to me was a bass that's so fantastic that I still use it. As soon as he put that bridge on, my sound improved at least 50%. That bridge is just one of the greatest inventions ever.

What kind of strings do you use?

Long-scale roundwounds made by Carl Thompson. They're gauged .100, .085, .065, and .045, low to high. I've been using them for several years now. They're without peer. For years I searched for the right strings — I used to mix my own sets with two of these, one of that, and one of the other. I did everything I could to get the sound. One day, a friend

of mine, Steve Friedman, who owns Stuyvesant Music in New York, said, "Try these Carl Thompsons." I did, and there they were! Boy, they've got life in them. And they sound so good when I play legato. I keep them on till they're just too dull to handle — usually a couple of months.

When you're onstage, do you change your bass' tone and volume controls?

I more or less leave the volume full for optimum sound. I move the tone around a little bit, but not too much, because I D.I. [direct input] into the P.A. board — I don't want to fiddle with the P.A. sound that much. I can actually change the sound as much as I need to with my fingers. I can go from a quieter, legato warmth to completely blasting out. It's all due to touch.

To produce such a powerful tone, do you use 12" speakers?

I like 12s, but I've got something with four 15" Gauss bass speakers that's awfully good; it was put together for me by the Stuyvesant Music people. Each speaker is housed in four separate maple cabinets that were specially designed for the 15" Gausses. I also have a Crown DC-300A power amp and an Alembic tube preamp. Altogether, it gives me an awesome sound.

When you're called for a session, do you bring your huge amp setup?

It really depends. I use my big equipment if that particular kind of sound is required. But most of the stuff is direct into the board anyway, so amps aren't generally that important unless you're going specifically for that miked sound. Sometimes I like to record onto two channels: one with the bass plugged straight into the board, and one with the miked amp.

What did you use before your current amps?

Ampeg SVTs. Until recently, I never seemed to have enough bread to score some really good stuff. I never really bothered about equipment, because it seemed that no matter what I played through, I seemed to have that midrangey, slightly grungy sound.

Do you think, then, that your approach affects your overall sound much more than your equipment does?

Absolutely! I can do it with almost any amp. If it's a great amp, I'm going to sound that much better. If it's a shitty amp, I'll just sound like normal, everyday me. I played Pat Metheny's guitar a few weeks ago, and nothing I did on that instrument would sound like me. Everything sounded like Pat. Get it? So it seemed that equipment is paramount for his particular sound and approach. If my equipment were an integral part of my sound, I'd find the same to be true with me.

What do you think of the high-tech, top-of-the-line basses?

I don't know. Companies make an awful lot of products these days. They're making replacement pickups, bridges, and switches — all kinds of stuff. It seems to me that if you were to find a good-bodied instrument, you probably wouldn't need to spend all that bread for a custom-made one. Some companies dictate to the bass players by saying, "Look, you should sound this way, and you should use this bass this way, and your neck should be like this." I think a bass player should find a great instrument with either a good sound or a good body — probably the good body. Afterwards, augment that.

Don't you think the sound of many of today's basses is too clean?

What's wrong with clean?

What if you want a little grit in your sound?

I can get grit. You can get grit out of the cleanest bass there ever was. Pickups won't give you grunge. If you want grit, you'll have to find some way of hooking up with a certain kind of power head and speakers. I love a clean sound; I really lean that way, although I also create a kind of smooth but gritty sound. People like what I play because it seems to make sense, and even if I have a distorted tone, they seem to hear the notes. Certainly that's what I was influenced by when I listened to players like Jack Bruce. You know, that farty bass sound — fantastic! But you could always hear the notes.

Who was the first bassist to profoundly influence you?

Stanley Clarke. I was in love with him at Berklee, because nobody else had such a unique sound. But it really hurt my progress. You see, I tried hard to sound like him, and it took me directly away from what I really enjoyed about my own playing. So I vowed that I'd never listen *that* closely to anybody again. My greatest influence on the bass is Jack Bruce. He's still the greatest — the most original rock bass player. Steve Swallow has also had a great effect on me. His playing is so rock-oriented, yet very jazz-oriented. He's also a tremendous composer.

What other contemporary musicians have shaped your thinking?

I'd say Gary Burton and the late [pianist] Bill Evans. Evans is my major influence in the art of lyrical music. As far as I know, I'm the only electric bass

"You have to keep your ego under control — you can't say, 'I'm great and everyone else sucks.'"

player to ever work with Bill. He invited me to sit in at the Village Vanguard one night, and I was so scared that I literally shook the bass off my shoulders. I've played with a lot of great musicians, but playing with him was a great event in my life. I also like Charlie Haden's upright bass playing. He doesn't have a lot of chops, but he can sure lay some astonishing grooves down. Eddie Gomez is also a great upright player. Different horn players — especially [saxophonist] Cannonball Adderley — are really important to me. I also like Tower Of Power; man, Rocco Prestia is such a hip bass player. And their horn section — they're the best out there.

How did you approach the percussive bass line at the beginning of "5G" [One A Kind]?

It's really neat, but it's nothing more than what a drummer would do: Use the left hand and right hand to tap out two separate rhythms. I employed several attack devices — the thumb, the heel of my right hand, my fingers snapping strings, my fingers tapping on strings individually, and my left hand tapping on the strings. With combinations of those techniques, you can come up with thousands of things.

How did you get into snapping the strings?

It's always been a gag with me. I remember the exact day when I started: August 4, 1974. That's when I saw Larry Graham on TV. And in about six months I developed just about everything I know about that style. And it was always a joke — you know, ha, ha, look at this. Isn't it cute? It was never meant to be anything real slick.

Do you follow any type of scheme for developing a solo?

Sure. I love improvising, but I always want to make sure that I spell out the chords clearly. That is, if the piano player suddenly went off and got a beer or got married in the middle of my solo — leaving me without chordal accompaniment — you would still be able to tell what key I was in. I think that's what makes a soloist successful: Being able to keep the flavor of the tonality. Naturally, I think in terms of melodies and lines, but I follow an inner voice. Anybody who solos might find it difficult to explain. But don't forget that chords, scales, and all those things are nothing by themselves. They're just tools: A hammer and nails and two-by-fours to build an architectural masterpiece. That's music.

Do you have a daily practice routine?

I'm at the bass every day at least a little bit. I'll re-iterate some of my old playing and examine it, and try to figure out what I was thinking of back then. And I've been working on my solo bass pieces.

Do you find any correlations between your boxing training and your bass practice?

I'm not a really smoking boxer yet, but I really work at it. My trainer will say, "Okay, let me see the jab and hook. No, go back and do it again." It's *detail for detail*, and after a while of concentrated practice, I could be a nasty good fighter. Now, can you imagine having a bass coach say, "Let me hear the G scale, the D scale, the A scale. No, I don't like that A scale. Let me hear you rehearse it again. Now listen to this. Now look at that. Listen to this guy; practice this tune." And do it detail for detail. How are you not going to get the working fundamentals like that?

Don't you worry about ruining your hands?

Not really. I've had my hands broken a couple of times, and I've damaged several fingers, too — mostly, when I was a kid — but they all healed cleanly. I'm not a masochist. I just want to get good. And that's been the name of the game my whole life in a way. My style is due to my fierce dedication. I never took it half-assedly. I'm a very intense student.

Is there any facet of being a musician that you find hard to accept?

I'm incensed that most musicians have the gall to think we're so fantastic, when all we do is pluck some strings or play a few notes on a keyboard. Where do we get off thinking that we're God's gift to humanity? We didn't invent penicillin or win the Nobel Peace Prize, and we don't come close to Bach, Beethoven, or Schumann. Record companies are responsible for some of this, too. They feed the musicians' egos and gear themselves to get the product out there, make the bucks. And anyone who cares to step off of the assembly line ends up playing clubs in New York forever. Music is entertainment, yet so many musicians think they deserve a place in immortality. They feed off of their own propaganda. You must grow up. You have to keep your ego under control — you can't say, "I'm great and everyone else sucks." I did that once, and I was wrong. I may be here today, but I know that the new guys or less experienced guys will be here tomorrow. I shouldn't dump on them.

Does anything else worry you?

Oh, yeah. I recently was turned down for a gig because I'm *white!* Another time I wasn't hired because I wasn't a Scientologist, and yet another time because I didn't follow Sri Chinmoy. It makes me sick that someone would be excluded from a band on account of their religion or color.

Do you think that success for a bassist hinges on how aggressive he is?

You've got to be, but you've got to do it with your head on your shoulders. What I mean is this: When you play, remember that you've got other musicians around you. It's not like you're performing a solo recital in Carnegie Hall. It's a band; it's an orchestra. You've got to play within that context. Nobody can deny you if you play stunningly beautiful bass, but don't blow everybody else out of the room. I always pull back on the reins a little bit. You've always got to do it your own way, but with cool. Play tough, play boss. But play it with your head on your shoulders. Play *music*, man; play music.

– TIM BOGERT –

BY STEVE ROSEN – SEPTEMBER 1979

EBET ROBERTS

IN 1967 A NEW YORK rock quartet called Vanilla Fudge interrupted America's fixation with British musicians to bring to the U.S. an insistent new version of "You Keep Me Hangin' On," a song popularized a few years earlier by the Supremes. With a boom, Vanilla Fudge was thrust into the limelight of stardom, and for bassist Tim Bogert it was a place where he would remain for the next decade as he took residence in some of the most potent bands in rock. In 1970, after five albums, Vanilla Fudge dissolved: Bogert and drummer Carmine Appice stayed together and moved on to new groups, leaving guitarist Vince Martell and keyboardist Mark Stein behind. Bogert and Appice first teamed up with guitarist Jim McCarty, who had been with Mitch Ryder And The Detroit Wheels and Buddy Miles. Completing their new quartet was vocalist Rusty Day; collectively they were known as Cactus.

After only three albums, the bass-and-drum duo left in 1972 to join forces with Jeff Beck, creating one of the most powerful rock trios of the early '70s. Touted as a supergroup of the highest magnitude, Beck, Bogert & Appice produced only one studio album, toured, and disbanded in less than two years. (A live Beck, Bogert & Appice album was released in Japan only.) In the past few years Tim Bogert has lent his explosive bass lines to the music of groups called Pieces, Boxer, And Pipedream. (Pipedream broke up in early 1979.)

Born on August 27, 1944, in Manhattan, Bogert grew up in Richfield, New Jersey, where he lived from the age of 2 until he was 22. He currently resides in Southern California. Tim began his musical development as a small child: "There was a piano in the house, and I used to plunk on it," he says. "I never really got serious with it, but I can play chords behind somebody if they're playing simple things." By the time he was about to enter high school, Tim was already developing his skills as a saxophonist, and by the time he was 20 he was on the road playing bass.

Saxophone was your main musical interest before you played bass. Was it your first instrument?

No, I actually started out playing clarinet in the seventh grade. I switched to saxophone in the ninth grade and then began playing in bands. When I was a senior in high school the band I was in had two guitar players, two saxophonists, and a drummer — the other sax player doubled on guitar. He was also the lead guitarist. Back then we were playing a lot of Ventures things. We did one song they recorded, "Pipeline," which called for three guitars and bass, so I started playing bass to let the other guys do the guitar parts. I just sort of shifted to it over the next two or three years. I played a Danelectro bass for a short while, and then really got into it with a Fender Jazz Bass with a Precision neck.

So you really didn't start playing bass until you were about 18 years old?

Yes, but I had been playing an instrument, so my head was musical, and the dexterity was already developed in my fingers. I remember when I wanted to get serious about bass and get professional jobs: It took me about six months of intensive practice in order to get the lines down properly and be good enough to get honest work.

Did you start off picking with your fingers?

I started off playing with my thumb, and it took me quite a while to learn to play with my other fingers. Currently I use my index, middle, and ring fingers. And now I'm learning again to finger pop with my thumb. So it's come full circle for me.

Didn't you start listening to bass players when you began pursuing the bass?

Well, I started picking up lines from [saxophonist] King Curtis' records. Having been a sax man, I knew he was extremely well thought of by saxophonists, and I was already familiar with his records. So I started listening to his records again — this time from a bassist's point of view, as opposed to a lead saxophonist's point of view — and a lot of my runs I do now are still based on a combination of bass and sax lines. My head still thinks lead from being a horn man, which is the reason I play a lot of lead lines. I picked up the rhythm things from drummers — the things that one needs to be a bass player — but my head still thinks lead lines.

Were there any bassists in particular who influenced you?

I suppose James Jamerson was my most critical influence, because those were my formative years. He was the hottest cat back then. I had listened to everyone and everything, but I had gotten to the point where I needed to be able to physically pick up something that I couldn't otherwise do for myself. It was from him that I picked up all those triplets and poplets and funky sorts of things. I still use a lot of them.

When did you first play professionally?

In 1965 I went out on the road full-time. I'd just gotten a Fender Jazz Bass then. Fenders were what everyone used then. You had to be like everyone else, so I had a Fender. I ran that into an Ampeg B-15, which I had used for my sax. I still have it. I later put an Altec 421A 15" speaker in it, and now I power it with a Fender Dual Showman head. That makes it sound about four times louder. I still use it to practice through.

Were you in any really substantial bands before Vanilla Fudge?

No. I did a lot of backup things. I used to go out on the road behind the Irwins and the Crests and

Camel. I never made any records with them, but I was in the backup band that went out to do tours and sock hops and those things.

Did you play their music from charts?

No. They did a record and we'd learn what was on it, and that was it. We would do it verbatim.

What kind of music were you playing?

Society rock, I guess you'd call it, where one does lounges but plays soft rock — no Screamin' Jay Hawkins. I played those for what seemed like years, and it was from a lounge band that I met [keyboardist/vocalist] Mark Stein. In late 1966 we formed the Vanilla Fudge out of a lounge band called Rick Martin And The Showmen. We played *very* society stuff like "Misty," and all of those things.

Was the concept behind Vanilla Fudge yours and Mark's?

Mark and I started the band, but the concept of what it eventually became was the result of all four of us putting in our ideas. It was also part of the times. That movement was happening in the New York area — the Young Rascals and us. There were a bunch of bands that got into this big concert-orchestrated production thing, and it was just that we were lucky enough to get a big record. We made the record that was the most popular. There were four of us in the group: Mark, Vinny Martell, myself, and a drummer by the name of Joey Brennan. We were playing a place called the Choo Choo in Garfield, New Jersey, which is where the Rascals tightened up their act. We were there for 10 or 12 weeks. Our drummer wanted to be a blues player, and we were starting to get into progressive things. We came back to the club one night when our group wasn't working and saw Carmine Appice's band. We thought this guy had a really good foot, so I approached him and asked him if he wanted to join our band. He said okay, and about four or five months later we had a record contract. Things went very well.

Did you know immediately that you were going to work well with him?

It took a while. He kept telling me to follow his foot, and I kept playing lead lines. Eventually, he played more lead lines and I followed his foot a bit more. We kind of met in the middle somewhere, and it turned out to be a very good style. We had a good partnership.

Do you think his playing shaped your playing?

Oh, sure. Whoever you play with shapes your style because you will either not play their lines because you don't like them, or you will play their lines because you think they're groovy.

When the British bands started coming over to the U.S., did you start listening to bassists like Jack Bruce?

Oh, yeah. I listened to everybody. Jack Bruce was getting outside in a different direction than I was getting outside, and I thought some of his lines and time spacings were really fine. He had a certain way of syncopating. It was all in the syncopation that the old James Brown things had, where you can go up and down on the feels; for part of the phrase you'd be on the upbeat, and on another part of the phrase you'd be on the downbeat — or you'd switch back and forth. He was phrasing things so differently, and I thought it was clever and liked it.

What kind of bass did you use with Vanilla Fudge?

I used an old Precision with a blonde Telecaster neck. I don't know what year it was made, but its serial number is 13000. I never took a spare bass with me on the road, so it was just the Precision. My Jazz Bass with the Precision neck was stolen early in the band's existence. I left it onstage when we went to do a radio interview, and when we returned it was gone. I almost cried — it was the bass I had done most of my learning on.

Did you use any effects?

I used a Mosrite fuzztone, and I played through five Fender Dual Showman amps. I tried phasers and synthesizer boxes — all sorts of things. I'll plug in anything at the studio and try it at least once. You never know; the sound you hear is so different that you often find yourself changing the way you play. It's like if you're playing through a big amp; you tend to play differently than if you're playing with a small amp. And the different sounds tended to kick off different ideas.

What kind of equipment did you use with Cactus?

I still had the Precision Bass. I also used three Acoustic 360s — the old stand-up ones with the amp in the bottom and the preamp on top. About halfway through Cactus, our guitar player, Jimmy McCarty, had his Marshalls worked on by Unicord, an outfit in Long Island that was the sole East Coast distributor for Marshall. There was a guy there named Tony Frank, who was one of those electrical wizards. He wanted to design the perfect concert amp setup.

"Whoever you play with shapes your style because you will either not play their lines because you don't like them, or you will play their lines because you think they're groovy."

What he came up with after four or five designs was the cabinets that I still use. They're great big black boxes with four 15" Altecs in them. They're all glued and doweled to cut down on vibration. I drove them with Sunn Coliseum amps.

Can you describe the construction of those cabinets?

Each box is divided into four sections — one for each speaker. In effect, each speaker has its own box, and nothing vibrates. The sound can be so loud that you can't stand it, but the box is hardly moving. All of the sound pressure is radiated straight forward, and there are almost no harmonics created by a vibrating box. Vibration is the reason that most bass cabinets don't project past the stage. Usually, the resonance that you hear from a bass just tends to be onstage — you can rattle someone's false teeth right out — but the audience doesn't hear much. With my setup, you don't get much rattle onstage, but after about the tenth row of people, their earrings are turning around on their heads. The sound just seems to go and disperse 10 or 20 feet away, and out there it's actually louder than it is right in front of the speakers.

How many of these cabinets did you use?

I used to have eight, but P.A.s are so sophisticated now that you don't have to stack 240-decibel equipment onstage anymore. The P.A. will take care of whatever I need, so I just use two of them now.

Do you think the sound made you play any differently?

Definitely. My tone became more distinct, and I began to be able to play faster because the notes would physically come out of the speaker quicker. The speakers were very tight, so they moved quickly and I was able to make notes pop where I couldn't get them to pop before.

Did you start using them in the studio also?

It's difficult because they are so loud, so I use the B-15, because then there's a fairly tight cabinet and it's almost the same size inside as each one of the compartments on my big cabinets. With the 421A speaker and my Sunn amp pushing a good 200 watts through the speakers, the sound's almost identical. It really sounds like what the big amp does live. Same head, same type of speaker.

Did you ever record with the big cabinets?

Yes, with Beck, Bogert & Appice, I had to be put in a separate room, which was frustrating as hell. The room was really small, so with that great big cabinet I had to wear the cans [headphones] just to block the bass out — it was that loud. I needed to play with the Sunn amplifier on at least 5 or 8 to get the clipping frequencies that I needed. Below that, it doesn't collect, and above that it clips too much. So there's a certain range I need to work in.

How do you feel about the Beck, Bogert & Appice band?

It was fulfilling to be able to play with musicians of that caliber. I wanted to play with Jeff because I always liked his records — he's a hell of a guitarist — and I already knew Carmine was a hell of a drummer. Playing with those kinds of people around you can only make you play better. But the band never panned out. It was sad. It didn't hold up for a multitude of reasons: our personalities, money, management. It seemed like it was dead from the beginning, and everything we did seemed to be wrong somehow. We couldn't win for losing.

Because you play so much like a lead player, do you think perhaps that you got in Jeff's way?

There were two things that happened there. Jeff missed Max Middleton [keyboardist with the Jeff Beck Group] very much in BBA, I think, because there were times when it seemed like Jeff didn't want to play. And in a trio, you don't have the prerogative of not playing much, because there's only one other instrument playing besides the drums. That's what I like about trios: One has to play a lot, and I like to play a lot. So I'm satisfied with trios. I think I got in Jeff's way *and* he missed Max, or he missed that opportunity of just being able to lay back for eight bars and fiddle around. He's very good at those eight-bar fiddles; there are moments of genius that come out of those little bits. We couldn't find a common ground, damn it. I tried and finally got discouraged, and I'm sure he tried and finally got discouraged. We just couldn't find it. It was a hell of a shame because I really had high hopes for that band.

Did you have any exceptional performances?

There were gigs that were absolutely awesome. I can remember gigs when I had the power. When the band was on and I had the power, it was just wonderful. Times like that were few and far between, unfortunately. Our level of consistency wasn't very high. We soared to some pretty unknown heights on some occasions, but our general performance was dodgy.

On the Beck, Bogert & Appice *album's second*

cut, "Lady," you riffed almost nonstop. Did you get that recorded in one take?

I can't remember how many takes that took, but I can remember in the middle — the solo section where I really let loose on bass — that was actually created from an attitude I felt. I was so frustrated being in that little six-foot room with my amplifier, not being able to see the other guys very well. I just let all that anger and frustration hang out during the solo, and it came out very well, actually.

Was there a second album in the making?

There were a lot of seconds in the making. We played a song from that tentative album, "Jizz Whizz," in Pipedream. It's a fun song. It leaves the way open to do a whole bunch of time-change things — I've written a lot of things in odd meters like 7 and 9, but I'm a bit wary to do them. Steely Dan's done a couple of time things, but you need to be established before you can start bending the intellect, because you don't have license to unless you're on the charts.

Do you view your tenure with Beck, Bogert & Appice as a positive experience?

It was the best teaming experience for me, or at least one of them. Instrumentally, it was the best teaming experience I've ever had, because Jeff is amazing. Being able to work with him for the year and a half that I did, I learned a lot of lines from him; it was like a one-hour course in technique each night. I was entertaining the audience, but I was in school, too. That's how you keep getting more lines together and hopefully improve.

What did you do after the group disbanded?

I moved to California and I met Steve Perry, Journey's singer; he and I put a band together called Pieces. We played around, but no record company would handle us. The timing just wasn't right. I stuck with that band for two years and couldn't sell it. I really believed in that band.

What did you do next?

I went over to Europe, and lived there for a year, and worked in a band called Boxer. We made one album, called *Absolutely,* and called it quits. We were scheduled to do an American tour, but our singer, Mike Patto, got cancer and died. When I came back to the States, we formed Pipedream.

What kind of equipment did you use with Pipedream?

I still use those big, black cabinets and the Sunn Coliseum heads. I also use the Mosrite fuzztone, and sometimes an effect that comes from Germany, but the name of it I don't know. It's just a red box that I got from [keyboardist] Jon Lord. He used to use it on his organ. It makes vibrato and tremolo, it can phase, it can follow an envelope with its filter. It can make a bass sound very Stevie Wonder left-hand, which is a very pleasing sound. I use that and fuzztones, and I use a Schaffer-Vega wireless transmitter as well. It's great — no wires to trip over.

What kind of bass are you currently using?

I use a black Kramer 4000 bass with an added DiMarzio P-Bass pickup near the bridge. There's a pickup selector switch and a phase switch for the DiMarzio, too. I use Picato round-wound strings, which I change every four or five months. I also use my old Precision with the Telecaster neck. It's got a black pickup on it; from where it comes, I don't know. It's the only P-Bass pickup I've ever seen like it. Usually, when you take the plastic cover off, there's a double-fiberboard sort of thing that has the magnets through it and the wire windings around it. Well, mine's black and the polepieces are longer, and it has very dark copper wrapped around it — very thin, dark copper. The pickup has no identifying marks of any kind, but I got it out of an old junked P-Bass.

How do you set the controls on your basses?

It varies. On some songs the bass is up all the way, and on some songs it's all treble. I always play with my volume control wide open. It's a matter of finger technique to control the volume. I never really change the volume settings on my bass; I either pluck it softly or hit it harder. The controls on my Sunn Coliseum amp are labeled Volume, Low Bass, High Bass, Middle, and Treble. I set the Volume on 8, Low Bass on 0, High Bass on 2, Middle on 5, and Treble on 6. Because of my cabinets, I don't need much bass on the amp. The design of the speaker cabinets will make the bass appear. Bass is more a matter of appearance than it is physically giving bass. A room will make bass if you give it a signal, so you use the room as the acoustic baffle instead of your cabinet.

What's the advantage to this?

You can project much further. So if I were to put more bass on the amp itself, it would cut the volume way back because the speakers would just flap and distort: It would be like trying to make a wave that can't be sustained by that much volume on only a 15" speaker.

> *"I've always approached bass as a lead instrument. It's not a complementary instrument, so you have to be as loud as everybody else."*

Do you consider yourself a loud bass player?

I try to be. If they can't hear you, they don't know you're there. You've always got to let them know you're there. I've always approached bass as a lead instrument; it's not a complementary instrument, so you have to be as loud as everybody else. You literally have to let them know that you're there, because if you don't grab their attention, then somebody else will. That's really the theory of high-energy rock, isn't it? Keep them moving and keep their eyes moving constantly, because there's only three or four of you up there. So, if you can keep it popping, you've got a show happening.

Are there certain patterns or scales that you work from?

Oh, sure. One's style is defined by one's limitations, isn't it? There's a certain repertoire that any musician has — lines that are safe. It's like a tumbling routine: There are certain tumbles that you know you can do. There are certain lines I know I can get away with. There are also certain lines that I know I can only play on a good night, when the dexterity's such that I can physically make those lines. One always tries to lay at the edge.

You play a lot of chords, too.

Being a trio player, I have to. I try to play a lot of three-string things, because it fills up the holes. I also do some string popping. There's a certain attitude that you have to take on when popping, because it requires a different frame of thinking than playing what I do normally. But I'm beginning to incorporate that pop thing into what I do, and it's starting to work out nicely.

Do you ever use a pick?

No. There was a time back in the early '70s where I recorded a couple of tunes with a pick, only because there were certain guitar lines that would sound closer to the guitar if I used a pick rather than if I used my fingers. I can now get a sound similar to picking by popping the strings. I can get that sort of *clack* out of the frets that I was trying to get from the pick, so now I would prefer to pop it.

Do you compose on the bass?

Yes, but I also have harmonies in my head to accompany my bass lines. I always say to the people I work with, "Play me an *E9* or a minor 7th here," or, "No, that one's not right; can you do this one for me?" All the colors are in my head, and all I have to do is express to the fellows what I would like, and they're always happy with it.

Do you have any aspirations of becoming known as a highly technical bassist?

No. I'm not that serious about it — you have to be serious to study for 11 years; you really do. I have too much fun working on my Harley or going out and having a good time. I'm not that serious about sitting down for five or six hours a day, which one needs to do in order to be a Stanley Clarke — I don't physically know the scales, nor do I give a damn, because I can do my tongue-in-cheek stuff and the audience will think that's even groovier than the other because my hand's moving and I'm jumping up and down.

Do you listen to any so-called progressive music?

I don't listen to a whole lot of it because much of it is too intense for me. I like intense music very much, but I mainly like rock and roll. I like the earthy sort of gut, up-and-down movement, and a lot of progressive things go past that, so it passes me. That's not a put-down in any way, shape, or form. It's just that I'm not up to it.

Some of your runs played with Beck, Bogert & Appice sounded complex.

They were and they weren't. It is because those particular lines and riffs are mine and are comfortable to me, whereas they might not be comfortable to someone else who would sit down and try to learn them. I'm sure that much of Stanley's stuff is very comfortable for him, but it's very difficult for other people. But there are lines I know that fall out easily, that are determined by my coordination.

Besides playing a lot of runs, you move around onstage.

Yeah, I've always been a ham, and I learned very young what got people off. I like to get people off. I enjoy the hell out of getting an audience up and out of their seats and jumping up and down and getting sweaty. It's as much fun as anything can be. There are certain things that work. Over the years, you use certain things that work, and you discard the ones that don't.

Does it take you a while to come up with a bass line that you're satisfied with?

The way I've always approached it, except, say, with BBA, is to have the parts worked out long before we ever walk into the studio, because it's far too expensive to go in there and *then* start learning things, no matter how fast you study it all. Getting the music tight with the band takes time, but it should be done before you walk in to record. You

may polish something in the studio, but when you hear it back you may say, "Oh, that's not really effective there, is it?" So you may change that part, but very rarely do I ever change a whole bass line for a song.

Will you ever do more than one bass line on a song?

Occasionally I'll do two. I'll play a counterpoint to something I've done, but I don't usually plan that. There's one tune called "Only Cause" on *Pipedream* where I've definitely conceived two bass lines running in opposite directions; one bass was played through my Mosrite fuzztone and a Colorsound Octave Divider. It made a very swooping kind of sound.

Are there any special effects or miking techniques that you use in the studio?

We always put the amp in a cabinet of sorts. We make it out of studio baffles by putting one in front, one in back, and one on each side of the amp, and then we cover the top. This makes the compression happen in there that you would otherwise lose in a room. There's a certain amount of popping push that you need from a speaker. You can put that on tape if you can capture it inside a box. Bob Margouleff showed me that; he's the guy who records Stevie Wonder. He was recording Jeff Beck when we first conceived BBA; I did a demo with him and he put my amp in this little box. The bass sound was great, so I've used that little-box concept ever since.

Can you hear a real development in your playing from the days of Vanilla Fudge until now?

I can hear a real maturity; I don't know if it's progress. What I'm trying to say is that I used to play lines I knew worked, and I would just sort of close my eyes and jump at it. But now I think more before I put my two cents in. I still go for it. I knew that I was going to be able to stop it on the one, no matter where I went, and the technique seems to work. You can just throw it out to left field, but if you come back on the beat looking sharp and clean, it becomes a happening, as opposed to being some sort of sloppy thing. It's a matter of timing rather than what you know. My timing that way has always saved me; it's better than my knowledge of music. It gets me through a lot of places. I never spent much time studying music; all I know is what I've picked up from the musicians I've played with.

How do you develop something like timing?

You don't. You can *groom* it. I've been grooming it all my life. Hopefully, it's not as groomed as it can be: I want to get smarter and smarter and tighter as I keep going.

Do you play any string bass?

No, not really. I do play a fretless Fender. It's a '68 Precision that I asked for with a Telecaster neck. It was a one-time thing that Fender made for me as a promotional item. They cut it out of a solid piece of maple; usually the bodies are laminated. They just shot a clear finish over it — this was before they offered their basses with a natural finish.

Why did you want a Tele neck? Why not a Precision or Jazz Bass neck?

Well, I guess for two reasons. Back in the '60s, before they started making Tele basses again, I played the original Precisions that had blonde necks. I just thought they were neat, and in all the psychedelic clubs I used to play back then, I could see them better under all those crazy lights than I could see dark necks. It's just a matter of looks; I just liked them, and they play as good as any other. I haven't used my fretless onstage, but I've used it in the studio, and I've done some fun things with it. It de-mands a whole different sort of approach; the lines that one could play on fretless tend to be very different because of the technique involved. It changes thought patterns considerably, so I like it, because it gives you a real variety of tone colors.

What song have you played that on?

I used it on the Boxer album, *Absolutely*; the song's called "Everyone's A Star." It was quite a good album, actually. It's a shame that band never did anything.

What are your plans now?

Now that Pipedream has dissolved, I've been doing various things. I've let it be known that I'd like to play bass on some sessions, and I'm currently trying to decide whether to join an Italian band called Giants. I taped five TV shows with them in Milan. It was great. Well, I'll just have to see. I'm lucky enough to be in my own situation where I can express who Tim Bogert is musically. I'm lucky enough to be able to do that, but what I am musically changes with every act I play with.

> *"Getting the music tight with the band takes time, but it should be done before you walk in to record."*

– JACK BRUCE –

BY DAN HEDGES – AUGUST 1975

CHUCK PULIN / STAR FILE INC.

WITHOUT IN-tending to be unnecessarily tedious about it all, bassist Jack Bruce truly is a man who needs no introduction. As electric bassist extraordinaire, he's made a sizable impression on contemporary music with his fluid, instantly recognizable playing style — sharing the stage with an impressive array of equally outstanding musicians over the years while becoming something of a household name himself.

Jack spent his early years in his Scottish homeland and was awarded a scholarship to the Royal Scottish Academy of Music, where he studied cello at the age of 17. With an underlying awareness that straight classical music wasn't exactly his cup of tea, he embarked on the erstwhile pastime of playing upright bass in various jazz clubs around Glasgow. Needless to say, it wasn't long before he moved into the realm of the professional musician.

In the early 1960s, Bruce joined the Graham Bond Organization, one of the pioneering exponents of a new brand of music (with Ginger Baker occupying the drum stool). After that, Jack served a short stint as a Bluesbreaker with John Mayall and Eric Clapton, followed by his enlistment in the ranks of Manfred Mann. By late '65, Jack had rejoined forces with Clapton and Baker, forming the ultimate powerhouse trio, Cream — considered by many to have created one of rock's finest hours. Lifetime, with Tony Williams and John McLaughlin, was next in line, but it wasn't long before the inherent complexities of their

music drove Jack in a simpler direction (and, subsequently, out of the band). That need for comparative simplicity took root with guitarist Leslie West and drummer Corky Laing in a more basic blues-rock format, West, Bruce, And Laing — a configuration that bore a marked resemblance to Cream in more ways than one.

Sprinkled throughout the last few years has been a collection of solo albums by Bruce, as well — *Songs For A Tailor*, *Things We Like*, *Harmony Row*, and the newest, *Out Of The Storm* — plus a collaboration with Carla Bley and friends on *Escalator Over The Hill*. Though cuts such as "Sunshine Of Your Love," from the Cream days, started from a bass riff, Bruce finds it easier to write using another instrument (usually a piano) or just to work his material out in his head.

Having finished a European tour last April and May, the newly formed Jack Bruce Band (Mick Taylor on guitar, Bruce Gary on drums, and Ronnie Leahy and Carla Bley both on keyboards) plans to cut its debut album on RSO records this fall and tour the United States.

Delving back into the dim past, how did you first become interested in music?

Well, I used to sing a lot when I was a kid, and my parents were very musical.

Did they perform professionally?

Oh, no. They were mainly into Scottish folk music and stuff like that. Later, I just started fooling around on the piano. When I went to school, I wanted to learn the [upright] bass, but I was much too small to handle it, so they sent me away and said, "Learn the cello!" Which is the next closest thing. So I started playing that, and in time, when I grew a bit bigger, I started playing bass.

What prompted you to switch from upright to electric bass?

About 10 years ago, it suddenly became a matter of necessity because I was working with Ginger Baker by then, who was a very loud drummer. It was impossible to use double bass, because I just kept running out of fingers — bits kept falling off! Actually, I think the first time I played bass guitar was on an Ernest Ranglin record in 1965. I borrowed a bass from a music shop and found that I actually liked it. I'd been quite against bass guitars up until that time because I was quite a purist about the bass. I didn't think I'd actually enjoy playing bass guitar, but I found that I did and could get a completely different kind of thing out of it. It was a whole new challenge.

Didn't you find it difficult to make the switch?

No, it was actually very easy. I think what I did was not try to play it the same way or get the same kind of effect. I just approached it as a different instrument — as a bass *guitar*, and that's probably why it was easy. The change came very naturally, really.

You definitely seem to have opted for a technique that's a bit beyond the traditionally uncomplicated role of the bassist.

That's because I was always playing jazz in the early days, and the technique for jazz playing at that time was set down by people like Charles Mingus and Scott LaFaro, who were among my influences. They played very melodic, very exploratory things. One of the reasons I never liked bass guitar was because most of what I'd heard up until then was nothing more than a lot of vague thumping, you know? Two to the bar, or something, which didn't really appeal to me. I haven't thought about it much, but I suppose I just have this free concept of playing music, where the only limitations are those of taste and my own feelings about it. There certainly shouldn't be a limitation that you have to fulfill a certain role *because* you're playing bass. Obviously, you have to fulfill that role anyway, but you don't *have* to do it in the prescribed way. I try not to play busily just for

> *"I try not to play busily just for the sake of it. I try to deal with each musical situation as I see fit."*

the sake of it, though. I try to deal with each musical situation as I see fit, whether the end result is simple or complicated.

Did you run into any opposition in the beginning from other musicians?

Oh yeah! I mean, what I was doing at the time didn't really make it with anybody, and I quite liked it, in a way! It was a while before people got used to it. I remember some American musician — I can't remember who it was — who came up to me when I was with Graham Bond and said, "You really play some amazing music!" Which was very encouraging, because most people didn't want to know about it.

Do you think the musicians you've played with have had to drastically readjust themselves to your style?

No. I haven't played in many situations where the music happened that way, where anybody was conscious of having to think along those lines. It was usually a situation where people's playing was an extension of themselves. You don't "find" yourself in a band. You have to be right for it. I don't consciously *not* play things, for example. As I said earlier, you have to fulfill a role to a certain extent, but there are all sorts of possibilities within that framework which you have to work out in your own way.

In other words, you can't readjust yourself too much, or your style ceases to be "your" style and the whole thing becomes unnatural.

Right. I wouldn't enjoy a situation where I'd have to be *uncreative*, though that doesn't mean I have to play a thousand notes all the time, either. In fact, I'm not playing half as much as I used to play, technically, in the past. It's altered itself into a slightly different style. It's still very loose and free, but it's changed a bit.

There seems to be a hint of classical influence in your playing, a touch of Bach, perhaps.

Yeah, he did some very, very interesting bass parts, you know. Obviously, the conditions he was writing under were very strict, but within his limitations, there's a lot to be learned in terms of bass lines and melody.

Do you think the electric bass is an instrument that's often taken for granted, even neglected?

No, I don't really agree with that at all. It *has* changed, though I think it was neglected for quite a while. I don't think that's been true for a long time, though. On all those Tamla things [Motown sounds of groups such as Stevie Wonder, the Four Tops, etc.] in the mid '60s, for example, quite often the most interesting part was the bass line. I mean, the bass should never be used as a lead instrument, because that's not its function. But I *do* think that the total possibilities for bass and drums have never been fully explored. The possibilities are really endless.

Are there any rock bassists who have particularly caught your ear in recent days?

Hmm. Well, I haven't really been around for a while. I haven't been listening, but I'm sure there are. I really like Stanley Clarke — quite amazing.

A lot of rock listeners consider him to be a jazz musician.

Well, I don't think that exists anymore — in my mind, anyway. There aren't any barriers. People still have to categorize everything, though, putting everything into neat little compartments. I gave up on that ages ago.

As far as equipment goes, are you still using that Gibson EB-3?

No, I'm using an old Fender Telecaster bass at the moment, and I'll occasionally switch to a Gibson Thunderbird. I always seem to come back to the EB-3, though. I enjoy it, and it's easy to play. For me, it's more flexible. I don't think anybody makes a really good bass, and I really wish somebody would.

Have you ever considered having one custom-built?

Yeah. I started to get that set up, but something happened along the way. Something went wrong. I don't think I should say any more about it. It's on the market now, or rather a very inferior version of it. But I won't say another word about it!

What sort of strings do you use?

LaBella. Sometimes they're light-gauge, sometimes medium, because I'm constantly switching back and forth. It just depends on how I feel, on how hard I'm playing at the time. I've never made a survey of different strings like some people have, though. For all I know, they might be the worst, but I just happened to hit on them somewhere along the line and grew accustomed to them. They're cheap, too.

You use both your fingers and a pick, don't you?

Well, I usually just use my fingers. I'd switch to a pick on occasion when I'm recording.

Do you see much difference between the two? Many people claim a pick gives them more speed.

I find that just the opposite is true with me. I get more speed from my fingers. I use a pick more for a specific sound quality, rather than for any technical aspect.

What kind of amp are you using now?

Well, I'm going to be using a Stramp. They're really very good, though most people have probably never heard of them.

How powerful is it?

That depends on which one I use and how I'm going to be using it. I don't want to be incredibly loud, though. The new band is really in the very early stages of development right now, so I haven't sorted out the equipment aspect yet. It'll be a far cry from all those Marshalls, though. Actually, with Cream, we didn't use *that* many amps. It just looked like a lot when compared to what other people were using at the time.

Were there very big differences between working with Cream and working with West, Bruce, And Laing, both of which had three pieces?

Well, there was the fact that they were basically different people, so the problems weren't the same. I went back into that format because I had gotten into another thing where I was developing in what I felt was the wrong way.

With all your formal training, do you place a lot of value on the ability to read music?

I found that I've had to forget a lot of what I learned. I think it depends on your ear. If you're very quick at picking things up, reading can be a disadvantage. I don't like to write things down if I'm doing something, because it gives you a different impression than if you just pick it up and play it off the top of your head and try to remember it. Reading can be useful for certain things, of course. Obviously, you couldn't do something with a large orchestra without being able to read. For a rock band, it's generally not necessary. I've done some things with Mike Gibbs and large orchestras, but the parts he'd write for me were usually just chord changes with occasional lines, if they were important. So in that kind of situation, reading is essential, though in rock there are very few people who can write good things for bass anyway. It's all in the playing.

What do you feel is the overall function of your bass playing in the context of working with a band?

I'd say that my position is that of a catalyst. When I played string bass years ago, for example, it was probably completely inaudible to the audience most of the time, but it was very important to the band, in terms of keeping them moving and providing something for them to take off on. In the band I'm forming now, it'll obviously be a bit different than if I was a sideman in somebody else's band. I'm the starting point, though not really the focal point, because the other people in the band will be too good for that. I really can't see myself doing bass solos all the time.

Actually, you're one of the few people who do solos on bass.

Well, I don't like solos too much. I only got into it with West, Bruce, And Laing. It's nice on occasion. There always were solos in jazz groups, and I'll do one if I feel it's appropriate. The bass obviously has its limitations, but the interesting thing is to try to push them to the side. If it warrants a solo, fine.

Do you play upright bass anymore?

I play it at home, on occasion, along with the cello. As far as using it onstage, there are too many limitations where volume is concerned. Acoustic instruments lose a lot when they're amplified. The thing I used to love about playing upright bass was the vibration, the sort of buzz you used to get in your groin. You can't get that with an electric instrument. You can't move around too much with an upright bass, either, though I used to manage to do it somehow.

Do you find singing and playing simultaneously at all difficult?

"Playing bass is an instinctive thing for me. I might forget the words, but the bass is no problem!"

It was difficult at first, because a lot of the things I write are in odd timings. It got really interesting with Lifetime, though. There was one thing we used to do that was in 11-something, and the bass part was basically a lot of E changes. The first note of the melody was C♮, and the rest of it centered around C and G♭, so it was strange trying to keep track of it all. Playing bass is an instinctive thing for me now. I might forget the words, but the bass is no problem! It was something that developed with Cream. I was voted to be the singer because nobody else wanted to do it. I didn't actually sit down and practice it, because it's something that you can get down only by actually getting up and doing it.

Anything in closing? A message for the up-and-coming bassist, perhaps?

Hmm. Well, I happen to play bass a certain way, but it doesn't really matter what you play. I think it's a shame that people get hung up in little boxes — "I have to conform to this," or, "Mustn't do that." You lose the excitement. The main thing is to believe in yourself and explore. After all, music is really an extension of the person playing it — or at least that's the way it should be.

– JOHN ENTWISTLE –

BY CHRIS JISI – AUGUST 1989

WITH NO LESS mighty a hand than Pete Townshend's, John "Thunderfingers" Entwistle helped transform one of rock's greatest bands into one of the greatest *performing* trio units in rock history. And in a typically peculiar fashion, his greatest reward as a bassist comes in knowing that by standard definition, he's hardly a proper bassist at all; more accurately, Entwistle is one of the first bass guitarists to play the instrument so improperly that through his own sheer aggression, technique, and sonic vision, the spare setting of his three-piece always seemed far, far larger. Today, though, as the freshly reformed, brass-augmented Who begins rehearsals for a massive 25th anniversary tour, Thunderfingers — anchor, propellant, big scary guy in the corner — looks a bit out of place. For the first time in the 25 years since the founding of this band, he's standing on a stage where the musicians outnumber the towering columns of equipment he uses to create his mammoth sound.

Out of place, maybe, but hardly out of sorts. As the run-through of the first song begins, Entwistle lays out briefly, steps back to survey the territory, and then lays back in with his patented thunder — and he's more overpowering than the other 14 pieces combined. "I don't intend to change my bass playing that much for this," he laughs, "but I suppose we'll have to be quieter onstage to protect Pete's hearing. I've devised a way of keeping the volume down, but

still getting the same impact with the help of about $30,000 worth of equipment — I've got to have my *sound.*" Then he turns away and continues his assault on the rafters. Long live rock.

John Alec Entwistle took to sounds quite early in life, singing along with tunes on the family radio in the West London town of Acton while still in his first three years. Upon urging from his mum, he began studying piano, with the stipulation that he also be allowed to pursue his interest in trumpet. That instrument carried him through the Confederates, his first band with schoolmate and banjoist-cum-guitarist Peter Townshend. Entwistle later took up the French horn and then the bass guitar, and was returning from a rehearsal with a band called the Scorpions (actually a less traditional reworking of the Confederates), axe and amp in hand, when a lead guitarist named Roger Daltrey confronted him and asked if he actually played the instrument he was carrying. Entwistle soon found himself in Daltrey's five-piece ensemble, the Detours, which suffered through several short, volatile periods of creative indecision before arriving at the concept and the sound that became the Who.

And their ever-changing sound concept altered the sound of rock. The Ox (as Entwistle came to be known, both for his girth of body and tone) had his hands fuller than any bassist working the idiom, straddling a tenuous rhythmic bond with the unpredictably flamboyant drum excursions of Keith Moon, and a melodic chasm split wide open by Townshend's

– 90 –

alternately slashing and introspective approach to lead/rhythm guitar. Before the turbulent but musically unrefined '60s had drawn to a close, Entwistle had forged a bass sound and sensibility that would never cease to evolve, but would preserve as its basis a stabbing, relentless pentatonic phraseology punched up by a brittle top end and a frightening low-end thunder — and enough stage gear to make Jerry Garcia blush.

Although Entwistle's first major bass showcase came in the form of his groundbreaking stop-time solos in "My Generation," it wasn't until the post-Tommy Who tours and albums that listeners began taking notice of the wild streams of notes emanating from the deceptively motionless figure at deep, dark stage right. On the band's growing commercial strength, each member undertook his own solo project in the early '70s, and Entwistle's strong debut, *Smash Your Head Against The Wall*, continued in the sardonically hard-edged vein of his previous contributions to the Who. With the 1973 release of *Quadrophenia*, the band's second double-record concept album, Entwistle became recognized as a bona fide bass phenomenon, hurling endless lines into the fray both onstage and in the studio. The Who's penchant for extended improvisation in concert was as unusual for the genre as it was exciting to witness, and 1970's *Live At Leeds* stands as one of the finest (legally recorded and released) documents of the period, of the power of the trio, and of the Ox' unparalleled ability to control the Who's impromptu motion while successfully dodging every bass convention in the book.

Despite personal problems plaguing the Who throughout the mid '70s, Entwistle's burgeoning musicianship and conviction strengthened the band. During the down time, he released two more solo albums and prepared the Who's 1974 collection of *Odds And Sods*, which he culled from the band's massive library of unreleased recordings. A year later he embarked on his first solo tour, in support of *Mad Dog*, a pumping retro-rock release by his new band, Ox. He returned to home base in time to provide the cover art, the industry-jibing 8-string showcase "Success Story," and some incredibly melodic 4-string lines for *The Who By Numbers*. Live, tunes like "Dreaming From The Waist" enjoyed the same bass-heavy readings they received on record, but the band's sound had evolved to where even straight rockers like

> *"I'd always been tempted to turn up the treble but didn't dare, because bassists just didn't do that."*

"Squeeze Box" were getting the full Entwistle treatment: Driving flurries, resonant snaps, and tom-tom-style fills, all of which figured with ease into the Who's characteristically unorthodox bottom end.

Entwistle continued to pursue production as an antidote for the lag between Who tours, and after the recording of the discursive *Who Are You*, the bassist settled in to oversee the scores for two Who films released in the late '70s, *Quadrophenia* and the "rockumentary" *The Kids Are Alright*. Then, on September 7, 1978, in the midst of the furious media activity surrounding their numerous projects, the Who lost Keith Moon to an accidental overdose of alcohol-combating pills. Their original sound and concept would never withstand the loss, and later that year, ex-Small Faces drummer Kenney Jones, who had done session work with members of the Who on various occasions, joined as a full-time member. With Jones, the Who was slow but certain to recongeal; their slightly unstable *Face Dances* gave way to a powerful resurgence with 1982's *It's Hard*, and although Jones' conventional approach tightened up the band's loose ends both onstage and in the studio, Entwistle found it refreshing to work with a stable timekeeper for the first time in almost two decades. With revitalized interest, he seized the opportunity between these last two Who albums to enlist frequent jamming partner Joe Walsh and multi-instrumentalist Joe Vitale and to produce his fifth solo release, *Too Late The Hero*. Less than a year later, he set off on the Who's farewell tour through North America, where they played their last official show at Toronto's Maple Leaf Gardens.

Five excruciating years of reclusion elapsed before the Ox returned to the scene in a curious context: Joining forces with members of the New York-based band Rat Race Choir (with longtime local hero Mark Hitt on lead guitar), he played a short club tour, performing mostly Who material and covers of tunes by the Who. The band also popped up at National Association of Music Merchants (NAMM) show parties and similarly oriented events, where throngs gathered to gaze point-blank at the hands of one of the preeminent figures in rock bass history. "We played the entire *Live At Leeds* album verbatim," chuckles John, "mistakes and all. In fact, I had to learn all my original mistakes, as opposed to performing the songs correctly." Since then, Thunderfingers has appeared at a "Say No To Drugs" benefit and played with Chuck Berry and Dave Edmunds at Berry's birthday celebration. Most recently, he laid down a basic track for a cover of The Crazy World Of Arthur Brown's "Fire," which appears as a featured Who track on Pete Townshend's new solo album, *The Iron Man*.

On this hazy spring afternoon, Ox is beginning full-time rehearsals for the Who's extensive reunion tour, which includes special stops in New York and Los Angeles for performances of the entire *Tommy* album, to benefit the Autistic Children's Fund. The band is augmented by some of the musicians who accompanied Townshend on his recent solo efforts and a set of benefit concerts he played in Brixton three years ago: The Kick Horns, percussionist Jodi Linscott, a three-piece vocal section under the direction of longtime Townshend collaborator Billy Nicholls, a second guitarist, frequent Who touring keyboardist John "Rabbit" Bundrick, and drummer Simon Phillips. Entwistle's tone is happening, his chops sharp as blades, his jones for the road soon to be satiated. And when cornered, he displays the same loquacity conversing about the bass as he does conversing with one.

Simon Phillips is an interesting choice for a drummer for this band — he combines elements of Keith Moon's adventurous style with those of Kenney Jones' more groove-oriented approach. How will he affect your role in the Who?

I'm looking forward to working with Simon because he uses a double-bass-drum setup, which I love. Kenney used one bass drum and insisted that it was really the same thing, but I like that sort of triplet rumble you get from two — I was weaned on it. Drummers used to throw that at me, and I'd shock them by answering back and then doing it twice as fast! I like the intricate way Simon plays, and I'm pretty sure I can pick it up and create some interesting things.

As explosively as you played with the original Who, you still appeared to be the most responsible for holding the band together. Was it a problem then that Keith played with such abandon, and then, later on, that Kenney didn't?

Not really. With Keith, a lot of times I would have to find a note and sort of hang onto it with my left hand — making sure I didn't hit it with my right hand, because it would be too loud — until I could figure out his next move. Or I'd play a part with my left hand that was roughly based on what I thought he

was playing until I could walk over and look at his bass drum to find the beat. But that was part of the way he played. I knew that if I went off on a tangent, he'd follow me, so if he went off on a tangent, I'd follow him. Kenney was very supportive, so I was able to go off on more tangents, and he'd stay right with me. But because of that, some of the things I'd done when Keith was in the band didn't work as well.

What was your initial attraction to the bass?

I studied classical piano at age six, took up trumpet at eleven during a period when jazz was the "in" music, and a year later played French horn in the school orchestra. Then rock and roll came along and changed my life. I guess I was attracted to bass for several reasons: Visually, the instrument was bigger and longer than a guitar, and soundwise, I liked that sort of sinister low drone that a lot of bands had at the time. Also, it had only four strings, so I figured it would be easy to play and a good way to get into a rock band, because no one wanted a trumpet player — about the only band that had one was the John Barry Seven, who played covers of American sax tunes like "Tequila." In fact, in the early days of the Who, we did "Tequila" and "Peter Gunn," and I'd play the sax part on a trumpet with a beer glass in front of it.

Anyway, I soon realized I'd made a wrong choice. I was playing what was supposed to be a background instrument. When I played trumpet in Dixieland and traditional jazz bands, I was the center of attention, and when I played French horn in the orchestra I had a lot of solo lines, but the only thing I was doing on bass was developing blisters. Then, one day, I had a brainstorm: I figured the piano had made my hands supple, the trumpet put speed in my right hand, and the French horn did the same for my left, so why not use all 10 fingers on the bass? I started slowly and eventually built up my speed and endurance.

How long did it take for your sound concept to begin developing?

Well, I'd learned to play by ear, by playing along with records by Eddie Cochran, Gene Vincent, the Ventures, Buddy Holly, the Shadows, and especially Duane Eddy — his guitar had the sound I wanted my bass to have. When I began experimenting, I still had a sort of thuddy, boomy bass sound, but I remember a turning point a few years later. We had our first hit record with the Who, "I Can't Explain," and showed up at a big hall for a concert, only to find the place empty because the promoter had forgotten to promote it. So we decided to make use of the situation by having a rehearsal. I had a Rickenbacker bass and

Marshall amps at the time, and after we started playing, our manager came up to me and said, "It's all very well, you playing that fast, but I can't hear the notes you're playing in the back. Why don't you try putting a bit of treble on it?" I'd always been tempted to turn up the treble but didn't dare, because bassists just didn't do that. So I opened up the treble on my amp and bass and started playing like Duane Eddy.

That was the turning point, but what I didn't realize was that I'd set quite a task for myself, because you can't play sloppily using that much high end. I had to clean it up and find a fluid way of damping the notes so they didn't blur into each other or vary in volume. Another turning point came when I went to Rotosound not long after we recorded "My Generation" [*The Who Sings My Generation*]. The LaBella strings I'd been using were going dead after each concert, so I visited the Rotosound factory and had them make me sets until they came up with what I was looking for.

You recently contributed to the audio portion of the memorial project Standing In The Shadows Of Motown: The Life And Music Of Legendary Bassist James Jamerson *[Hal Leonard Pub.], by playing bass and speaking of "the bass player from Motown," as you knew him. Certain Who tracks, such as "The Relay" and "Squeeze Box," use some of the rhythms, chromatic passages, and tonal elements popularized by Jamerson. How much of an influence was his playing?*

It was a lot of fun doing that project, but I can't really say he influenced me, first of all, because he was a peer of mine, and second, because to me he was a real bass player, and I never considered myself to be a proper bass player. I've always been a bass guitarist, emulating guitar players and using a guitar sound, so I couldn't get worked up about straight bass players. I admired his playing and feel and probably nicked a couple of his syncopated rhythms, but I was always more excited by lead players. As far as the sound similarities, that wasn't my doing. The producers and engineers used to be so frightened of the treble I used that they would turn the treble all the way off in the mix!

How did the "My Generation" solo come about?

Originally, we wanted to feature the sound of a Danelectro bass, which had thin strings. We did three takes, all of which were faster, more trebly, and more complex than the final one, and I kept breaking the strings. You couldn't get replacements, so I had to keep buying Danelectros. When the store finally ran out of them, I bought a Fender Jazz Bass, put on LaBella strings, and used it to cut the recorded version.

The solo suggests that electric bass was entering a freer, more improvisational phase. Where was the line drawn for you with regard to extended soloing?

I guess you'd have to ask the others about that. Maybe they wouldn't let me do more of it for personal reasons concerning themselves, although there was a similar break on "Call Me Lightning" [*Magic Bus — The Who On Tour*]. A lot of times, I would sneak in a lead part and everyone would think it was Pete playing. That's why I like playing live, especially in clubs, where the audience can get close and really see what my hands are doing. I did a seven-week solo tour recently during which I devised a way to lay down the low part while playing the melody on top, so that both parts ring on.

So, such flamboyance wasn't too far out for the time?

Oh, no. I mean, if you listen to *Live At Leeds*, I'm soloing the whole time. I'm making sure I'm holding the band together, but at any chance I get to play something flashy, I play it. That whole album is like a free jam. We would have "islands," certain riffs or ideas that we could clutch onto if what we were doing between the islands wasn't working after a while. We knew we'd have this or that riff coming up, so in between we would play completely off the top of our heads. If I had an idea, Pete would follow me, and vice versa. There's a section on *Leeds* where Pete introduced a lick that I'd never heard before, and you can hear me working it out until I finally get it under my fingers, and then we blast through it. That used to happen every night. There were a few solos after that: "The Real Me" [*Quadrophenia*] was more or less a solo, and there was one on *The Who By Numbers* ["Dreaming From The Waist"]. But I was never really satisfied with what the Who did with my bass playing, because I always found things very restricting. We never managed to get the sound or style on record. The only Who stuff I feel happy about is the live stuff, but on a lot of it the bass is mixed so low you can't hear it.

Were you ever tempted to quit, especially given the number of other great musicians in England at the time?

> "*I was never really satisfied with what the Who did with my bass playing, because I always found things very restricting.*"

[Laughs.] I was going to leave the Who every other week! At one point, Keith and I were going to form our own band with Jimmy Page. Keith said, "It'll probably sink like a lead balloon," so I said, "Why don't we call it Led Zeppelin?" and Keith agreed. We even planned an album cover with a picture of the Hindenburg going down in flames and the band's name in red letters on the top. Anyway, our driver at the time, Richard Cole, had just lost his license for speeding so we had to let him go, and he went to work as a production manager for Jimmy Page. So Led Zeppelin was formed without me or Keith. I also remember Chas Chandler asking me to come and jam with this brilliant black guitarist he'd found in the States, who, of course, was Jimi Hendrix. At that time he was just playing the blues; I'd see him in audiences around London checking out Page, Jeff Beck, and Pete with us. Eventually, he took a little bit of all of them, joined it to what he already had, and *pow*. A few years later I was tentatively called to join the Experience, but the Who was doing so well at the time, so I declined. When they found Noel Redding, who was really a guitarist, he rang me up and asked what kind of equipment I used, which was a Jazz Bass, Rotosounds, and Marshalls, so that's what he went with.

Did your solo career evolve for the same reasons?

Actually, it was more out of boredom than dissatisfaction. The Who would have two or three years off between records and I would go nuts wanting to play. Also, I was writing a lot of songs and had no vehicle for them.

Are you satisfied with the five albums you made?

They were successful economically, but I made the mistake of writing songs around my voice instead of around my bass. I mean, I'm not a rock idol or personality; I'm a rock performer, and I'm known for the way I play bass. So to have a successful album, I'd have been better off playing bass solos than singing. A lot of the stuff I wrote, I like, and a lot of it was crap. The idea was to record an album and then get a band together and do a little tour. My first few attempts didn't work out, but I finally got it together after the fourth album with the Ox band. Then a Who album and big tour came up, so I had to disband it.

I think the first two albums I made, *Smash Your Head Against The Wall* and *Whistle Rhymes,* are my favorites. The ones that are great for parties are the next two, *Rigor Mortis Sets In* and *Mad Dog.* I think they would have been successful if I'd done them five years later, when the rock and roll revival took place.

Actually, *Too Late The Hero* was my favorite record of all of them, in terms of production, which was very good at the time.

What inspired the offbeat, black-humor tone of the songs you wrote for the Who?

A lot of it stemmed from an idea our manager had after "Whiskey Man" and "Boris The Spider" [both from *Happy Jack*], my first two Who songs. Those songs were popular among kids, so he asked me to write a black-humor sort of album for kids. I wrote "Silas Stingy" [*The Who Sell Out*] and "Dr. Jekyll And Mr. Hyde" [*Magic Bus — The Who On Tour*] for that reason, but no sooner would I write one than we'd need it for the B side of a Who single. From there I moved to writing ironic songs like "My Wife" [*Who's Next*], which, ironically, came true [laughs].

Conceptually, things seemed to open up for you around the Who Are You *period, when you became more involved in songwriting and preserving the sound of your bass within the band.*

Yes, on that album and on *Too Late The Hero,* I started writing more commercial songs, and recording techniques were getting better, so it was easier to use the treble on my bass. Actually, there were a couple of songs on *Quadrophenia* where the treble is there. The problem was not only with engineers ducking the treble in the mix, but the tendency at the time to mix everything at a high volume — the bass would always *sound* loud enough, and by the time it got to the record, it had disappeared. On *Too Late The Hero,* I managed to get the treble right. One thing I think I taught the people who worked or co-produced with me is that you don't have to be frightened of putting bass on record, which, as I said, is a fear that had an unfortunate effect on my Who stuff. A lot of people put the bass drum up too high and lose the bass itself. I can remember saying to producers, "Yeah, you can hear and feel the bass, but you can't hear the actual note. I want to hear the note."

In the studio, do you find you have to boost the bass more than one would expect?

Yes, especially if you're listening to it loud. Once you lose all those nice, woolly frequencies from the big speakers and you play it on little, flat speakers before you decide how loud it should be, you won't hear any bass. You need to put bass in the little speakers before you decide how loud it should be, just like you do with vocals. I was there for the mix of *Who Are You,* and the funny thing was that it was done on one of those old computerized boards with the automatic faders moving up and down. So I'd ask to do another mix with a bit more bass and I'd push up the fader, and the next time they played it through, I'd see the fader go down! While I wasn't looking, the engineer had brought it down again.

Why wasn't the proof in the finished products?

I don't know. It's a weird thing with musicians. I mean, with my band, I found that I could play back a horrible mix that had the guitars nice and loud, and the guitarists loved it! That was a syndrome that I suffered from, too. I was thought of as the bass player who always wanted the bass louder, not because it sounded better but because I was the bass player. For our last album, *Who's Last,* copies of the final mix were sent to each band member. Unfortunately, on the first three tracks, the bass was too loud, but it was fine on the rest of the album. Of course, the band heard the first three tracks and said, "The bass is too loud," and wanted to remix them. I told my manager that if they sent it in to be remixed without me, the engineer would overcompensate and there wouldn't be any bass on the record. So they sent it in, the guy overcompensated, and we came out with the shittiest live album we've ever released. I refused even to do interviews because I didn't want anything to do with it — I played the first side and threw it away. I don't even own a copy of it. In fact, this is probably the first time I've ever mentioned any of this. I mean, I even wanted to remix the first three cuts because the bass was far too loud.

But by today's standards it probably wouldn't have seemed loud.

By today's standards the Who don't have a bass player [*laughs*]!

Is it difficult to sing while playing your complex lines?

In the Who, we all sang backup vocals to Roger — except for Keith, who used to double a note because he couldn't find one of his own. Of course, we all had to sing them while we played. That was another mistake I'd made on my solo albums, because I didn't actually write them while playing the bass. A lot of my best songs were unperformable because I couldn't play the bass part and sing the melody at the same time. I managed most of the time, but "Talk Dirty" from *Too Late The Hero,* which had two vocals and a busy bass line, was impossible. People like Paul McCartney and Sting are different than someone like me or, say, Jack Bruce. They write their bass parts around their vocals, and it's very effective. I wrote

> *"I always make sure that there's a clean bass sound that's the backbone of whatever band I'm in."*

"The Quiet One" [*Face Dances*] and "My Wife" that way, since I knew I was going to sing and play them live. But that approach was a little restrictive for my solo LPs because I wanted to have nice, moving bass parts and a different kind of vocal. I've got four new songs in the can now that I'm very proud of, from a contemporary and songwriting point of view. We performed them on my solo tour in late 1987 and they went over well. I'm going to use them on my next solo album, and we might even do them on the Who tour.

Can you hear your influence in the playing of other bassists?

Yeah. A lot of people have been influenced by my sound. As I mentioned, Noel Redding rang me up directly to find out what I was using. I guess Chris Squire was imitating my sound, and Greg Lake as well. Later on, there was Billy Sheehan.

How was Jack Bruce's approach different from yours?

Jack was and is a good technical bass player who can play fast when he wants to, but he's more of a straight bass player. He was trained on upright bass.

Were you aware of players like Stanley Clarke and Jaco Pastorius?

Yes. They were virtuosos who took bass in a different direction than I did: not in a rock way, but in a funky, jazzy way. If you draw a family tree, you have me going up there in one direction, then you have James Jamerson, with a branch for Jack Bruce and the female bass player for Tamla [Carol Kaye]; they're sort of the early funk, real bass players. They lead to Larry Graham, with branches for people like Stanley Clarke and Jaco, which then lead to people like Mark King and Pino Palladino.

Where do you see current rockers like Sheehan and Doug Wimbish fitting in?

Doug Wimbish is kind of on the Larry Graham branch. Billy Sheehan is my branch, but his sound isn't quite there. I know I influenced him because he sent me a fan letter and some tapes back when he was with Talas, and I've met him a few times — he's a nice chap. But there doesn't seem to be anyone using the amount of treble and distortion I use, plus, I always make sure that there's a clean bass sound that's the backbone of whatever band I'm in. Then the treble is the part that makes it fun for me.

The only really in-depth documents of your approach are your Hot Licks instructional tapes.

Well, I enjoyed making them as a representation of

what can be done with the instrument and to give players inspiration, but I'm glad that it hasn't caught on. Luckily, no one's managed to imitate me. It's nice to be uncopyable.

Aside from your normal two-finger approach, pick playing, use of bass chords, and slap, pull, and pop methods, how does your technique differ from, say, Sheehan's or Wimbish's?

What they call "tapping" is actually the use of hammer-ons, which is easier than my tapping method, because they use two hands. When I tap, I strike the strings at the base of the neck with my right-hand fingertips to sound the note, and then lift off quickly, in a typewriter-like motion. You have to develop tremendous strength in your fingers to make the note come out. From there, I'm able to imply drum-like rhythms, by damping the notes, or I can move my right hand to different points on the string to bring out various overtones. I use standard hammer-ons, too, as well as "flicks," where I strike the strings with the back of one or more fingers, and "crab-claws," where I grasp the strings with my thumb and fingers to play octaves and similar two-string lines.

Do you keep up with the latest technology or attend trade shows to seek out devices that might help improve your sound?

Yes, although it's getting impossible to go to the shows anymore. Ever since the Who broke up, we each draw huge crowds when we're in public. I've got an Akai 12-track at home, along with the regular 24-track studio that I can rent out. Pete did his solo album there. I like using drum machines and sequencers to write because they help the process — sort of a musical shorthand system.

What current music do you like?

I like what's out there: Van Halen, Bon Jovi, that sort of melodic metal. "Heavy Tinsel" — pop metal, I call it. My songs are in the same direction. I don't like dance music much because I find it rather bland. And my TV's just barely escaped destruction a few times after I saw some of those rap videos.

Apart from the Who tour and the possibility of a solo album, what does the immediate future hold?

I plan on spending some time in Los Angeles, where I'm going to be writing a book about the Who. Whenever I get into a conversation about the original Who, I think of so many funny stories that aren't in any of the books about us. All the books I've seen so far are about someone else's idea of what it was like back then. Well, I'm going to tell the hilarious truth. Take our first tours through the U.S., for example:

We'd be in some city like Baton Rouge, Louisiana, where if you didn't shave in the morning, they'd have killed you! If some truck driver didn't like the color of your hair, you could have had a gun held to your head. Flower Power had caught on, and we were considered hippies. I'd be wearing a $500 black suit and tie with a white shirt and had relatively short hair — we were leftovers from the mod days — but because I had long sideburns, I'd be called a stinkin' hippie and be thrown out of bars.

Then there's the whole hotel-smashing thing. No one ever said *why* we smashed 'em up. A lot of times it was because Keith and I had this running gag: He'd bring a couple of girls to his room and then he and the road manager would start talking about me, saying what a horrible person I was, how frightened they were of me because I bullied everyone, and how I hated girls and liked to slap them around — you know, really building it up. Then Keith would ring me up and I'd knock on the door and the girls would see me, and their eyes would bulge. So I'd come in and start knocking the guys around, breaking furniture and mirrors, and then I'd say, "You girls are next!" and they'd run screaming from the room! Just a little levity [*laughs*].

Would you do a solo tour to support an album now?

Yes, but it would be a little different. It would be John Entwistle and band. I've even got a name for the band, Thunderfingers, which is my nickname. And as I said, I've got four great songs that are the best I've ever written, and I'm writing about eight more. One of the million reasons I'm doing the Who again is so I'll have money to lose on my solo career [*laughs*].

What role does the bass play in your new songs?

One has a hammering bass intro, and I've written the rest to feature bass in certain spots so I can sing them, as well.

What advice do you have for the young bassist, especially the one striving to become a soloist?

That person is letting himself in for a lifetime of trouble. Solo bass players are a small-numbered breed. You get less work because you're too flashy. You'll get more work as a straight bass player. If you really want to be a soloist, then take it up, but you can't sit back on your laurels. You've got to keep getting better and better, or people are going to catch up with and overtake you. Experiment. Play anything but bass on your bass. Listen to a piece of classical music, for example, and try to play it. The way I discovered all my different hand positions was by messing around and trying to get different noises out of the bass. I was always petrified of losing a finger, so I used to make believe I didn't have a certain finger, and I'd practice playing without it, even to the point of working with my right-hand pinky alone! Play a lot with a drum machine; it will keep the beat while you go off on tangents and will help give you inspiration, because it can be difficult to play bass to nothing. Think up counter-rhythms, like drummers do, and always be prepared to approach things from different directions.

It's also important to work with other musicians. Lots of bass players have their impressive "party piece" for the NAMM show booth, but you can't play three songs at once when you're performing with a band. The thing to do is learn licks that you can use in any situation. Build up a mental collection of licks you can play in any key, so when you get to a given point in a song, you'll know, "Ahh, *that* one will fit in." The reason the Who was able to perform live as we did was that we had a huge amount of such licks and ideas, so when we did the free-form bit, we could afford to take some chances. And sometimes, you'd come up with something you never played before and think, "Christ, I hope somebody taped that!" [*Laughs.*] Work towards developing a telepathic relationship with everyone in your band, especially the drummer. To be a bass player, you have to think like a drummer anyway. I mean, if you play

> *"Work towards developing a telepathic relationship with everyone in your band, especially the drummer."*

a run off the top of your head that matches what the drummer just played off the top of *his* head, you're going to sound like a couple of geniuses.

So you'd advocate becoming a good straight bass player before trying to become an innovator?

Oh, yeah. There aren't any shortcuts. Guitarists who go right for the whammy bar and screaming noises have to, at some point, go back and learn the chords and basics. Because when the style changes and whammy bars become such old hat that everybody hates them, then they'll be in a real bind.

Likewise, bassists can't go right into slapping; they have to learn the basic method, which is, you know, *finger on the string, perfect note, perfect note.* Another thing that keeps your brain alive in the process is to play in different styles. I'll occasionally sit down and play along with a jazz record, not imitating a walking bass, but creating something in my own style that goes along with the jazz beat. I had one of those old, cheap drum machines that had bossa nova, merengue, and rhumba rhythms, and with a tool like that, it's amazing what you can come up with. Kids today never get to hear that. But there are so many different styles of music today that it's hard to tell a kid what to do. What it really comes down to is finding whatever it is that turns you on emotionally. To me, performing music is emotion. It's probably the strongest emotion I get. It's the biggest kick I know.

– STUART HAMM –

By Tom Mulhern – August 1988

EBET ROBERTS

WHEN STUART Hamm was born in New Orleans on February 8, 1960, Leo Fender's pioneering 4-string electric — the Precision Bass — was but nine years old. Today, just 28 years later, Hamm is expanding the relatively young instrument's vocabulary by fusing the diverse techniques of slapping, plucking, and hammering with integrated right- and left-hand fretting. Like his contemporaries Billy Sheehan and Kjell Benner, who utilize the right hand to hammer notes, Hamm commands the listener's — and viewer's — attention in his own unique way. He seamlessly segues between rapid-fire slapping and two-handed, multi-voiced harmonizations and counterpoint.

You may recognize Stuart Hamm as the bassist on Steve Vai's *Flex-Able* and *Leftovers* records. Hamm has known Steve since the late '70s, when they were both freshmen at Boston's Berklee College of Music. "I played on his audition tapes for Frank Zappa," Stu says. "Later, I was starving and things were pretty slow, and Steve called and convinced me to move to California. We did some trio gigs, and then I played on his tracks."

Ever since his big onstage splash with Steve Vai's mentor, Joe Satriani, at Chicago's Limelight in June 1987, Stuart has been at the guitarist's side, touring the U.S. in support of Joe's *Surfing With The Alien*. At each gig, Hamm not only pours on the power to support the guitarist's pyrotechnics, but he gets to

solo extensively. The crowd screams as he lays down the familiar groove to Vince Guaraldi's "Linus And Lucy" (also known as the "Peanuts Theme") on one of his three Kubicki Factor basses; using his left hand to hammer out the ostinato, he attacks the melody and chords with his right hand, bringing to mind a jazz pianist. Stu also launches into a "greatest hits" phase, dazzling the audience with highlights from his solo album, *Radio Free Albemuth*. Stuart feels lucky to have the freedom to do his own music, as well as to improvise in Satriani's group: "I don't know what most people think jazz is, but for me it's when people get together and do group improvisation. We do a lot of that in Joe's band, not just play hits. Even though it's a rock band, there are sections where we take it someplace different every night. For me, that's more jazzy than a fuzak band where there's a set thing going on for a number of bars and a guy just blows over it. It's great with Joe's band, because we get a lot of younger players checking out the improvising, and I think it exposes them to something new."

Although the bassist didn't play on Satch's album, Satch did play on his; Stuart's spotlights Joe on three cuts, and on one of those he appears alongside Allan Holdsworth. But make no mistake: Even though there is hot guitar on a few tracks, *Radio Free Albemuth* is a bass showcase. Hamm's originals, including the beautiful "Flow My Tears," and the red-hot, funky "Sexually Active," are juxtaposed with his bass renditions of piano works such as Debussy's "Dr. Gradus Ad Parnasum" and Beethoven's "Moonlight Sonata." His pianistic two-handed approach maintains the beauty of the pieces, and his performance seems so effortless that the listener might mistakenly think that this is standard bass repertoire.

After growing up in a household full of musical diversity — his dad is a musicologist and his mother taught opera, plus his older brothers exposed him to Miles Davis, the Mahavishnu Orchestra, and Pink Floyd — it's no wonder that Stu covers many styles. He learned piano and oboe while growing up in Champaign, Illinois. "I started playing flute, but in junior high band there are always 84,000 flute players," he laments, "so I switched to oboe, because there weren't any oboe players. I was immediately first chair, but I wasn't really that good at it. I basically kept playing piano — mostly classical music — until I moved to Vermont. I still compose with the piano, but I'm not terribly proficient. I just bang out chords and work out melodies."

Stu switched to bass in high school, and taught himself enough from Mel Bay books to play in the school's jazz band. When his family moved to Vermont in 1975, he continued playing bass, but found that his options in a school band were limited. Working with bands at Dartmouth College, he got more into rock and roll and became a devotee of Yes' Chris Squire. When he first heard Stanley Clarke, he decided to become the fastest bass player alive. "I went to Berklee College of Music when I was 18," he adds. "On November 8, 1978 — I'll never forget it — I had a ticket to go see Weather Report, and before then I hadn't really been exposed to Jaco Pastorius; it was right in his heyday. It changed my life; I had never seen anything like it before. The control! The bass was like putty in his hands. After the concert, a few friends and I just stayed up all night. It was just the most incredible experience. Jeff Berlin was there in Boston a lot, so I got to see him play." Although an avowed jazz and fusion fanatic from then on, he took a year off from Berklee to tour in a band backing an Elvis Presley impersonator. He returned to the school for one semester, but then decided to get out into the club scene. After a couple of years working in various groups, he was ready to head for California to work with Vai.

Today, his *Radio Free Albemuth* is testimony to

"Interpretation is an art form. It's one of the nice challenges of music."

his determination. His excellent instructional video *Slap, Pop & Tap For The Bass* (available from Hot Licks Productions) showcases him in a solo setting, picking apart most aspects of his playing — including his pianistic approach to two-handed musicianship.

What prompted you to transcribe piano pieces for bass?

At Berklee I experimented with laying down the root and fifth with the left hand on the bottom two strings and then playing, say, Latin rhythms on the top. And when I was first with Steve Vai's band, I worked out the Vince Guaraldi thing, "Linus And Lucy." It was a slow process, but once I learned it, I figured I could do harder things. So I took the hardest thing I could do and practiced it slowly every day, and sure enough, it became part of my vocabulary. So now I've even got a couple Gershwin pieces worked out. I was messing around one day and worked out the first part of the "Moonlight Sonata." So I bought the sheet music, and spent about six months figuring out how to get my fingers to play all the notes. Then it took about another three months to make it sound musical. It's a rewarding experience. But even when you think you've got it down, you haven't really mastered it. It's just the tip of the iceberg. It takes constant encouragement to keep going.

Why did you choose such an obviously pianistic song as Debussy's "Dr. Gradus Ad Parnasum"?

I used to play it in my classical piano repertoire, and I rediscovered it. It works out great because the left hand plays the accompaniment, and the right hand plays the melody. Not everything I've picked up is feasible, but that's one of the pieces that works. I started working on that at Berklee. But I didn't have a clue how to get it all, until I started doing the hammer-ons with the right hand. I spent a lot of hours with it.

An unusual aspect of your technique is the inclusion of your right-hand thumb in fretting.

Yeah. It's just that necessity is the mother of invention. It came up in the "Moonlight Sonata." The middle two strings are doing the triplet pattern, and the E string gets the roots while the melody is on the upper strings. I had to take that piece apart beat by beat.

Did you ever work out a section's fingering, only to find that you've hit a dead end, or at least a very difficult fingering transition in the next part?

It's tough sometimes. I had to go through a lot of alternate fingerings, because you want to make it flow and have some consistency to make it smooth. You can't be jumping all over. So you experiment with different fingerings to keep it even, making it a little more musical, which is the key. I try to make it not just an exercise, but real music. I really like classical music, as well as improvisation. Interpretation is an art form; it's one of the nice challenges of music.

Before you wrote "Country Music (A Night In Hell)" — the breakdown on your album that's similar to "Foggy Mountain Breakdown" — did you listen to much banjo music?

I'm not really a big fan of country music, but I always dug bluegrass and the fast banjo double-picking stuff. One day I was messing around, and I came up with that. Using the open *G* string, I'd hammer-on from *F* to *G* on the *D* string. I came up with a lot of ideas practicing. And we've all been in situations where in clubs someone's yelling for you to play something that you aren't doing. I just wanted to get a laugh onto the album. I unwittingly encouraged hecklers to harass me the rest of my life. Wherever we go, there's always a handful of Stu Hamm fans, and the drunker they get, the more they yell between songs, "Hey, play some country — ha, ha, ha." And every time it gets quiet: "Hey, play a polka — ha, ha, ha." I really didn't think ahead on it.

Among the pieces demonstrated on your instructional video is Bach's "Prelude In C." Why didn't you put it on the album?

I didn't know it back then. That's something I worked out later. It's really interesting to play because there are many different places where you can do a lot of different fingerings. I was trying to always keep the bottom string ringing. There are sections that I could have fingered in an easier way, but I wanted to make it sound smooth. I'll probably put it onto the next record as a segue into another piece I've written.

You did a lot of right-hand slides on "Flow My Tears."

Yeah. That's just laying down a root, 5th, and 9th of an *Em* chord with the left hand and then sliding my right hand for *Em* and C triads. I really like that piece. Joe sounds just beautiful on it; it's really special to me. The middle part of that piece is ridiculously hard to play. I do the triplets on the *E* and *A* string with the 1st finger of my right hand and the 1st and 4th fingers of my left hand, and with my right-hand pinky I play the melody notes on the *D* and *G* strings. It's quite a stretch.

With such intense hammering and stretching, have you ever developed tendinitis or suffered from stretched tendons?

Not really. On the road, with playing every day, my hands are looking pretty chewed up, but they're okay. It's really important to warm up. I do a set routine. Playing the Bach piece is a good warm-up. You can't just pick up the bass and go. I get to do stretching exercises during the soundcheck. Playing a lot, especially doing double shows, my hands are getting really strong, and I've even been able to raise the action on my bass a little bit. When I'm off the road, I lower the action.

When you first began fretting with the right hand, did you have to lower the action drastically?

Way down, but those Kubicki Factors are great. The necks are laminated maple, so they are very stiff and steady. I don't lower the action to the point of excessive fret buzz, but it's low enough so that you just have to put your fingers on the fretboard; you don't have to push them way down. It certainly helps. I use medium-scale GHS Boomers strings gauged .045 to .105. I'm thinking of putting heavier ones on my red Kubicki and using it more for the rock stuff, but keeping the .045 to .105 set on my blue one with a black front for the tapping stuff. I use heavier strings on my yellow fretless, too. I play the melody to "Simple Dreams" [*Radio Free Albemuth*] on the fretless. I do a lot of sliding on it; it has a beautiful action.

Do you use the Kubicki's extension, which lets you flip a switch to get a low D and D# on the low E string?

Oh, yeah. I use it on Joe's "Surfing With The Alien" and sometimes in the solo. It lets you compete with the 5-string players. Of course, with my old Fender Jazz Bass I used to tune the *E* down to a *D*, but to play octaves I had to think in terms of fingering like a minor seventh. On the Kubicki, the harmonics change, but otherwise everything else stays the same up and down the neck. It's like a classical extension on the upright bass.

Did you ever play string bass?

I did when I was with the jazz band in Champaign. When I moved to Vermont, they didn't have one for me. It's really a whole different instrument, like 5-string. If I could only learn to play 4-string, maybe I'd think about switching to 5-string [*laughs*]. Four's quite enough, thank you.

Have you ever taught bass?

Yeah. I have some students, and sometimes when Jeff Berlin's on the road, I do some teaching at B.I.T.

It can get kind of frustrating sometimes. I like teaching someone who wants to really learn to play, but if they're just taking their parents' money and trying to steal my licks during a half-hour, it's not the most rewarding experience. You learn a lot about your own technique through teaching.

How much does slapping and popping enter into your technique?

A lot. I've been doing it since I was 18. I keep coming up with new ways to do it, like adding triplet raking and stuff. I really try to put things into the context of a song. You know, some bass players, when it's time for them to solo, just let fly with five minutes of fast funk stuff in *E*, which is cool. But I much prefer to work it into something more compositional, such as "Foggy Mountain Breakdown." It's a lot of slapping and popping, but it's more than just a bunch of fast licks in *E*. I'm a big one for thumb. You know how a lot of players use a pick to get eighth- or sixteenth-notes? I do it with my thumb. You get a brighter ring with the fingers, and it's a part of my sound. And if I want to rock out, I use my thumb. I even use my whole hand sometimes.

"I've never wanted to be thought of as a lead bass player, because as long as I'm grooving, I'm happy to stay down in first position."

Because you use such a broad range of hand dynamics, do you find it necessary to use a compressor?

No, but my amp has a bit of a limiter in it — although I try to stay away from that. So much of your tone comes from your hands, and I want to keep as much control over that as possible. Obviously, you sometimes have to get a little limiter in there.

What's your main onstage setup?

I use a Fender Dual Bass 400 amp, plus an Energy B-215 cabinet. It sounds great. I change my strings before every set, and I crank the treble on the bass all the way up, so I get the distinction and brightness from all the strings. And the Energy cabinet gives me the low-end kick that lets me know, "Yes, I'm still the bass player, not a frustrated lead guitarist."

Do you use any effects?

Absolutely none. I worked to develop a sound, and I like the purity of the tone. When you plug in a chorus, for example, you get too much top end and lose your sound. I did some gigs with a keyboard player, like opening up for Jeff Berlin, doing mostly a classical repertoire, and I mostly let the guy at the board add a little reverb, like on "Moonlight

Sonata." But in general, I like the straight sound.

When you record, do you go direct?

Yeah. I usually get a real good sound direct. When I did my record, I plugged in direct and miked my amps. I can never get the exact sound I get live just by miking the amp in the studio. So I ended up going direct and putting in a little bit of the amplified sound. Usually, when I do sessions I go straight into the board, using a direct box.

Your song "Sexually Active" sounds like a cross between Allan Holdsworth and Nile Rodgers.

Actually I was thinking Miles Davis when I wrote the melody. He's always been one of my favorites. One of my big dreams was always to play with Miles Davis, and the other was to play on a Steely Dan or Donald Fagen album.

Do you find that as a bassist it's harder to communicate your song ideas to a band than if you were, say, a keyboardist?

Actually I played some keyboards on the album, and I have a 4-track recorder and I work with some of the other guys. It's funny. Most of the time, everyone else tells the bassist what to play, and with my own material I get to tell them what to play. It's great having Allan Holdsworth and Joe Satriani playing on an album. I sometimes wake up and say, "Allan Holdsworth is on my album." I mean, I grew up idolizing him.

Had you worked with Allan before he laid down guitar tracks for your album?

Well, I auditioned for his band — one of the worst auditions of my life. I had learned all of the songs from his *Road Games* album, but then Gary Husband flew into town that day, and Allan said, "Let's play stuff from the first record." I said I didn't know anything off that album, so Allan started writing down chords for me, like $Dm7\flat5add9$ and $E\flat13sus\flat6$ [*laughs*], and then he said, "Let's go." So Allan's flying all over and the drums are doing everything but keeping time, and meanwhile I'm saying, "$E\flat$, two, three, four; D, two, three, four." It was a nightmare.

Have you listened back to your album since it was released?

Twice. It's so hard to listen to your stuff, because you're so critical. I can't even look at my videotape. Hearing yourself play is one thing, but when you see yourself, you go, "Oh, no!" Anything even close to a mistake seems to get bigger and bigger. I can't wait to do my next album. I hope by playing with Joe that some of his audience will go out and buy my record, and then they'll be exposed to Beethoven and Debussy — encourage them to broaden their musical horizons. It's sure fun to play in Joe's band, with all the rock energy. I like that I get to do some of my solo material with him, but even with all the tapping and stuff, I still function as a bass player, laying down the root and grooving. I've never wanted to be thought of as a lead bass player, because as long as I'm grooving, I'm happy to stay down in first position. I try to tell that to some kids who come to learn only chops. And I say, "Hey, man, go listen to what Marcus Miller does." You're the bass player, the foundation that's holding everything together.

Is there anything you'd like to do to improve your playing or your music?

I'd like to be locked up in a room for about two years with some equipment and not hear anyone else's music, so that I could work on something really original. Obviously, when you're young, you have to go through learning all of Stanley Clarke's licks, as much Jaco as you can figure out, and so on. But then you reach a point where it has to come from within yourself. I haven't seen Billy Sheehan play live, and I refuse to see Stanley Jordan, because I'll start comparing how they approach everything in relation to how I do it. I don't know if what I'm doing is unique, but at least it's original.

– JIMMY JOHNSON –

BY TOM MULHERN – MAY 1989

THOSE WHO FEEL that the 5-string bass, with its gut-shaking low *B* string, is a new phenomenon probably haven't been following Jimmy Johnson's career. He's been rattling ribs with his 5-string since 1976, onstage and on record with the likes of Flim & The BB's, Allan Holdsworth, and the Wayne Johnson Trio. Make no mistake: That fifth string alone isn't what makes Jimmy Johnson (sometimes called Flim) such a standout musician. His deftness, un-canny sense of melody, clever lines, and rock-solid crafts-manship keep him in de-mand. He was the house bassist for the short-lived *Late Show* on the Fox net-work, and since the dawn of the '80s he has been a busy Los Angeles studio bassist, doing jingles, TV and movie sessions, and record dates with the Rippingtons, Steve Hunter, Lee Ritenour, and Albert Lee.

It's no surprise that the 32-year-old Minneapolis native is so musical: His mother is a piano teacher and an accompanist, and his dad is an orchestral string bassist and piano technician. (On the Flim & The BB's *Neon* album, Jimmy and his dad, Cliff, played togeth-er on "Fathers And Sons.") After piano lessons in his youth, he studied clarinet all the way through high school. At 11, Jimmy took over on electric bass in his brother Gordon's band. (Today Gordon plays bass with fluegelhorn player Chuck Mangione.)

Bass became a big part of Jimmy's life, and after high school he started doing jingle work in Minneapolis. There he worked in the studios with keyboardist Billy

Barber, saxophonist Dick Oatts, and drummer Bill Berg, and in 1978 they formed a jazz ensemble and recorded *Flim & The BB's*. Tracked on a prototype 3M machine, it was one of the first digitally recorded albums. It was also the ad hoc band's first of six digital projects with engineer Tom Jung, who, in 1982, coaxed the musicians — then scattered to the East and West Coasts — to record for his fledgling compact- disc-only Digital Music Products label. Their first CD, *TriCycle*, was released in 1984, and their fol-low-up *Tunnel* was named Best Jazz CD of 1986 by *Digital Audio* magazine. (Three BB's CDs — *TriCycle*, *Tunnel*, and *Big Notes* — were in the *Digital Audio* Top Ten that year.) Subsequent BB's al-bums, *Neon* and *The Further Adventures Of Flim & The BB's*, have featured equally fine musicianship.

But Flim & The BB's has always been only a small part of Jimmy Johnson's career. In 1978 he moved to Los Angeles, started doing session work, and linked up with another Minneapolis expatriate, guitarist Wayne Johnson. With Bill Berg on drums, they formed the Wayne Johnson Trio. Like *Flim & The BB's,* their 1980 debut album, *Arrowhead*, show-cased Jimmy's formidable bass work. And since 1985's *Metal Fatigue*, he has been the main bassist for Allan Holdsworth. Meanwhile, Jimmy is busy in L.A.'s studios, working on a new project with Flim & The BB's. Recently, he appeared on the Wayne Johnson Trio's *Spirit Of The Dancer*.

You were among the first 5-string bassists.

Yeah. I got my first one in '76 — unfortunately, it was stolen out of Allan Holdsworth's truck a year and a half ago. Anyway, the idea came from my dad, because all the orchestral basses have extensions that let you go down to low C. They have a machine just for that, and I started talking to my dad about how I could do this on electric bass. He said that they make 5-string upright basses, too, which he might have been playing at the time; at least, he's changed over now with a low *B* string. I decided that would be simpler than having an extension, so I got in touch with Alembic, who was making 5-string basses, but with the high string on top, rather than the low one. Nobody had asked for a low *B*. I got in touch with GHS and asked for their largest gauge; it was basically a huge *E* string — a .120. I'm using .125 now. Some guys use really huge ones, like a .140.

Was it difficult to adjust to the fifth string?

It was kind of a shift. There is an adjustment time, but it's not as bad as you think. It takes a little while because you'll be looking one way and trying to play low *G*, and it's wrong because you plucked the wrong string.

Are your strings spaced like a standard 4-string's?

It's narrower for the right hand. It's pretty close on the Alembics, and I like it that way. It seems that the East Coast bass makers are building them really wide. It might be better to have more space down there if you're into popping.

Have you ever ventured into 6-string bass?

No. I don't think I'm going to get into it. It seems like this 24th-fret *G* on my Alembic is as high as I need to go. If I want to go higher, I play harmonics.

From Metal Fatigue *through* Atavachron *and* Sand, *Allan Holdsworth's music has grown increasingly complex. How has this evolution affected you?*

It's always been a pretty free situation. Actually, that's an interesting view; I hadn't thought about it. I know that his stuff keeps changing, but I don't consider myself to be any kind of influence on where he's going. I was just hanging on, holding onto the railing. He's got amazing talent; I can't believe it when he just keeps coming up with new things. It's a lot of fun, and it's a real ear stretcher, too.

On Metal Fatigue, *"In The Mystery" has an unusual, almost funk-like feel. How did you approach it?*

Next to the singer, I was the last to put a part on it. It was basically a machine track that Allan had done on a computer. There was already a synth bass track on it. And I just came in and tried one, and came up with all that overplaying that I did. Oops. [*Laughs.*] Well, you know, sometimes it's fun because

machines keep the time, leaving a lot of space. It was really different for Allan. Usually, there's a drummer wailing on the track, but "In The Mystery" had so much room in it that I just played like crazy.

Do you often work with sequencers on other jobs?

On occasion. A lot of record things start with sequencers. Occasionally, I get to play along with a synth bass part, and I actually enjoy it. It's fun. You have to pick and choose, and play a part that works. Sometimes the synth bass parts can be really busy and very effective; then I can't play all those notes and have my part make sense. So I pick some parts in it, and it ends up being kind of a two-bass part.

To construct a part, do you think very much in terms of the chordal structure or a strict melody?

I try to think "bass" first, and then kind of embellish it. That seems to be my thing: Sign my name here and there, but basically try to play the foundation — and hopefully be within the harmonic structure if I'm lucky [*laughs*].

How well do you get along with click tracks?

Oh, fine. It depends on the drummer, though. If anything, I think I'm often ahead of the beat. I tend to get kind of excited and take off, but there's nothing wrong with a click. It's good practice. If you have a drum machine, you can set up a pattern and play along with it and try different tempos. Sometimes you get into a situation where you're trying to get a groove to work with the click, and it's like it wasn't meant to be. Sometimes it's too hard to make it groove at a particular tempo, for some reason, and if you push it up a couple notches one way or the other, it makes a big difference. But I have no objections to it. There are some drummers who just make the click disappear completely. You just hear the *time*. Like Carlos Vega — he can make any tempo groove, and it just feels great. There's no problem at all. Other guys, the click drags on them, or you have to catch up to it.

It's a lot like practicing with a metronome.

Well, if you do that, then you're better prepared to work with a click when the time comes. My whole practice thing was to play along with records, and that's good time practice, too. I mean, that's like a glorified metronome. At least you get to play with somebody. It's good to practice with someone or with time. You can practice technique all day long, but when you get with a band, all of a sudden you realize that you can't groove at all. It's good to have something to refer to.

On Atavachron's *"The Dominant Plague," you play an ostinato that keeps the time, but it's always* *changing.*

I don't remember how much input I had into that. On some tunes, such as "Looking Glass," Allan has this progression of chords, but he's not really specific about the bass notes, and you sit down with him and work it out, because four or five different bass notes can all work under certain chords. By working it out different ways, I sort of get to write a bass part.

You also do a short solo in "Metal Fatigue."

I was just being silly there. I have these moments where I go, "Oh, maybe I'll try this." And if I don't derail it too badly, it stays.

You play many quick lines, but you don't do very much slapping and popping.

I challenge you to find *any*, actually. I'm not really into it. I never pursued that approach, and I don't know why. I have a lot of respect for the guys who can really wail on it, because it's cool. I've been lucky in the regard that here in L.A. the people who call me generally know that I don't do that. They call the guys who play a lot of it.

So, is your approach primarily based on two-finger plucking?

No, I use three. On the 5-string, I put my thumb between the two bottom strings, and I can hold all of the strings quiet with my hand. Then, when I start moving around, the thumb moves from between the strings and the whole thing shifts down. I don't think about it very much. I think the approach comes mostly from holding everything quiet. I can play the A, D, and G strings with those three fingers just the way they're positioned.

Do you ever long to be in just one band?

No. I like the variation. It's kind of scary if you're in just one band. I've always done different things, so I guess that's the way I like it.

But you have done a few tours with Allan.

Yeah. Well, I check in now and then, but I go. It's worth it to go out and play that music. I tell you, it's one of those bands that you're proud to be in. I know the music isn't for everybody, but I'm sure glad to be involved in it.

With the BB's, who do you cue off of most of the time?

I never really have to think about it. The parts just come. I think that applies to everybody in the band, because we've been playing together for so long, even though we don't get together very often. We kind of know what the others are going to do. We write a lot

as a group, too. Billy Barber has a good sense of melody and groove, and he's got a good, round sense of everything. Then Bill Berg and I try to get some grouping going, and if there's a spot that needs a melody, I volunteer. It just *happens* — I can't explain it very well.

You used a lot of harmonics in "Rokeby Garden" [The Further Adventures Of Flim & The BB's]. Did you ever go through a period of heavy practice to perfect them?

Well, Jaco Pastorius had everybody's ears several years ago. He had a great influence. I had to figure out what he was doing, what his harmonics were. That was a revelation. Then the idea was to not use them, because he had done them. On the BB's stuff, I do the harmonics mostly to extend the fingerboard a little bit. I guess I'm contradicting what I said about 6-string basses. If I play a melody that goes above G, I play it with fingered harmonics. For instance, I fret the D and then find the halfway point between that and the bridge, and finger the harmonic with my right-hand thumb while I pluck with my right hand. You can play melodies like that if your thumb follows the midpoint between the fretted note and the bridge.

What's your basic equipment setup?

I've got two Alembic basses, both 5-string Series II models. The fretless has a graphite neck. It's kind of an oddball that I got in '80. I use GHS Boomers, gauged .045, .065, .085, .105, and .125. I have two different amp rigs. I have a small one for clubs and rehearsals, with a Walter Woods head and two 12" Electro-Voice speakers in Thiele cabinets. Really handy. For playing bigger places, I have an overkill rig that I put together about a year and a half ago. It's essentially part of a P.A. system: It's Meyers Sound Labs speakers — one subwoofer cabinet with two 15s, plus two of their UPA-1As, which each have a biamped 12" and a horn. So, it's a full-range rig. I power it with a Yamaha power amp. I have an ADA Stereo Tapped Delay that I use for chorusing, just on the bridge pickup. I run this rig in stereo. I also have a Simon Systems rackmount unit with four direct boxes. I use that as buffer amps for the active crossovers and for the direct out to the P.A. It sounds a little more complicated than it is, but essentially it's a stereo triamped rig.

Do you use any echoes or other processors?

No. When I do studio calls, I just bring my direct

> *"I try to play the foundation — and hopefully be within the harmonic structure if I'm lucky."*

box and my bass, because if they want to put an effect on the bass, they have a better one at the studio than I do. I mean, it's not like the guitar players, who have to deal with the switching in and out with their stuff. They either want an effect on the bass or they don't.

Besides "Panic Station," are there other examples of your double-tracking?

Yeah. I also did two bass parts on "Walk In The Country," on Wayne Johnson's *Spirit Of The Dancer.* I overdubbed the top part to keep that accompaniment going. I should clear something up: On the BB's record *Neon*, there's a song called "Fish Magic." The liner notes said that we never overdubbed or remixed. But that part would be impossible if I hadn't done two bass parts on it. I have guys call me out of the blue and ask me about it. I had to do two passes. I'm not *that* good.

Because you often play complex, intricate lines, do you do any exercises to keep your hands under control?

Nothing specific. I practice a little bit, but not as much as I should or as much as I used to. There was a phase where I practiced a lot — everybody goes through that. My technique is all pretty illegit — I don't actually even know positions. So, it's all just fingering. Something that I learned from clarinet, believe it or not, was that you should lift your fingers up only as far as you need to, in order to get the sound to come out of the hole, so you're not flailing around. The further you have to move, the slower you go. So I don't move too much. My right hand looks pretty sleepy, and the left hand, hopefully, kind of stays on the fingerboard.

When you do a jingle, are bass parts written out for you, or do you face chord charts?

It varies from writer to writer. There's almost always something weird about it. Like, there will be a seven-bar phrase or an odd bar or tempo somewhere because they're trying to match it up to video. Lots of times, it's really strange to read, and it's kind of a challenge to try to make music out of it. You're trying to catch a camera cut, and all of a sudden, out of the blue, on the "and" of three, there's a big *pop.* I

kind of get a kick out of it. Those guys I work for know they're not curing cancer, so they don't treat it like the ultimate art or anything. We just go in and get the job done and have a good time.

Do you ever get tied up for several days on one project?

Well, a recent Lee Ritenour project lasted for five days. That's always fun because then you get to dig in. That's quite a contrast from jingles. You get to hone your parts, punch things in, and fix them. You have the time to work on it and get it to where you feel it's the best you can do. I like that, too.

Doing all these sessions must keep your sight-reading pretty sharp.

For records, reading generally isn't a big problem. You're into the project and you get maybe a chord chart, and you know unless they have a really specific thing in mind, it will be pretty open. At least, that's been my experience. Some of the TV film stuff might be the trickiest sight-reading. For jingles, it's usually a short piece, and you get to decode it. When you're doing a film call with a big orchestra, the stuff is flying by; you get to maybe run it by once, and then you've got to record it.

Don't feel any pressure, right?

Oh, man! I did one of these Disney things that was almost like cartoon music, a real fast two-beat thing. Man, I was on the edge of my seat. So that might be the hardest. They say that cartoon music is actually the hardest to play.

With all the work you do, is there ever a time when you feel as if you can't come up with anything?

Sure. I have big doubts sometimes. There are tracks where I think it's just not happening at all. But those kinds of thoughts are usually more internal than external. I can have what I think is a really awful day, and listen to it a week later and say, "Well, I wasn't *that* awful." So, you've got to have some faith that something's happening, even if it doesn't seem like it. I definitely have bad days. Sometimes I feel like I'm having good luck. It's like, "Oh, gosh. I hope they don't find out that I really can't do this." You know what I mean.

– PERCY JONES –

By Tom Mulhern – August 1980

SEEING BRAND X'S 32-year-old bassist Percy Jones in action, you can only wonder where he gets his stamina. Perhaps his 17 years of bass playing has toned his muscles. He rips through fast-paced ostinatos, twisted melodies, and rapid successions of harmonics almost effortlessly, yet with obvious concentration. Besides acting as Brand X's source for low-frequency tones and rhythms, Jones creates virtuosic solo lines from series of harmonics and natural tones on his fretless electric bass.

From the time he started on the bass 17 years ago, Percy, a native of Llandrindod Wells, Wales, has been self-taught. Born December 3, 1947, in the central Welsh town, Jones was given a few basic lessons by his mother on the family piano; his father wasn't musically inclined, so other than the bits of musical guidance he received from his mother, he was without tutelage.

Percy's first bass was a Vox Clubman solidbody which he characterizes simply as *cheap.* "It cost about £10," he says, "and it had plastic machine heads that used to break off. I later got a Gretsch bass, a wide-necked hollowbody with a spike that came out of the end so that it could be played upright. I put Fender Precision pickups in it, and kept it until 1974."

In 1966, Jones left Wales to study electronics at the University of Liverpool. And although he had played in pickup bands in his teens, it was there that he started to develop a serious interest in music. From 1968 to 1971 he worked with a band called the Liverpool Scene. With them he wrote poetry and music, but he says, "The stuff was pretty bad. Nevertheless, it was an interesting phase to go through, and I learned a lot. We played mostly rock, and I became frustrated because I was actually more interested in jazz. I was really into Charles Mingus' bass music."

In fact, much of what Percy learned on bass was derived from hours of listening to jazz records and picking up techniques from acoustic bassists. During his early development in bands he found few electric bassists that he liked well enough to emulate; in fact, it wasn't until the mid '70s that the status of the electric bass was sufficiently elevated so that Percy became interested in its exponents. For a short time he even played string bass: "I bought an old Czechoslovakian model with a big crack in it. I had it fixed and had a new bridge nut put on, and then I practiced quite a bit. I never got very proficient on it; I never really grasped the bowing."

When the Liverpool Scene broke up in 1971, Percy abandoned music and spent about 18 months working a construction job in South London. After his hiatus, he returned to playing bass, wading into studio work and doing sessions with singer Roy Harper, Nova (an Italian jazz-rock band), and synthesist Brian Eno. The association with Eno produced three albums (*Before And After Science, Another Green World,* and *Music For Films*), and with Nova he recorded *Vimana.* Jones later toured Europe for six weeks with Soft Machine as an interim member.

In 1974 Percy bought a fretless Fender Precision bass, which he used until mid 1978. He originally installed Rotosound flatwound strings on it, but after two years he switched over to Rotosound roundwounds; he felt that they offered greater harmonic response, especially in the upper ranges.

Living near Jones in South London was keyboardist Robin Lumley, who told Percy that he had been sitting in with a rehearsal band — the germinal Brand X. He asked the bassist if he would like to come along and jam. Jones spent about three evenings with Lumley and [guitarist] John Goodsall, and the following week they were all called for an audition at Island Records. Brand X got the contract, but weren't satisfied with their first recording, and it was never released. However, their move to Charisma and their release of *Unorthodox Behaviour* firmly established them as a serious band.

Jones' techniques with Brand X are varied, but all come from his years of experimentation with intricate styles. He plucks the strings with his fingers, rather than using a pick. Says Percy, "I've always played this way. I never really liked the sound of a plectrum used with a bass. It sounds good with certain types of music, but I don't think that it suits the sort of material we do."

One of the more prominent features of Jones' style is his use of artificial harmonics in melodic contexts (e.g., his solo on "Not Good Enough — See Me!" from *Product*). To execute them, Percy frets a note with his left hand and then plucks the string with his index finger, while lightly touching his right-hand thumb to the string between his right-hand index finger and left hand. In order to vary his harmonics, he changes his right hand's proximity to the bridge, and to further augment them, Percy sometimes slides up or down the strings with his left hand after striking a note. Another common technique in Jones' work is sliding the left hand after striking a natural tone or a double-stop.

Percy's equipment contributes as much to his overall sound as does his unique playing style. The heart of his system is a custom-made fretless Wal JG Custom bass; in fact, he has two nearly identical axes (one has a leather pickguard). "Actually," Jones adds, "that was the first one that Ian Waller made for me. It was a prototype built for [bassist] John Gustavson. I think he wanted a fretless with markers in the fingerboard, and this one didn't have any. So Wal built him another and I took the original one."

The pickups on Percy's basses are made by Wal, and each has a small switch for selecting series or parallel wiring of the coils. There is a standard pickup selector, separate volume and tone controls for each pickup, and a master volume control. An active bandpass filter with its center frequency at 3,000 Hz can also be switched into the circuit for more punch. On the side of the bass are dual outputs: One is an unbalanced $\frac{1}{4}$-inch plug wired for low impedance, while the other is a balanced low-impedance 3-conductor XLR jack for plugging the bass directly into recording consoles. Ground-lift switches are located next to each jack; these enable Percy to eliminate ground loops caused by using either both outputs or a direct box (he uses the unbalanced output via the direct box when recording, as well as onstage). Carbon fiber strips and a truss rod are located under the rosewood fingerboards; Schaller tuning machines (the only parts of the hardware not made by Wal) and huge brass bridges further enhance the instruments.

Percy has only found one audible difference between his two Wal basses: "They're almost identical, yet one sounds better to me," he says. "I couldn't figure out *why*, but it turned out that the nut on the first one is fractionally lower. This gives more of a growl — more like a stand-up bass. The string vibrates against the fingerboard just a bit, and creates the sound I happen to like."

On both of his basses, Jones uses Superwound strings. In fact, before he obtained his Wals, he used SuperWounds on his Precision. Percy says, "I like them a lot — they sustain very well. It's interesting that the core of the string goes over the bridge, although none of the windings do. This caused problems when I first tried them on the Precision, because after only a few hours' use they'd break. I was a bit disconcerted and called up the manufacturer and asked what was happening. They couldn't understand it. We found out that my Badass bridge on the Precision was allowing the strings to move back and forth on the saddles, literally sawing through the cores. The solution was to saw a narrow groove — the width of the core wire — in each saddle to keep the string in position. I have the bridges on the Wals similarly prepared."

Aside from the initial problem with core breakage, Jones has experienced no other difficulties with the SuperWounds. He advises bassists that these strings have a very lively, bright sound: "You've got to watch out; they can sound very clanky. When I first switched from flatwounds to roundwounds I experienced a similar difference. Also, they're much less stiff, and have far more accurate intonation as you travel up the neck."

Also contributing to Jones' onstage sound is a dbx 160 Compressor/Limiter (which keeps his signal level even, whether he is playing natural tones or harmonics), an MXR Digital Delay, and a special flanging unit that he designed and built. Putting his electronics knowledge to use in creating an unusual and very subtle effect, Percy made an amplitude- and frequency-sensitive flanger. The amount of flanging effect can be regulated by which notes he hits (high- or low-frequency range) and how hard he hits them. Between his bass guitar and effects devices is a Countryman Type 85 Direct Box that matches the instrument's impedance to the effects.

"If you have to play by ear, the parts sink into your brain quicker."

On past tours Percy has used an Ampeg SVT amp with two cabinets, each housing eight 12" speakers. His current amp is a new British make called Front, which Percy says gives him a cleaner sound because of its solid-state circuitry and specialized speaker complement: One cabinet has two 15s in a horn-loaded arrangement, and the other has four 12s in a standard configuration.

In communicating his musical ideas to the other members of Brand X, Jones either plays lines on his bass or explains what he is trying to achieve; he says that because his facilities in reading music aren't very developed, writing out parts for each player would be far too time-consuming. And sometimes he uses a cassette to tape rough drafts of songs. Another method involves keyboardist Pete Robinson; Percy plays the part, and Pete writes down the notes. "I did some recording for [percussionist] Morris Pert a while back," Jones says, "and he gave me a tape of the material so that I could listen to the songs and learn parts for them. I learn quickly by ear, and therefore it's the way I prefer to learn songs."

Percy Jones acknowledges the value of being able to play from written music, but also defends playing by ear: "I think that in rehearsal situations especially, it's sometimes quicker if you are able to read. Both Morris and Pete are excellent sight-readers — just stick the parts in front of them, and they can play through them immediately. But on the other hand, if you have to play by ear, the parts sink into your brain quicker. So, while reading has definitely got its advantages, it has — maybe in subtle ways — disadvantages, too. Taking all that into account, I believe it's good to have a balance between the two abilities. If you've got a good grasp of both approaches, you've got it made."

– GEDDY LEE –

BY TOM MULHERN – JUNE 1980

PAUL NATKIN / PHOTO RESERVE INC.

SINCE THE AUTUMN of 1968, Toronto's premier power trio, Rush, has been tirelessly slugging its way up the rock ladder, playing quick, complex, and loud material that embraces both progressive and traditional rock styles. The members' persistence has paid off: They are one of today's most popular groups, and their most recent album, *Permanent Waves*, has hovered in the Top 20 almost since its release this spring.

Perhaps the most prominent member of Rush is the 26-year-old son of Polish immigrants, Geddy Lee, the hard-hitting bassist, synthesist, and lead vocalist who's well known for his peripatetic stage movements — it's dazzling to see so much sheer energy expended without a nervous breakdown. Riffing away almost constantly on his black Rickenbacker 4001 bass, Geddy sets forth low-frequency melodies while loosing his piercing vocals. Additional harmonic work on his Taurus bass pedals further creates the image of a one-man rhythm section which complements Alex Lifeson's nimble guitar work and Neil Peart's intricate drumming. Nevertheless, Geddy's self-taught style goes beyond merely supplying the pulse for the band — it is an indispensable factor in Rush's melodic lifeblood.

When did you start getting interested in music?

When I was about 14. I always took music in school; I tried various instruments — drums, trumpet, and clarinet — all for really short periods of time,

though. Learning an instrument in school didn't really turn me on, so I took piano on my own when I was very young — rudimentary stuff. It wasn't until I was out of grammar school and listening to rock music that I became interested enough to seriously learn to play.

Was there any particular band's music that inspired you?

Yeah, Cream was actually the first band that really got me interested. From then on, I listened to people like the Who and Jeff Beck. I was mainly interested in early British progressive rock.

Did you start out on bass?

No, I began with guitar, although I didn't play it very long. I was about 14 then, and I got my first acoustic guitar, a beautiful acoustic that had palm trees painted on it. Other than that, I have no idea what kind it was. I got a bass about six months after that, a Conora, which was just a big solidbody with two pickups. It had a real big neck — sort of like a Kent. I had a little amp, too, but I can't even remember what kind it was. We used to borrow and rent amps — Ace amps, Silvertone amps — whenever we needed them. The first *real* amp that I got was a Traynor with two 15s; I was almost 16 then. It was just before I joined Rush, actually.

Did you play along with records?

Yeah. That's how I learned to play bass — emulating Jack Bruce and people like that. I was always trying to learn riffs to all their songs.

Did you use a pick or your fingers?

I never used a pick. In fact, I can't even play guitar

very well with a pick. It's all right for rhythm, but when I write songs, I always just fingerpick. I find a pick very awkward for some reason.

Were you playing in bands or just jamming?

We had little bands floating around, but we didn't actually play gigs, except maybe occasional talent shows at school.

How did you come to join Rush?

I knew Alex from school. We were pretty good friends, and we had always wanted to play together, but we never had the opportunity. He used to call me all the time to borrow my amp, though, because in those days, an amp was hard to come by. He would say, "How are you doing?" and I'd say, "Oh, not bad." Then he'd say, "Oh, by the way, can I borrow your amp this weekend? We've got a gig." I used to loan him my amp all the time. Well, I received a call from him about two weeks after he started Rush with our original drummer, John Rutsey. They had an excellent bass player, but he decided to quit the band at the last minute before a gig at a local coffeehouse. That was big stuff back then. So I got this panic call from Alex: "Do you want to come out and fill in for the gig?" I said, "Sure!" You know, in those days it was typical for a band to rehearse for four hours, get all the songs together, and just go out and do it. I did that one gig, and they asked me to stay in the band. We've been together now for about 12 years.

Once you were in Rush, did you keep the same equipment?

I had the same Traynor amp for years — in those days we couldn't afford very much. I changed basses, though. I got a new Hagstrom, which was a light solidbody shaped kind of like a Gibson SG. It was quite a step up from my Conora. It had a couple of slide switches and really weird-looking black pickups with silver dots. I liked that bass a lot because it had a thin neck, which made it easy to play really fast — and it had a really raunchy sound. I had that bass for quite a while.

Did Rush play in Toronto?

We played all over Ontario, actually. Originally, we played only at this one coffeehouse called the Coff-Inn; it was a local drop-in center in the basement of a church. We used to play there on Friday nights and make perhaps seven bucks each. Then we'd go wild afterwards — go to a restaurant and

buy some Cokes and chips. We thought it was great! Other than that, we didn't play many gigs. But then Ray Danniels — sort of a local street-type, hustling kind of a guy — said he wanted to manage us. He started booking us into Ontario high schools, and he's still our manager today.

How did you branch out into other jobs?

I just turned 18 when the law changed, lowering the drinking age from 21 to 18, so we could finally play bars. You see, rock bars were the real thing to get into. It was important for local musicians in Toronto to get into those clubs and be seen by more people, older people.

What kind of music were you doing?

We were doing half original and half copy material, mostly in a blues-rock vein. We used to have this running argument with our manager because we were always writing songs. And whether they were good or bad didn't matter to us; it was only important to write, just to get the experience. And just to get work, our manager would say, "Look, you can't just play originals, because people in these bars don't want to hear your original stuff." In those days, we were doing five sets a night, so we agreed to play a couple songs each set by somebody else. But we would pick known tunes by people like John Mayall and Cream.

When did you start playing music more akin to your present material?

It's funny — there was a sort of a crossover point, I guess around 1970 or '71, when we started going to other types of music, such as stuff by Procol Harum. And then Jeff Beck started getting heavier, and Led Zeppelin was happening. They really blew us away. We became real students of that heavy school of rock, for sure.

Didn't your reluctance to play Top-40 music make it difficult for you to get work?

Yeah. We once went through a summer with only three gigs because we couldn't get any work. We didn't want to play other kinds of music; we wanted to play mostly ours. And our manager said, "Well, you're just not going to get work." Another problem we had in bars was that we were too loud. We used to get a lot of hassles because it was important that the barmaids could hear the orders from the customers. And we'd get up there and play Led

> *"We were too loud for bars. We got hassled because it was important that the barmaids could hear the orders from the customers."*

Zeppelinish, screeching, loud music. The bar owners would get really upset, and fire us.

Was Rush just a three-piece group then?

On and off. We had an electric piano player for a while, in our bluesier times, but he left the band. Then we got a rhythm guitarist for a short period, and he also left. We always seemed to return to a trio format; it felt most comfortable.

What kind of bass were you using then?

By then I had a 1969 Fender Precision. In fact, before we started playing the bars I traded my Hagstrom for it. I used that Precision for years and years — I still have it.

What kind of strings did you use?

I was using LaBella flatwounds for a few years. Then, around 1972, there was a big turning point for my sound when I discovered Rotosound roundwounds. It was like, Wow — high end! And at the same time, I got interested in Sunn amplification; John Entwistle was using Sunns, and I really loved the sound that he used to get. So I got a 2000-S tube head and two cabinets with two 15s in each. I didn't care for the speakers that were originally included, so I eventually took those out and put SRO speakers in. My Sunn had much better transient response than my Traynor — it was really a live-sounding amp. I had it up until about two years ago.

Was the band becoming more popular?

Yeah. All of a sudden we had a following that would come out to every bar we played. Eventually, our manager started taking notice of the fact that we were attracting quite a following. They were trying to get record people interested in us, and time and time again they'd say, "Well, you can do a single or something." And it would always fall through. We'd really get our hopes up and say, "Hey, it's going to happen and get us out of the bars," and then we'd be disappointed. So around 1972 or '73 we were getting really frustrated because all these record companies were turning us down left and right. And our management was getting frustrated, too, because they started to really believe that the band couldn't make it. So they talked about forming their own record label — which they did in 1974. It was called Moon Records. And they fronted some money for us to go in and do an album, but we had to record under the worst of conditions.

Were you still playing in bars?

Yes. We'd start playing at 9:00 and finish playing at 1:00 in the morning; we played three or four sets a night. Afterwards, we'd take all our gear out of the bar and move it into an 8-track studio. We'd set up, and then record from 2:30 to 8:00 in the morning. In

addition, the producer didn't know what he was doing. It was just crazy.

Did any of you have a nervous breakdown?

Very close to it! Fortunately, we were really young. We were so fired up that it was finally happening that we didn't care what hours we had to work. It eventually turned out to be our first album, but it went through a lot of changes along the way. After we finally heard the original mixes, we went, "Wow! There's something wrong with this. It doesn't sound good." You know, it sounded really dinky and wimpy. And we were disappointed. So we figured that the guy in charge of the production just didn't know what he was doing. He was a good engineer, I guess, but he was no producer. So we were freaked out, and our managers were freaked out because we'd spent all this money and it didn't sound right. So one of our managers knew an engineer/producer named Terry Brown who'd come over from England; he had his own studio in Toronto. We took the tapes to him, and after listening to them, he couldn't believe how poorly recorded the stuff was. So we made a deal that we'd work 48 hours straight in this studio in an effort to fix up the tapes — that's all the money we could afford. So in that 48 hours, we redid three songs from top to bottom, and fixed up all the other tracks as best we could, and then remixed them. It made quite a difference — it's still a real raw-sounding album, but at least it has some balls to it.

Did you plug your Precision right into the mix board, or did you use an amp?

I tried both. At that time I didn't know anything about recording basses; I was still just learning about what kind of sound I wanted to have. Actually, for the first few albums, that was the basic *modus operandi* — just experiment and try to get a half-decent sound on tape.

Did you double-track any bass parts?

No. We mainly did that with guitars. Since we were a trio, we had a basic way of recording: Put the rhythm section down, get a meaty guitar sound, and double it. Then we'd stick the lead guitar and the vocal on. Sometimes we doubled the vocals, too. But other than that, it was all really simple, with no fancy production techniques, except an occasional repeating echo. That was as fancy as we could afford to get. And soon after, *Rush* was released in Canada, on Moon Records.

How did you happen to end up on Mercury Records?

Someone sent a copy of the Moon album to a radio station in Cleveland; they played it as an import, and found that they were getting tremendous response from listeners. We were all freaked out. So we started getting phone calls from record companies then. We got a real nice offer from Mercury, and signed with them. That was really the beginning of our professional phase. We officially became a *concert* band. We said good-bye to bars and started playing local Toronto concerts. Then we got on a tour of the United States, and that was our big chance. But at that time, we were having some problems with our original drummer, John Rutsey, who'd been with us for five years — in the bars and through all the other work. Just when we were getting our first big break, he was becoming disinterested, so we decided to go our separate ways. And we were sitting there a week before our first American tour without a drummer. We were going out of our minds. So we held auditions, and we listened to about six drummers; then Neil Peart walked in and blew us away with his playing. We said, "Okay, you're in; let's go." We rehearsed for a week, and *bing*, we were off to the States. We hardly even knew him, and we were off on our first tour, backing Uriah Heep. We were the first act of a three-act show, and we had exactly 26 minutes to play — it was a little tight.

Were you still using your Precision then?

No. When we got our first advance, the first thing I did was run out and buy a Rickenbacker 4001. I was a big fan of Chris Squire back then, and he was using one. He and John Entwistle, to me, had the most innovative bass sounds, although they were very different. I always admired that, so I figured if I wanted to try for the type of sound that Squire had, I'd have to get that kind of bass.

Did you still have your Sunn amp?

Yes. And I decided to go stereo onstage, so I bought an extra bass setup: two Ampeg V4B bottoms and an SVT head. For my low end, I would run the bass pickup through the Ampegs, and the treble went to the Sunn. I would always keep everything full up on my basses — I still do — and just crank up the treble on the amps. I have my low end directly fed into the P.A., while the speakers for my high end are miked.

Do you use any effects?

On the first tour I was still using just straight licks. Seeing as we only had a half-hour at the most to play onstage, I just wanted to get a good bass sound that I could set up quickly.

As the band's lead vocalist, do you find any prob-

"We opened for everybody! All we cared about was playing and touring."

lems trying to balance your concentration between singing and playing bass?

Well, I have always been a singer. I just happened to be the only one that could sing in every band I was in, even before Rush. In Rush, I became more adept at both singing and playing bass at the same time. And as our material became more complicated, it was naturally a little more difficult for me to get it together. But with practice, it all worked out. On our later albums, we'd start writing songs in the studio, and I'd put down the bass tracks; then I'd overdub the vocals afterwards. Then, when it would come time to rehearse, I'd realize, "Whoa! I've got to do both of these things at the same time." So in rehearsals, I would always stick to the very elementary playing whenever I was singing. But eventually it got to the point where I became very good at adapting. It all balanced out pretty well. I can sort of split my head and think different songs — and it works! It just takes a lot of rehearsing.

Did you record the second album, Fly By Night, *immediately after you completed the first tour?*

Yeah. We actually started writing material for that album while on tour. It was a real big step up from the first album: We had 16 tracks to record on, we'd already rehearsed the material, and we had a drummer who could really play. We were getting into some different areas of music, too, like different time signatures. It was a real breakthrough for us. And it was the first time we could really zone in on sounds and try to get good tones.

What basses did you use on Fly By Night?

I used the Rickenbacker on every track. On one song called "By-Tor And The Snow Dog," a fantasy tune that featured a character representing evil and a character representing good, I was given the role of By-Tor, the evil one. And I developed an interesting sound — there's a monster sound that sort of growls around during one really chaotic musical segment. I put my Fender bass through a fuzztone — I can't remember what kind — and then into the board. It was distorted all to shit, so we added phasing, and ultimately put in everything but the kitchen sink. I had all that sound going through a volume pedal, so every time the monster was supposed to growl, I would lean on the volume pedal. When we fit it into the song, it sounded like a real monster!

After you switched to roundwound strings, did you sometimes have problems with poor intonation?

Yeah. It happens even now. But at that point, the money wasn't really happening yet, so I would be doing stuff like boiling my strings to get them back into shape. Strings cost about 20 bucks or so, which was really expensive back then.

Were you still opening up for other bands on your second tour?

We backed up other people until about two years ago. So, we were constantly touring. We opened for Kiss, Aerosmith, Billy Preston — we opened for everybody! We didn't care; all we cared about was playing and touring. We were working real hard, and were away from home for months at a time, but success was coming very slowly. We just seemed to have a sound that would do great in concert but just didn't seem to have the right kind of push on a record. It just seemed so difficult to get ahead.

Did you ever consider disbanding?

We went through a period after we recorded our third album, *Caress Of Steel*, where our music wasn't well received at all. It was a pretty naive album in retrospect, but still it was a very important one, because it was the first time we actually had almost four weeks to record. And we did a lot of experimenting with sounds; I used a different bass sound for every song.

What basses did you use on that album?

I was just going back and forth with my Fender and my Rick, trying them with different combinations of direct feeding and miking the amp. That's when I discovered that the best way for me to record my bass was to approach it as if I were playing onstage: Use the direct bass from the low-end pickup, and mike the amp for the high-end pickup. I've just been refining that ever since.

And despite your efforts, the album was poorly received?

Right. And there was a time when we thought, "Well, maybe we should just hang it up and go home." I remember we were on an overnight drive to Atlanta, Georgia, and we were all real depressed, saying, "Oh, this is never going to work! What are we doing here?" We were still getting a lot of pressure from people to commercialize our sound. But we always felt that if your music is interesting, people will like it. It's a very simple philosophy. We didn't want to try to aim our music at a lowest common denominator. In fact, we felt compelled to do the opposite: Try to make the music more interesting. And therefore, if it's more interesting, then it will succeed.

So you thought your individuality would be the key to your success?

Yes. We were growing, and we were going through changes, becoming a little more complex. No matter how raw your music is in its original form, it seems only logical for musicians to want to make it better and more interesting. The more we played, the better we got at playing; and the better we got at playing, the better we wanted to become. And that was basically the only way that we figured it was worth having success. And so we sort of said, "Well, fuck everyone else! We don't care if they want to do this. We're just going to do what we want to do! So let's not pack it in; let's keep going." Just after that tour, we went in and we did our *2112* album, which was our first real success. And the whole theme of the album was based around individualism — it was sort of a passionate statement saying, "Leave us alone, we're okay, we will still get along."

Were any of the cuts on 2112 particularly difficult to play?

The whole *2112* suite — side one — was a real challenge for us. Parts of it were in odd time signatures, and were very up-tempo. And it was the first time we ever attempted to play for 20 minutes around one concept, without breaks. That was our first major epic. It was a challenge to play it properly every night, so it was real important for our development as musicians.

Do you think it was one of your most important albums?

Well, *2112* was the first album where we achieved something that we felt resembled a Rush sound; it was the first album that, while you could still hear our influences, you knew there was something else happening there — the beginnings of a sound that said, "This is us." With so many bands and so many styles of music happening, I guess all you really look for is that little, tiny space — no matter how small it is — so you can say, "Okay, this is us. This isn't anybody else." It might have been made up of a sum of all the knowledge that we accumulated from other people, but *2112* was the first time we sort of carved a little niche and said, "Okay, this is a Rush sound, so let's develop that." The next album we did was live, so we had 18 months to just play and get to know our instruments even more before we went in to do *A Farewell To Kings*. And when we did that, we brought some other instruments in the band, too. I started playing synthesizer, [Moog] Taurus bass pedals, and a double-neck Rickenbacker [4-string bass/12-string guitar].

Isn't it like a juggling act, playing all those instruments and singing?

It's really difficult to keep on top of it, and it was especially hard at first because it was a departure from what I'd always been doing. Playing bass and singing was just a matter of practice, and adding the bass pedals was much the same story. So I had to learn to carefully balance the things I was doing onstage. And some nights, things would go wrong until I got the hang of it. But it's been two years now since we started using all those other instruments, and it's quite natural. It's never *easy*, though, and I think that's what makes it so challenging: I can't just walk out onstage and float through the night. You can't be high, and you can't be too *anything*, because you have to know *exactly* where you are at all times. Aside from just the actual physical singing and playing, I now have to coordinate a whole bunch of changes, as far as changing guitars and so forth. I have to set up my Oberheim 8-voice synthesizer for the next song, which means that I have to switch this octave and change these oscillators . . . . So as soon as I finish one tune, I'm already thinking about the next one, and making changes for it. It's a constant chain of actions and reactions for me to perform and set myself up for the next song.

"Playing bass and singing was just a matter of practice, and adding the bass pedals was much the same story."

Did playing the keyboard give you much difficulty?

Well, it was sort of a revelation at that point, because for years I'd been thinking in terms of the fretboard, and all of a sudden I had to deal with a keyboard — all the notes are laid out differently. It was a real education, and my all-around musical sense really had a shot in the arm because I could listen to things and write from a different perspective. So, rather than just write a bass riff, I could think in terms of composing a melody. I'd go over to the synthesizer and work out a melody, transpose that to bass, and have a more interesting bass line to work with. And coordinating my bass work with a footpedal sound makes the rhythm section a whole lot more complete. So before the guitar even comes into the song, there's Neil and I, putting down the basic rhythm tracks. And there's all kinds of melody happening, creating sort of an ambience and a subterranean rhythm. It's almost like having another person sometimes. Then when Alex comes in, he can just lay his solo on top of whatever melodies and rhythms are already there; it gives him a much freer hand, especially since we're only a trio.

When you write songs, do you use primarily bass, or guitar?

I use guitar a lot for chordal and melodic things, but if I'm working on a riff to a song, then I will usually choose the bass. And sometimes now I use the keyboards. So it really depends on what I'm looking for. It feels more natural that I should pick up the bass because I'm obviously more adept at that instrument. If I'm having trouble getting an idea across to Alex, I'll grab my bass. When it comes to guitar, though, I'm just a basic rhythm player, so it takes me a longer time to convey the same idea. Nevertheless, guitar is very helpful for writing verses, choruses, and melodic things.

What instruments do you currently use in concert?

Just my Rickenbacker 4001 and two Rickenbacker double-necks. One has a 6-string guitar and a bass, and the other has a 12-string guitar and a bass. The doubleneck's bass has a really nice tone because of the larger body size. There's so much wood that it's got a better low-end response than the standard 4001. I really like Rickenbackers. But because of the wear and tear I put on them, they must constantly be refinished and rebuilt: I put a lot of miles on all of them.

What other basses do you have besides your 4001s?

I have a 4002, which has low-impedance pickups and a beautiful ebony fingerboard. It has Schaller tuning pegs on it, and I've had a Badass bridge installed. I sometimes use the 4002 in the studio. I also have a 3001, which has a single low-impedance pickup and a thick, heavy body. It's got a really meaty sound. I haven't found too much use for it in recording, and I don't use it live, but at home I use it a lot for writing and jamming.

Do you have any Gibson basses?

No, but I recently lucked out and found a '69 or '70 Fender Jazz Bass in a pawnshop for an unbelievably low price of $200. Some Jazz Basses have chunkier necks, but this one is thin and smooth. It was in beautiful shape, and I just love it. In fact, I used it on about half of *Permanent Waves*.

What kind of bass strings do you use now?

Rotosound Swing Bass, long-scale. I change them every four dates. This is usually as long as the tone lasts. This tour, I had a really weird problem, though. I hadn't broken a string in about two years, and on this tour I broke about six in just the first few weeks. After about three weeks, we found out why: the bridge was placed wrong. You see, I had Badass bridges put on all my basses, but they put one on about a half-inch closer to the neck than it should be. The strings were resting on the saddles in the wrong place, placing undue tension on the weaker part of them — the section of the strings with the red fiber covering. Besides causing my strings to break, this was cutting down on my sustain. So I had the bridge moved back to where it should be.

Do you wipe your strings between songs?

No. They're cleaned quite vigorously before each show, and that's enough. I think they use Finger-Ease on them. It takes all the grunge off, and keeps them nice and slippery. And although I usually wait until after four shows to change them, I'll replace them if they sound like they're getting a little too dull. Now, I don't change the strings on my 12-string as often, because I only use it on two songs a night, "Xanadu" and "Passage To Bangkok." They seem to retain their sound a lot longer than bass strings.

Do you have a pedalboard of bass effects?

No. I don't use any effects on my bass, except for a Boss Chorus on perhaps one song in the course of a concert. Sometimes the sound engineers will add a little bit of digital delay or Harmonizer in the mix, too.

Are you still using separate high-end and low-end amps for bass?

Yes, but now I have a whole different bass setup. I have two BGW 750 power amps — one for highs and one for lows. I also have two Ashly preamps. And I also have two new high-end cabinets that I believe are based on an Electro-Voice design. It's a pretty simple configuration — just two front-loaded 15s built into each cabinet, with a separation between the two speakers. For the low end, I still use two Ampeg V4B speaker cabinets. I split them up, though, so that I have a high/low setup on my side of the stage, and Alex has an identical setup on his side so that he can hear what I'm playing. I have one of his Hiwatt cabinets on my side so that I can hear him, too.

Do you generally pluck the strings close to the bridge?

I move around. I usually rest my hand towards the back, and place my fingers between the bridge and the treble pickup. Occasionally, I'll work up a bit more toward the neck, depending on what kind of sound I need. Also, I sometimes rest my hand on the E string and pick with my nails. I use them a lot, in

"In rock music, it's not necessary to know all the terms and theory, but it certainly doesn't hurt."

fact. My nails extend just over the ends of my fingers, so if I want a pick-like attack, I can get it with my nails, rather than having to use a pick.

When do you play harmonics?

It depends on the tune, but often when Alex is playing acoustic guitar. There's one song on the new album called "Different Strings" in which harmonics become quite an integral part of the piece. The bass part was very simple — a punctuating sort of rhythm — but in between the notes, I popped a couple harmonics on two strings at the 5th fret.

Are chords often employed in your bass playing?

I use a lot of double-stops: roots and thirds, and those kinds of things. Sometimes I use full chords to fill things out. Outside the band, I've been playing around with a piece of music by [guitarist] John Abercrombie called "Timeless" [from *Timeless*]. When you figure it out on bass, you find that it's full of interesting chords and intervals. I haven't been able to work that kind of playing into our music yet, but it's something I practice on my own, nonetheless.

Do you do any warm-ups or practice exercises before you go onstage?

It really depends on how I feel at the time. I got into a habit of working out a lot before we went onstage, but I found that because we do such a long show — over two hours — I sometimes started getting aches in my hands about three-quarters of the way through. All together, with my warm-ups and the show, I was actually playing for three-and-a-half hours. So now I don't warm up before the gig, except in the soundcheck, which only lasts about 45 minutes. Now I no longer cramp up, and my fingers are a lot fresher and I have more enthusiasm for the show.

Who are your favorite bassists today?

I really like Jeff Berlin — he's about my favorite right now. His playing on *Gradually Going Tornado* [by Bruford] blows me away. I listen to Jaco Pastorius, and Chris Squire is still a big thing for me. I also like Percy Jones, the bass player in Brand X. He's great.

Do you have any favorite jazz bassists?

No, not really. My introduction to jazz is strictly through rock. People like Jeff Berlin, Brand X, and Weather Report sort of dabble in rock and jazz, and fuse the two. It's an interesting way for me to get into jazz, and it's something I'd like to get into heavier. But my background is strictly rock, so the introduction has to come through rock.

Do you think lessons are a necessity?

I think they're very helpful. I mean, there are lots of things I wish I would have done in terms of learning the language of music. In rock music it's not necessary to know all the terms and theory, but it certainly doesn't hurt. Once again, it all boils down to the language of music. Once you know it, it's a lot easier to talk to another musician and sit down and say, "Let's do something together." Rather than picking up your bass to show what you mean, you could just sit there and explain it. So, it's a time-saving measure, and it's a communication form that I wish I would have learned at one point. It never hurts, but

obviously it's been proven time and time again that it's not necessary for everyone.

Can you suggest any shortcuts that might help a young bass player become successful in the rock field?

That's a difficult question that a lot of young musicians ask me. There's really no formula for success. Everyone's got to find their own speed and realize their abilities. I think that the important thing is to realize what you want to accomplish, set that goal for yourself, and just go for it any way you can. I don't believe that shortcuts are possible without a sacrifice of some of your musical integrity.

– PAUL MCCARTNEY –

By Tom Mulhern – July 1990

BOB GRUEN / STAR FILE INC.

DURING EACH two-and-a-half-hour show on Paul McCartney's first tour since 1976, his warmth and natural showmanship — a blend of personality, 25 years of hit songs, and musicianship — convert the sell-out arena crowd from an expectant but "show me" audience to a frenzied throng. That should inspire confidence in anyone. That's onstage.

But when it comes time to write and record a new song, there's always that uncertainty factor: After so many years of turning out a stream of catchy tunes and creating some of the most influential bass lines in pop music, is there still magic waiting to be brought forth? Every time he sits down to write, and every time he plugs in the bass, it's back to square one.

Yeah, he was a Beatle. Yeah, he's incredibly famous. And, yeah, he's likely more successful than any player in history. But above all else, he's a *musician*, and like any of his peers — famous or not — past accomplishments are no guarantee of future success.

Paul's had ups and downs, and to most people it would seem that being in the world's biggest band would be a virtually impossible act to follow. When the Beatles broke up, he could have walked away from the music business, and who would have blamed him? There's just one catch: This man *loves* music. At 48, he's leading his latest band with the enthusiasm characteristic of players half his age. From the minute he hits the stage for an afternoon soundcheck until the last note of the evening's encore, he's *into it*.

Before he had money, fame, or even a decent guitar, Paul McCartney was digging Chuck Berry, Little Richard, Elvis Presley, Jerry Lee Lewis, and Fats Domino, tapping into rock and roll to inspire his budding writing, singing, and playing abilities. Those influences are a strong part of early Beatles music, the propulsive force behind the Fab Four — Paul, John Lennon, George Harrison, and Ringo Starr. But as time passed, Paul's songwriting and playing evolved dramatically, becoming practically a genre unto themselves, almost as far removed from Chuck Berry as from Beethoven or Bach.

Despite decades of evolution, McCartney never lost touch with his roots. He returned to them for *Back In The U.S.S.R.*, a 1988 album on which he covered '50s gems by his early heroes (the album was originally released only in the U.S.S.R.). During the jams that culminated in the LP Paul also started playing *guitar* in a band, something he hadn't done since long before the Beatles conquered the world. Of course, he hadn't given up for all those years: He picked guitar in the studio with the Beatles and Wings, as well as on solo recordings. However, he had almost always appeared onstage with his violin-shaped Hofner or his Rickenbacker 4001 bass.

Besides picking up the guitar again, Paul — at the insistence of new songwriting partner Elvis Costello — dusted off the old Hofner that had been in hibernation since the Beatles did "Get Back" on Apple Studios' rooftop for *Let It Be* in 1969. He applied it

– 118 –

to Costello's "Veronica" on 1988's *Spike*.

For 1989's *Flowers In The Dirt,* McCartney used a variety of guitars and basses, including his old Hofner friend and his new 5-string Wal. Partly as a result of the *Flowers* sessions, partly as fallout from the *U.S.S.R.* album, and partly as an outgrowth of weekly jam sessions, a new band evolved, featuring McCartney on bass, guitar, piano, and vocals, his wife Linda on keyboards and backing vocals, Chris Whitten on drums, Hamish Stuart on guitar, bass, and backing vocals, Robbie McIntosh on guitar and vocals, and Paul Wickens (a.k.a. Wix) on keyboards. Since last year, McCartney and band have played to packed stadiums all over the world (including a 150,000-person venue in Rio de Janeiro).

Over the years, Paul has participated in charitable events, including Live Aid and the Prince's Trust concerts. He is currently promoting Friends of the Earth, an environmental group. For musicians, though, few projects that he has lent his name to can equal his participation in *Standing In The Shadows Of Motown: The Life And Music Of Legendary Bassist James Jamerson* [Hal Leonard]. Acting as emcee to the accompanying cassettes, the English bassist had a rare opportunity to pay tribute to one of his contemporaries — and influences — from the '60s, a man who, like Paul McCartney, played a major role in shaping rock bass.

You contributed to the book on James Jamerson. When did you first hear about him?

Well, I didn't realize who I was hearing for all those years — like a lot of people on the Motown stuff. I was always attracted to the bass lines. They had their own guys in Motown and their regular house band.

You knew who the fronting artist was, but not the support players.

Exactly. It was just an artist on Motown. And we loved all those backing tracks and all those sort of "Heard It Through The Grapevine" songs. They were huge pieces of music for us. Just the backing tracks — never mind the great vocals in front of them. When they used to ask me who my favorite bass player was, I would say, "That Motown guy. The guy who plays in the band." But I never really knew who he was. Then James Jamerson, Jr., wrote and said, "I'm doing this big project to kind of get my dad's name known a

"We lifted a lot of stuff from Motown, but quite unashamedly. I'm happy to have done it."

bit more." I didn't even know who he was. So I did that, and it was very nice. I was happy to be of some use.

By the time you first heard James Jamerson, you'd formed your own style. But was there anything that made you say, "Oh, I'll take a little of this or a little of that"?

Oh, sure. I'm always taking a little of this and a little of that. It's called being influenced. It's either called that or stealing. And what do they say? A good artist borrows; a great artist steals — or something like that. That makes us great artists then, because we stole a lot of stuff. If anyone ever said to us, "Wow! Where's that from?" we'd say, "Well, Chuck Berry," or that the "I Saw Her Standing There" riff is from [Berry's] "I'm Talking About You." We took a lot of stuff, but in blues, anyway, you do: People lift licks. It's part of the fun of being alive, too. You hear somebody's incredible riff and you go, "Oooh." You hear a new chord somewhere and you go, "Oh, my God, that's it!" We used to travel miles for a new chord — literally — in Liverpool. We used to take bus rides for hours to go visit the guy who reputedly knew *B7.* None of us knew how to finger it. He was like the guru. We went to his house, and we sat there, and he played it a few times. Then we all said, "Brilliant, thanks," and we went home and practiced it. Yeah, we lifted a lot of stuff from Motown, but quite unashamedly. I'm happy to have done it.

Listening to the "I'm Talking About You" bass line, it's easy to see where the line to "I Saw Her Standing There" came from.

Actually, I admitted it about 20 years ago. I admitted it more recently, too, and in an article it said something like, "He admits *perhaps unwisely.*" I said, "Come on, guys. I'm not going to tell you I wrote the bloody thing when Chuck Berry's bass player did." Actually, it's a guitar part. It's such a great riff. And most of the people we played for didn't know the song, so we were pretty safe.

It was reasonably obscure.

Yeah, we worked on obscure songs with the Beatles. There was a good reason, too: All the other bands knew the hits; everybody knew "Ain't That A Shame." Everybody knew Bo Diddley's "Bo Diddley." But not everybody knew [Bo Diddley's] "Crackin' Up." Hardly anybody knows "Crackin' Up" to this day — it was just one of his B sides that I loved. I don't know how dynamite it is, but I like it. We used to look for B sides — a good, smart move, too! — and obscure album tracks, because if we were turned on by them enough to bring something special to them, just by being in love with them, you sing them good. John, for instance, used to sing "Anna" on the first Beatles album. And that was a really obscure record that we'd just found, and guys would play in the clubs. We'd take the record home and learn it. We learned a lot of songs like that: "Three Cool Cats," "Anna," "Thumbin' A Ride" — millions of great songs. And still to this day, I keep them filed in the back of my head in case I'm ever producing a young act, and they say, "We haven't got a song." I can go, "Wait a minute! Try this one. It's an old rock and roll thing, but it's got something."

Assumedly, you started out left-handed.

Yeah, I'm left-handed.

Some right-handed people actually play lefty.

I know! We were just in Japan, and there was a little kid there who had a Hofner bass, so I tried to be the elder-brother guy. I said, "Hey, do you know this one?" I played the "I Saw Her Standing There" riff. I expected him just to say, "Oh no, but wow, thanks for teaching me." But he said, "Sure," and he turned the bass wrong way around. They explained that he's really right-handed, but he just plays it left-handed because I do. And he went [*imitates bass*] do do do do do do do do — totally on top of it. His brother then picked up his Rickenbacker guitar and goes [*imitates rhythm guitar*] mmm Gah! mmm Gah!, and kicks in John's rhythm part. They had it word-perfect. But I'm actually left-handed. You know, Jimi Hendrix was left-handed, but played a right-handed guitar.

Did anyone try to talk you out of playing left-handed?

No, I was lucky. In school, I was allowed to be a left-handed writer, although Hamish [who plays right-handed] apparently started off as a left-handed writer, because his school was more strict up in Scotland. A little bit more *dour* up there. But I was okay; they let me do that. And so when I came to play guitar, I bought a right-handed guitar, a Zenith, an old acoustic which I've still got. I sat down at home with a little chord book and started trying to work it out. It didn't feel good at all; it felt very awkward. It felt nothing natural about it. It was only when I saw a picture of Slim Whitman in a magazine, and I saw he was left-handed and was holding it all the "wrong" way, that I thought, "Oh, he must have turned his strings around, then." So I started on that problem, which is always the nut: I could never change the nut.

I had the strings changed around, but the thick bass string never fit in the little first-string slot in the nut. So I had to gouge that out, which I could do reasonably successfully. But then I always had my little thin string in this whacking great cavern of a hole originally cut for the bass string. So I used to actually take matchsticks and build up the bass nut that way. It was only later that I was able to buy a left-handed guitar.

You used a Hofner, even though most bassists in the U.S. had Fenders.

Yeah, most of the players were using Fenders in England, too. They still are better instruments. But, for me, it was a matter of expense. That's all it was.

Really? Hofners aren't cheap basses in the States.

Yeah, but I was in Germany, where they're made, and I think they were about 30 quid, which is about $70. I wasn't earning that much. And the thing is, the way I'd been brought up, my dad had always hammered into us to never get in debt, because we weren't that rich. I think he'd got in debt when he was a bit younger in the marriage. He used to bet on the horses a bit; he was a bit of a naughty boy — in a very small way, but he got embarrassed at his finances. So John and George went easily in debt and got beautiful guitars: John got a Club 40, and George had a Futurama — which is like a Fender copy — and then, later, Gretsches. Then John got the Rickenbackers. They were prepared to go into hock and use what we call hire/purchase credit. But it had been so battered into me not to do that, I wouldn't risk it. I thought the world would cave in if I did that. So I bought a cheap guitar. And the other thing was that the Hofner was violin-shaped and symmetrical, so being left-handed didn't look so stupid. And once I bought it, I fell in love with it. That's why I'm using it again now. For a light, dinky little bass, it has a very rich bass sound.

You did switch to a Rickenbacker eventually.

Well, it was when Mr. Rickenbacker gave me one, when we were in L.A. I'm a cheap sort, I am. I had always wanted to get a Fender — I've got a Fender now, which I sometimes record with — but funnily enough, it never was my thing to get a Fender. It wasn't always the expense, because later I could afford it, but by then I'd kind of made the Hofner my trademark. And really, it was only when Mr. Rickenbacker said to me, "This will record better than what you've got." It looked nice, and I said, "We'll see." And, obviously, a free guitar was a pretty hefty thing. You know, I'm still impressed by stuff like that. People expect you not to be impressed when you get a bit of money, but I'm still impressed by that. And the guys used to do anything for guitars — they'd sell their souls [*laughs*] to get a free guitar: [*shouts*] "Yeah! Yeah! We'll do it, whatever it is. Can I have it now? Can I take it home?" It was just like sweets to a baby, just to see new guitars in their cases. Well, you know — readers of the magazine know what that one's like. If you're a guitar fan, it means more than getting a new car, just opening that new case and seeing it and smelling it.

Well, a car is just a car.

A car is only a car, but you can't play a car!

If you went to a party and saw a guitar standing in the corner, it wasn't likely to be a left-handed model. Didn't that frustrate you?

I had to learn backwards. I can play right-handed guitar a bit, just enough for at parties. Hopefully, by that point everyone is drunk when I pick it up, because otherwise they're going to catch me. But I could do that, and the guys obviously wouldn't let me re-string it. Certainly, they wouldn't let me gouge out their nuts. And at a party, you only want to play it for 15 or 30 minutes or so, and by the time you've goofed up their guitar and you hand it back to them, they've got to string it back again, and it's silly. So I had to learn upside down. It's funny: John learned upside down, too, because of me — because mine was the only other guitar around for him, if he broke a string or he didn't have his. That's more unusual; left-handed guys can nearly always play a straight guitar. Actually, Robbie is very accomplished that way. He can do both. He can actually play rather well: [*in a stage voice*] Dirty swine! The rest of us can just play passably, but he's actually pretty good the wrong way around.

How did the Rickenbacker change your approach? Did you have to really labor with it?

No, the Rickenbacker was very nice. They were right: It recorded better. It had sort of a fatter neck, and it was much more stable — didn't go out of tune as easily. Also, it stayed in tune right up the neck; the Hofner had problems when you got right up near the top. So I hardly ever went up there — although some of that stuff in "Paperback Writer" is Hofner, so it did actually stay in tune for that. But it was a little more difficult to work with, being a cheaper instrument. I guess you pay for that precision.

By the time you got the Rickenbacker, recording technology was starting to catch up to what you and George Martin were trying to accomplish, too.

That's true. On the early stuff, the drums and bass were really mixed towards the back of the records.

Not by the time of "Rain" or "Paperback Writer."

Well, it started to move forward, and we *noticed* it was moving forward. There was also the kind of thing you get in groups: John would have his volume on 8, and George would have his on 7. The next time you looked, George would be on 8, too. You hadn't noticed him doing it. So John would casually go to 9. That happened on the recording desk, too. We each had a fader, and you'd say, [*slyly*] "Oh, I think the bass ought to be a little louder there." Techniques gradually improved. The other thing was that records originally couldn't actually take that amount of bass.

You obviously didn't abandon guitar altogether, but did you ever feel that you had hopelessly locked yourself into the role of the bassist?

It's funny, actually. I have problems with one of the books that's been written about us, because the guy obviously didn't like me. That's fair enough. But this guy started to make up a whole story of how I was so keen to be the bass player that I really did a number on Stuart Sutcliff, the original bass player. He made it sound as if I had planned this whole thing to become the Beatles' bass player. I remember ringing George up shortly after this book came out, and I asked him, "Do you remember me really going hard to chuck Stu out of the group and be a bass player?" And he said, "No, you got lumbered with bass, man. None of us would do it." I said, "Well, that's how I remembered it." Because it's true: We all wanted to be guitar players.

Sure. Bass players were never frontmen.

The fat boy in the back was the bass player, and who wanted to be him? So I really wasn't too keen to do it, but I'd had a real bad guitar — because of my fear of getting in debt. When I went to Hamburg, I had a thing called the Rosetti Lucky 7, which is a really terrible British guitar with terrible action. It just fell apart on me — you know, just the heat in the club and the sweat made it fall apart. Eventually, I sort of busted it — early rumblings of the Who! In a drunken moment it was busted somewhere, and it had to go. So I ended up with my back to the audience, playing piano, which was then the only thing I could do unless I could get a new guitar.

So, yeah, I did pretty much get lumbered into playing bass. I didn't really want to do it, but then I started to see some interesting things in it. One of the very earliest was in "Michelle." There's that descending

> *"The Hofner bass was violin-shaped and symmetrical, so being left-handed didn't look so stupid."*

chord thing that goes, [*sings bass notes*] "*do do do do words I know do do do do do my Michelle*" — you know, the little descending minor thing. And I found that if I played a *C*, and then went to a *G*, and then to *C*, it really turned that phrase around. It gave it a musicality that the descending chords just hadn't got. It was lovely. And it was one of my first sort of awakenings: "Ooh, ooh, bass can really change a track!" You know, if you put the bass on the root note, you've got a kind of straight track. But later I learned how to make other notes work for me, as Brian Wilson was to prove on the Beach Boys' *Pet Sounds,* a big influential album for me. If you're in *C*, and you put it on something that's not the root note — it creates a little tension. It's great. It just [*takes a long, expectant, gasping breath*] holds the track, and so by the time you go to *C*, it's like, "Oh, thank God he went to *C*!" And you can create tension with it. I didn't know that's what I was doing; it just sounded nice. And that started to get me much more interested in bass. It was no longer a matter of just being this low note in the back of it.

Also, once I got into it, this engineer in Hamburg named Adrian made me a great bass amp that he called the coffin. It was a quad amp with big, round knobs — just bass and treble. No sophisticated graphics. He had these two 15" speakers in a big black box that looked a bit like a coffin. And, man! Suddenly that was a total other world. That was bass as we know it now. And, in fact, they wouldn't let me record with that. They were too frightened. It was like reggae bass: It was just too *right there*. It was great live.

So the recording engineers wanted you to tone it down?

Yeah. They said, "Look, the other groups use a Fender Showman or Bassman amp. We've got one here. Wouldn't you like to try it? Oh, that sounds much better." So I got persuaded out of that. It probably fell apart, as well. I started to get into bass more, although I never put down the guitar. Obviously, you can't write on a bass.

You can come up with a groove, though.

You come up with a groove, but when you're writing, you need the guitar or a piano. So I would always remember that first and foremost I started off as a guitar player. That's one of the reasons I'm playing guitar on this tour.

But you're also playing bass.

Oh, I'm playing a lot of bass still, yeah. Mainly, I play bass — and piano and acoustic guitar — but for the first time on tour I'm playing electric lead.

During your soundcheck, you were playing your Les Paul on a bluesy number, and it had a terrific tone.

Yeah, I got a nice tone on my bass pickup on that guitar. I had it on the bass pickup through a distortion unit. It sounds really good, like an Isley Brothers thing. It gets that lovely sort of fuzz sustain. So I guess I think of myself as a guitar player, really. Mainly acoustic — that's my main instrument, I suppose. If I couldn't have any other instrument, I would have to have an acoustic guitar. I always take one on holiday, and most times I have one in the dressing room.

Do you have any favorite guitar parts that you played with the Beatles?

I liked "Taxman" just because of what it was. I was very inspired by Jimi Hendrix. It was really my first voyage into feedback. I had this friend in London, John Mayall of the Bluesbreakers, who used to play me a lot of records late at night — he was a kind of DJ-type guy. You'd go back to his place, and he'd sit you down, give you a drink, and say, "Just check this out." He'd go over to his deck, and for hours he'd blast you with B.B. King, Eric Clapton — he was sort of showing me where all of Eric's stuff was from, you know. He gave me a little evening's education in that. I was turned on after that, and I went and bought an Epiphone. So then I could wind up with the Vox amp and get some nice feedback. It was just before George was into that. In fact, I don't really think George did get too heavily into that kind of thing. George was generally a little more restrained in his guitar playing. He wasn't into heavy feedback.

So, even hearing Jimi Hendrix and John Mayall's records didn't make you think that you should give up bass to pursue guitar?

Not really, no. I'd always felt that the bass thing was really it, because we had to have a bass player. At the very beginning, I did think, "Well, that's put shot to any plans I had of being a guitar player." But I got interested in bass as a lead instrument. I think around about the time of *Sgt. Pepper's* — "With A Little Help From My Friends" and "Lucy In The Sky With Diamonds" — there were some pretty good bass lines. Like Motown. Like Brian Wilson's lines in the Beach Boys. So, it was okay by the time I came to do that. But with "Taxman," I got the guitar and was playing around in the studio with the feedback and stuff, and I said to George, "Maybe you could play it like this." I can't quite remember how it happened that I played it, but it was probably one of those times when somebody says, "Well, why don't *you* do it then?"

Rather than spend the time teaching someone else?

Rather than spending the time to get the idea over. And I don't think George was too miffed. But when people say, "Great solo on 'Taxman,'" I don't think he's too pleased to have to say, "Well, that was Paul, actually." I didn't really do much like that — just once or twice. I also liked the part I did on "Blackbird" on acoustic; that was one of my favorites.

How did you react when, in the late '60s, a new breed of lead bassists such as Jack Bruce and John Entwistle emerged?

I thought it was quite interesting. To me, it depends who you're talking about, and what record, but often I thought it was too busy. I often felt it was like the bass as lead guitar, and I don't think it makes as nice a noise as a lead guitar. It's sort of like speed merchants. I've never been one. I remember reading where somebody said that someone's the fastest bass player ever, and I thought, "Big deal." You know, there used to be a guy in Britain — I think he's still around — called Bert Weedon, who used to come onto the children's TV programs. He used to say, "I'm now going to play 1,000 notes in a minute." And then he'd get one string and go *dididi-didid* and play up and down, hitting it very, very fast. It was quite funny, actually. It's one thing to be fast, but that's short-lived. I think I'd rather be melodic, or I'd rather have content than just speed.

Any favorite bass players or guitarists today?

I like Stanley Clarke. We only really met once, and just had a bit of fun in Montserrat. And he played on a couple of tracks. I admitted to him, "Hey, I'm trying to steal your licks, man!" He said, "Oh, you've got licks of your own." So, we just had a bit of fun. I decided not to steal his licks after all; he was right. He's got his style; I've got my style. And he's a great guy. I like Eddie Van Halen as a player. He gets it *right* quite often. I like a lot of heavy metal guys because they wind it up. What I usually like in a heavy metal band is the guitar player. But when it's just miles of scales, I lose interest. I like some of the hot sounds. And I also like David Gilmour. I think Clapton is real good, particularly these days. But I still like Hendrix the best.

Have you ever had any doubts about your playing?

Definitely. Often. Probably every time I've done a bass part. I have some self-doubts because I think, "Oh, my God; I've made so many records. How am I going to make this sound fresh?" But if you're lucky, you just get a little thing, like, you know, in "Rain," where there's this sort of high stuff. Then you go,

"Ooh, I've got it!" And the rest of the part flows because you've got something to feel special about. "Paperback Writer" — there's something. Or the lines that I discovered in "With A Little Help From My Friends." And what gets rid of the self-doubt is just plugging at it, keeping at it, and finding something to sort of release myself with.

On guitar, do you mostly fingerpick or flatpick?

I normally use a flatpick. John learned — I think I read recently he'd learned off Donovan or one of Donovan's friends, who were more into the folk thing, so they would fingerpick in the proper way, first string, third string, and all that. The proper thing. I got my own little sort of cheating way of doing it, so on "Blackbird" I'm actually sort of pulling two strings all the time. But then, when it gets to the little fingerpicking sort of thing, it's not real. I figured anyway that everyone else was doing that correct stuff, so it wouldn't hurt.

It certainly doesn't sound like strum, strum, strum.

No, it's more like fingerpicking. I kind of liked it. I was trying to emulate those folk players. John was the only one who actually stuck at it and learned it. If you listen to "Julia," he's playing properly with fingerpicking on that. I was always quite proud of the lad. I think he just had a friend who showed him, and so that's really a nice part on "Julia." But I could never be bothered, really, learning things. You know, I'm a great learner. I always sort of figure something out. Like, I've never had guitar lessons, bass lessons, piano lessons, music-writing lessons, songwriting lessons, or horse-riding lessons, for that matter, or painting — I do some of that. I always jump into things, and so by the time I'm ready for my first lesson, I'm beyond it. I always did try to have music lessons. I always tried to have someone teach me how to notate music, because I still don't know to this day.

You're doing okay.

But I figure I'm doing okay, yeah [laughs]. I tried when I was a kid, and I couldn't get it — it just didn't seem like nice fun to me. It seemed like hard work. I tried piano lessons when I was 16, but then I'd already written "When I'm 64" — the melody of it, anyway. And so the guy taking me back to five-finger exercises was really just *hell*; it was *torturing* me. I'd been plunking around on little chords, and I had a little bass line. So I never got on with that. And it was the same with everything — like I say, fingerpicking or anything else. I've always just sort of busked it and

> *"The fat boy in the back was the bass player, and who wanted to be him? We all wanted to be guitar players."*

learned, and I enjoyed the accident.

You used fuzz bass very early. Was it a sort of substitute for playing guitar?

I love fuzz bass. Yeah, it helps you be a bit more lyrical because it makes the notes linger, gives you a bit more sustain. That used to really turn the whole thing around.

The Rickenbacker bass seemed to do that without fuzz.

Well . . . the thing now is, the new fuzzes are not quite as good as the old fuzzes were. The technology's changed. And there were a lot of primitive things that we used to use in the Beatles, prehistoric machines. One of my theories about sound nowadays is that the machines back then were more *fuck-uppable*. I'm not sure if that's in the dictionary. But they were more destructible. You could actually make a desk [recording console] overload, whereas now they're all made so that no matter what idiot gets on them, they won't overload. Most of the old equipment we used, you could get to really surprise you. Now a brand-new desk is built for idiots like us to trample on. We used to do a great trick with acoustic guitars like on "Ob La Di, Ob La Da." I played acoustic on that, an octave above the bass line. It gave a great sound — like when you have two singers singing in octaves, it really reinforces the bass line. We got them to record the acoustic guitars in the red. The recording engineers said, "Oh, my God! This is going to be terrible!" We said, "Well, just try it." We had heard mistakes that happened before that and said, "We love that sound. What's happening?" And they said, "That's because it's in the red." So we recorded *slammin'* it in the red. And these old boards would distort just enough and compress and suck. So instead of going [*imitates staccato "Ob La Di" riff*] *dink dink dink dink,* it just *flowed.* So, a new fuzz box just won't go as crazy as an old one would. And it does make it all a little bit cleaner, which I'm not wild on, actually, because I'm a big fan of blues records and stuff, where there's never a clean moment. Nothing was ever clean. It was always one old, ropey mike stuck somewhere near the guitar player, and you could hear his foot more than some things.

Do you ever just sit around at home and tweak your amp to explore its tones?

I do that mainly in the studio, which is almost like home. I can go in and just goof, and sometimes I just work on guitar sounds. I can get a nice clean sound fairly easily. It's the pumped-up sounds that I like to experiment with. I've got one of the old Vox AC-30s that Jeff Beck used to call "the old Beatle bashers." I

once asked him if he used them, and he said, "What? Those old Beatle bashers?" Then he realized what he'd said [*laughs*]. But I love the sound of them; I actually love the *straight* sound. It's pokey. It's not too clean. I'm not a big fan of clean in rock and roll. It's funny in a way, because I guess I've got a reputation for being a fairly clean rock and roller. But my taste doesn't extend that way.

If you really want a clean sound, you can always go to acoustic.

Yeah. Or, [*whispers*] you can just turn down. That's the perfect way to get clean. But that's no fun at all! This is *Back To The Future,* guys. You want a whole wall of this stuff. So, yeah. I sit around and experiment with pedals, too.

Have you ever gone on an equipment-buying spree?

Very occasionally. My first Epiphone was one of them, where I just went down to a guitar shop after having heard B.B. King, Eric Clapton, and Jimi Hendrix, and I wanted something that fed back. He said, "This Epiphone will do it, because it's semi-acoustic." And he was right. The only reason I don't use it onstage is because it's a little too hot. It's great in the studio. You've got to stand in the right position for it not to feed back — I always had to do that in the studio, but nowadays guitars don't do this.

That's a right-handed guitar, isn't it?

Yeah, it's right-handed, but I play it left, and I had the nut changed.

Do you run your picking arm into the knobs all the time?

Yeah, but that's all I know. It was only much later in my career when I got the luxury of having it my way 'round. You know, I'm kind of used to playing what we call in Liverpool *cac-handed*. Spell that as you will; nobody's done it yet. Or *gammy*-handed, which is what they also call left-handed people.

When did you get a 5-string bass?

I was doing some jams in London that eventually turned into the Russian album, and one of the people who kind of volunteered to come along was Trevor Horn, the producer. I didn't know it, but it turned out that he'd been a bass player; I just knew his work as a producer. So he showed up with a Wal 5-string, and I just loved the extra string, the extra depth I'd been noticing on some records. I went to see Peter Gabriel, and there was always that [*makes a low growling sound*] somewhere in the show, and I was wondering where they were getting it from. Half the time it was the synths. But I noticed bass players getting that noise, and when Trevor showed up with the Wal, I said, "Oh, I like those." In fact, Linda bought it for me for my birthday.

Did you use it on "Figure Of Eight"?

Yeah. And there's a real low bass on "Rough Ride." It's doubled with synth. "We Got Married" is nice and low, too, and in the show it kind of shakes your booty.

What about "My Brave Face"?

That's the Hofner.

How does it feel to switch back to the Hofner after playing the Wal?

I think it's great. I was working with Elvis Costello, and when he was doing his album [*Spike*], he asked me if I'd guest on it. And he asked me to bring the Rickenbacker and the Hofner, because he's sort of a fan of older instruments. He often uses Hofner guitars because they've got a real honky sound that he likes. It's a period sound. During the work on *Flowers In The Dirt,* he said, "Why don't you try the Hofner?" It was a little bit like pulling it out of mothballs. I had resigned myself to not working with it again because it's not very precise, but he said, "Oh, I love the sound, and you must be able to get it in tune." So we fiddled around, and we did a bit of work on it. We just about got it so it was in tune everywhere on the neck, so that was great after all these years. You've got to have the bridge at a very acute angle to get it to work. But anyway, it started to sound really good and he was very happy with it. He asked me to play it on "Veronica." So it reawoke my interest in it. And the other thing is, I saw a little bit of the *Let It Be* film of the Beatles on the roof doing "Get Back," and I realized that the way I was holding the Hofner was not like you hold a big, heavy thing that weighs you down and you sort of become a part of it. It's as if it were just a little jacket or something; it's so light, it's like a little piece of balsa wood.

The Wals are considerably heavier.

Yeah, and the Rickenbacker's in between. So when I saw this *Let It Be* footage, I noticed how easy it looked to play. And because it's so light, you play guitary stuff on it; you play quite fast stuff. It just kind of flows more naturally than if you're on a physically heavy bass.

The bass line to "Ebony And Ivory" is very tasty, but the melody and harmonies are so strong that many people probably don't even notice it.

Yeah, that's right.

"Voices should be first, guitars and drums should be second, and then you should kind of get a feel of the bass."

How do you feel about it after doing so much work?

Oh, I don't mind. Obviously, I sing it, too, so if they notice the singing, that's great. I wrote it, and if they notice the writing, that's great, too. I don't mind; you can't have everything. The thing about that song, working with Stevie Wonder — Stevie is such a *consummate* musician — working with someone that good really keeps you on your toes. He did the drumming on that, but we started off with a rhythm box, one of the first Linn drum machines. He brought it to Montserrat, and as you know, he's blind. He kept opening the top and fiddling in it, sticking his hand in it. The guys would say, "Stevie, watch out, man, it's switched on; it's live." And he'd say, "Yeah, I know." Bloody hell! I'd never stick my fingers in there. I'm not mechanical, you know. Stevie just knows what he's doing. So while he's sticking his fingers in there and adjusting stuff, I'm saying, "I hope he doesn't hit a live wire in there."

After we put a track down with that, Stevie did the drums, and then we did the vocals. So then I figured I had to put down a good bass part. I sat around and tried to work out something that would sympathize with the record; I was quite pleased with it.

Do you ever splice bass parts together, or create a line by punching it in bit by bit?

I like to be more intuitive. It depends if I'm in good form or bad form. If I'm in bad form, I go on forever and I don't really find anything. And that's very frustrating. But we all have those days, right? But if I'm in good form, I'll goof around with it a few times and find some really good ideas that I'll then solidify and pull into an actual part as if it was written, and then just be free in certain little bits, but mainly put in what I think is a bass part that kind of sympathizes with the song. I don't really like to come too "out of the song" with a bass. Because in my view, it's kind of like film music: You shouldn't really notice it. You should be watching the acting. You shouldn't ever hear the beautiful theme from *Dr. Zhivago*, because it means they're not acting that good. They should be acting so good, you should just feel the music. And in bass I like to do a similar thing. If you're a bass player, I like to have something there for you to check out. But I don't necessarily want the bass to stick out more than anything else on the record. I want it to be probably about *third* on the record: Voices should be first;

guitars and drums should be second; and then you should kind of get a feel of the bass.

But on a number like "Silly Love Songs" [All The Best], the bass is louder than anything.

Now, that is the opposite of what I just said, because that is the bass in your face. And that was really just because we were making a dance record on purpose. I had been accused around that time of singing too much about love. I said, "Hey, wait a minute! It's the best thing!" Love definitely beats hate, and it's definitely kind of cool, at least in my book. But it can be perceived as sort of soppy. So I wrote this song, and asked, "What's wrong with silly love songs?" I wrote it out on holiday in Hawaii; I just had piano and chords, and I then wanted to have a melody on bass. We really pushed the bass and drums right out front. But it drove the song along quite nicely. Pushed it hard. We wanted to make something you could dance to, so you *had* to.

Do you generally mike your bass in the studio, or go direct?

All my career, I've miked it. But these days I do both. I have the option. I run out a lead into the studio. I've always worked in the studio, but the tendency these days is to go into the control room and plug straight into the board. I've always liked the liveness of an amp. By doing a split, they can get me live or clean — direct through to the board — or put a mike on the amp. We can mix the two, or go for one or the other, depending on what we want in the end.

Does it make it easier to get the sound you want when you work with Geoff Emerick or George Martin, who've been engineering or producing for you on so many projects, including the Beatles recordings?

Yeah. Geoff Emerick's very good. He reads me. He's really good to work with. Geoff is a very deep engineer. He knows what he's doing, he's emotionally involved, and he has all the chops. And having known him for that amount of time, he knows what I've done. He keeps you on your toes. If an engineer doesn't really know your work, you think, "Oh, I can get away with that stuff." I don't mind trying to get away with stuff, actually, because in the early days of the Beatles, with George Martin, you used to do a take and you'd think, "I hope that's right." And if George said it was okay, I'd say to the other guys, [*whispers*] "Listen. I played a mistake in the middle." And they'd say, [*whispers*] "If he doesn't notice it, don't tell him." The bass was a lot further back, back then. And a lot of Beatles records have what I thought were mistakes. So it was cool if it got through: Hmm,

passed the exam! I won't complain. We always thought we'd left school, and we were always so glad to see the back of school, but then, when we came into *life*, all the people from school came into life, too! They fooled us, man; they all came! So all the school sneaks became the bad reporters, and all the teachers became the judges, and all that.

How did you get this band together?

We started during the making of *Flowers In The Dirt*. First of all, I wanted to play live, because I was in the studio every day doing bits and pieces. And the easiest thing to do was to have a jam once a week — invite a few people, see who shows up. The original idea was to have a kind of thing where anyone who wanted showed up. But that started to get a little too inexact, because one week you might have no one show up, or you might have 50 people show up. So we invited people to a Friday evening jam, and each week was a different lineup of people. Basically, when I'm jamming, I just run through all the old rock and roll numbers that I know. So that's songs like "Lucille," "Matchbox," "Lawdy Miss Clawdy," "Bring It On Home" — you know, all those kinds of standards. And the drummer who impressed me, among others who also stood out, was Chris. He wasn't too set in his ways.

And?

[*Laughs.*] Well, we're talking *drummers* here, and if you get a drummer who's absolutely set in his ways, sometimes you'll get one who'll say, "I can't play to that." So you need someone who's a little bit flexible. He's young enough not to be set in his ways, and good enough to hold a good, strict tempo. Younger guys normally have trouble with things like shuffles. They're not from those times. People like Ringo have an automatic shuffle — it's just part of his repertoire. It's like a gear he can go into. And I know from the little bit of drumming I do that a shuffle is pretty hard to do — to get a nice loose shuffle. Apparently, Chris was nervous as all hell, and it was the worst day of his life. But he played great anyway, so we invited him back, and he became a regular. I decided to do some recordings from those, because the jams were feeling good and we were building up a loose repertoire. So we did what became the album that was released exclusively in Russia.

Are you as concerned about the quality of the guitar player?

I'm *very* fussy about guitar players. I go back too far to be satisfied easily. I knew Jimi Hendrix when he was playing in London, and I was a major, major fan. In fact, he still is my favorite guitar player — just through his whole attitude and his playing. I mean, I like attitude, but it's no good unless you can play. And in fact, some of the attitude kinds of things, like picking with his teeth, Jimi didn't really want to do. It was just show, and he got fed up with that very quickly because he was a real proper guitar player. He played lovely acoustic, too. He was the first guy to really wind it up, to get into heavy feedback. I caught his first gig in London, and I used to follow him around London like a fan. It's a very small area, and people would ring me up and say that Jimi's playing at Blazes tonight, or at the Bag O' Nails. And I was there.

One of my greatest memories was that we released *Sgt. Pepper's* on Friday night, and on Sunday night Jimi was playing at the Savile Theatre, which Brian Epstein used to run, just for something to do on a Sunday night.

There was never any entertainment on for Sunday night, so Brian began to book people in, like Chuck Berry and Fats Domino. And we could go into a little special box, and not be bothered, and we could watch all these great acts. So Jimi came on, and he opened up with *Sgt. Pepper's*, which had only been released on Friday. That was a great, great memory. Since then, I've seen people like Clapton, who I admire a lot, and David Gilmour. And there's just something there about what I'd call a real guitar player. They hold the instrument right, they play it right. They have the right attitude about it, and they've got something individual that each one of them that's special brings to it. In the jams, I suppose I was mildly disappointed that I never really found the guitarist who really blew me off my feet — although there were some really good players. Johnny Marr showed up, and we had a great time. The kind of guy I was looking for was more of a Hendrixy type, where Johnny's more of what I'd consider a rhythm guitarist cum lead. All these guys were brilliant.

This is the first permanent band you've had since Wings disbanded in 1976.

It's the first sort of definite band, yeah. You know, after the Beatles, anyone could be forgiven for saying, "Well, that's it. I've *been* in a band." I heard Brian May of Queen say, "You're only ever in one great band." I kind of know what he means, spiritually, but I think I've been really lucky. The '76 lineup was real good — with little Jimmy McCulloch. Strange little lineup, but a magic one. I'm very excited about this band, because it's pretty musical. We can sort of go

"A lot of Beatles records have what I thought were mistakes. So it was cool if they got through."

anywhere with it, which is very interesting, and a little bit daunting, because if you can go *anywhere*, where do you go? It's like going on holiday: If you've got the power to go anywhere, you're really stuck for choices. But I'm not really worried about that, because I've got a pretty firm direction of where I want to go with the next stuff, so I'll try that out and see what comes of it.

Do you like having someone full-time who can pick up, say, bass, if you want to play guitar?

Yeah. That was one of the big attractions of Hamish. He's interested in bass — not just as a minor instrument; he's quite into it. I started on acoustic guitar, and I played Hamburg on guitar, and all. As I said, when it got busted I had to switch to piano. Which was quite good, because I'd had a piano at home. My dad was a good pianist, but not trained. Like I've picked it up, he picked it up; he learned by ear. I used to say to him, "Teach me some of your stuff." And he said, "No. You've got to learn properly." He felt he wasn't good enough to teach me, which was okay, actually. I just did what he did; I emulated him and just picked things up that I heard off records. We all sort of started with middle C, found the chord of C, found F and found G, and then we found *Am*, and then the rest of it — got into all the augmented and that sort of stuff as we went along.

So, I never really got to go back to guitar, except for the odd solo with the Beatles, where I'd do odd little things, like "Taxman." "Tomorrow Never Knows," I played some stuff there. "Paperback Writer," I played the riff on that. Then there were the acoustic things like "Yesterday" and "Blackbird."

You played with Carl Perkins on "Get It" [Tug Of War]. How did you two get together?

I rang him up, and he was in the States playing clubs. We met him in the very early days with the Beatles, and he was a good old friend, such a down-home boy. I love Carl — he's so great. I'll tell you a story about Carl; I don't think he'd mind me telling this. We were recording at Montserrat, and a musician friend was sailing around the world on a yacht — a bit of a tax dodge, I think [laughs], and he sailed into Montserrat and came to see us. He invited us to his boat. There was this British naval crew piping us aboard this spotless yacht. Carl was really impressed with the buffet and the champagne, and the way it was all laid out. He came over to me and said, "Paul, where I come from they call this shittin' in high cotton." It's one of my favorite expressions. After that, we recorded "Get It," and at the end both of us are laughing, and that's the joke we're laughing at. We had to cut it, because otherwise we'd have never gotten it played on the radio.

Did you both play guitar on it?

Yeah. I just played a little bit, and Carl did a rhythm part. The fun tended to come when we had a free moment, so he and I sat on the floor of the studio and we were talking and there was a mike on. I was just telling him about some of his old songs we loved, like "Lend Me Your Comb" and "Your True Love." I told him we were big fans of his and we used to do "Your True Love." And then we'd sing together. Then we'd stop, and he'd say, "Well, you know, Paul, I used to do this," and he'd show me some fingerpicking thing he used to do.

Back in the early days of the Beatles, you did "Matchbox" and other songs by Carl Perkins. Were you awed to meet someone who, to you, was a legend?

Absolutely. Anyone who was a legend in our formative years is still a legend. I haven't grown out of that. Carl is still the guy who wrote "Blue Suede Shoes," and he can never do any wrong. It only took one guy to do that, and he did it. Elvis recorded it and beat his version, but still Carl wrote it. There's some magic stuff. We used to love those early albums — very primitive, very simple, but just such *soul*. Carl has lovely stories about how he was taught by an old black gentleman [John Westbrook], and he speaks of him with great reverence. It's very nice to hear. He said, "You know, Paul, I used to pick cotton in the field, and when we had a break, we'd sit down and this old black gentleman would show me some of his licks." It was very exciting for us kids. We'd grown up in a kind of urban world, and we didn't really know about that stuff. He's still an idol. Little Richard was another idol. And in the same way, the magic didn't fade any when we met him. He's great — wacky. He always gives me a bit of fun: Whenever he does an interview, he looks into the camera and says, "Now Paul, you know I taught you how to do that *woooooooo.*" It's true; he did! He says it like I don't admit it, but I admit it quite happily. In fact, the first thing I ever did showbiz-wise was at the end of term, when on the last day of school you'd have a bit of a blowout. All the kids would party around and there wasn't a lot of work, and the teachers were too busy cleaning the desks and getting out of there. I remember standing on a desk in Cliff Edge's room; his real name was W. Edge, the history master, and we used to like him because he was a bit looser than some of the other teachers. We called him Cliff Edge. I was standing on the desk — it was like a scene out of an old rock and roll movie —and I was clapping and singing "Tutti Frutti" like Little Richard, and all the guys in the class were going, "Yeah!" and rockin' around.

I still owe a great debt to Little Richard and a lot of those guys, just because they turned us on. It's something when people turn you on, something I don't think you ever forget. It's so deep when you're young, too. The turn-on, when you're younger, is so intense. It burns itself into your soul, hearing "That'll Be The Day" and "Heartbreak Hotel" and "What'd I Say?" They burned themselves into my being.

And you can't get them out.

I wouldn't *want* to get them out, ever. That's something I'm really proud to have burned into my soul, *branded* in me.

– BILLY SHEEHAN –

BY TOM MULHERN – DECEMBER 1986

THERE'S MORE to Billy Sheehan than two-handed hammering, flashy solos, and onstage cavorting with singer David Lee Roth. He's as much influenced by Jimi Hendrix' pyrotechnics as by Tim Bogert's bass work. Between hot licks, though, he holds down the bottom with a firm, commanding groove that comes from years in the bars of Buffalo, New York, where he plugged through everything from Led Zeppelin to Three Dog Night and Loggins And Messina. At 33, Sheehan estimates that he performed at least 3,000 gigs — mostly with his former band Talas and all with his "wife," a mongrel bass consisting of Fender odds and ends — before joining forces with Roth, guitarslinger Steve Vai, and drummer Gregg Bissonette for Roth's *Eat 'Em And Smile* album and tour.

Despite his firm grasp of the basics, it's his awesomely aggressive approach that's propelled him into the limelight. For years Billy worked with Talas, with whom he recorded a pair of albums, *Sink Your Teeth Into That* and *Live Speed On Ice*. He recorded with Michael Schenker in 1979 — although the tracks weren't released — and toured Europe in 1983 with UFO. Sheehan and Talas hit the road in 1980, opening for Van Halen. He also played on Tony MacAlpine's debut LP, *Edge Of Insanity*. Even though he doesn't read or write music, he gives clinics at Musicians Institute in Hollywood whenever he's in town. After more than 17 years in rock and roll, Billy Sheehan's ship has come in. In the follow-ing interview, he talks about his work with Vai and Roth, his specialized gear, and his diverse influences.

You're not a schooled musician, and yet you give clinics.

Well, I mostly talk about seat-of-the-pants playing. I know if I'm playing a wrong note and how scales should sound. And I know a little about modes, too. But I'm basically a pattern player. When video games were big, I saw guys playing PacMan, and they racked up giant scores. I couldn't figure out how they did it, until I realized that it was just patterns. Once you learn them, you just follow them. And that's pretty much how I play. I use three basic patterns, and everything else is variations on them. A major scale has eight notes, but only two intervals in it: a half-step and a whole-step. So I employ three patterns on a given string: two consecutive whole-steps, a whole-step followed by a half-step, and a half-step followed by a whole-step. I have the same options on each string, so when you combine them, there are a lot of combinations [a total of 81] available at each position.

Do you follow any sort of practice regimen?

A real strong one, where I force my hands to do a lot of exercises. When I warm up, I exercise my hands for quite a while, always forcing them to do the things they're worst at, and trying to avoid the things they do best. I used to practice by doing lots of *wrong* notes — just patterns for the sake of patterns, even though they weren't musically correct. Then, when I discovered the modes, I started to do variations on the patterns across all four strings to make them correct.

Have any of Steve Vai's abilities rubbed off on you?

It's hard, because we speak a different language. Steve says, "It's that *E* demented, cemented, fermented chord with the . . . ." And I say, "Oh, you mean *this*." And I play a chord that I saw Jimi Hendrix do in the *Woodstock* movie. I don't have a name for it, but I know the fingering and sound. I leave that up to Steve because he's the one who has to transcribe it [*laughs*].

How did you get started on bass?

I tried drums for about a week, but then I realized that I couldn't get a drum set because it was too expensive. I used to sneak into my sister's room and try to learn chords on her folk guitar. Around the corner from me was a guy named Joe Hesse, who is [keyboardist] Chick Corea's road manager now. He was the most popular bassist in Buffalo for years, and I used to sit outside his basement window while his band practiced. Of course, the bass was the loudest thing traveling through the walls. I wanted to play bass because Joe was my hero, and the bass was so cool: It had cool strings, and its amp was always bigger than the guitar amps. It was *obviously* the most important instrument in the world. Finally, my sister gave up possession of her guitar because she couldn't get it out of my hands anymore, and I knew more chords than her. I learned some bass lines and a little lead, but I never got beyond the Young Rascals for lead; I couldn't get the hang of it. And when Hendrix came along, I said, forget it. So I decided to get a regular bass and amp. Later I realized that I loved Jimi so much that there was no way that I could *not* try to learn his stuff, but I didn't have a guitar anymore, so I had to learn on bass. I learned Jimi Hendrix, Frank Zappa, and Bach keyboard stuff on bass because nobody told me that you weren't supposed to do that. After I learned the bass parts, then I picked up the keyboard and guitar parts; soon I knew them all. When it was time to play in a band, of course, I just played the bass lines.

What kind of band were you in?

A copy band, which was the best training I ever had. We did other people's music night after night, often 21 nights in a row, three to five sets a night — playing for a *living*. And if you couldn't entertain

> *"Once you learn patterns, you just follow them. And that's pretty much how I play."*

people and get them dancing and interested in watching the band, you couldn't pay your rent. Nowadays, most kids have a day job, and it's harder to get gigs, so they don't really depend on their playing to survive. That was the greatest influence on me. It forces you to be good.

Did you listen to any bassists for early guidance?

Yeah, Tim Bogert. He was my biggest influence. He pushed me — unknowingly, with his Vanilla Fudge recordings — into being a fingerstyle player. He did things with his fingers that guys with picks just couldn't do. And to this day, I still say that the most articulate way of playing a guitar is with the fingers. I'd rather listen to Paco de Lucia than a pick player, because using the fingers gives you the most options. I have relearned guitar, and I use a pick, but using the fingers is the real secret of so much speed and so many types of licks. And that came from Tim Bogert. Plus he played all over the place; he didn't necessarily play in the pocket. Apparently he listened to a lot of saxophonists, which Jeff Berlin also did — and Jeff's probably the best bassist *anywhere* right now, as far as command of the instrument goes. And Jaco Pastorius' transcription of the Charlie Parker sax solo, "Donna Lee" [*Jaco Pastorius*], set a new standard for bass. I listen to a lot of sax players, but I could never quite get the hang of sax lines on the bass, probably because I didn't like jazz as much as classical. Rhythmically speaking, classical music is pretty steady, and it fit more with rock. I've always been a rock guy, rather than a fusion guy. It seems that every time somebody gets very good on their instrument, they turn into a fusion or jazz player. I got into Stanley Clarke and Jaco for awhile, but no girls would come to see me play if I did play that kind of music. So I didn't want to do it. I learned it, but it wasn't rock. It wasn't long hair and tight pants and meeting lots of girls after the show. I mean, that kind of stuff is as much a part of my career as my playing, which may make some people cringe. But I like the lifestyle. I don't do any drugs, but I like partying and hanging out with people after shows. It's been a big part of my life.

Was there ever a time when you had to pull in your own reins because you were straying too far from the basics in favor of wild playing?

Oh, sure. Actually, I now find it enjoyable to lay back and listen to what Steve is playing. Like in "Ladies Nite In Buffalo?" he takes an extended solo, and I just barely hum underneath with the bass. He's an amazing and unusual soloist. Plus Dave's such an eclectic personality, and he can solo just by talking — the Jimi Hendrix of the mouth. It's easy to lay back with this band. I always felt in Talas that I had to make up for the lack of personality or guitar playing or other factors. Fortunately, it's no longer the Billy Sheehan Show — which Talas turned into, much to my distaste. It was a drag, because I prefer being a band member.

Do you get a lot of room to solo in this band?

Yeah. Steve and I do our infamous guitar duel now, though. Instead of doing equal solo spots, we decided to make it more like professional wrestling or like a tractor pull [*laughs*]. He starts playing; I start playing. He stops; I stop. And then we go back and forth. It's really entertaining and it keeps us on our toes. It's a friendly battle, and at the end we play together, doing this super-fast wild stuff together. Actually, I'm sick of people soloing alone solely for that effect. A lot of guitarists forget that you can't just play solos all the time; you have to know chords, too. Good rhythm players are almost impossible to find. Everybody's a lead player, the world is lead guitar crazy.

The unison lines that you and Steve play in "Shy Boy" are pretty tricky.

Yeah, and a lot of people don't realize that there's bass in there with the guitar. They think it's a guitar with an octave divider. It's cool to be able to do something like that; it's the first time I've been able to work with a guitarist instead of behind or in front of one. Steve is an amazing player.

Did you work out those unison lines before you recorded the song, or did you leave a space for dropping them in later?

We worked it out in the first rehearsal of the song. I did half of what I did, and Steve did half of what he did. We've only scratched the surface of what we can do when we interact. I'm sure that after a year on the road, we will be very used to each other's playing and do even wilder stuff on the next album.

You play octaves during the second chorus in "Elephant Gun."

Yeah, it's been a habit that instead of playing just one note, I always find its octave — whether it's higher or lower — and even if I don't play that octave, I

> *"I learned Jimi Hendrix, Frank Zappa, and Bach keyboard stuff on bass because nobody told me that you weren't supposed to do that."*

finger it. Then the string sympathetically vibrates, giving a sound like more is going on. I always had to fill in more than my share as a bassist, so now I almost never have my hand hold a single note. It's practically all octaves.

You also use a number of harmonics in "Goin' Crazy!".

I've always been a heavy harmonics player. Because of my amp setup, I've always been able to make them ring out. They ring, even without the bass plugged in; it's just the sound of a new set of Rotosounds. You know how Billy Gibbons gets those harmonics by sliding the pick off the string and touching the string with his thumb? The fingernail of my middle finger acts as the guitar pick, and the skin of the thumb damps it. I pinch the string between my finger and thumb, and I pluck the harmonics. I can't quite go as fast as a guitarist. I can also tap the harmonics on the fingerboard if I want, because the amp is very sensitive. I got right-hand hammer-ons from watching Billy Gibbons in 1974. I guess I owe him a lot more than I thought. He was always one of my favorite players because he's a real Hendrix devotee.

What's your main bass for this tour?

I want to do at least the first part of the tour with my "wife." I can't bring myself to *not* let it play on the tour, because it's the high point of my career. That Fender has been with me for over 3,000 gigs. I also have my Yamaha BB3000S, which is much better than my Fender. There are no shortcomings to it; it has a flat-radius fingerboard, a thick neck, a perfectly comfortable body, an angled headstock so that it stays in tune all the time — it doesn't need string retainers, which almost always catch on roundwounds. I also had it equipped with a Hipshot Bass Extender Key. [*Ed Note: This is a retrofit tuning machine with a lever that allows the player to detune the low E string to as low as C.*] Before I got it, I used to retune my *E* to *D* for some songs because it's such a cool tone. It's one of the best retrofit ideas I've seen. It's cheap, easy to use, and it doesn't change your bass. And I can flip it to *D* quickly, like for the breakdown in the middle of "Yankee Rose."

What songs do you use the Bass Extender Key for?

"Ladies Nite In Buffalo?" and "Goin' Crazy!" And "Yankee Rose" is in the key of *D*, so I use that all the way through the song. The only thing you have to remember is that the notes on your *E* strings are now different, but you get used to that after a while. I even use it on some of my soloing. If I'm running down the *E* string, I get to the bottom and then flip the lever to take it down to a *D* — it's a cool effect. I'm thinking of getting another to put on the *G* string so that I can retune the *G* up to *A,* giving me *D A D A* tuning.

What's the biggest improvement in the Yamaha over your old Fender?

The Yamaha has a neck that goes through the body. The weak point on a Fender is the bolt-on neck, because I use a lot of vibrato by pushing the neck from behind. The neck always shifts from side to side and goes off axis. Then I have to pound shims in between the neck and body. You wouldn't believe all the old razor-knife blades and pieces of metal pounded in there on my Fender. Whenever I do clinics and get hold of a student's bass, I say, "Here's the inherent problem with a bolt-on neck." I push it a little bit and it gives out a loud crack — like the bass chiropractor. [*Ed. Note: This isn't a recommended procedure; it may damage your bass, and it will certainly void your warranty.*] And the strings are then off the neck at one side. To get my bolt-on neck on as solidly as possible, I put the bass on the floor and stand on it while I bolt the neck on. I just torque the bolts on as hard as I can without stripping them. The Yamaha's neck is very stable, but I don't notice any difference in the sustain.

Your Yamaha has non-stock pickups.

I put all DiMarzio pickups in. The Yamaha has two volumes, and I added another pickup at the bridge. Its volume is the knob that would normally be the P-Bass pickup's tone control. It's experimental still. Like my Fender, it has two outputs. On the Fender, there's an old Gibson EB-O pickup near the neck. I send that separately to a straight bass amp with the low end trimmed off, so that you get a lot of bottom end and clarity. Two outputs let me mix how much clarity and definition I get separately from the low end. I got the idea for the EB-O pickup by listening to Paul Samwell-Smith with the Yardbirds. He was so far ahead of his time. But even though he was all over the place, his bass sounded so deep; my Fender never sounded like that.

What kind of strings do you use?

Rotosound Swing Bass. They're bright and they

rip your frets to death, but I don't care, because I'll get my bass refretted every eight months if I have to. I tried using other strings, and it was a nightmare. They were too smooth, and my hands kept slipping off of them. They were finished roundwounds, which were smooth on purpose so that they wouldn't eat up the frets. But with my right-hand technique, I need my right hand to grip as I pluck. That's what makes Rotosounds so perfect, besides the great tone. I have to wear a lot of wrist bands because I sweat so much, but my hand still gets wet, and the strings get slippery. The roughness lets me grip through all that.

Are they changed often?

Every gig. If I could, I'd change them halfway through the gig. I sweat so much that there's practically a steady stream of water dripping off my chin onto that low *E* string. I have Jimbo [equipment manager Jim Neal] pour Brut in a towel and go over the *E* string during a drum solo, and that brings it back to life a little bit. I usually keep the previous night's strings on for the soundcheck, and they're dead as doornails; then Jim changes them before each show.

Do you bend strings a lot?

Yeah. I bend the *E* string quite a bit because it's the easiest to bend. I actually bend from a *C* note at the 8th fret up to the *E* octave. It's really wild, because to approximate how a guitar player drops a low *E* note with his vibrato bar, I take the *E* string at the *C* note, bend it up to the *E,* and then pluck it and let it down. So it sounds almost exactly like a guitar.

Is your action very low?

Pretty low. I lower it to the point where it buzzes, and then I back it up just a little bit. Someone told me that there are two ways to set up an electric instrument acoustically or electronically. Electronically, you can have fret buzzes and noises; you can't tell when you hear it through an amp. But if you were to play it acoustically, you'd say, "This is buzzing all over the place." I try to reach a happy medium, because I do practice without an amp most of the time. I practice getting a clean sound, trying to eliminate all the clickiness. If I do practice with a little amp, I turn the treble up to 10 and all the bass off, which forces me to play less clicky. Then I try to eliminate the pops and string noises that are inherently part of fingerstyle playing and roundwound strings.

What kind of onstage equipment are you using?

I use all solid-state gear. The Pearce preamp is my

"Good rhythm players are almost impossible to find. Everybody's a lead player."

main piece of gear for shaping the tone. It has a warm, kind of wooden tone. I have six of them, but I only use two at any given time. The rest are spares, although I've never had one fail. I depend on those so much that if one ever did go down, I'd want to be sure that I could still go on playing. They have two modifications. The one for my low end and clean sounds is padded [electronically altered to reduce the input level] so that it's almost totally clean and can't be distorted. The other one has an extra stage of distortion so that I get a screaming, reaming distortion. It has no noise, no tube microphonics, no changing from moment to moment, and none of the problems of tubes. I have six Yamaha PC2000 power amps that drive eight cabinets made by Flagg Systems in L.A. Each one has four 15s. I overamplify everything so that I can run my amps lower and get more dynamic range and a cleaner sound.

What are your effects?

My main one is an Eventide Harmonizer or a Yamaha SPX90. I have two Eventide H910s, one of the Eventide 969s, and two SPX90s. They aren't used at the same time, just in various spots. I usually split my distortion signal, sending it straight to one amp and through a Harmonizer set to about 1.01 and then to another amp. This gives a good chorused sound.

You have a variety of basic tones on Eat 'Em And Smile. *How did you get them?*

I mostly played through my amp — we miked the distortion and clean sounds and sent a clean low end direct; when we mixed, if I needed a grindier sound, we dialed in more of the amp. We also had a direct signal, so we mixed them. For example, on the middle part in "Yankee Rose," we just dialed in a bit more distortion from the amp. It's mostly a real woody tone; it's an example of tons of electronics approximating the sound of the unamplified bass. And on "Shy Boy," for the doubled things that I did with Steve, I dropped some low end off. Otherwise, it would be hard to articulate those high-speed, intricate lines.

Do you really try to approximate the sound of an unamplified bass?

Yeah. I do most of my practicing with no amp at all, so I find when I plug into a regular old off-the-shelf amp that the dynamic range is completely different than when you're playing the bass with no amp in a quiet room. Therefore, what my amp mim-

ics is what the bass feels like when it's not plugged in.

With your huge amp setup, do you still get the same intimate feeling?

In a way. Even though it can be very screaming with the distortion, it has a real *touch*, too. The change in the dynamic range when I plug into any other amp really throws my hand off.

On songs such as "I'm Easy," you have a real old-time round tone.

That comes from turning the distortion of my amp down or off. That's the beauty of my amp setup. And I can just mix the pickups on my bass to get the tone I want.

When you're working in a stadium, do you think the audience can hear the subtle differences?

I think so, because it's all miked up pretty well, and we've got a good sound company. We purposely didn't skimp on the sound; we wanted it to be something special.

Onstage, where do you usually get your cues?

The drummer. It's funny because he was used to cueing things himself, but I'm used to watching a drummer, as is Dave. But now it's a natural thing for all of us to cue off the drummer, because we always know where he is — he's the only one who isn't wireless. When you look for a cue, he's right there. I always like to be able to see the bass drum; I stand stage right. That way I can see what the bass drum is doing — most drummers are right-footed. I always like to lock into it. The guy who started me out, Joe Hesse, used

> *"I always stand stage right. I like to be able to see what the bass drum is doing and lock into it."*

to practice a lot with *just* a drummer. And when I was with Talas, to get songs tight before we played them out, I would get together with the drummer rather than have the distraction of guitars and vocals. I did that with Gregg, practicing just the bass and drums to all the songs together. Now we know each other's vocabulary of moves, so if I go to take a chance, I kind of know where he's going. The chanciness is what makes it fun, makes it magic. I don't know exactly what street he's on, but I know what city he's in. The guy who can make or break a band is always the drummer. When I started to play with a more active style, rather than just following the bass drum, I got into following tom-tom fills, snare shots, and bass drum and tom figures. If the drummer was doing triplets, so was I. I learned to play along with the whole drum kit. I'm just a frustrated drummer.

Drum machines can be good therapy.

It's true. It's a great advantage for bass players to be able to sit down with a machine, playing a flawless rhythm and practicing all day. In my day, we had metronomes or those drum machines that accordion players used to accompany them on weddings. Now we have John Bonham In A Box. It's really good for players to be able to work with drummers. I notice in my clinics that a lot of guys are concentrating on themselves as solo performers, rather than being ensemble players. They say, "I can solo, I can solo. Here, Bill, watch this solo." I say, "Yeah, that's good, but here comes the drummer. Now what are you going to do?" I try to stress that soloing is great and it's fun, and if anybody is guilty of overplaying, I sure am. I hope I do it effectively, but who knows? It seems to be going over okay. But the only reason I think it's effective is because I learned how to play *bass* first, rather than how to solo first. So when it comes time to play Motown or solid rock or solid blues-based stuff, where the bassist is hanging on that one note forever, I can do it, because I grew up with that. I like to stress to all the young players that if you don't know how to play the bass first, you'll never get a gig. I'm a specialized player, an unusual player, a square peg in a round hole of bassists. If you can walk really well, you can always learn to run.

– CHRIS SQUIRE –

BY LEONARD FERRIS – OCTOBER 1973

CHRIS SQUIRE IS a giant. Not just physically (he's well over 6' tall), but musically. His innovative, original, and powerful bass playing is the core of the brilliant English group Yes. And no matter how exceptional singer Jon Anderson, guitarist Steve Howe, and keyboard player Rick Wakeman are, without Chris Squire they'd probably be just another band — a marvelous one, certainly, but not a Yes.

Squire is a very soft-spoken and, at times, seriously introspective man. Music has been his major love since he was a teenager, and his devotion to it and to Yes is virtually all-consuming.

Though his parents had no musical background, Chris studied music theory in a London suburb school, even singing in the Gifford Cathedral Choir. At 16, he and some friends decided to form a band, and since Squire was the biggest and could best hold the bass, he was elected. But during this time Squire was "into school rebellion" and was expelled. "But my parents were quite good about it, actually. They never hassled me about music at all," he says.

The band continued on an informal basis, playing weddings and the like, and mostly copying Beatles and Chuck Berry tunes. In 1965 Chris and the group's organist split to join a better-known local band, Syn. For two years they worked casuals all over the country and played frequently in London's Marquee Club. Syn's guitarist was Peter Banks, who was later to be Yes' lead player through the group's

first LP (he was subsequently replaced by Steve Howe).

Syn lasted into 1967, but disbanded because some of the members, according to Chris, didn't want to make music their careers. "But the seeds of Yes were there," he says.

Then followed a nine-month period in his Kensington flat, sitting at home studying and practicing his bass. For a few months he played with "a freaky band in UFO-type clubs." The group, an experimental trio, was called Mabel Greer's Toy Shop, and Chris still cracks up when thinking about the strangeness of it all.

In 1968 Squire met singer Jon Anderson in London. Together, on 300 borrowed pounds, they formed Yes with Banks on guitar, drummer Bill Bruford (later replaced by Alan White) and organist Tony Kaye, who would give way to Rick Wakeman in 1971. For nine months they rehearsed, tried out, and worked on getting the group to unite. Then, when Sly And The Family Stone canceled a London club date at the last minute, Yes was called on. The overwhelming reception they received that night hasn't died down yet, and Yes continues to be one of the most popular and critically acclaimed bands to emerge from Britain.

A Futurama bass, "probably made in Italy and exported to England," was Squire's first instrument. At the time he joined Syn, Chris was also working at Boosey & Hawkes' store on Regent Street in London as the shop assistant and salesman. The company also had a shop in Piccadilly which sold electric guitars. As an employee, the bassist took advantage of available discounts to get a two-pickup Rickenbacker which he later converted to stereo. It's still his primary instrument, though the Rickenbacker company recently custom-made a 6-string bass for him.

"I didn't like their amps, though," Squire recalls, "so when I was with Syn, I got a Vox AC-30 head with two Vox speaker cabinets. It had a treble-boosting circuit on it. In the studio, it's one of the best amps. I still use it."

When Yes was being formed, Chris turned to a Marshall 100-watt amp, but a year after the band started going on the road he switched to two Fender Dual Showmans with four Fender speaker cabinets. He says, "I was used to that size of a unit, but not to the 15" speaker sound. I wanted something like them, though, so I decided on two Sunn cabinets with six 12s in each one."

He was still using Fender amps, though, when Yes planned its first U.S. tour, but was told there'd be plenty of American equipment available. He was given a Sunn amp with 4x12 cabinets, but didn't like the bass sound. As a result, he played the first tour using the lead guitar amp.

"When we returned to London," Chris says, "I went to Sound City to order a Sunn. They said Sunn had given one like I wanted to Eric Clapton and he had sold it to Sound City. It was the Coliseum lead amp. So I bought it right then. It's the one I still use."

Squire also utilizes a Cry Baby wah and a Maestro Brassmaster. "The Maestro is the best fuzz that's made for bass. It gives me the amount of fuzz I want, plus the perfect blend of fuzz and straight tone." He also uses an unnamed bass pedal, similar to what organists play with their feet. It was found in kit form in Europe by the Yes equipment manager, who put it together. It's tuned to the deepest organ tones "for extra depth," and had a sustain switch built in. There is also a graphic equalizer to boost various frequen-

cies in order to compensate for differences in halls the band plays.

Additionally, Squire uses a Herco pick (though he occasionally plays with his fingers) and prefers Rotosound strings, which he says "are great for one night, so I change them before each show."

When Yes goes into the studio for an album, Chris Squire hauls in nine different basses, including the Rickenbacker, a Fender, a Guild, and a Danelectro 6-string. "I like to try them all out on the different songs, just to see what sounds best," he says.

About the only thing he ever does the same in the studio is refuse to plug directly into the board, preferring to mike his amp. "The board takes all the character out of your sound," he claims. "It rules out all that you've previously done to get your own sound."

Squire is a very precise musician, especially when it comes to his equipment and amp settings, feeling that "My sound is a combination of the amp controls, the guitar's controls, and the volume we're playing at." The settings on the Sunn, which Chris states without hesitation, are 6 on the volume knob, 4 on the low-frequency control, 3 on the high-frequency, 5 on the mid-frequency, and 10 on the treble. The volume and tone controls on the treble pickup are both run wide open. The volume on the bass pickup is near full, and the tone knob sits at 4.

Traditionally, the function of the bass has been to lay down a steady beat, to be the anchor for the rest of the band. Squire is changing all that, preferring instead "to be an integral part of the band, to be as equally important as the other instruments." In this, he is — philosophically, at least — akin to such bassists as John Entwistle, Jack Bruce, and Felix Pappalardi, among others, who are altering the instrument's entire future. "The bass," Squire feels, "is just as much a solo and melodic instrument as the guitar or even organ. It just depends how you want to play it."

– BILL WYMAN –

BY JON SIEVERT – DECEMBER 1978

BILL WYMAN IS often called the quiet Rolling Stone. It's not that he has nothing to say, but rather that hardly anyone ever bothers to ask. In the 16 years of the turbulent existence of the Stones, the focus has always been upon the lead singer and chief guitar player, as journalists have scrambled for a few words from Mick Jagger or Keith Richards.

In fact, Bill Wyman proves to be a wellspring of information as he reflects upon his years as part of the foundation of perhaps the quintessential rock band. His unobtrusive, almost immobile stage manner may make him the least recognizable member of the world's most recognizable band. And yet his steady, deceptively simple bass lines have provided an anchor for a band that depends upon rhythm as an indispensable element in its sound, both onstage and in the studio.

Born 37 years ago in the working-class London suburb of Penge, Wyman's first encounter with music came at age 10 as a result of his parents' decision that he should play piano. Two years of lessons allowed him to pass a couple of early exams at the London School of Music, but Bill wasn't interested in the practicing required in order to proceed with an academic career. He then tried the clarinet, but the cost of renting an instrument from the school coupled with a lack of real interest ended that endeavor after only a few months.

Though he continued to occasionally "mess about" on the piano, Bill did not again get interested in playing until he was nearly 20 and in the British Air Force in Germany. This time it was an acoustic guitar tuned to an open chord that attracted him, and he was especially inspired by a particular kind of music called skiffle, which swept England in the mid-'50s. The foremost practitioner of skiffle (which usually featured a broomhandle bass, a jug, and handmade percussion instruments), was Lonnie Donegan, who had several hits with American folk songs such as "Rock Island Line," "Stewball," and "John Henry."

When Wyman left the Air Force, he returned home and rounded up some friends and formed a band that consisted of a singer, a drummer, and three guitar players. Somebody had to play bass, and Bill, as leader, took on the responsibility. Unable to afford the luxury of an electric bass, he tuned the bottom two strings of his guitar down an interval of seven frets and attempted to improvise. Before long he bought his first electric bass, a nondescript Japanese thin-body model, for the sum of $15. To this day he treasures it as the best-sounding, easiest-playing instrument he has ever owned, and he frequently uses it for recording.

Wyman's early band, called the Cleftones, gained something of a local reputation playing Chuck Berry, the Coasters, and Fats Domino tunes. Bill settled into a scratch existence supplemented by a day job and gradually began to build a reputation that got him calls in TV and recording studios in London, backing up-and-coming musicians. In December of 1962, the drummer in his band, Tony Chapman, answered an ad in a music newspaper. When he returned from the audition he told Bill that the group also needed a bass player, and Wyman went to the next rehearsal. The band already had a name — the Rolling Stones, inspired by a line from a Muddy Waters tune — and at the time consisted of Mick Jagger on vocals and harmonica, Brian Jones on guitar and an assortment of other instruments, Keith Richards on guitar, and Ian Stewart on piano. The band's raw blues sound riveted Wyman, and he signed on. Three weeks later, Charlie Watts replaced Chapman on drums, and the last piece of the Rolling Stones snapped into place.

Within six months the band acquired a manager and released their first single — a Chuck Berry tune, "Come On" — which made the U.K. Top 30. A year later they had their first #1 hit, "It's All Over Now." Stewart soon became road manager and a part-time Rolling Stone.

Through all the incredible craziness that has seemed to follow the Stones around for the past 16 years, Wyman has seemingly remained the most untouched. Musically, he has always been the most active member outside of the group, turning up at a wide variety of recording sessions. He is also the only member of the band to produce a solo album and, in fact, has produced two, both on Rolling Stones records: *Monkey Grip* and *Stone Alone*. Both consist primarily of original material penned by Wyman.

This interview was conducted in Los Angeles three days after the completion of the Stones' 1978 American tour. Wyman was there relaxing and receiving treatment for a chipped bone in a knuckle on the middle finger of his left hand; the injury was incurred near the end of the tour when he fell from a stage in St. Paul, Minnesota.

What were the circumstances surrounding your recent accident?

I fell off the back of the stage. They had a balcony behind the stage with kids hanging off it, and between that and the stage was about seven or eight feet of black curtain, which I assumed covered a wall. As we went to leave at the end of the concert, I ran behind the amps, and there was this girl leaning over the balcony, shouting, "Shake my hand, shake my hand." So I jumped about six or eight inches to reach her hand, and when I landed, one foot went through the curtain and one was on the stage — I had no support. I threw out my left arm to get the wall — which wasn't there — and went through the curtain and fell

seven feet to a concrete floor. They thought I might have concussions, because I had all these lights going off in me eyes.

Did you miss any concerts because of the injury?

No. I was laying in the hospital the next morning and phone calls were going back and forth saying, "Are you going to do the gig?" because it was one of the few times when the gigs were back to back. I had to make a decision at 7:30 in the morning whether I could do it or not. So I thought of all those people and all that crew going out to build the stage and things like that, and I decided I wanted to try. I figured that if I couldn't do it, Woody [Ron Wood] could always come across and take over.

How did you pull it off?

Well, I wasn't sure I was going to, because by midday the pain killers they'd given me had started to wear off. They hadn't done any real treatment to me — they just told me what was wrong. I didn't want to take pain killers, because I thought that I might not feel the pain when I used the fingers, and that I might make them worse. Then the doctor told me that I should have the wrist and hand in a cast for three weeks, because he suspected a hairline fracture of the wrist. And I just told him there was no way, because I had never missed a gig in 15 years and wasn't about to start now. I just basically told the doctors what I was going to do, and they said, "Okay, if that's the way you feel about it." The way I got away with it was by taping the middle and ring fingers together and noting with the index and little fingers. It was harder on some songs than others, but overall it turned out easier than I had anticipated. It was kind of like playing piano with one hand. I played five gigs like that. The lads in the band were great about it.

It is remarkable that you've never missed a gig in all these years.

Mick and Keith have never missed one, either. Brian missed a lot, but that was later on when he was ill a lot. Charlie missed one once — he was on holiday in Gibraltar and came back a day late because he didn't know we had a job. We found a drummer overnight; that was way back in 1963, so it was all right. The only gigs we miss are the ones where people say we're coming and we don't know about it. There've been a lot of those.

How did you first get interested in music?

Basically, I think my parents wanted me to study piano just because we had one in the house. The fundamental music lessons in school were actually quite good, the theory lessons. They were good for teaching you about crochets [eighth-notes] and minims [half-notes] and all of that. I was always messing about on the piano instead of doing the right things. I used to speed them up and slow them down and put twiddly bits on and all of that, and my parents used to get very angry.

Did you have access to much recorded music?

Only on the radio. And if you would listen to the BBC in those days, there was really nothing on there. The first person I heard who I thought was really amazing was Les Paul. He was the one who turned me on to the sound of guitar music. I was listening to singers before that, mostly English ones doing covers of American hits by people like Frankie Laine and Kay Starr. Johnnie Ray was one of the first to make me really open my ears. That was like two or three years before Elvis. A few jazz records made it across and, though I'm not really interested in jazz, I do have some nice memories of some records by Dizzy Gillespie at the time and by a band led by Kenny Graham called the AfroCubists.

How old were you then?

In my late teens, I guess. Then rock and roll appeared, and it was a whole other thing. Just about then I was called up for the National Service and had to serve two years in the Royal Air Force in Germany. When I got there I started listening to American broadcasts, which we used to pick up in the British sector. Suddenly I was hearing things like the *Grand Ole Opry* show when I'd never heard country music before. I used to really like waking up at 6:00 A.M. before we'd go on duty and lie in bed and listen to all the great singers like Roy Acuff and Flatt & Scruggs. I'm still a great collector of that kind of music. Then we started to hear things by Bill Haley and Elvis, and then Little Richard and Chuck Berry. Little Richard and Berry really blew me away. I saw Berry in a film called *Rock, Rock, Rock,* where he was playing "You Can't Catch Me," and I was completely won over.

Is that when you started playing skiffle music?

Yes. Lonnie Donegan was doing really well playing three-chord folk songs and old blues tunes. It seemed pretty simple, so I got a few guys together and we tried it.

Did you play washtub bass?

No, I was playing guitar. I wasn't interested in the bass until it became necessary for the band. I think a lot of bass players have started that way.

> *"I wasn't interested in the bass until it became necessary for the band."*

How did you decide that a seven-fret interval was the right amount to tune down the guitar strings?

I'm not exactly sure, but it seemed like they couldn't go any lower without the strings getting too soggy to play. I used to play Chuck Berry riffs under the band or just maybe do a walking thing on two strings. And then I remember going to see a band that was playing at a dance for maybe 800 people in an old cinema that had been gutted to make a dance hall. I remember walking from the stairway and through the door and being floored, just rooted to the spot, by this amazing sound. It took me a moment to realize that it was the sound of the electric bass, and I was just thunderstruck by it. I thought, "Well, I've got to get a bass, because this it where it's at." I could see the difference immediately.

What did you finally choose?

Well, there wasn't much choosing involved. When I went looking, I found out that basses were something like 115 pounds, which you can multiply by two if you want a rough idea in dollars. I didn't have money like that. I was earning about eight pounds a week then and about to get married, so there was no way I could purchase it. So then the drummer said he knew a guy who had a bass guitar to sell. He wanted eight pounds for it, and I thought about how terrible it had to be. But I wanted a bass, so we went and looked at it and, sure enough, it was a mess.

What kind was it?

I never have found out. It was Japanese and had a thin, flat body with one pickup. The body was big, but it had an incredibly thin neck. The tuners were really bad, and the strings went straight over this solid piece of thing for a bridge and through a hole and hooked on the back; it was also a horrible brown color. But it was a bass, and it was in my price range, so we scraped half of the money together and promised him the other half later. It was a little disappointing, because I'd been looking at photos of Jerry Lee Lewis and Little Richard's bands, and they had all these wonderful-looking guitars which I had never seen in England. Of course, they were mainly Fenders and Gibsons. Little Richard's band used some really obscure-looking ones.

So what did you do with your prize?

Well, I got out some of the pictures from guitar catalogs and came up with a drawing of a bass body as I would like it to be. It was kind of a Gibson shape, and I drew it out on a piece of cardboard and cut it out. Then I took the piece of cardboard and put it on the back of the bass and drew around it. There was like two or three extra inches around the edge, and I went down the road to my uncle's house and cut it out with his saw. Then I pulled all the frets out because they buzzed badly. I figured I'd still have the lines in the fingerboard to go by if I took the frets out. Then I rubbed it all down so there weren't too many holes in the fingerboard, and got the body very smooth, with a bit of shape on it. Then I stripped all the finish off and painted it with three coats of shiny black paint and rubbed it down to a fine finish. I bought some Framus strings and plugged it into this tiny little amp I was using. It sounded fantastic.

What kind of amp was it?

It was like an 8-watt Watkins that had cost 30 or 40 dollars. It had four inputs, and we would all go in. One for bass, one for lead guitar, one for rhythm guitar, and one for the vocal. It even had a reverb on it.

How long did you use that first bass?

I still use it even today for recording certain songs, because the sound is so pure and deep and rich. With no frets, you can really slide around on it like a stand-up bass, only you can see where the frets are supposed to be. I could never see my way about on a fretless with no markings; on this you can actually see where to put your fingers, but you have to be very careful because you have to be dead-on to be in tune. I've used it on nearly every single record, with the exception of the *Some Girls* album; I used a Travis Bean for that.

What other instruments have you used?

After I'd been playing a couple years and started getting the studio gigs, I decided I had to have something that looked a little more respectable. So I bought this big flashy-looking Vox. I think it was called a Phantom. That's what I was playing when I went to audition for the Stones.

Did you have an idea what you were getting into when you went to that rehearsal?

Well, sort of. The drummer had brought back a tape from that first rehearsal so that I could learn some songs. He played it, and it was so slow and funky. It was a Jimmy Reed tune, actually, and I had never heard the blues before, apart from early jazz-blues things like Jelly Roll Morton. None of that stuff had ever been released in England. I got real interested in the sound with the harmonica and all that. So I went in with this big flashy Vox, and the band didn't like it at all, because they were using the most crude equipment you could believe. They had two little amplifiers with blown speakers, and when they

riffed on them they'd crack and growl — it sounded so authentic. Keith had this weird guitar with a sliding pickup on it, a Harmony or something.

So what made them decide you were the man they were looking for?

By that time I owned a Vox AC-30 amplifier, which was really something in those days. It was like your Fender Twin, if you like, which was quite a valuable asset. So they thought, "Oh, really good amp; bass player's nothing special, but we'll keep him so we can use the amp." That was the general opinion, I have since learned. You know, they are real con artists, that lot.

How long did that Vox last?

I went back to my homemade bass about a month after I had joined the band. It just had a sound that couldn't be beat. After a while I got really scared to take it on the road because I was afraid it would get stolen. That happened a lot in those days, with the kids pouring onstage and all that. I had to find a substitute, which wasn't easy, because my bass had such a narrow neck and my hands are really tiny. I've probably got the smallest hands in show business, at least among bass players. I would say the scale on my bass is at least 6" shorter than a Fender Precision.

So what did you settle on?

I've never really settled on anything. About the only thing around at that time that was suitable was a Framus Star — you know, with the big cherry body. I played it upright, because it was still quite a long guitar, and my arms are short as well. I just found it physically easier to stretch up and down than sideways. I played one of those way up through about 1968. I tried a few Vox guitars, some Gibsons, and various Fenders, because of the sound. The boys always used to say, "Why don't you try a Fender — you get a really good sound, and it's easy to record," and all that. And I would agree, but I could not play the bloody things. I tried the Mustang, the smaller version, and there were a couple more which I can't remember. I actually did an album with the Mustang, though I can't remember which one. It was just too hard for me to play. After that, I tried a Gibson for onstage, but the bottom strings were really dull sounding. You could never get clarity on those lower strings. I always ended up using my old one for recording.

Could you mention a few tunes that you feel it was particularly appropriate on?

"I've Got The Blues" [*Sticky Fingers*] was probably one of the best songs I ever did with that one. "Sister Morphine," from the same LP, is another — a lot of the slow, bluesy things, the ballady things, songs where I wanted it to sound like a string bass. I can sort of slide on it because there are no frets, and I can almost get a little bit of that slap sound playing it with the thumb. I play every other bass with a pick, but I use my thumb on that one.

Have you ever changed the electronics on it?

Yeah, we added another pickup, a Baldwin. That's about it, though — just changed a bit of the electrics, put new tuners on, and gave it another coat of paint. Still, it's the most amazing guitar. Everybody that tries it is flipped out. Billy Preston says it's the best bass guitar he's ever messed with.

Why don't you have somebody duplicate it so that you can have it on the road?

I've tried to have it duplicated by guitar makers, and they just aren't interested. They look at it and they just say, "Forget that one; why don't you have one like this?" I had a long correspondence going on with one guy over a period of years about duplicating it as near as possible. He couldn't do it — or wouldn't do it, I should say. They all want to sell you their new invention. Also, I'm scared of leaving it with someone for three months. I would like to say something right here and now that I hope will be heard by someone. I wish manufacturers would make small basses, mainly because there are a lot of kids who want to play coming up who can't do it because their hands are too small. I think it would really be smart of somebody like Fender or Gibson to come up with a mini-bass with a thinner neck, smaller body, shorter scale, and lighter strings. Bass is really hard to learn if you're a kid, and it would be a great help. I'm amazed it's never been done, because it seems like it would be a good selling line.

What other basses are you using these days?

I've had a Dan Armstrong that I've used onstage since 1975. They built it for me, but the first one was Plexiglas and incredibly heavy. We thought of ideas to lighten it, like drilling holes in it and still keeping it strong. In the end Armstrong finally said, "Well, why don't I make you a wooden one?" So off he went, and he came back three or four months later and says, "Try this." It was quite good, but I still couldn't find perfect strings for it. It's very difficult to find short-scale strings, because even the few that are made are designed for a guitar that has the tuners

"I've probably got the smallest hands in show business, at least among bass players. I wish manufacturers would make small basses."

spread out in one row. All the short-scale basses I've owned had two on one side and two on the other, so I would find that they didn't fit. We had a hell of a job trying to find strings that would match. I finally found some Rotosounds that fit and sound good. They give it a harder tone, but it still sounds fat, which is important to me. I love that fat, heavy sound underneath; I like to hear a lot of bottom.

Have you found another guitar suitable for recording?

Yes. I've now got a Travis Bean that was built to my size specifications. I played one of their full-size models and was really impressed by the quality of it. The bottom notes were clean all the way down, which was something I was really looking for. I asked them to make me a short version, and about six months later along came this guitar. I used it on *Some Girls* exclusively, and it's probably the best bass sound I've ever had on record. And if you can hear yourself sounding that good, you can play that good, too. You know what I mean? It always takes you to that step beyond, and you never get that encouragement if it sounds bad, no matter what you do. So I love that guitar, and I've asked them to make me another one like it.

How do you see your development as a musician since those early days?

I thought I improved very quickly in the first two to three years, as the whole band did. The only exception was Brian, who after a couple of years reached a saturation point and started to deteriorate. Keith, Charlie, and I were improving fast on our instruments and Mick was, of course, also improving as a performer, dancer, and singer. We were all trying new things, experimenting on other instruments. Brian was the best at that. Even when he wasn't playing any better on his guitar, he was picking up all sorts of instruments in the studio and playing them well. He'd try just about anything — dulcimers, sitars, flute, full-size harp. We used to experiment quite a bit, but then it kind of leveled out. The scope for experimenting with the band just seemed to close up. Mick and Keith are always looking for something different, but the songs and the chord structures don't give you much of a chance of doing anything different, except perhaps on the slower ones. "Loving Cup" [*Exile On Main Street*], for instance, offers a few possibilities where you can turn some runs around or do some little slide things, but basically if you're into "Brown Sugar," "It's Only Rock 'N' Roll," and "Jumpin' Jack Flash," there's really not a whole lot you can do.

What inspired you to record your own album?

I got pretty frustrated about five years ago and felt that I needed to break out. I'd always been aware that I was no Jack Bruce or Stanley Clarke, but I was feeling really cramped by the material we were doing and what was left for me to actually perform on. I wanted to play with some different musicians and instruments. I've always done more outside session work than anyone else in the band because I need that variety. The Rolling Stones have gotten so big that it's just not practical for us to mess about and experiment with new instruments. If you want to mess on piano, Billy Preston or Nicky Hopkins is there. If you want horns, you have to have a horn section. If we want vocals, we can call up three of the best in the world. So all the fun of playing around on other instruments — like finding a glockenspiel and doing something on that — just faded away. It got down to just playing the bass on the track, and sometimes it wasn't even that if you didn't happen to turn up the day it finally came together. I might have been working on a song on and off with the band for five days, just trying to get together and working it out from a basic riff. Then maybe on the seventh day my kid gets sick and I call in to say I can't make it to the session. And they'll say, "Oh, that's okay; we might mess about, but we probably won't do anything." Then I come back the day after and find that the track is done, and Keith has played bass on it because it suddenly happened.

So that explains why you don't play on all the tracks?

Yes. And it's no fault of anybody's, apart from the fact that things just happen. And, of course, there was nothing else to play on the track after it was recorded by somebody else. Whereas if it had been Keith or Mick Taylor that hadn't been there one night and we'd done the track, they would overdub the guitar. But you can't overdub the bass, because it's already there, you know? It would mean just copying it, which would make no sense whatever. So it gets terribly frustrating when you finish an album you've been working on for six months — the same as everybody else — but suddenly you're only playing on seven of the ten tracks.

Did the solo albums satisfy your need to diversify?

Well, I lost that frustration I'd been living with for two or three years. After I'd done those two albums,

I felt very differently about playing and recording with the Stones. I became much more confident and unafraid about experimenting in the studio, rather than sticking only to the safely solid. I could experiment more and see what the guys thought. I might do something on one song and Mick would come up and say, "That's really great," and I'd get all puffed up. Another time I'd come up with an idea which I thought was equally good, and people would come over and say, "Hey, man, there's one thing wrong with the track. The bass isn't quite right, and maybe you should do it a bit more like Motown." And then I'd have to adapt, and I'd be disappointed. That's the way it is with all musicians — let's face it. But it did give me that chance, and I've felt more daring over the last four years. I took a lot more chances on *Some Girls*, and I was very pleased because most of the things worked out really well.

The lines on "Miss You" [Some Girls] are especially strong.

Especially different. The idea for those lines came from Billy Preston, actually. We'd cut a rough demo a year or so earlier, after a recording session. I'd already gone home, and Billy picked up my old bass when they started running through that song. He started doing that bit because it seemed to be the style of his left hand. So when we finally came to do the tune, the boys said, "Why don't you work around Billy's idea?" So I listened to it once and heard that basic run and took it from there. It took some changing and polishing, but the basic idea was Billy's.

What kind of process do you and Charlie go through in preparing to record? Do you rehearse rhythm tracks?

No, there's no rehearsal, as far as recording is concerned. Basically, Mick will come in with a cassette of a completed song, usually the slower, more ballady things. You usually have to work out the middle eight bars and the tempo, intro, and ending — if there is one — but usually the words, melody, and basic chord sequence are there and just need tightening up. Keith usually just comes in with something like a basic riff, and we all start working off of that. Charlie will lay something down and Keith says, "No, use the bass drum different," or, "Bill, change that note, because I'll have to adapt to that." We'll just work things out amongst ourselves while putting it all down on tape. And then we'll get to a point where someone will say, "Naw, we're not doing anything like where we were an hour ago." So we'll run the tape back and see that "Oh yeah, you were using the other beat, Charlie," and, "Why don't we go back to that?" and, "Bill, you do what you were doing."

So it's often pretty loose.

It's done very casually, and it's really jamming. We won't work it all out or anything like that. Actually, it's quite easy that way, but it can also be very boring. If you've got your bit together, but the whole thing isn't together, you can play it for eight hours. And by the time you go to bed that night, all you can hear going through your head is that riff. It drives you mad. Then you get all tuned up to do it the next night and they go, "No, let's leave that one. We're a bit bored with it." And so, by the time you get back to it 10 days later out of the blue one night, you've forgotten it and have to start all over again. But it's the way we record, and it seems to work.

Why do you think it works so well?

I don't know, but our band has always seemed to function very well against the rules. None of us are superb musicians in a technical or performing sense. It's just that we have that mixture within the band, and Ron Wood has really dropped into that. Mick Taylor didn't, really. He's very technical and a very clever musician — much more clever musically than the rest of us, I think. That's probably why he didn't jell with us as well as Woody does. Woody's a very good musician, of course, but much more "Stonesy," if you like, more like Keith's playing than pretty.

What do you think gives the Stones their characteristic sound? Why does no other band sound quite like them?

That's something I've tried to analyze with a lot of people. We have a very tight sound for a band that swings, but in amongst that tight sound, it's very ragged as well. Leon Russell and I finally came up with a theory that goes something like this: Every rock and roll band follows the drummer, right? If the drummer slows down, the band slows down with him or speeds up when he does. That's just the way it works, except for our band. Our band does not follow the drummer; our drummer follows the rhythm guitarist, who is Keith Richards.

And that makes the difference?

Yes. Immediately you've got something like a 1/100th-of-a-second delay between the guitar and Charlie's lovely drumming. Now, I'm not putting Charlie down in any way for doing this, but onstage

"I became much more confident and unafraid about experimenting in the studio, rather than sticking only to the safely solid."

you have to follow Keith. You have no way of not following him. You know there's no rigorous 12 bars and then we break and do that bit and then we come in with four more bars and then Mick does his part — it doesn't work like that. The tune is basically worked out, but it changes all the time; it's very loose. So with Charlie following Keith, you have that very minute delay. Add to that the fact that I've always been able to pick up chord structures very quickly, so I tend to anticipate a bit because I kind of know what Keith's going to do. We've been playing together for so long that I know without even thinking about it. That's why I might be standing there looking at the ceiling when everybody else is looking at Keith to see when the final thing is coming down. I mean, we all make mistakes but basically I don't need to watch Keith as the other guys tend to do, because I can feel when it's coming. So I tend to anticipate the change, and that puts me that split second ahead of Keith.

What's the result?

When you actually hear that, it seems to just pulse. You know it's tight because we're all making stops and starts and it is in time — but it *isn't* as well. That's what we think is the reason for our sound, apart from our style. Everyone thinks, "Oh, Rolling Stones" as soon as they hear one of our fast tunes. And yet sometimes the whole thing can reverse. Charlie will begin to anticipate, and I'll fall behind, but the net result is that loose type of pulse that goes between Keith, Charlie, and me.

How did that begin to happen? Was it a conscious decision or just a matter of personality?

Probably a matter of personality. Keith is a very confident and stubborn player, so he usually thinks someone else has made a mistake. Maybe you'll play halfway through a solo and find that Keith has turned the time around. He'll stop a half- or quarter-bar somewhere, and suddenly Charlie's playing on the beat, instead of on the backbeat — and Keith will not change back. He will doggedly continue until the band changes to adapt to him. It doesn't piss us off in any way, because we all expect it to happen. He knows in general that we're following him, so he doesn't care if he changes the beat around or isn't really aware of it. He's quite amusing like that. Sometimes Keith will be playing along, and suddenly he becomes aware that Charlie's playing on the beat, and he'll turn around and point like, "Ah ha, gotcha!"

Like Charlie made the mistake?

Yeah, and Charlie will be so surprised and suddenly realize he's on the beat for some reason, and he hasn't changed at all. And then he'll be very uptight to get back in, because it's very hard for a drummer to swap the beat. So it's a mite funny sometimes, but it does happen, especially on the intros. Some of the intros are quite samey-sounding. I mean, if you're doing a riff on one chord with the inflections that Keith uses, and you're not hearing too well with the screaming crowds, you cannot tell if you are coming in on or off the beat. "Street Fighting Man" is a tune that this tends to happen on.

Doesn't Charlie have monitor speakers?

Well, he's got monitors, but in those circumstances it's very difficult to hear the accents — the difference between the soft and hard strokes. The problem is that he's often totally unaware that he's on the wrong beat, and he shuts his eyes and pulls his mouth up, you know, and he's gone. You can't even catch his eye because they're closed. Someone has to go up and kick the cymbal. I don't think that happens too often with other bands; I don't hear those very simple kinds of mistakes going on with other bands. But I think that's a little of the charm of the Stones. They're not infallible, and we know that. Everybody else might as well know it, too.

How did you get one of your original compositions, "In Another Land," on Their Satanic Majesties Request?

The only reason that went on the album was because on the night that it was recorded, Charlie and I were the only ones who turned up for the session. Glyn Johns was engineering those sessions, and they seemed to go on forever because the drug busts were on and we didn't know whether Mick and Keith were going to prison for God knows how long, or what. Mick was maybe getting three years and Keith was getting a year — we didn't know. They were out on bail and there were appeals, and the tour had been canceled. It was a very, very weird time about then. So on this particular night, I turned up as usual and Glyn told me that the session had been canceled but that I'd already left home before he could reach me. So we listened back to a few things, and then Glyn asked if I had any songs I wanted to do. It so happened I had been fooling about on the piano, and so we had a go at it. We thought we'd use sound effects because we didn't have much instrumentation.

Did you do all the vocals by overdubbing?

The Faces were recording next door, and Steve

Marriott came in and volunteered to help out. I had never sung before, so I used a tremolo on my voice. Nicky Hopkins showed up to play some piano, and we just messed about until we finally got it down. And the next night when the boys came in, Glyn played it back and they really liked it but decided they had to put some backing vocals on. So it came out because it seemed to work with the rest of the songs on the album. But you have to look on it as a complete coincidence. I mean, if everybody had turned up that night, that song would never have appeared on record. That's the way it is.

What kind of amplification are you using?

Right now I'm using Ampegs, though I have no idea what model or anything. In the studio I'm using an old piggyback Ampeg I've had since the '60s. It was the first guitar amp I ever saw used in little clubs in America and in recording studios, so I decided to get it and I've used that practically always in the studio. With my old bass I usually go directly into the board, because it has such a pure sound. I used a Vox almost exclusively up until the end of the '60s.

Didn't you have some kind of endorsement deal with Vox?

Yes, in the early '60s. They had the best amps in England. When we came over to America for our first tour, we had to use Fenders. The guitar players loved them, but not me. They sounded too thin; they had no body. Then Vox came up with these 50- or 100-watt cabinets that were completely enclosed and had concrete in the bottom of them. They really sounded fat and rich. We used to blow them every other night, but Vox would always come up with a new set right away. Vox was invaluable to all those early English bands, and a lot of them never would have kept it together without that equipment. Then the Who arrived, and they started to use Marshalls and Sunns, and a lot of people jumped on the bandwagon.

But you stayed with Vox?

Yeah, because I never could find a better amp for my sound and the way I played then. That's also why I still use that old piggyback Ampeg in the studio — it suits my sound and the way I play, and that's important. Some guys would look down their noses or squirm at the sound of it, but it all depends on the way you play. If it suits *you*, that's all that counts.

Who are some bass players that have influenced you or that you really like?

James Jamerson. He was the Motown bassist during all those great early years. Duck Dunn was great on all those Stax things. I loved all those Booker T. and Otis Redding records he worked on. I like him because he was basically a very simple player, yet every now and again he'd throw in a tasty surprise. Like he'd play a line, and every other time he'd do it, he'd time the last two or three notes differently. You knew where he was at, but he'd always come up with these interesting little deviations from the very simple line. And for the same reason I like Carl Radle very much. He used to go by fairly unnoticed in a lot of bands, like Leon Russell's, but I could relate to him very well. On some tracks with that band I would sit back and say, "Sweet Emily, that's me playing the bass on that track." It sounded just like something I would do. And I used to say to Carl, "What's going on here? Are you copying me, or am I copying you?" He'd just give this little wry smile. I admire other bass players for their flash and brilliance, but I don't want to play like that. I probably couldn't anyway, and even then it would not fit in with the Stones' sound.

Are there other players?

There's one amazing player that I must mention named Colin Hotchkinson. He played in an English band called Backdoor about four years ago. I saw him at a Montreux Jazz Festival playing chords on a Fender bass and accompanying his vocal on a Robert Johnson blues song. He had the strings tuned up some, but he was playing it like an acoustic guitar and singing. I think it was the most amazing bit of bass playing I've ever seen. When I run into guys like that, I think about going into photography or something. He's just phenomenal, and yet hardly anyone knows of him. I often wonder why people like that don't resent people like me. Maybe they do. I get very sensitive about that sort of thing. In the past, there has been a lot of resentment between jazz and rock musicians, but that seems to be slowly disappearing because the level of musicianship is climbing.

"I admire other bass players for their flash and brilliance, but I don't want to play like that."

Do you have any more plans for solo albums?

No, I finally got bored with it. I mean, I had a great time working with all those great musicians like Dr. John, Leon Russell, [drummer] Jim Keltner, Van Morrison, Tower Of Power, and the Pointer Sisters. It was fun, but I don't think that it's my calling. It got off a lot of petty frustrations and made me think differently from a musical standpoint. It made me play better with the band.

Do you hope to write more songs for the Stones?

Basically, there's not really any room for another songwriter in our band. I'd like to be involved if I could, and I'm sure Ronnie Wood would. And Mick Taylor definitely wanted to be, which was one of his frustrations. So it's a little bit of a drag, but if you only record one album every 18 months or so, which is what we've done for the last eight years, there's not much room for anyone else. By the time we get around to recording, Mick and Keith have so many songs ready that they have to weed tunes out. Besides, the kind of things I write may not be the right kind of songs for the Stones.

So what do you want to do to keep from getting bored again?

Actually, I've been working on an idea for a film score lately. I'd like to do some electronic music. Nothing heavy or complicated, but something very simple. I've got a Polymoog and an ARP synthesizer that I've been using to put some things down on a 4-track. What I'm looking for is a chance to write descriptive music for a visual thing. I got turned on by all those spaghetti westerns by Sergio Leone, and they got me trying to write descriptive music. I've gotten quite hung up on that in the last year or so, and I'd like to experiment with it some more with some new instruments just to see what happens. That's really my next goal. Now all I need to do is find a filmmaker who will trust in me.

– STUDIO & POP –

– NATHAN EAST –

BY TOM MULHERN – OCTOBER 1985

BOB GRUEN/STAR FILE, INC.

ONLY FIVE YEARS ago, Nathan East told himself, "I want to be *everybody's* bass player." So far, he's on the right track, contributing to hit albums by the likes of George Benson, Kenny Loggins, Phil Collins, Philip Bailey, Eric Clapton, the Jacksons, Al Jarreau, Julio Iglesias, Barbra Streisand, Diana Ross, the Eurythmics, and the Tubes. The recipient of two NARAS (National Academy of Recording Arts and Sciences) Most Valuable Player awards — in 1982 and '83 — he is a powerhouse session man, as well as a touring member of Kenny Loggins' band. Nathan also wrote the music to the Philip Bailey/Phil Collins hit "Easy Lover" [*Chinese Wall*]. Sometimes working 10 hours a day in the studio, the 29-year-old can be heard on a number of soundtracks, including *Footloose, Private Benjamin, Mr. Mom, Brewster's Millions, and Dr. Detroit.* Turn on the TV, and he's in there punching up the theme to *Fame;* when commercials for McDonald's, Budweiser, and Coke punctuate the main attractions, he's laying down the groove. Switch over to pay TV, and besides hearing him on the many soundtracks, you'll hear him on the logo pieces for HBO. Indeed, he seems to be everybody's bassist.

As a kid growing up in San Diego, Philadelphia-born Nathan East wanted to play piano, but only traditional band instruments were available in the junior high bands. "Violin and viola were too small, and string bass was too big," he laughs. Young East studied cello for about three years. His brothers played

guitar in folk masses at the nearby Catholic church, and Nathan often tagged along to their rehearsals. When he was about 14, he picked up a bass and started plunking. "It was really magic," he says. "I learned a few bass lines, and I took it to a school dance. I got up and played with the band, and everyone went crazy. All of a sudden, I had a bunch of girls talking to me [*laughs*]. I said, 'This is the instrument for me!'"

Once he reached high school, Nathan began playing bass in the stage band and soon enrolled in the chorus, pep band, jazz band, and orchestra. He also joined a local group playing proms and dances. An admirer of Tower Of Power's Francis "Rocco" Prestia's bass work, he tried learning all his material, as well as lines by Peter Cetera of Chicago, and Larry Graham of Sly And The Family Stone. "I couldn't figure out how Graham was doing some of the stuff," Nathan says. "That was before everyone knew what thumping and slapping were." Other influences included Verdine White of Earth, Wind & Fire, Chuck Rainey, James Jamerson, and upright player Ron Carter.

East never took electric bass lessons, but he obtained heavy sight-reading experience by performing in the school ensembles; he supplemented his learning by attending concerts and playing along with the radio. When he enrolled in the University of California at San Diego, he studied classical technique on string bass with Bert Turetzky (electric bass wasn't included in the curriculum). Although he enjoyed the acoustic instrument, he found the lure of the electric irresistible. During his first three years at UCSD, East took physics, chemistry, biology, and calculus, in addition to music courses, "in case I needed something to fall back on." He finally declared his major in music in time for his fourth year — while working in a band six nights a week. College was briefly interrupted when he went on the road with his band, Power, backing singer Barry White. After a two-quarter hiatus, he returned to UCSD, finished his requirements for his bachelor's degree, and plunged into a master's degree program.

After hearing Nathan's recital (which included pieces by Jaco Pastorius, among others), Bert Turetzky convinced him to move to Los Angeles and pursue a studio career. He quit his gig in San Diego and began working with Barry White again, touring for three months before settling in L.A. in 1979. "I spent the first six months waiting for the phone to ring," he recalls. "I called the phone company a couple of times to make sure my phone worked [*laughs*]. And the only sessions I had were with Barry — and he didn't put the names of the musicians on the album cover. So, that really didn't do much for my career."

Things began to pick up when keyboardist Patrice Rushen referred Nathan to flutist Hubert Laws, culminating in a tour of the Philippines and an album titled *Family*. Some of Laws' band members in turn introduced Nathan to various producers, and his name soon appeared on about a half-dozen records. Beginning in January 1980, work started to come in, and arranger Gene Page took him under his wing, using him on jingles and records and referring him to other producers and arrangers. His workload ballooned, and the bassist was soon working almost every day. Nathan also cites the exodus of several top bassists from the studio scene as a catalyst for his newfound success. "My phone was ringing off the hook," he says. "People were impressed if you could read really well and play. That was the calling card. I had no problem reading, and I was used to a lot of playing. I said, 'Hey, this is painless!'"

Before working in L.A.'s studios, Nathan had limited jingle experience from San Diego, and admits that he had little idea of the inner workings of the recording scene: "I just knew that once you got into a 24-track studio and the red light went on, you were being charged megabucks to be there; you needed profes-

"Reading is just a means of communication, so that you don't have to hear someone sing it to you."

sionalism, good equipment, a good attitude, and a good sense of time. I didn't know that so many studios existed, and it was a new experience for me. The first session I walked into, there was Ray Parker, David T. Walker, Lee Ritenour, [drummer] James Gadson — all these heavyweights on the same date. I was really nervous. They all introduced themselves to me, and I found that they all had a very respectable, professional attitude. It was really exciting for me, and I used to keep a diary of every gig, saying who was on the date. It read like a who's who of studio players."

Nathan quickly felt at home, although he found a few dates exceptionally formidable — especially those combining complex bass passages and a full-sized orchestra. "Going to the soundstages at Universal or Fox, and playing with an orchestra full of 'pro' guys, and knowing you have to get it on the first take — that can get you a little nervous. And guys like Lee Ritenour and Jay Graydon were so slick and professional that it was just a little bit intimidating."

Nathan has performed with a broad range of musicians, attesting to his ability to work under vastly different circumstances. "I noticed by the end of one year that it was easier to keep busy if you were versatile," he says. "Lionel Richie was introduced to me at a Motown session, and later he called me in to play on the song 'Lady' [*Kenny Rogers' Greatest Hits*]. That was my first working introduction to him and Kenny Rogers." After the song became a hit, both singers tapped the bassist for their respective albums. Nathan explains, "One thing leads to another, and the producers at Warner Bros. — Lenny Waronker and Russ Titelman — used me on Randy Newman's "I Love L.A." [*Trouble In Paradise*] and some of Rickie Lee Jones' stuff. They produced some of Eric Clapton's songs on *Behind The Sun*, and I got called for that. I think they get comfortable working with you, and it becomes sort of a loyal situation."

Longtime favorite musicians are also included among those who have employed Nathan's talents. "After working with Earl Klugh, who was on my hit list, I said, 'This is great — I could quit playing now.' It was like a dream to work with him because I was such a big fan." Likewise, working with drummer John Robinson was a dream come true: "I used to listen to him with Quincy Jones, and I always wanted to work with him. The first session we played together, we hit it off just great. Now we play so much together that it's like being married [*laughs*]."

Despite his sight-reading skills, Nathan often comes into a session with nothing written for him, especially on rock dates. For the Eurythmics' "Would I Lie To You" [*Be Yourself Tonight*], he was asked to play a bass line that would complement a straight eighth-note bass part played on synthesizer. "In those situations," he explains, "I just listen to it and get all the changes in my head. Then, when they start to roll tape, I experiment with different ideas. In those instances, they want *you* to come up with a part. Other times, everything is written and I don't have to come up with anything. It goes from one extreme to the other." To be successful as a studio bassist, Nathan feels that there are several crucial elements. "In sight-reading," he advises, "one of the most important things is identifying the rhythm, because most of the music isn't that difficult. Reading is just a means of communication, so that you don't have to hear someone sing it to you. I learned that there are a few rhythms that always come up, particularly the dotted eighth-note followed by a sixteenth-note, and certain things that are tied together. What really helped me was reading drum music. If you get the rhythms under your belt, the pitches are almost secondary. There are only so many notes in the scale, but there's an infinite variety of rhythms. I wanted a good grasp of rhythms so that I could concentrate on the notes."

Although he has found the ability to read treble clef helpful, Nathan believes that a strong understanding of the bass clef is usually sufficient. "The more you know, the better off you are," he says, adding the caution: "You never know what they're going to pull on you in the studio [*laughs*]." He also suggests that a good attitude is a key to success, and believes that it is one of his most valuable assets. And even though he used to practice prodigiously, he rarely does so today. "My fingers are sometimes connected to the bass for 10 hours a day," he explains, "and that's about as much practice as I get. I don't sit down and run through scales like I used to. Mostly what I practice is getting a good feel."

What does Nathan East take to sessions? Generally, he has a trunk containing at least a half-dozen basses, including a Yamaha fretless, a Yamaha BB-5000 5-string, a Roland G-77 synthesizer bass, a Fender Precision Bass with a '65 neck on a 1970

"Because the bass is so low, I've always looked for the clearest note I could get out of it, while still getting a full sound."

body ("I always fall in love with a neck and put it together with my favorite pickups"), a '70 Fender Jazz Bass, a Yamaha BX-1, and an Alembic piccolo bass for popping parts. "The notes *really* pop out with the piccolo," he says. "I played it on Jeff Lorber's *It's A Fact* album, and on 'Sushi Monster' and 'Really Scary' [*In The Heat Of The Night*]."

An endorser of D'Addario XL Reds copper-coated bass strings, Nathan uses them on all of his basses (except the Yamaha BX-1, which is strung with Rotosound round-wounds), because he prefers their piano-like tone. He states, "Because the bass is so low, I've always looked for the clearest note I could get out of it, while still getting a full sound." To ensure the best recording of his lines, he usually goes direct into the mixing console. Engineers sometimes can't get the sound he's looking for, so he carries his own direct box, a Fat Box, which he reports gives a fat, warm sound. Supplying his own gear for the mundane linking of the bass to the recording console reveals his conscientiousness: "They know you mean business, especially if your direct box is better than theirs."

Occasionally, he employs a Polytone Mini-Brute amp with one 12" speaker, which has been part of his arsenal for several years. Aside from its pleasing tone, engineers like it because it doesn't drown out the other performers. Nathan also has a couple of effects racks for unusually adventurous sessions. Included in one rack are a Yamaha PB-1 preamp, a Yamaha P-2200 power amp, a Yamaha E-1010 analog delay, and an Ibanez digital delay. In another rack, he has a Lexicon 200 digital reverb along with a DeltaLab Effectron digital delay and a dbx 150 compressor. Despite the sophisticated signal processors, Nathan often opts for an unadorned sound, or just adds a touch of Boss chorus: "A lot of times, the guys are so busy with the synthesizer and guitar players and their racks that I just go for the no-frills approach. It makes the engineer's job easier." (On the road, he uses the same effects setup, with an added Yamaha graphic equalizer and two Yamaha speaker cabinets for added volume.)

Since last year, East's primary bass is his Yamaha 5-string, which is tuned B, E, A, D, G (low to high). Producers were so enthusiastic in their initial response to the distinctive sound of the 5-string that they often called him prior to sessions to remind him to bring the instrument. "Now I swear by it," he exclaims. "It was one of my answers to having to tune the *E* string down all the time. It allows you to get down with the synthesizer's range."

East is often called to double or replace synthesizer lines. "Many people were concerned that the synthesizer would put a lot of bass players out of work," he says. "My feeling is that you really need *both*. A lot of guys who have me come in to replace or double synth bass tell me that it doesn't have that fat sound, that it isn't complete enough, that it's too synthetic-sounding, or they just needed some pops in it." (He also uses his Roland G-77 bass synthesizer occasionally to provide a keyboard-like sound.) In fact, about half of his work today entails going into the studio alone to overdub bass in such situations. Although he misses the interchange between musicians, he can sometimes can get away with a lot more when he's alone: "I have maybe three hours to work on one or two songs, and I can put the bass part down and suggest an alternate part or a guitar part to go on top of it. It gives you time to kind of tailor-make the track."

As much as he likes the 5-string now, Nathan admits that there was a necessary period of adjustment to the slightly narrower string spacing and the altered eye-to-hand coordination: "That was a challenge. Now a low $A\flat$ isn't on the bottom string; it's on the second to the bottom. Since I was involved in the bass' design, it wasn't too difficult to get used to." Even more than the playing aspects, Nathan was concerned about lack of definition in the low end's recorded tone, and therefore specified that the pickups be wired so that the low *B* have a tighter response than the other strings. "When I first started to use it in the studios," he explains, "I thought, well, my bill for woofers is going to be pretty high" [*laughs*]. I try to be economical with it, but you can really tell when I drop those low *B*'s every now and then — you can feel it."

Further adding to his palette of sounds, East occasionally uses a pick, particularly on country dates (such as with Kenny Rogers) and pop sessions. Recently, he has grown his nails, giving him the option of nail or finger tone. "Whenever I want the more percussive sound, or if I'm playing chords," he says, "I use the nails. A lot of times, I overdub some high guitar-like parts using nails, and you wouldn't even know it's a bass."

"I don't run through scales like I used to. Mostly what I practice is getting a good feel."

Nathan often has to turn down invitations to go on the road due to scheduling conflicts and the difference in pay. However, he has been touring with Kenny Loggins because his three-weeks-on, two-weeks-off schedule affords the bassist the opportunity to get a balance between playing live and in the studio. "It gives me a chance to see what makes the people move and bring that energy back into town," he says. "It keeps my studio chops fresh. Drummers I work with have told me that they notice the difference in my playing when I come off the road. Working with one really good drummer, such as Tris Imboden, is great. Actually, playing with different guys almost whets your appetite. It's like you're away from your woman for a little while: It makes you more anxious to get back to her. And the studio is my woman now. It feels really fresh, and the ideas are a lot fresher than if I were in the studio all the time."

Adequate compensation is important, although East insists that he simply wouldn't do a road gig if it weren't fun. "I can't see doing something just for the money," he says. "I have a lot of fun with Loggins and Al Jarreau. And I could make a living just fine by not going on the road. Nowadays, I have to compete with what I would lose in town. Otherwise, I couldn't afford to leave. Nothing's worse than just sitting there out on the road and getting calls from Lionel Richie or Quincy Jones or Linda Ronstadt, and having to say no to them."

Nathan admits that with all the sessions he does, some of the work becomes a blur. This is especially true of TV. "I think just about anybody with good reading could do many of those sessions," he says. "So, I usually like to be called for the kinds of things that they want *me* for. I also prefer records because I get a credit on the jacket, which documents what you do. It's kind of like a calling card at the same time. I like doing commercials, though — the residuals don't hurt, either, so I do about four or five a week."

When laying down tracks, East likes working with a click track or, in many cases, a drum machine. A Roland TR-808 drum machine provided a simple beat on most of Philip Bailey's tracks, and on the extended-play version of "Easy Lover," it was included in the mix.

Ever since "Easy Lover" became a hit, Nathan is busier than ever writing songs for Kenny Loggins, Al Jarreau, and others. Although he writes some pieces at the piano, he often composes a song in his head, sings it into a microcassette recorder, and later transcribes it. "The entire song 'Wildfire' on Hubert Laws' *Family* album came to me in the car," he says. "I couldn't get home fast enough. I just sang it into the tape recorder; then all I had to do was write the music and take it into the session. Songwriting gives you the freedom to do other things. If you have one hit song, that brings in what 100 sessions would generate."

Nathan's future schedule shows no signs of letting up, although his roles will certainly be expanding. "Five years ago, one of my goals was to be everybody's bass player," he reflects. "I guess I've kind of covered that one." He has been asked by the Eurythmics to tour with them, and he has been offered the bass job on Philip Bailey's next

"There are only so many notes in the scale, but there's an infinite variety of rhythms."

album. And besides wanting to get further into his songwriting, he and his guitar-playing brother Marcel have plans for an R&B/pop band. Nathan believes that changing his direction is practically inevitable: "Ray Parker is a great example of a really busy session player who turned into a public figure. He had a long talk with me, and he said that it's pretty hard to know where you stand. If everyone is saying you're at the top, you have to realize there aren't too many places to go in that league, unless you change directions or graduate to another level. He was really trying to talk me into the artist/producer/songwriter thing. I see the bass becoming a bit less of a studio instrument but more of an onstage instrument. And there are only so many dates you can play on."

– JAMES JAMERSON –

BY DAN FORTE – JUNE 1979

JAMES "JAMIE" Jamerson, "the Motown bass player." Regardless of the countless studio dates he has played on since moving to Los Angeles in the early '70s, Jamerson will always be known for his unparalleled tenure in the house band of black music's hit factory of the 1960s — Motown Records, in the heart of Motor City, Detroit, Michigan. And when one considers the profound and lasting effect the Motown/Tamla/Soul/Gordy record conglomerate has had on popular music, and then considers Jamerson's prominent role in defining that sound, it is difficult to overestimate his importance as both stylist and innovator.

Jamerson's bass was an integral cog in the machine that produced the Motown sound, which was also known as "The Sound of Young America." Evidence of the magnitude of his contribution would include any of the company's overwhelming number of hit singles, but possibly the best example of James' style is found on "Reach Out, I'll Be There," the Four Tops' #1 hit of 1966. The song opens with an echoey chorus of piccolos, a slapping percussion sound, and Jamerson's electric bass laying down a galloping one-note rhythm. Levi Stubbs enters with his vocal line, flanked by an army of tambourines and a falsetto choir, as Jamerson bounces from octave to octave, propelling the song forward. The bass line, mixed high enough to strain the woofers on a bottom-of-the-line stereo system, is not particularly complex, although few bassists of the day

could pull it off with the imagination and intense sense of urgency he injected into it.

Jamerson's impact and influence on all electric bassists is incalculable. Rock producer/bassist Felix Pappalardi's comments concerning Jamie in the April 1972 issue of *Guitar Player* magazine probably reflect the feelings of many bass players: "That cat really killed me."

James Jamerson, Sr., was born in South Carolina 41 years ago. He grew up in Detroit and received a four-year music scholarship at Wayne State University, where Motown president Berry Gordy heard him and hired him as the company's staff bassist — as part of the rhythm section which included drummer Benny Benjamin, percussionist James Giddons, keyboardist Earl Van Dyke, and guitarists Joe Messina, Robert White, Eddie Willis, and Dennis Coffey. Though they remained anonymous for the most part and worked around the clock for a flat salary — while their Memphis counterparts Booker T. & The MGs turned out hit singles — the Motown band was nonetheless impressively talented and obviously influential.

During his tenure at Motown from 1959 to 1973, Jamerson laid the foundation for most of the label's hits by acts such as the Supremes, the Temptations, the Marvelettes, the Four Tops, Stevie Wonder, Mary Wells, Marvin Gaye, Tammi Terrell, Smokey Robinson And The Miracles, Gladys Knight And The Pips, Jr. Walker And The All Stars, and Martha And The Vandellas.

Since moving to Los Angeles, James has recorded with artists as diverse as Tom Jones, Robert Palmer, Joan Baez, Bill Withers, Dennis Wilson, Bloodstone, Al Wilson, and Marilyn McCoo And Billy Davis. He has also played on a number of television and film scores, including the popular theme from the TV show *SWAT*. His 21-year-old son and protégé, James Jamerson, Jr., is also an accomplished bassist and appears on the Crusaders' album *Street Life*.

In the following interview, the soft-spoken Jamerson offers some valuable insights based on his 25 years of experience as a bassist.

Were your bass lines on those innumerable Motown hit records usually your own ideas?

Yes, they'd give you a chord sheet written in pencil and say, "You're on your own." They'd use the numbers [Roman numerals that denote chords, such as I, IV, V, etc.], like the people down in Nashville use.

How did you first connect with Motown?

Well, I was playing upright bass in the late '50s, doing some sessions with other people at Berry Gordy's first wife's studio. Berry heard the lines I was playing and fell in love with them. He asked me if I'd be interested in coming over and being part of the company, and I told him yes.

Was upright bass your first musical instrument?

Yes, I took it up in high school, in 1954. I played sessions on upright until 1961.

Was the transition from upright to electric difficult?

No, it just took a little while to get the feel of the neck, because the neck is smaller, you know. It took me about two weeks [*laughs*]. I bought my first electric, a Fender Precision, in 1961 when I had to go on the road with [singer] Jackie Wilson. I played with Jackie almost a year.

Were your first influences on the bass mostly jazz players?

Right. Modern jazz players like Percy Heath, Ray Brown, and Paul Chambers. Back then I was working with cats like [pianist] Barry Harris and [flutist/oboist/saxophonist] Yusef Lateef. I played dances in high school in a jazz group — modern jazz with a little bebop mixed in. That was during the Ivy League days.

When you started playing on rock and roll and soul dates, where did you get the non-jazz influences from?

> "Bass players want to know what type of equipment I use. I tell them, but that's not what's important. It's the feel."

That was automatic. But I had worked with blues players like John Lee Hooker and an old fella called Washboard Willie. Also, I was raised a Baptist, and I heard a lot of gospel music.

Did your formal training at Wayne State come in handy on any of the gigs?

Yes, because after I played a line, they'd have an arranger write it out. Then if I'd go on the road, I'd have to relearn and memorize the line, because I never played the same thing all the time.

Did you tour much with the Motown acts?

I toured till '64, then came off the road completely to be on the staff. I quit traveling with the Miracles in '63. Nobody at Motown would record anything until I came off the road.

Did you record for any other labels during that time?

I didn't do too many things for other labels. We were told we'd get fined if we moonlighted. It's illegal for a company to fine you for that, but I didn't know it then. I did do a few Chess things with some vocal groups. At that time we'd just do the rhythm track, and I never even heard the records.

Do a lot of bass players ask you for playing tips?

Bass players call from all over, wanting to know what type of equipment I use, what type of bass, what kind of strings — things like that. I'll tell them, but that's not what's important; it's the feel. The strings don't make the sound, it's the feel. It's all in here, in the heart.

Do you still use a Precision?

Yes, none of the other basses get that sound. I just put La Bella heavy-gauge flatwounds on it. I think they're better than the Fender strings that come on the bass.

What kind of amplifier do you use?

I have an Ampeg B-15 for sessions — I use it on gigs, too. On the road now I plug the B-15 direct into the P.A.

How do you set the tone controls?

It depends on the producer and the session. Some people like the treble up; I like the bottom end, because that makes the record sound fuller. It gives a rounder tone, a fatter sound.

How many basses do you own?

Four. I have an old German upright, a Fender 5-string, a Hagstrom 8-string, and the Precision. I've had two Precisions stolen from me, but my present one

I bought new in '63. When I got it I immediately took the Fender strings off and put La Bellas on, and I've had the same strings on it ever since. You don't need to change strings all the time; you'll lose the tone. It's like a new car: The older it gets, the better it rides.

Do you use any effects devices?

Not unless people ask for them. It's all in the fingers, man. I don't think a bass should sound in any way different than it's supposed to sound. It should sound like a bass.

Do you ever use your thumb for any slapping effects?

I'm not into that; my son's into that. I can get the sound without having to slap. It's in the way you pull the string. I just use my index finger.

Did you teach your son how to play?

Oh, I sat down with him and showed him things. He discovered some on his own and asked me if they were right or wrong.

What advice would you give to beginners?

Well, I think the first thing you should do is play upright bass. That would strengthen everything — your wrist, your fingers, the joints of your fingers.

Do you still practice your upright?

Well, I don't practice [*laughs*]. I just practice when I'm doing a gig or a session.

Do you prefer studio work to live gigs?

Since I've been in the studios such a long time, I need to get out sometimes. I like to get out and change the scene, especially if the price is right. It's easier; if you make a mistake, you just keep going straight ahead.

What players do you listen to today?

Well, I never have listened to too much. I just create my own thing. The stuff on the radio is somebody else — that's old. I try to come up with something different. What I'm hearing these days from other people has all been played. Most of the bass players don't play *bass;* they're just playing at it. They're not really saying anything. It's just a lot of gimmicks, and actually I don't think they know what they're doing. A lot of the younger guys who I like copied me. Most young guys try to copy Stanley Clarke or Larry Graham.

How often are you in the studios these days?

It varies. It's not like it used to be. I had to go into the studio every day at nine in the morning and come out at three the next morning.

Do you still create most of your own parts?

Sometimes; some leaders come into the session with the bass lines written out. They want it nice and simple now.

Do you still get a lot of calls asking for the "James Jamerson sound"?

Yes, the sound plus the name.

Do you think you get more dates because producers want your own distinctive sound, or because you are capable of handling whatever they ask you to play?

I don't know [*laughs*]. I think a little bit of both.

Do you think Motown's records started sounding different when the label moved from Detroit to Los Angeles?

Yeah, altogether different. They lost the sound, man. They moved to L.A. looking for something different, and they didn't find it. And all along everybody else was searching for the same sound they had.

– CAROL KAYE –

BY JAS OBRECHT – MARCH 1983

I N THE BEGINNING, there was Carol Kaye. She came on the scene when Elvis and Chuck Berry were the rage, and the Beatles still years away. A jazzer turned studio ace, Carol added guitar and bass to a huge string of hits in the '60s, including many Phil Spector productions with the Righteous Brothers, Ike & Tina Turner, the Crystals, and the Ronettes, as well as numerous sessions for the Beach Boys, Sonny & Cher, the Supremes, Temptations, Four Tops, Monkees, Ray Charles, Joe Cocker, Glen Campbell, Stevie Wonder, Harry Nilsson, and others. In the '70s Carol concentrated on film work and her movie credits — too numerous to list here — are headed by *Butch Cassidy & The Sundance Kid, In The Heat Of The Night, Valley Of The Dolls, The Pawnbroker, In Cold Blood, Airport,* and *Walk, Don't Run.* Carol is regularly heard on TV in *Ironsides, Love American Style, Mission Impossible, Hogan's Heroes, Soap,* and *Hawaii Five-0* reruns. Since 1969 Ms. Kaye has directed Gwyn Publishing and authored all of its method books and a video course. Currently, she keeps residences in Northern California and Los Angeles, where she occasionally plays sessions. Carol also does seminars and some select teaching, but most of her efforts are focused on producing educational videos for bass and other instruments. Carol remains rock's most often-heard woman instrumentalist.

— JO

In the late '50s I didn't know of any other women who were playing rock and roll. Around then I was playing a lot of bebop guitar in the nightclubs in the south part of Los Angeles. Most of the time I was the only white person there, let alone being the only woman. As far as I felt, there wasn't any discrimination in those days. There were times when I felt I wasn't playing up to par, and I went home and practiced on the areas I needed work in. All of a sudden I was very much in demand in jam sessions and jazz work. I played in Jack Sheldon's band in back of [comedian] Lenny Bruce. [Pianist] George Shearing asked me to go on the road with him, but I was eight months pregnant and couldn't handle that. It was a real honor.

I got into rock in the studios. I remember my first session very well. It was 1958, and producer Bumps Blackwell came into the Beverly Caverns, where I was playing guitar with a jazz group. He asked me if I wanted to do a record date. I went down and it was a session with a soul group featuring Sam Cooke. Lou Rawls was the singer on that date, and it was his first record, and Jesse Belvin was the other singer. I thought it was fun, like gospel music. So I got into studio work that way.

I started to play a lot of gigs and record dates for H.B. Barnum, who was an arranger. He put a lot of the town to work and wrote a lot of hit records in the early '60s, Motown-type stuff. I soon found out that most of the groups in the '60s didn't want people to know that they did not record their own

– 157 –

music. Occasionally, I would get a call to go out on the road, but I couldn't afford to because I was making so much money and I had my kids.

Back then I didn't feel that anyone in the studios looked down on me because I was a woman. I guess I had the reputation of being a pretty good live jazz player. If you were a successful jazz musician, you were very respected by all the players. But in my mind it was very hard to make that transition from being an up-and-coming giant in jazz, which doesn't pay any money, to doing studio work, which was really dumb until I got the idea that it's fun to make a hit record. Even though it's rock and roll and 8/8, it's got its own groove. I'm kind of a schizophrenic because I've been voted #6 Electric Bassist in the *Playboy* Jazz Poll, yet I consider myself a rock/funk bass player. When you are able to think in both styles like that, it's amazing. When I started playing on all the #1 hit records that were coming out of the West Coast, I definitely thought of myself as a guitarist. I didn't feel like I was a bassist for a long time. I always felt that I was a jazz guitarist who picked up bass.

From about 1958 to 1964 I played guitar, then switched to primarily bass. I was the #3 or #4 call on guitar in those early studio years, making pretty good money. Then, when I switched to bass, I put a lot of bassists out of work. In those days they were using acoustic bass and Danelectro 6-string bass guitars. They'd use three bassists on a date. As soon as I started on bass, I put the other two bassists out of work because I played it with a pick and got a really good sound. I was the only one in town who was really working their tail off. In those days, the bass was a real physical instrument. I used a Fender Precision with a Super Reverb amp, and kept the strings high. They always miked me. They never took it through the board. I got a pretty good sound. They even miked my amp for some of the Motown dates, like the Supremes' "Love Child" and the Four Tops' "Bernadette."

From 1960 to 1969, I played guitar or bass on all of Phil Spector's dates. He wouldn't do anything without me. I mostly played guitar, and bass towards the latter part. In fact, at first I used my [hollow-body] jazz guitar, an Epiphone Emperor. That was the secret of Phil Spector's guitar sound: They would mike an electric guitar acoustically and dump a lot of echo on it, like on the Righteous Brothers' "You've Lost That Lovin' Feeling." The acoustic guitar fills you heard on the Sonny & Cher stuff was me. One of the earlier hits I played electric guitar on was "Zip-A-Dee-Doo-Dah" by Bob B. Soxx And The Blue Jeans.

In those days sessions were long. It would take anywhere from 20 to 35 takes to cut a record. Phil took his time and knew what he was looking for. The whole band would sit around. Hal Blaine used to have to play drums for about an hour to get the balance before Phil would get to the bass and then the guitars. The horn section would play chess. I saw a lot of *Playboy* magazines with the guys [*laughs*]. We used to use several guitarists, too. I played guitar on Ike & Tina Turner's "River Deep, Mountain High," for example, but I would have to listen to the record to tell you exactly which part I played, because Phil always used two or three guitars. He always used me, Barney Kessel, and [producer/guitarist] Mike Post. Another rhythm guitarist, David Cohen, came in about 1963. Leon Russell and Mac Rebennack [a.k.a. Dr. John] played keyboards on those sessions. Glen Campbell also played guitar on a few of those dates.

It seemed like Phil Spector set the standard: It was okay to go six hours on one tune, which we did. He had such a phenomenal success that everybody thought they had to take six hours. Just like doctors practiced on their patients, producers started practicing in the studio to make hit records. That's why it took so many hours. Now people have it pretty well down, but I'm not really thrilled with most of the music that's coming out. The feeling is not there.

It took a lot of takes with the Beach Boys, too. I played guitar on their early records. The first hit I did with them on bass was "Help Me Rhonda." The band couldn't get that studio feeling that we got, so they used all studio guys except for Carl Wilson, who would be in the booth on 12-string. Lyle Ritz played acoustic bass. You can hear him on "Good Vibrations," where there's two parts — for a while I played the higher part. Brian Wilson wrote that song. In fact, he wrote all of his lines. Once in a while I would play a fill that was mine, but I can't lay claim to any of Brian's bass lines. If you listen, "Good Vibrations" has a walking feel: That's pure jazz. Brian was greatly influenced by jazz, as well as the way the Four Freshmen sang. Barney Kessel, Howard Roberts, and I were on the dates, and we were constantly amazed by Brian because he's the one who came up with all the ideas and arranged it all. We would sometimes have to recopy his music, but it all came from his head. His *Pet Sounds* album, on which I played bass, was very creative.

With Spector, we mostly had skeleton charts. At times there would be no music written and you'd have to skull out the parts with chords and come up with a bass line. With others I had to be able to sight-read all kinds of music, depending on if it was films or records. There were some dates — especially with Sonny & Cher — where [saxophonist] Harold Battiste had written some pretty intricate arrangements, in the sense that they were different. The style of every hit Sonny & Cher put out was different, which really made them successful. One of their tunes just kind of laid there like a dead duck. It was a one-chord tune, and I started to figure out a bass hook on my Epiphone. Sonny heard it and said, "Ooh, I love that line. Give it to the bassist." And that's the bass line to "The Beat Goes On." So we were called upon to read music and/or make up hook lines. The secret of a lot of hit records is in the bass line and the drum licks — mostly the bass lines.

People are not aware of how important the bass is to arrangers. A lot of people love to play bass because it gives you a lot of control. It's the foundation, like the basement of a house. In the '60s and early '70s I played on all of Quincy Jones' films. Quincy would occasionally write some great bass parts, like the *Ironsides* thing. Other times he would bring in a rhythm section and tell us to just jam. We would sit there and play funk for a couple of days. I went to the movies one time and thought, "Gee, that stuff is really familiar." The name of the movie was *The New Centurions,* and what Quincy had done was very hip: He wrote the horn lines on all the off-beat, Latin-type bass notes I played. It sounded like it was arranged, but it wasn't. This shows you how important hook lines are to arrangers. When I played on [Glen Campbell's] "Wichita Lineman," they took one of my bass licks and milked that for the string part.

The hardest sessions I tackled were the ones that weren't very musically satisfying, like the Hondells, because you'd be playing that dumb stuff for hours. Howard Roberts was also on those dates, and we would just space out: "Oh, God. I should have turned this down." But you don't turn down a lot of money. Some of the Dick Dale stuff was hard. The most difficult stuff was the music that took hours and shouldn't have.

Eventually I got so much work that I didn't know what was what, and I didn't care. I just wanted to find a parking space, get in, get out, and get paid. I was in the clique that was playing on all the hit records. All we did was cut a hit from 8:00 A.M. until midnight, every day of the week. Some of the people

"I quit doing studio work at the very peak. I just couldn't stand the coldness of it."

I worked with were Johnny Mathis, Henry Mancini, Petula Clark, Andy Williams, Sam & Dave, Gary Puckett, Ray Charles, Jerry Vale, and a lot of pop stuff. I played on Stevie Wonder's "I Was Made To Love Her" and Joe Cocker's "Feelin' Alright." I was on thousands of records, and it's hard to remember the mountains of work you do. Sometimes I hear a rhythm or lead part and say, "Yeah, I played guitar on that." Remember the Alka-Seltzer ad that became a big hit for the T-Bones in the '60s? That was me on lead guitar. I also made the Maxwell House commercials. I played 12-string on the early Herb Alpert & The Tijuana Brass albums, and got a lot of money when they used one of his cuts for a Wrigley's gum ad.

In 1969 I started Gwyn Publishing on my kitchen table because everyone was bugging me — "How do you do this and that?" I wrote my first bass method book — *How To Play The Electric Bass* — and nobody wanted to publish it. They said it was too hard and wouldn't sell. So I started my own company, and it sold hundreds of thousands of copies. I also put out *Electric Bass Lines I* through *VI* and other books for rock bassists. I named my publishing company after my last baby; I've had a couple of girls and a boy.

I quit doing studio work at the very peak. I just couldn't stand the coldness of it. It was pretty cut-throat, and I just couldn't take it anymore. I wanted to live a better life. But I kept coming back to it, and in the '70s did more and more film work, where they wanted to hear the rock-funk bass. It was pseudo-rock, not the real rock that we did on the Phil Spector dates. Remember *In The Heat Of The Night?* I'm the fuzz bass player. I was the first bassist to use effects in movies. I used all the effects, but not like they are doing now — I never used a flanger or anything like that. I also got into playing a lot of TV.

Cutting down on studio work gave me time to go out in the public. See, when you are in the studios, that's the only life you know. It's like being locked up in jail. You don't interact with the general public. You're cutting hit records and they are listening to you, but you don't grow in any other way but in your music. The last couple of hit records I was on were "Memories" by Barbra Streisand and "I Heard That" by Quincy Jones. The shape of the bass was taking its toll: Sitting there for so many hours in a twisted position began to affect my spine.

I had to find out if I was really as great a bass

player as they said I was in the studios. They would flatter me all the time, and I would be sitting there playing dumb music, wondering if I was good or not. So I had to step out and find out if I could play. The only way to do that was to get onstage. So I toured and recorded with [pianist] Hampton Hawes and started to get back into jazz. It was fun to find out I could really play. That's a woman's thing, anyways, because she really doubts herself all the way because of this identity thing that we're supposed to back up the men. I even researched philosophy and found out that over 2,000 years ago things were a lot different: Women were worshipped, the children took our name, and we had the money and all that stuff.

Eventually, I began to become aware of other women guitarists and bassists. I realized that the attitudes that women have to develop today are really not much different than when I got started. I never thought of myself as a woman. I thought of myself as a guitar player. Now I'm seeing women in groups who seem to have the notion, "Well, I've got to play like a man." That's not it, either. You either play or you don't play. The ones who seem to come across the best have that attitude. If somebody puts you down, you just have to put the blinders on and keep going. Forget other people's trips: It's their hangups. The women who will be successful are those who can exploit their own talent and get it across with strength and conviction. The ones who are trying to put men down or to be cute with their boobs and that kind of stuff tend to die out pretty soon.

I've seen a lot of women players that I really like. The women in Heart aren't technically fantastic players, but I like what they do onstage. I like the way up-and-coming women groups put themselves across without being real cute and coy. They are taking care of business without saying, "Look at me. I've got the curves, too."

– JOE OSBORN –

BY DAVID PERRY – APRIL 1974

ON A TYPICAL Monday morning, as Ahmet, Clive, Bones, and the rest of the record business are checking this week's new *Billboard* charts, a bright orange truck is roaring across the Ventura Freeway toward Hollywood. Behind the wheel is Joe Osborn, and bouncing around the back seat is the chewed-up old Jazz Bass on which he averages two of the Top 10 records each week. Over the past 15 years, with the possible exception of Hal Blaine, Joe has played on more hit records than any other musician in the history of the record industry. As one of the fabled heavyweight Los Angeles studio men, Joe has worked himself into a position where he handles half of the hits to come out of L.A., and in the process has become one of the best-paid studio men in the business. His long, smooth, crisp bass lines have become as recognizable and familiar as some of his gold records, which stretch from the doo-wop period of the late '50s, through the California Rock Explosion in the '60s, right up to the latest Top 10 record by Neil Diamond.

By any definition of the term, Joe is a studio musician, solidly rooted in the dozen or so recording studios that line Sunset Boulevard. What traveling he does is principally to New York, Chicago, and San Francisco for artists and producers he is close to. Joe's client list is as impressive as it is loyal. He has played on virtually every record ever cut by the Carpenters, Fifth Dimension, Johnny Rivers, Mamas & Papas, and Glen Campbell, and fills in the gaps with dates for Quincy Jones, Helen Reddy, Sergio Mendes, and virtually every other act to set foot in Southern California. Transplants from New York such as Neil Diamond and Simon and/or Garfunkel have picked up on Joe, and now he handles a majority of their dates also. Recording in Los Angeles really means recording with Joe Osborn.

Relative to most studio men Joe is an equipment freak. His axe is a 1959 Jazz Bass that the Fender factory gave him in return for the endorsement. Joe recalls, "I asked Fender for a Precision because that's what I had been playing, and I was accustomed to that fat neck." But they sent a Jazz Bass instead because they were introducing that model the following autumn. "I was very pissed off," Joe remembers, "and it took me a good while to get used to that thin Jazz Bass neck. Now, I wouldn't trade it for anything." The serial number on the back plate can be traced to a manufacturing date in March 1959, and is most likely a prototype rather than a regular production model.

Although Leo Fender deserves credit for that initial vintage year, the sound and timbre of Joe's bass owe less to its bloodlines and more to the type and caliber of work he has put it through. No other axe can say that it lost its virginity with Lou Adler and the Mamas & Papas, or with Karen and Richard Carpenter in their early days out in Joe's San Fernando Valley 4-track garage studio. On the surface, the bass is a disgraceful old hulk of wood and wire with half of its original sunburst chipped off, and enough gouges and scars to give away 15 years of steady, grueling daily studio work.

The strings are heavy-gauge 1963 La Bellas which have worn smooth and shiny up past the 15th fret, which is an indication of Joe's technique as well as the strings' age. The G and D strings have begun to notch where they meet the frets, but this has not affected their tone or tensile strength, since the strings are held taut by their core rather than the wrapping. The strings are absolutely dead, having been stretched, vibrated, gummed up with finger oils and dirt, and otherwise having suffered the kind of abuse that three to four sessions a day will provide.

Grammy-winning engineer Armin Steiner says, "In its own way Joe's bass is a Stradivarius. It has the same warmth and clarity that you get from a 300-year-old violin. And his strings are magnificent. There has never been another set like them." Joe says, "I'm not superstitious, but I've never tampered with it. In fact, I don't even wipe it clean." Those scratches are proud battle scars won in the War of the Top 40, and Joe would no more restring and refinish than Les Paul would take up with a Telecaster.

Like several other top bassists Joe plays with a pick, and indeed his whole sound and technique are predicated on that little 10¢ piece of plastic. "I started using a pick on my old Precision," he says, "while I was in Las Vegas with Bob Luhman in 1958. One night I would be on the guitar and the next I was on bass, so I just took the pick with me as I went back and forth. All the other bass men in town were picking with their fingers. The attitude was that the bass should be felt but not heard." But Joe was more comfortable with the pick, and it gave him the treble he needed to be heard by cutting out all the low-end clutter. "Now people were actually hearing my notes," he says, "and not just the booming sensation that the other guys were sending out. I also found that I was blending better with the bass drum. All along we had been fighting for the same frequency range, and now I was cutting through and giving the bottom end a tonal, melodic quality."

By 1963 the California Rock Explosion was about to take off and Joe was just settling into the studio business full-time, having paid his dues on the road, in clubs, and playing all those infamous publishers' demos that somewhere along the line everyone has done. One afternoon, Lou Adler called a session at Western Recorders' Studio 3, bringing together for the first time the now-legendary rhythm section of Hal Blaine, Larry Knechtel, and Joe Osborn. They were to become the rhythmic core of most of the L.A.

groups to emerge from that era with classic records like "California Dreamin'," "MacArthur Park," "Up, Up, & Away," "Aquarius (Let The Sunshine In)," "Bridge Over Troubled Water," and other giant hits.

Producer Bones Howe remembers engineering some of the trio's early sessions: "My first reaction to Hal, Joe, and Larry was that they were the tightest rhythm sound I had ever heard, and they still are. They were like one instrument. In particular, Joe and Hal locked into a drums-bass blend that stuck, no matter what kind of music they were called for."

For many years there was a noticeable decline in the number of sessions booked in Hollywood during the weeks that Hal was in Las Vegas with Nancy Sinatra, or when either Joe or Larry was out of town and the unit couldn't be called. Producers just postponed sessions and worked around the group's availabilities. Nobody was going to tamper with success.

Ten years later, the three occasionally still find themselves on the same date, but not every date, every day like it was in the '60s. "We started breaking up," Hal recalls, "when self-contained groups would call just one or two of us to beef up their rhythm sections without actually taking it over. For instance, Joe and I have been doing the Carpenters' dates without Larry because Richard [Carpenter] is an excellent keyboard man. On the other hand, Larry joined Bread without us because they had bass and drums covered."

Up until the late 1960s Joe was picking up only "head" dates where he had to sweat and beat his brains out to come up with his own lines. As a nonreader, he worked from chords, and every note he played was his own. It was creative but very tiring. "Eventually," Joe says, "Tommy Tedesco convinced me that studio life would be a lot easier and I would earn a lot more money if I could pick up some of those easy-reading dates where all they ask is that you follow a part."

Joe started teaching himself to read from an instruction book, and got "all the way up to page 8. The rest I learned on dates. I began by bouncing back and forth between the chords and the written part. Pretty soon I could run through a whole take without once looking up at the chords." Joe says that reading is a prerequisite to a full schedule, but he still emphasizes the importance of being able to work up "head" charts: "Most arrangers and producers depend on their rhythm players to create hooks, figures, turns, and even chordal variations on which the string, horn, and vocal writing can be pegged. We have to keep our minds not only on how our lines are working, but also what the arranger can make out of them in the sweetening dates that follow. It's a responsibility, and those guys who lay down just ordinary lines don't get asked back." Most arrangers want Joe to experiment with the written line, and usually what emerges is a collaboration between the two.

While Joe's axe is a one-of-a-kind freak of nature, the main ingredient to his success and style is his basic philosophical approach to music. "If I have one rule governing my style," he says, "it is: The simpler the better." And Joe's work with the Carpenters is a perfect example of how simple, basic lines can be the most effective. "Richard's charts demand a clean, uncluttered part from me," Joe says, "so we generally work out bass lines that are streamlined and clean, but still rhythmic and supportive to the vocals. Richard usually doesn't double my lines with his left hand, so I'm all alone down there on the bottom, except when Karen or Hal has a bass drum line in unison with mine."

Richard's charts also leave lots of room for Joe to get into his famous slides, which have really become his trademark. He has gotten many letters from arrangers and other bass players asking just how he pulls those slides off, but, says Joe, "there is just no way to explain." They come off best when there isn't too much going on in the track, because they are fairly delicate and lack the power of a regular note. The Carpenters' records have given Joe his best opportunity to further develop and explore his slide technique, and on songs like "For All We Know" he has used slides exclusively. There is a clean, smooth fretless sound to the slides, and except for the presence and bite of Joe's pickups, they sound like they're coming from an upright bass. The best slides seem to be the long descending ones on the *G* string. They have a fragile, pastel quality that doesn't sound like a bass part. Even though the slide may last only a second, Joe says, "I usually check in with some chord notes on the way down. Otherwise, it's just another long gliss. I can't explain how I do them except that you need a very sensitive set of left-hand fingers that can sense and deliver an infinite variety of pressure on the strings. It is all a reflex action."

The development and growth of Joe's bass style parallels the maturing of pop music itself. Back in the

"I started using a pick on my old Precision, and now people were actually hearing my notes, and not just the booming sensation."

'50s, bass lines were either the dotted-quarter/dotted-quarter/quarter-note style, or the four-to-the-bar walking bass left over from the Big Band era. When the electric bass came along in the mid '50s everyone played it like the acoustic. That is, everyone except guitar players like Joe who saw this new instrument as a deep-throated guitar rather than an electronic miniaturization of the acoustic bass. He was so used to using all four of his left-hand fingers on the neck that when he switched over to the bass where he needed only one finger at a time, the remaining fingers were still searching out the chord notes they had been taught to play. The result is, says Neil Diamond, "Joe has a very chordal style. He manages to work up bass lines that take you on a trip between chords. He is one of the most lyrical and melodic bass players I've ever worked with, and whenever I can get him to do one of my sessions, I consider it a big plus."

Despite Joe's technique, style, and agility on the bass, Bones Howe says that Joe's greatest asset is that "he is the only bass player in the business who knows how to cut through a tiny radio speaker. When a producer hires Joe, he can be comfortable in the knowledge that all those fantastic things he is laying down in the studio will survive mixdown, plating, and stamping and still come charging through on the radio; and there's where you sell records."

Producer/engineer Roy Halee prefers to run Joe directly into the 16-track recorder without any board equalization. He remembers, "In the course of recording the tracks for 'Bridge Over Troubled Water,' I learned that Joe could EQ his signal better out in the studio than I could on my board. It's only in the mixdown if we want Joe's lines to do something different than we had asked him for at the session that I'll give his track any EQ."

The Los Angeles chapter of the record industry's association of the most successful producers, arrangers, sidemen, and engineers has just handed out their first annual Most Valuable Player awards to the best player on each instrument. Some winners were newcomers, some were veterans, but no choice was so obvious and overwhelmingly popular as the winner on electric bass: Joe Osborn.

– CHUCK RAINEY –

BY DAN FORTE – SEPTEMBER 1976

CHARLES WALTER Rainey III is one busy bass player — probably the most in-demand electric bassist in the business. And "in the business" is exactly where Rainey can be found.

Even if you've never heard of the man, it's doubtful that you haven't been exposed to his playing. Whether your tastes lean toward jazz, rock, blues, soul, pop, or country, you probably own a record for which Chuck supplied the bottom line. His recording credits include artists like Cannonball Adderley, Sergio Mendes, Joe Cocker, King Curtis, Ray Charles, Albert King, Laura Nyro, Aretha Franklin, and The Jackson Five. His rock-steady bass has also been heard in motion pictures such as *Midnight Cowboy*, *Lady Sings The Blues*, and *Fritz The Cat*, television series like *M*A*S*H*, *Hawaii Five-0*, and *Sanford And Son*, and even commercials for Annie Green Springs Wine, Arrid Extra Dry Deodorant, Wheaties, and any number of other salable commodities.

Obviously, to cover all this ground with just a Fender Precision, a man has to keep on his toes. And when Rainey isn't in the recording studio, he's usually heading a seminar or giving private lessons. A "day off" might mean flying out of town for a weekend of club gigs with, say, Tom Scott or maybe Sonny Rollins — which sometimes necessitates a quick return hop to fit in an afternoon workshop before that night's opening set.

Chuck was born in Cleveland, Ohio, June 17, 1940. He attended Lane College in Jackson, Tennessee as a music major, at that time concentrating on horn, and he began playing bass at 20.

What was your first instrument?

My career's kind of strange. I started out at a very early age on piano — that's preschool age. The family was very musical: my sister and my mother sang, and my father played piano. My mother also played piano, but she was really a flutist. When I got into school, I took piano lessons for a couple of years, and then I took violin lessons for about three years. In the sixth grade I started playing trumpet, and that's where it really started. I played trumpet all through grade school, high school, and college. Except when I got into college I majored in brasses, so baritone horn became my main instrument.

What made you switch to the bass?

I was trained exceptionally well on the horn; I can attribute a lot of knowledge that really helped me get into the business when I started playing bass to my schooling on the brasses. But they didn't teach me how to play, you know; they taught me how to perform and function in a symphonic situation. Like reading charts, orchestration, breathing, and stuff like that. When I was in school I realized that I was an excellent musician, but I couldn't "play," if you know what I mean. I went to a jam session when I came home one summer and took my horn out and attempted to blow, but I couldn't without any music

- 164 -

in front of me. They were playing the blues in *F*, and I was 20, and there were guys 17, 18, and 19 — they were gettin' it, they were *playing!* And I wanted to be good at whatever I did, in any environment. I had always fooled around a little with guitar, and with some friends we started rehearsing some things in the house, and we got a gig. I played the guitar for about six months.

Did you start playing bass on an electric?

At first I played bass on my guitar. I tuned the low *E* string down as far as it would go without clanking. I used a thumbpick and then switched to a fingerpick, but I had to take the pick off to play jazz. So one day I saw some group that had an electric bass — I had never seen one before — and I'd always thought that sound was a 6-string bass guitar. And here was this great big long thing, and I liked it, so I got one. I loved it as soon as I got my hands on it. I was almost reborn. Where I came from, in Ohio, it was all upright and organ basses, so when I got the instrument I was the only guy in town that had it. Everyone seemed to like what I played; popularity just started spreading.

What type of music was your local group playing?

When I started on bass the first things we played were blues — like rock-blues or blues from a jazz idiom, but more blues than jazz. Blues was first, then it jumped right off into standards and ballads and [saxophonist] Big Jay McNeely walking a bar with "Rhythm" ["I Got Rhythm"] changes.

Did you find that the electric bass gave you more freedom than the horn?

Now that I look back on it, yes, in that it was new, and I could use my ear — which is how I found out that I could play. I felt reborn, because I could do something where I could really express myself. There's only one bass player in a band; I felt that power, and it was a challenge. When I stop to think about all those years on other instruments, they really weren't wasted, because without that knowledge I would've had to start at the beginning. That's why it took me just a matter of a minute to do it. And my style of playing came from all my other musical experiences too — with motion or speed on the bass. As a baritone horn player, I could only express myself when I played a written solo or when I blended well with the brass ensemble. But with the bass, I could relate myself to Charlie Mingus, to Ray Brown, Keter Betts — the bass players that sort of inspired me to

"There's only one bass player in a band. I felt that power, and it was a challenge."

play. Keter Betts was the first to really make me sit down and go "Wow!"

What was your first professional gig?

After I'd been playing about a year, I worked with Big Jay McNeely for a year in Cleveland. Then [tenor saxophonist] Sil Austin came through town without a bass player. Sil offered me a little more money and a chance to go to New York. At the time, with Sil and with Big Jay, the charts that I thought I was reading, I wasn't reading. It was all ear. And the situation never got to be such that anyone knew I wasn't reading. I'd improvise, it always sounded good, nobody said nothing. But my day came when I had to sight-read an Etta James show at the Apollo, and they had to let me go. I worked in the garment district in New York for about six months.

Were there many other electric bassists in New York?

When I got to New York it was another kind of trip. In the early '60s, the jazz musicians didn't really accept the electric bass. The only people in jazz that accepted it were leaders, because they were always looking for gimmicks, trying to get over with different things. Lionel Hampton had used Monk Montgomery, who was the first electric bass player [on record]. Monk is a very thorough bass player, but he was working in an all-black band in an all-black circuit, except every once in a while, so he didn't get that kind of a pure shot, the way [James] Jamerson or I did. My shot was right in the media, producing and making records. At first I had a tremendous ego about my playing. I had sort of a chip on my shoulder about the older cats, the older bass players especially, who talked negatively about the instrument not so much putting me down, but putting the *instrument* down. So I always did what I wanted to do first, and I would take chances. Not that I try to tell other bass players to take chances, but I would rather make a mistake than to not try it. And there was always a big love affair between me and the rhythm section.

In the studios, did you find that your freedom to improvise was limited?

Most orchestrators don't really involve the bass player in what they're doing. They arrange the horns and the strings, and very few orchestrate the rhythm section, because it's really hard to put a "feel" on paper. Oliver Nelson would write out parts, and all he was concerned about was the orchestra; he don't want no rhythm player asking him nothing. You'd say, "Do you want me to walk here?" He'd go, "I don't care; *you're* the bass player." You know, as long as you don't play a major run against a minor chord. He's trying to get these four horns to blend; he doesn't want to hear from any bass player. Some guys will write a part and want you to play it or embellish on it. Then there are some who I don't have to ask anything — if I want to change it, I just change it.

Is the West Coast studio scene different from the East Coast?

I don't like L.A. at all. It's a business in Hollywood. It's a business in New York, too, but there's more music involved; the integrity of the business is in the Apple. I'm not picking on Los Angeles, but there are a lot of orchestrators and arrangers on the West Coast that would be better bus drivers. Back East, if you claim to be a producer or an arranger, that's what you better know how to do, because if you can't, there are thousands of guys in the wings just waiting for you to blow your cool. They'll take two weeks to cut an album in L.A., where in New York it'll take them about a week to do the same album — they just go ahead and do what they've got to do. When I moved to Los Angeles, my income almost doubled. Scale is $100 now for three hours. For people like me, [guitarist] Larry Carlton, [tenor sax man] Wilton Felder — the guys people really want to use for name's sake, to help sell the record — they'll give double or triple scale in L.A., because they have the budget.

Stanley Clarke views the electric bass and the upright as two different instruments. He said, "The electric instrument is a bass, and it's a guitar." Is that how you feel?

No, I look at it as a bass. You have an instrument that has the same written range, the same sounding range, the exact fretboard as an upright. And it has the same tone — because electronically you can duplicate a natural wood sound. See, a guitar player can play an electric bass, but he'll play it like a guitar. The things Stanley plays on his electric bass, I think, would be accepted a lot more if he just played them on his upright. His electric bass sounds like a rock and roll bass, and my whole concept is to *never* sound like a rock and roll bass — just to sound like a bass. I don't have anything against the rock and roll sound, but it doesn't have as much finesse. I don't look at it as a guitar at all. I've always had a chip on my shoulder when people say, "Can I see your guitar?" I'd say, "It's a bass." You listen to music and

"I don't have anything against the rock and roll sound, but it doesn't have as much finesse."

hear the bass — it seems like people should know where it comes from.

Has the electric bass as an instrument suffered from being made by guitar companies?

Absolutely! The people that manufacture that bass — like Fender — they never have a musician in on the setup of the instrument. Why don't they get a bass player to help them design it, or a *commission* of bass players? Everybody that has a Fender, it's modified. I mean everybody. The pickups are modified, with more coil. You cannot go to a store and buy a bass without fixing the bridge. And for so many years they'd put this little thumb guard under the neck, not realizing that no one plays with their thumb. I thought that was so dumb! When you play an upright, you anchor your thumb on the body of the bass. So the average cat, when he plays the electric, wants to play it like he sees the upright players playing. So they take the thumb guard off and put it on top; then they take the plate off, because that's just about the best place to hit the strings. I play right next to it. I anchor on the plate, but I don't have any pressure on my thumb. I usually just use one finger, seldom two. Now I play with my bare fingers. The most natural thing you got going is your hands. It's a lot more intricate than a lot of people would believe. There are some things you can play with two fingers that you can't play with one, and there are some things that you can play with one that you can't play with two. Most of my notoriety has come from people noticing me playing with speed.

Do you still do any exercises?

Sure do. I don't sit down and practice, per se, for an hour a day, but if I'm not working in the studio, I'm teaching someone else. So that's like practice to me. Usually for woodshedding, I'm always suggesting to people that if they don't have imagination, don't play — because music is imagination. My teaching is designed to let the player see what I did and where I got my ideas. I get my ideas from other people — and they're good ideas.

How many basses do you own?

I have three Fenders, a Gibson, a Hagstrom fretless, an Ampeg "baby bass," and a Hofner Beatle Bass. The bass that I use in the studio is perfect — a '59 or '60 Fender Precision.

What about amplifiers?

I use an Ampeg B-15 in the studio; it's got a good quiet sound. For gigs, I use a Benson 40-watt.

What type of strings do you favor?

For piano-type strings, or roundwound, Fender, in my mind, makes the best — although they have big problems. The low *E* is always dead. Always. So I try to liven the strings up a little; put oil on it, stretch it as much as I can. If you pull that string, it's going to cancel itself — it's low enough as it is. I play very lightly. I play right on my fingertips, and my nail has a lot to do with the sound I get. You've got to have a little bit of nail on your attack. I made too much money from good bass players — some who were better than I am, but you just couldn't hear them, so they had to have me overdub. The best drummers in the world have got it from the wrist down. Most players want to dig in, but it's all in the wrist and the fingers. [*He flexes the small muscle between the thumb and forefinger like a weight lifter would flex his biceps. Rock-hard.*] I just never play hard. It's all finesse. And finesse can be taught if you just have a book or a teacher that will show you how.

Do you ever play the upright?

I think the upright is a beautiful instrument, and I like to play it. I do every now and then, but so far I don't really have enough rapport with the upright to use it on gigs. I feel that given the right situation I can make my electric bass sound like an acoustic — which I have done. It can swing like an upright, sound like it, have the touch; or if you want to get raunchy, you can do that, too.

Did you listen to acoustic players to get that sound?

I didn't search past Keter Betts. He and Earl May and Jymie Merritt — after hearing them, I didn't search anymore. Charles Mingus, I never understood, and a lot of people have tried to tell me to go to Mingus. He used to come and sit in, and he'd take my bass and put it on a bar stool, to play it like an upright. Charlie Mingus, George Duvivier, and Bob Cranshaw never said anything intimidating or negative about the instrument. I have the most admiration for Cranshaw. I think he's one of the few upright players who can play the electric bass as an instrument. People like him, Bill Lee, and Milt Hinton really turned me on, as far as cats saying, "That's all right; I wish I were young enough to start all over and get into it." Ray Brown and Ron Carter, every interview they get, they say, "I wish these younger bass players would learn the 'real' bass." But what is

> *"When I get to be 50, if they're playing a bass that's only a foot long, you better believe I'm going to be right in there."*

a *real* bass? Ninety percent of the music that's being played or recorded uses the Fender bass, an instrument that they can't play. I think it's a drag when a man can't realize when things change. When I get to be 50, if they're playing a bass that's only a foot long, you better believe I'm going to be right in there. Brown and Carter changed the style of bass playing when they came up, and they were put down, so how can they forget? That's where the generation gap is. The first time I met Ron Carter, he said, "Do you play the upright?" I said, "No, not really." He said, "You should learn to play the upright." So I said, "You should learn to play the Fender, because I make as much money as you, playing my Fender." When I met Ray, on the other hand, he was beautiful. And Ray Brown can play about everything on his acoustic that I play on the electric. I have a lot of respect for Ray's ability and what he does. We were together in Quincy Jones' band, and we learned a lot from each other.

Why did you become a musician?

Music makes me daydream; it makes me plan and set goals; it makes me smile or feel sad; it makes me say something to somebody I wouldn't ordinarily say. In my jazz feeling, [pianist] Oscar Peterson, the Modern Jazz Quartet, the Three Sounds, [organist] Jimmy Smith, [trumpeter] Lee Morgan — those were the people I *heard*. And in those groups, whoever was playing bass, I heard it — that nice, soft *wang, dang, dinka, doom, bom*. In rock things, I still heard the bass. Jerry Jemmott was a great influence on me, as was Mervin Brunsin, who's been working with Larry Coryell, and also James Benjamin, who's with [tenor saxophonist] Sonny Rollins. Back in the early '60s, my favorite bass player was James Jamerson. He played on all the Motown stuff from 1964 to '72. Carol Kaye will say stuff like she did all the Motown things, but she didn't. They used Ron Brown and James Jamerson. And she'll put Jamerson's lines in her books! [*Ed. Note: James Jamerson concurs that some of his bass lines have appeared, uncredited, in Kaye's manuals. Carol, however, states, "All of the lines in all of my books are patterns that I played on records. Ninety percent of the runs were made up on the spot by me — the other ten percent were things that were written out but that I deviated from. The only line, in fact, that I ever played note-for-note, as written, was on the Beach Boys' 'Good Vibrations,' where Brian Wilson had written out a specific pattern."* Kaye adds that while Jamerson played on the bulk of the Motown material from late 1964 through 1967, she played bass on Motown sessions cut on the West Coast as "demo tapes" at $25 for two sides — and later sent to Detroit to be used as records. Hal Davis, who was A&R man on those West Coast sessions for Motown, says that Carol Kaye was used on bass.] Carol is a good guitar player; that's her instrument. I wasn't a good trumpet player, and I wasn't a good guitar player, and my bass playing might have inflections from those two instruments. But it's a schooled thing of listening to Ray Brown, Bob Cranshaw, Ron Carter, Keter Betts, Mingus, and George Duvivier. It's bass-oriented.

Do you consider yourself mainly a jazz bassist?

I hate to be categorized. The first thing they try to do is figure out if you're jazz, rock, or blues. And the way I feel, I can fit into all of those. I could play a bar mitzvah and get over. Basically, though, if any kind of label is going to be put on me, I'd rather for it to be a jazz label, because I understand jazz, it's a very high art form, and the average rock or blues player cannot play jazz. In the bands I worked with, there was always a big love affair between me and the rhythm section. And when you're playing jazz, the drummer and bass player should complement each other — they should be listening to, looking at, and loving each other.

– Funk & Blues –

– BOOTSY COLLINS –

BY TOM MULHERN – APRIL 1979

JON SIEVERT

FUNK IS *THE* WAY of life for William Collins, the bass guitarist better known to his fans as Bootsy. At the age of 27 he is already a veteran, having lent his bass lines to James Brown, Bill Doggett, Etta James, and Parliament/Funkadelic. He is currently the leader of his own group, Bootsy's Rubber Band.

Flashing his star-shaped spectacles and star-shaped bass, and sporting his star-emblazoned attire, Bootsy looks like something from outer space — or as he envisions, from a cosmic cartoon. His sidereal demeanor, however, doesn't end with the visuals — armed with an arsenal of electronic effects, Bootsy is the epitome of the astral bassist. The sounds he makes don't always seem to match up to the physical characteristics of the instrument; indeed, they sound as if they were produced by a synthesizer, or even several synthesizers.

Bootsy's message of space-age funk is obviously getting through. Of his three albums with the Rubber Band released since 1976, two have gone gold: *Aah. . . The Name Is Bootsy, Baby* and *Bootsy? Player Of The Year.* The only album that didn't reach the mark was the first, *Stretchin' Out In Bootsy's Rubber Band.* All over the United States, the Rubber Band plays to sell-out crowds in large halls.

When did you first get into music?

What really started me off was listening to my brother Catfish [Phelps Collins], who was playing a guitar all the time. He had a little band that I was always seeing around the house. Hearing them play really got me into it. As a matter of fact, when I was about nine, I used to play my brother's guitar when he wasn't around.

What kind of guitar did he have?

At that time he had an Epiphone solidbody electric. In fact, it had the red-colored wood and two pickups. What was happening then was the single pickup, but this guitar was one of the first double-pickup guitars I ever saw, and it had a tremolo bar.

So Catfish was your first inspiration to play?

Yeah. He was, and so was Lonnie Mack, who was playing a lot of guitar then. Everybody was trying to play like him. Both Catfish and I were, too; I wanted to play some of those tougher things.

Did your brother teach you any licks or techniques?

No, he didn't really teach me; I just watched a lot. He *wouldn't* teach me — he was older. You know how older brothers treat younger brothers: "Get away, kid, you bother me," and all that.

Did you learn from any chord books then?

Not really; I just listened to the radio and played what I heard.

Did you use your brother's guitar when you first started playing in bands?

No, I didn't. I just used it to learn. I kept asking my mom about getting me a guitar of my own, so she finally got me one. It was a Silvertone — a $29.95 job. It was a greenish-blue solidbody electric with a white pickup on it. That guitar was really pretty nice, and I turned it into a bass later. I just put four strings on it. Actually, my true ambition was to play guitar in a group with my brother, but he played guitar and was much better at it than me. So, I said I might as well change this thing into a bass.

What kind of amp did you use?

I didn't have one of my own, so I used to sneak my brother's. He had a Gretsch — a little bitty job.

What was your first band experience playing bass?

Well, in school we used to have talent shows, and I just messed around then. But the first band I really got into was my brother's. There were three of us in it — myself, the drummer Frankie Waddy, and Catfish. We called ourselves the Pacemakers. That was around 1967. We were doing things by Lonnie Mack and songs like "Peter Gunn," and of course we were into James Brown. We did the stuff that was happening. When I was about 15 or 16 at King Studio [in Cincinnati] we started being a studio band, and we did that up until about 1969, when we joined up with James Brown and became the JBs.

How did you get into working in the studio?

Well, there was a guy named Charles Burley, who was sort of an A&R [artists and repertoire] man, who did singing on the side. He went to record and he needed a band, so he grabbed us and took us into the studio.

Being so young, weren't you nervous about working in the studio?

Not really, because we wanted to record. We weren't scared. And I was the type of guy who would say, "Show me a stage."

How did you come to record with popular artists such as Hank Ballard, Bill Doggett, and Etta James?

In much the same way as we worked with everyone else. They were signed to King, and everybody saw that we were the best thing happening around Cincinnati, so everybody wanted us. We played on Bill Doggett's "Honky-Tonk Popcorn" or something and Hank Ballard's "How Are You Gonna Get Respect When You Ain't Got Your Process Yet" — those kinds of tunes. We were mainly on the last things they did at King Studio. Phelps, Frankie, and me went with James Brown when I was 17 years old, and there we stayed until about 1971.

What did you do then?

Three or four months later we got into Funkadelic. We left James, and there were still the

three of us — Frankie, Catfish, and me — plus we had two horn players [Maceo Parker and Fred Wesley]. We called our band the House Guests. So we were traveling around doing gigs for different headliners, such as the Dells. It was like an opening act. We just happened to be in Detroit playing at a club, and I was introduced to George Clinton [Parliament/Funkadelic's leader]. At that time he needed a band because they were losing members and going through a bunch of craziness, so we just hooked up. Working with them was great. It was just what the doctor ordered. It was something we needed, because when we were working with James we were restricted to certain things. That was cool, because we learned a lot from it. But just getting into the band with George, we found that we could do whatever the funk we wanted to do.

What kind of bass were you using then?

It was a 1967 Fender Precision. I used that with an Acoustic 360 amp. I didn't have any effects then, although later I added a Big Muff fuzz [made by Electro-Harmonix].

Then you quit the band in 1975?

Yeah, I guess you could say that. I just had to come off the road because it had started to take too much out of me. I formed the Rubber Band about four months later.

Where did you get the band together?

We got it together in Detroit — at the studio, really. I was flying everybody in and we would record, but we didn't actually start getting together as a band until after the album was done and we had a deal with the record company. Then we started really putting everybody together, rehearsing and so on.

What made you decide to be a front man?

Well, that's what I really wanted to be all the time, anyway. But I just had to go through different things to really find out *that* was what I really wanted to do. I had to learn different ways to handle myself, because I'd always been in the background.

Did you think it might be difficult to gain acceptance as a front-man bassist?

No, because it was already happening for people like Larry Graham. He came through and opened it up for bass players. I am not going to say it was really easy for me, but I think it was a little *better* because the bass thing was happening.

Who made your star-shaped Space Bass?

I had it made by a guy named Larry Pletz. He worked for Gus Zoppi Music on the outskirts of Detroit. I designed it. As a matter of fact, I first went to a guy in New York named Alex [Carozza], who made Rick Derringer's guitar. He said he would have done it, but he didn't want to put a guitar with that shape together because it would mess up the sound. He got really technical, but all I wanted to do was have the star-shaped bass; I didn't want to hear any of that. So I had to find somebody. I just ran into Larry.

What are some of the features of the Space Bass?

Right off, it has a star shape, and it's covered with rhinestones. It had Fender pickups on it when it was first built; one was a Precision pickup and the other was a Jazz Bass pickup. Originally, I had it wired for stereo, but last year I decided to go three-way. It now has three DiMarzio pickups, and I've got my bass going through three different systems.

What kind of amps do you use in your setup?

The entire system is divided into three different parts — high, mid, and low. But we're not just talking about amplification; we're talking about the effects in each part. On my highs I use a Big Muff fuzz, a Mu-tron III [envelope-following filter], an MXR digital delay, a Morley Fuzz/Wah, a Morley Power Wah, and an Eventide Harmonizer. The Harmonizer sits in a case that looks like R2D2 from *Star Wars*. It looks just like a little robot, so I call it R2FunkU. There's a sign hanging on it that says, "Can I Play?" Inside of it, there's also a keyboard for the Harmonizer that enables me to preset harmonized intervals to what I'm playing. That way I can play a note and have a fifth or a third coming out at the same time.

All of that equipment just for the highs?

Right. For the mids, I have a Big Muff fuzz, a Mu-tron III, and an MXR digital delay. On the lows, I use a Mu-tron Octave Divider, two Roland Space Echos, a Big Muff fuzz, and a Mu-tron III. I keep all my effects in one box called the Space Case. The highs and mids each have an Alembic preamp, two Crown DC-300A amps, and four Cerwin-Vega speaker cabinets.

What's in each cabinet?

The cabinets used for the highs are called V-32s. They have two 12s, one midrange horn, and two tweeters. The midrange cabinets are basically the same, except there's one 15" speaker instead of two 12s. Those are called V-34s. On the bottom end are three Acoustic 370 heads and six Cerwin-Vega cabinets. Two have one 18" speaker and one 12", two more have an 18 and a 10, and two have one 18" and an 8.

"Just as there was a time for lead guitar playing, it is now time for lead bass playing."

Isn't that a lot of equipment for onstage?

I don't play it that loud. I've just got it there so that I don't have to strain the equipment and everybody can hear. As a matter of fact, the whole stage is set up like that. The guitar player, the keyboard player — everybody is set up like that so there is no real strain.

Do you use the guitar and bass with this setup?

Just the bass. I haven't really got a guitar setup yet, and that is what I am going to be working on for the next trip out.

Are you using that setup in the studio, too?

I use about half of it in the studio. To get a good live sound, I use maybe two of each of the cabinets — two of the highs, two of the mids, and two of the bottoms.

How many basses do you have?

I have five. I've got two Space Basses and one Space-Face double bass; that's the one with the two necks and the star shape. It has a 6-string guitar and a bass. All three were made by Larry Pletz, but they've been modified since. I also have two Fender Precisions, but I had the guts altered to the way I wanted them: Instead of having the one stock pickup that comes on the Precision, I have three. The basses also have pickup phasing switches, and they've been wired with stereo outputs. In addition to those, I'm having another bass made right now.

What's it going to be like?

It's wired with lights and it talks by itself; it's got a built-in tape recorder — a cassette unit that plays back a rap, or interviews, or radio conversations.

What kind of strings do you use on your basses?

I use Rotosound Swing Bass roundwound strings. On my electric guitar I use Fenders or Ernie Ball Slinkys. I kind of like Ernie Ball bass strings, too: I tried them when they first came out with the nylon tape-covered ones, but I think I like them more in the studio than onstage — they give more of a point-blank sound than a ringing tone.

How often do you change your strings?

About once a month, probably. It's sometimes a hassle with that many basses. I take care of my instruments on a day-to-day basis, too.

Do you use flatwound strings on any of your basses?

I used to, but I don't get that really rough sound from flatwounds that comes from the round ones, which actually *feel* rough. Roundwounds make me play harder, and I like my bridge fairly high, so that makes me have to pull the string and stretch my fingers more.

When you record your bass, will you usually go back and double it on another track, or will you just play it once?

I just play it like I'm on the set. We record it on four tracks at once — three are direct into the board and one is the miked amp. This way I can use three different sets of effects as I would onstage. When we mix down, I can select the final sound. If I want the echo to be louder or if I want to get straight bass, we can play with it.

When you lay down tracks, do you usually start out by recording the guitar?

Yes. Guitar and "electric drums" — a rhythm box. My brother Catfish and I usually lay the guitars down first.

And later you erase that track with the rhythm box?

Right. After we get the guitars and stuff down and I've got my timing together, then Frankie lays down the drum tracks. I play rhythm guitar mostly, and my brother plays the melody parts.

Do all of those tracks usually end up on the final recording?

The only thing that gets erased is the rhythm box, which is replaced by real drums. About a week or a week and a half later, everyone else comes in and plays their parts.

Are there any particular fingering patterns that you work around?

It depends on the song. For instance, on the solo things I like to play in A or E. And whether I go to the upper or lower section of the bass depends on my emotions. It also depends on how the audience makes me feel. When I'm onstage, my playing is strictly a fill-in type of thing.

Then onstage you don't try to play the same way as you would in the studio?

No, I just play what I feel — all the time. I don't try to get it note-for-note. I couldn't do it that way. I mean, I could if I just sat down and practiced and practiced. But I don't think like that. I just play what I feel and what the audience feeds me. I also key off of my brother and especially the drummer. We all play off of each other.

Do you have any songs arranged so that you can just jam onstage?

When we are onstage, we usually have it together already, but certain parts of the show allow for us to play what we feel. But for the most part, it's pretty well set, like which songs are going to come first and which ones are going to be last.

When you pick with your fingers, do you play over the neck, or closer to the bridge?

Right in the middle. I'll snap notes for certain things; it depends on which effect I hit on the floor. However I attack the note and whatever pedal I use will determine the sound that comes out. It takes a while, but once you get it down, you know how to treat all of the effects.

Before you start playing, do you do any warm-up exercises?

Not really exercises. We usually have a sound-check onstage before our concerts to make sure everything is cool, and that's basically when I get to warm up.

Do you do any practicing on your own now?

Yeah. I have to because I am always writing songs. I don't practice as much as I'd like to, though, because a whole lot of other things are going to be happening now with the business. I'll have to get my practicing up to keep it together.

Do you think your bass playing has gotten better over the years?

I would have to say yes, with the different effects and things that keep me crazy. I keep expanding.

When you compose your songs, do you work alone, or do you get together with people from the band?

I work them out myself in advance. I have one of those little portable cassette tape recorders, and when I come up with something I'll record it. I might hum a little line, or I might come up with a new bass line and tape it. Then I push the "pause" button and sit there in space for another minute until another part comes to me. I'll record that, and the next thing I know, I've got a whole tune. Now my brother and I are starting to collaborate on some songs. We just really started that on the last album [*Bootsy? Player Of The Year*], because at first I was just doing everything by myself, and now I want to expand. I also work on my material with George [Clinton], who comes up with ideas for the lyrics and some arrangements. We try to make the music so that it really gets you moving. We try to keep an "up" feeling.

What do you look for when you're putting a bass line together?

The basic thing I want to create is just something catchy — a good, catchy line or something that moves me — because usually when it moves me, it usually will move the people, too.

What do you think the bassist's role should be?

I think it is time for bass players to come out

front. Just as there was a time for lead guitar playing, it is now time for lead bass playing. Larry Graham really opened the bass thing up, and I think he should have gotten more credit for it. His style became so popular that it looked like *everybody* did it. But it was Graham who really brought out a new dimension in bass playing — pulling the strings and all that. He simply should have gotten more credit. And just like my friend Sly Stone, it's a drag to see things go down like that. Larry actually started a musical thing, and it seemed like everybody jumped on it.

Just what is the essence of funk?

Funk is dependent on the rhythm. It's on the count of "one," you know; everything is on the "one." It's just like a pulsating heartbeat type of thing. I just usually stay to the basic beat, the basic funk beat; I don't really try to stand on any certain pattern for playing, just the movement of the funk, the rhythm. That's really the basic thing.

What made you head toward funk?

Well, I was always in it, but I just didn't know what to call it. I grew up in it, and it was a part of living and everything. I didn't know it until I did *Stretchin' Out*.

Since you use a lot of effects, do you think you were influenced by any guitarists?

Well, you know that everybody listened to Jimi Hendrix — he was the main one. I was more interested in his guitar playing than in Noel Redding's bass lines. There were just so many things Jimi could do with a guitar, and that's what got me off.

Is there any other instrument you would like to play?

Not really. I would have loved to have learned how to play the piano. But, you know, that is the only thing. I can play the drums. That was just something I wanted to do while I was in school — in the marching band — but they stuck me on clarinet because I was good at it. I had the first chair on that, although I really wanted to play drums. I stayed after school and messed around with the drummers. I was learning to read music drumming, but I had already learned how on the clarinet.

Do you write out any charts or anything like that?

No, I don't get into that. I'm more interested in whatever sounds good. That's what it all boils down to, anyway.

What kind of advice would you give to young players starting out in funk music?

According to my Pinocchio theory, don't fake the funk or your nose has got to grow with it. It's the main thing. Be honest and play on the "one." You have to move the people. The main thing is getting them up, getting them on the floor. And it's not just dancing; it's getting you up and getting the vibe up. It's all in the vibe, you know.

> *"I was more interested in Jimi Hendrix' guitar playing than in Noel Redding's bass lines."*

— LARRY GRAHAM —

BY TOM MULHERN – MARCH 1980

SELDOM WILL A single bassist influence a generation of his peers through the use of one technique. But Larry Graham's popping and thumping style has been adopted by countless bass guitarists in the rock, jazz, funk, and disco veins. He didn't devise his percussive approach simply for glorification or to influence other players, though. It was developed by his piano-playing mother during his teens so that he could deliver the same kind of punch as a drummer.

His snappy sound caught the attention of Sylvester Stone (a.k.a. Sly), and in 1967 Larry became a charter member of Sly And The Family Stone, the preeminent psychedelic rock/soul/R&B group of the late '60s and early '70s. Numerous hits by the band owe their distinctive sound as much to Graham's insistent, unique bass lines as to Sly's energetic vocals and arrangements. "Dance To The Music," "I Want To Take You Higher," "Stand," "Thank You (Falettinme Be Mice Elf Agin)," "Everyday People," and "Hot Fun In The Summertime" are just a sampling of the long line of songs that reaped numerous gold records and earned them a solid standing on the rock and pop charts.

In 1972, Larry Graham left Sly And The Family Stone, played a few studio sessions, and decided to team with a group called Hot Chocolate. The amalgamation became Graham Central Station, a driving, dance-oriented band that in many ways took up where Sly And The Family Stone left off. In 1973, the new band launched its debut album, *Graham Central Station*. Six years later, a succession of seven albums, almost constant touring, and a string of TV appearances have brought them well-deserved prominence in the disco and pop fields. In 1976 the band won *Ebony* magazine's R&B and pop award for "Group Most Worthy of Wider Recognition." Today Graham Central is busy preparing its eighth album (tentatively titled *Finger Pluckin' Good*), and Larry is honing his skills with the objective of recording a solo album in the coming year.

The only child of musician parents, Larry Graham was born in Beaumont, Texas, on August 14, 1946. His father played guitar and his mother was a professional pianist. When Larry was three, he and his mother relocated to Oakland, California. The lure of playing music was strong for Larry, but when he was five his inclination was to learn dancing. By the time he was seven years old, though, he had begun piano lessons, which continued through junior high school.

In seventh grade he began playing drums, and shortly after that, his father gave him his guitar — an Epiphone single-pickup hollowbody electric — and an old Fender amp. After nailing down his first guitar rudiments, Graham joined a band of friends. "It's funny," he says. "I was such a little fella, and everybody used to crack up when they saw me with that big guitar. It was a riot — the guitar was almost as big as me." He eventually grew into the instrument, and continued using it as his main axe for the next few years. Then love at first sight occurred when Larry saw the rock and roll guitar of his dreams in the window of a local music store. "I saw this skinny, white, solidbody Supro that was trimmed in black and gold, and I just ran home," he recalls. "My grandmother, who was taking care of me while my mother was on the road, was there, and I said, 'You've got to see this guitar; you've got to see it!' So she went down there with me and bought it for me."

Equipment fever caught hold of Graham, and he soon bought a new Supro amp to match his new guitar. With this gear he was ready to cook, and he began writing songs. His band, the 5 Riffs, played original music and Top 10 songs, as well as some from the rock and R&B veins. In 1960, the group recorded a single for Sphinx Records, a small company which distributed it in the San Francisco/Bay Area. It didn't move mountains, but it gave Larry a chance to play in the studio.

By the time Larry was 15, his mother had quit playing on the road, so the two joined forces, and along with the 5 Riffs' drummer formed the Dell Graham Trio. They performed in Bay Area lounges and clubs, and Larry doubled on guitar and organ. He also began using the organ's bass pedals while playing his guitar. The added bottom end quickly became a major part of the group's sound, and when the organ broke down just before a busy weekend, Larry decided to rent a bass guitar. "I got a solidbody St. George," he says. "I liked the way it felt and sounded, so I kept it. Eventually my mother and I decided we would just be a duo, and we let our drummer go. That's when I started to develop the style of playing that I have now — thumping and plucking. I tried to get the rhythm thing happening in order to compensate for the lack of snare and bass drum. I had gotten used to hearing those drums, so I just had to fill in for them."

For the next four years Larry developed his style and began catching people's ears in local lounges. While working in a club in San Francisco in early 1967, he earned an anonymous admirer who had heard that a disc jockey and record producer named Sly Stone was starting a group. She called the radio station constantly, urging Sly to check out this incredible young bassist. Larry says, "She was bugging him for a long time, and finally he came to see what she was talking about. He was impressed by my style of playing, and seeing as how he was trying to start a

"I tried to get the rhythm thing happening in order to compensate for the lack of snare and bass drum."

whole new thing, my style was perfect. Unfortunately, the lady who told Sly about me split — I never saw her again, and I don't know who she was. Maybe one day a little old lady will walk up to me and tell me."

The new band consisted of Larry, vocalist Sly, guitarist Freddie Stone (Sly's brother), drummer Greg Errico, trumpeter Cynthia Robinson, vocalist/keyboardist Rosie Stone, and saxophonist Jerry Martini. The group blended jazz, psychedelic rock, soul, and rhythm and blues into their own distinctive style, nurturing it in practice sessions in the basement of Sly's San Francisco home.

Their first gigs were local — San Francisco, Oakland, Hayward, Redwood City — but by the end of 1967 they had kicked up enough dust to get themselves booked into major clubs and concert halls in Los Angeles, Las Vegas, New York, and Chicago, usually as a backup group for better-known rock bands. Larry was using a Fender Jazz Bass with a Fender Bassman amp but found that he needed a more powerful setup for larger halls, and he bought four Sunn amps and cabinets with two 15s in each. Sly And The Family Stone's first album, *A Whole New Thing,* was released in October 1967, but it was their hit single "Dance To The Music," put out in February '68, that brought them a burst of national recognition.

"Our first headline gig was in New York at the Fillmore East," Larry recalls. "Jimi Hendrix opened for us. That was something!" Now that he was playing bigger venues, Larry began using four Fender Dual Showman amps, eventually switching to four Acoustic 360s. If people got a dose of prominent bass work on records, they got an equally large dose in concert. "One thing everyone remembered was the floor shaking from the bass," he says. "Those Acoustics were right on the money, and they had a built-in fuzztone. When you turned that on, it just rattled your chest."

In the studio, Larry used his Jazz Bass, his Bassman amp, and a Maestro fuzztone. The fuzztone was overdubbed on "Dance To The Music" [from *Greatest Hits*] and "Sex Machine" [from *Stand!*] Larry says that he didn't overdub on other songs, though. "Because of my thumping and popping, everyone thought I was overdubbing. And on 'Sing A Simple Song' [*Greatest Hits*] I sang the line, 'Livin', lovin', overdubbin',' and everyone thought, 'That's how he does it.' Even on 'Thank You (Falettinme Be Mice Elf Agin)' [*Greatest Hits*], I didn't overdub, although it sounds like it. But I did have a different bass — another Jazz by then. I called this bass Flash. I used a Dual Showman with a lot of treble and a lot of bass to get that sound. Plus, all basses — even the same model — sound different. Flash was the bass I loved the most out of all that I've had; it was stolen in New York, though — a real heartbreaker."

Less than two years after the band's inception, they played at Woodstock in August 1969, before a staggeringly large crowd of well over 300,000. Larry and the band dazzled the audience as they blasted out a set of their best material at 3:00 in the morning. And Larry was no less dazzled by the size of the crowd: "I didn't expect to see that many people. I didn't know what it would feel like until I walked out onstage; I just had no conception of how many people were there, because most of the time we were in the backstage area. But when you get up onstage you can really appreciate it. Boy! There were people for days, as far as you could see left and right. When we finished, they were all hollering; it was really something to hear."

Other festivals — such as the Isle of Wight — were livened up by the group, and Larry's unique style became better known throughout the world. "I'm really glad I didn't listen to other bass players," he says on reflection. "There was nobody else doing what I was into — no one to listen to who could encourage me to keep going in that direction. By the time the Family Stone started, I already realized that I was doing something different.

"I never was too interested in listening to any particular bass players, because I was playing such a variety of music that no one bassist covered all my interests. My mother and I had played some Top 10 tunes, a lot of standards and jazz songs, a little country and western, and some blues. My favorites were a lot of old standards and Ray Charles things. We mixed up a good variety because the nightclub clientele wanted to hear all different things. If I were to only listen to an individual musician, I wouldn't have benefited as I did from all the different kinds of music."

In 1972 Larry left the band, even though he had no solid plans for the future. "Sly And The Family Stone got into the wrong direction, and I just ended up not being into it," he says. "My intentions weren't to get

"Because of my thumping and popping, everyone thought I was overdubbing."

out so that I could start my own group. I didn't know what I would do — what direction I would go in."

Since 1969, Larry had spent a great deal of his free time producing Hot Chocolate (a different band than the one of the same name that hit the charts in the late 1970s). He was writing songs for them, but wasn't seriously entertaining thoughts of joining them. But after a few sessions as a sideman for B.J. Rogers and Betty Davis, Larry was convinced that forming his own group might be the right idea after all.

The sextet, formed in late 1972, consisted of Larry, singer Patrice Banks, drummer Willie Sparks, keyboardists Robert Sam and Hershall Kennedy, and guitarist David Vega. They wasted no time, and by January 1973 they were playing concerts. By the end of the year, their first LP, *Graham Central Station*, was in the stores and getting airplay nationwide.

The band's slick, high-technology sound demanded changes in Graham's gear to give him more punch. His equipment manager, Chris Becker, designed a mammoth amplification system. A custom-built preamp with volume, treble, midrange, bass, reverb, and master volume controls is used in conjunction with three Cerwin-Vega power amps in a triamplification arrangement. A total of 18 speaker cabinets, made of birch plywood with combinations of 18s, 12s, 10s, and 5s — a total of 52 speakers — is used to handle the 3,000 watts of power. An add-on unit, consisting of a fuzztone from an Acoustic 360 amp, is integrated into the setup.

Larry also has an MXR Flanger and a ProCo Sound Juggernaut fuzztone. He has other effects, such as an Eventide Harmonizer and a 360 Systems bass synthesizer, but he uses them sparingly in recording and never in concert.

His main instrument is still a Fender Jazz Bass, which he ordered with a special silver-sparkle finish. It has had a Plexiglas mirror pickguard added, as well as a Leo Quan Badass brass bridge, a brass nut, and DiMarzio pickups. Graham uses this bass not only for live performances, but also as his main axe for recording. To obtain the most clarity, he runs it directly into the recording console, although on some songs such as "Earthquake" [from *Now Do U Wanta Dance*] he uses his huge amp setup for the sheer massiveness of the sound.

In the past decade, Graham has accumulated several other basses, including an Alembic long-scale, a Kramer, another Jazz Bass, a Fender Precision, an

Ibanez Musician, a Fender Bass VI 6-string bass, a Mexican acoustic 4-string bass, and a Vox Sidewinder IV, which he describes as "a big hollowbody with the Mickey Mouse ears [two cutaways]. It has built-in distortion and treble and bass boosters, plus an electronic tuner that gives you a G note." Larry also has a few guitars, including a Fender Stratocaster and a Gretsch Chet Atkins, even though they don't get anywhere near as much use as his basses.

Ever since he began playing bass, Larry has used his fingers; even with his guitars he uses his fingers. But with the development of his thumping and plucking style, he found that he needed all of his right-hand fingers free and in motion in order to achieve the powerful attacks used in his music. He hits hard with his thumb and yanks on the strings, giving the resounding slap to his sound. Graham realizes that he has left quite a mark on the bass world, and doesn't want to change his style.

He is aware of what his playing has done to the sound of the electric bass in general, but doesn't view his style as an unapproachable pinnacle. "It makes me feel really good when people say that they picked up their popping from me," he says. "I feel like I've contributed to the world of music. But if anyone's ever seen me at a gig or on TV, they can see what I'm doing; the style isn't hard to figure out. You just have to watch and try it."

New embellishments, including harmonics and a variety of snapping attacks, are always being worked into Larry's approach. He plays daily, and believes that his improvement is steady because of his efforts. "As time passes, I feel I'm better at what I'm doing," he states. "I feel myself getting stronger now — not only as a bass player, but as an all-around musician."

Of course, he mentions that his years spent with piano lessons and playing drums, guitar, clarinet, and saxophone paid off in many ways. But one of the most important things he can prescribe for a solid foundation is hard practice: "A lot of people have the desire to play, but they don't really work at it. You have to make time to practice, no matter how busy your schedule is. You've got to be really serious about it. There are a lot of people who say, 'Yeah, I play,' but they're wrapped up in 90 million other things and playing is just something they do as a hobby. They have to realize that practice is the number-one priority if they want to be professional.

"I have to change strings constantly, because I hit them so hard that they're always breaking."

"It's also a good idea to take lessons. I don't know of a single serious musician with training who has regretted taking formal instruction, because even if they don't play the kind of music that they were taught, the concepts come in handy somewhere down the line — when they're writing songs, playing sessions, or whatever. If you ever have a chart put in front of you and you don't understand it, you'll wish that you'd had a few lessons."

Graham sees his diverse training as the basis for a unified style whose many facets help to keep his music fresh and unique. They also afford more freedom to think of music — and not just lines for one instrument — while composing: "I often think up a melody and then record it on my microcassette recorder that I carry around with me. I save ideas — bass lines, lyrics, solo runs — and then put the songs together. I record the tunes myself, I play all the instruments; and then I bring them to the band so that they can learn them. Then we record together. I occasionally write out chord charts, but it's not really my thing. It's easier to convey the ideas with a tape."

Meticulous attention to detail not only in arrangements and concerts but also in everything he does is another of Larry Graham's prominent traits. Graham Central Station has appeared on dozens of TV shows since their founding in 1973, including the *Mike Douglas Show, Rock Concert, Midnight Special, Dinah's Place, Soul Train,* and various Grammy Awards presentations. And although the majority of the shows are live performances, every so often one will come along that requires the band to mime their parts to a recording. "I'm really conscious of how I played the parts originally, how I breathed while singing, and little things like that," he says. "If I'm not going to be actually playing, it will at least *look* right. I think it's important; I watch other groups do it on TV, and I can see when they aren't paying attention to what they should be doing. Of course, I can't really be sure how much it all matters to the public watching the shows."

On the whole, Graham would rather be playing live, and playing hard. It's what he's used to after a decade and a half of hard work. His intense approach to playing causes him to break a lot of strings, though. "I have to change them constantly, because I hit them so hard that they're always breaking," he explains. Changing strings so often gives him a chance to try a variety of brands, but despite years of experimentation he has no real preference: "I don't stick to anything. I've used GHS, Rotosound, D'Addario — you name it. And I keep switching between roundwound and flatwound. They don't last very long in any case, so they hardly get a chance to lose their tone, regardless of what I use."

Graham's staying power in the music business can to a large extent be credited to his ability to look at his position in the world clearly without letting his ego take over, and assess his efforts so that he can plot a course — and not just try in an abstract way to top himself album after album. He says, "I don't look over my shoulder to see if anyone is gaining on me, but I do hear what's on the radio. And even if some-one thumps twice as fast as me, or plucks twice as fast, or plays two or even four strings at a time, it still boils down to nothing more than thumping and plucking. I guess I'll always be what I am, so I'm not trying to compete with anyone."

Unless the bass returns to the background of popular music, and thumping, plucking, and other Larry Graham stylisms fade from the scene, he plans to stay on his own side of the musical street, doing what he has done all along. "I guess I won't really be checking out what other bass players are doing," he says. But he also hastens to add, "At this point, a lot of them are still checking *me* out."

—JERRY JEMMOTT—

BY GENE SANTORO – MAY 1984

COURTESY HOT LICKS PRODUCTIONS INC.

WHILE HIS name may not ring any bells, you've heard his bass before, setting the groove for Aretha Franklin, B.B. King, Wilson Pickett, Roberta Flack, King Curtis, and Jerry Jeff Walker, among others. "The Thrill Is Gone"? "Killing Me Softly"? "Mr. Bojangles"? They all move to the Groovemaster's beat.

Jemmott is a classic musician's musician. Jeff Berlin admires him. Jaco Pastorius announces to anyone who will listen that "Jerry's the best." Arlen Roth, who's played with Jemmott in a variety of formats, calls him "the complete bassist." B.B. King declares, "As far as I'm concerned, he's superb, and all that he can get he's earned, and he deserves it. He's helped many people make many hit records." The list could go on.

And yet, despite the recognition of his peers, Jemmott remains largely unknown to the general public. He's paid his dues — 25 years in the music business playing one-nighters, running through countless jingles in the studios, gigging in house bands behind a variety of performers with new charts to learn every week. He's a consummate pro, but he wants more. "This is going to be my year," he says hopefully, and he slaps the table with his long hands for emphasis. "I once heard [trumpeter] Louis Armstrong talk about some cat that nobody ever heard of, and say that he owed everything to the way that guy played. And nobody's heard of him." He pauses. "I said to myself, 'That's gonna be you, Jerry,

unless you do something about it.' Well, I'm doing something about it. I don't want to be like that cat."

Jemmott started doing something about music early on during his childhood in the South Bronx. "Before I discovered music, I didn't have an interest in anything," he asserts. "When I was about 10, my sister, who's four years older than me, got into jazz and picked up a lot of Miles Davis records, so I heard Paul Chambers (the bassist for Miles during the '50s). Once I heard him, I said to myself, 'That's what I want to do.' It was as clear and simple as that."

Jemmott's mother had to find him a private teacher because the bass wasn't among the traditional instruments taught in the public schools. His formal training was in classical music, "but when the sun went down," he grins, "I was out messing with the fellows." At that point he was a member of the Boys' Club and played in their band, lugging his bass the half-mile to and from home. "Then one day this guy stopped me on the street and said, 'Hey, do you play that bass? Well, I want you to play in my band.' It was my first professional gig." The band's name was Smilin' Henry And The Rhythm-Makers; Jemmott was 12 years old.

It wasn't until around 1962 that Jerry got his first electric bass. "I was very much into jazz at the time," he remembers. "But the cats playing jazz were very much into themselves — it was all very free and they had no regard for the audience. That really turned me off. Now, I'd been going on some jobs where there would be two bands — an acoustic one playing jazz and an electric one playing dance music. It seemed to me that the people playing electric bass were playing music for people, not just for themselves. It was a real turnaround for me, because when I first heard the electric bass I swore I'd never play one. I just hated the sound — it wasn't wooden, it didn't sound natural to me. I messed around on it for a while. It seemed like child's play." So Jemmott bought himself a Zimgar bass and an Epiphone amp: "I thought I could figure it out right away. I had a gig that Friday, so I practiced for [*rolls his eyes in mock horror*] a whole *week*. When I started to play on-stage, I had such a hard time with the electric that I had to borrow the other band's acoustic to finish out the set. After that, you'd better believe I went home and did some serious woodshedding."

While Jemmott was switching instruments, he was also expanding his musical tastes. "I really fell in love with rhythm and blues," he recalls. "Junior Walker, New Orleans groups, all the Motown stuff — I discovered James Jamerson at that point. That was my inspiration. I learned one Jamerson line and that was it — I've probably been playing it ever since," he laughs. "He had the same background as mine — acoustic bass training, jazz, all that. He was a great musician."

Another great musician who changed Jemmott's musical direction and life was saxophonist King Curtis. "I met him in 1967," Jemmott reminisces fondly. "His bass player at the time, Chuck Rainey, was leaving the band and told King Curtis to check me out. I was working out of Small's Paradise, a jazz club, and so he came down. By then I'd gotten married and started a family, and my old dream of becoming a studio musician slowly started to fade. I was working in First National City Bank during the day as a document checker, and I wasn't interested in making music a full-time thing. I had a little girl, and even though the marriage wasn't working, I was still determined to do this family thing. But the bank job wasn't working either — I was tired of getting off playing at 4:00 A.M. and getting to the bank by 8:00 A.M." It was at this point that Curtis, impressed by Jemmott's talent and facility, asked him to join his band, the Kingpins. "I said nahhh," Jemmott smiles. "In fact, I turned him down several times. Then in March 1967, I had a vacation scheduled, and I went to visit my father in New Jersey. Curtis called me down there, and I said, 'Well, if he's going to call all over the country trying to track me down, okay, I'll

give it a shot.'"

Jemmott gave it more than a shot, and in return he learned a great deal about the art of performing. "I've never been in awe of people — I've respected their ability, but I've never been in awe of them," he explains. "And since I was coming from a jazz tradition, King Curtis wasn't that prevalent in my mind, although I enjoyed his music. But when I started playing with him, I got to experience the magic — the man was a giant. Working with him opened me right up. He showed me how to perform for an audience — his enthusiasm, his ability, his spontaneity, all created magic on the stage. It doesn't matter what kind of music you're playing; when you start moving step-to-step with somebody, when you start making the same moves at the same time, that's when you make magic from the music. We went on some musical voyages that were incredible, very spiritual; I'd never experienced anything like that."

Curtis had also used the lure of studio work to pull Jemmott into his band, but that aspect took a while to come through. "One of my dreams had always been that I would be a studio musician," Jemmott remembers. "I had this image of myself going from studio to studio carrying my acoustic bass. King Curtis promised me studio work, so it looked like everything was coming together for me. We were working together in the band, but there was no studio work. I said, 'Hey, what's going on? I want it now.' Ed Pedant, a friend of mine who was [vibraphonist] Lionel Hampton's bandleader, asked me if I wanted to play with them. So I said, 'Curtis isn't giving me studio work — well, *later* for Curtis. I'm going to play with Lionel.' He was going to Japan, where I'd never been; and after all, he was Lionel Hampton, the great jazz musician, and jazz was my thing."

His tenure with Hampton's band was brief, due to a falling-out with the bandleader. He returned to New York in November 1967, and started looking for work. "I said to myself, 'All right, I'm going to make this studio thing a reality, because that's what I really want to do.' Now, I had gotten a few dates with other members of Curtis' band — Melvin Lastie in particular. When I got into a real studio for the first time I thought, 'Wow, so this is it; you hear the music coming back at you and all.' That made me even more hungry for it."

While he kept trying to break into session work, Jemmott continued to play around town, making connections wherever he could. Six months after he had promised it, King Curtis delivered some work to

Jemmott — but not just any old session. Jerry explains, "He asked me to come down to Atlantic Records because the bass player didn't show up. That was the beginning. I'd done some other dates for RCA and Columbia, but nothing really major, nothing consistent. This was it." The session was for a Wilson Pickett tune called "Donna," which was released in Italy. "It was a big hit over there," smiles Jemmott. "There must have been 30 musicians for that session: Donny Hathaway had done the charts, and [drummer] Bernard Purdie and King Curtis were on the date. It was an all-star lineup. Well, I took care of business. I took it *out*. I followed the chart until I saw a place where I could put a little something in; I put it in, and they loved it. That was it. After that, they started asking me back for more work, and my studio career was happening."

Aretha Franklin, Wilson Pickett, the Rascals, and Jerry Jeff Walker were just a few of the people who benefited from Jemmott's blossoming musical talents during that period. Along with the likes of Duane Allman and Bobby Womack, Jemmott helped lay the rhythmic foundations for the Atlantic soul sound, which was in some ways as influential as Motown. Just ask Jaco Pastorius: "When I was 15 or 16 years old, I used to sneak off from school and go down to Criteria [Atlantic's studios in Miami]. I'd hide in the bathroom bent all over, just so I could listen to Jerry Jemmott. It was incredible; those were the sounds I wanted to make. He was my idol. That stuttering kind of bass line, bouncing all around the beat but keeping it right in the groove — well, they don't call Jerry the Groovemaster for nothing. He's the best."

Jemmott remembers those days well, especially playing with Allman, Atlantic's in-house session ace at the time. "We used to call him 'Skyman,'" he says, "because he had that long blond hair and, well, he was *out* there. I think maybe Wilson Pickett named him. Anyway, he'd come up to New York to do sessions, I'd go down to Muscle Shoals to do sessions, and so we played together a lot. He was great to work with, had great insight into music. Call it insight, intuition — all the great players have it. They listen ahead; it's about knowing where it's going. He was one of those people who could do that. The last time I ever saw him, he told me he was leaving to get a band together with his brother, and he sure did it."

Another guitar superstar who reaped the rewards of Jemmott's musicianship was no less a figure than

"I learned one Jamerson line and that was it. I've probably been playing it ever since."

B.B. King. In the late 1960s, the blues revival was in full swing, and large, appreciative audiences of white kids were paying to see bands fronted by Muddy Waters, James Cotton, Charlie Musselwhite, and Paul Butterfield; with guitarists such as Mike Bloomfield, Eric Clapton, and countless others playing and publicizing the blues. B.B.'s time had come. In 1969 he released two albums that helped put him across to that big white audience, *Alive And Well* and *Completely Well*. Both feature Jemmott's bass funking up B.B.'s blues, creating a catchy, upbeat fusion of sounds that challenged B.B. to move in new directions — with spectacular results. "The Thrill Is Gone," released as a single off of *Completely Well*, rose to #15 on *Billboard*'s chart, the highest slot by far that a single by B.B. has ever occupied. Jemmott recalls the night B.B. received his Grammy award: "I went back to his dressing room to say hi, and — well, he fell down on his knees [*shakes his head*] and started bowing down to me. I was so embarrassed. But B.B.'s like that — just a real warm-hearted nice guy."

Asked about his time in the studio with B.B., Jemmott is expansive: "Those are my favorite albums. We had no arrangements, no set patterns. The idea was to be innovative — and I'm very proud that the albums I made with him were instrumental in getting him to where he always deserved to be. Basically, the way it worked was like this: B.B. would stand there with the guitar, play and sing, and we'd get a feel off that. Although I'd never thought of myself as a blues player, this was the perfect situation for me, because I love to create. And here I was with the King of the Blues. So, I watched his foot. No matter what he sang, I watched his foot to tell where he got the feeling from. So whatever his foot did, I created a different kind of line based on that. That kept the feel of the music. And Herb Lovelle [the drummer on both sessions] is a real innovative musician himself, partly just because he's left-handed, and everything he plays is a little different. We'd worked together before, and we were familiar with each other's playing. We just went crazy doing what we wanted to do. And whatever he needed, we gave him. Some of those tracks are eight or nine minutes long. We'd just get into a groove and go on. He'd sing chorus after chorus of blues, and each time I'd come up with a different line, because that's always been my key principle in terms of bass playing — that's the Paul Chambers school. You start off here and just keep going. Never play the same thing twice; that's a no-no.

"Start off simple and develop to a climax," Jerry further advises. "Of course, with R&B you usually have only three or four minutes, but with B.B. we were allowed to do that in a more leisurely way. I played things I'd never played before. You can really hear it on those records, the way things just develop. They're really classics." He pauses, savoring the memories, and grins. "I remember at the end of one take — it's right there on the record — he said to us, 'What are y'all trying to do, kill me?' [*Ed. Note: This occurs at the end of "You're Mean" on* Completely Well, *which stretches out for almost 10 minutes; Jemmott and the other musicians on the session are credited with B.B. as co-writers.*] We *were* trying to, in a way; each chorus he'd play a different solo, and so we pushed each other, really. It was incredible."

B.B. King, for his part, remembers those sessions and Jemmott well: "He is a great guy, very quiet, very creative. In other words, he never does anything just because it's right to do — he likes to do it because it feels good doing it. He would come up with things that fit. Somebody may say, the chord goes this way; what you're playing isn't right. But what's right as far as the arranger is concerned, on paper, doesn't mean every artist is going to feel comfortable with it like that. Quincy Jones has a way of working with people where he'll get them all together and start them playing and just say, 'Okay, get into something.' This is before he writes anything. That way you start to play and gel together. Once you're doing that, then he writes from it. Jerry was the same way. He was very helpful with suggestions, very concerned."

The only time Jemmott played onstage with B.B. was at the Fillmore, where he met keyboardist/producer Al Kooper and Mike Bloomfield. He and Bloomfield hit it off and did a few live spots together, making tentative plans to record. Fate had other plans. "I saw Mike about a month before he died," Jemmott recalls. "I'd arranged for him to meet [guitarist] Cornell Dupree. A month later he was dead. He was a gentle guy and a good musician who knew exactly what he wanted."

Aside from a handful of live gigs, though, the period from November 1967 to December '72 saw Jemmott leading the full life of a busy studio musician: "My dream had become reality." He stopped

touring with the Kingpins — though Curtis still used his bass for all recordings — because he wanted to stay in New York and keep his jingle and record dates rolling. Then in 1971, Curtis called him about a special tour he was putting together. "I didn't want to go," Jemmott recalls. "I was doing my studio thing, so I said, 'Call Chuck Rainey.' And Curtis said, 'No, I want *you* to do it.' I didn't really want to, but my love for him and the experience of playing with him made me do it."

So Jemmott, Curtis, Cornell Dupree, Bernard Purdie, and keyboardist Billy Preston formed a high-powered nucleus, with the Memphis Horns on overdrive, for the band that recorded *King Curtis Live At The Fillmore West*. Among the inspired tracks on that LP is "Memphis Soul Stew," which sounds like a swinging encyclopedia of R&B bass lines, showcasing Jemmott's talent to fine effect.

> *"I've never been in awe of people. I've respected their ability, but I've never been in awe of them."*

"The promise of recording finally convinced me to leave New York," Jemmott says, reminiscing about the tour that took him all over the U.S. and Europe. "Ever since I was a 10-year-old kid I've had a tape recorder, and my passion has been to get down on tape, put it on wax. That's why I enjoyed studio work so much." When the tour ended, Jemmott left the band and resumed his studio life, hooking up with singer Roberta Flack in time to anchor her breakthrough record, "Killing Me Softly With His Song" [from *Killing Me Softly*]. He notes, "She was doing weekend work plus studio work, which was perfect for me; so that happened until I had the car accident in December of 1972."

It took Jemmott a long time to recover from the ill effects of that accident. His left shoulder broken, his nose smashed, and various muscles damaged, he spent two weeks in the hospital. Two days before Christmas, he was released, with a brace around his neck and his arm in a sling and bandages. While Christmas shopping, he was mistaken by the Yonkers police for a suspect they were seeking, arrested, and held overnight. One of the officers broke his right wrist with a karate chop. "My muscles, coordination, everything was all messed up," he recalls. "I couldn't play at all for a long time, and even after a couple of years I still couldn't do all the things I used to do. Sometimes I'd just get so embarrassed and frustrated . . . ." His voice hangs. "These things happen all the time, but you never believe it until it happens to you. It's made me a champion of peace and justice. I became a Buddhist in

1974, and that kept me cool going through 10 years' worth of legal hassles. It gave me a focus when I couldn't play. But now it's finally over and behind me, and I can get on with my life." [*Ed. Note: It wasn't until nearly 10 years after the arrest that the City of Yonkers fully settled the suit for false arrest brought by Jemmott, in his favor.*]

During his long convalescence and rehabilitation, Jemmott counted himself lucky that he had done so much studio work. "I lived off my residuals," he says, shaking his head. "I had gotten fed up with the record scene, where everything was so haphazard that they might give you a chord chart or they might say, 'Hey, it goes like this, pssst, pssst, pssst. I'll hum it and you play something with it.' I was writing tunes for people without getting credit. That made me turn toward doing jingles, which was a lot more lucrative and better organized. You come in, and 40 minutes later you're out; plus you get overtime and residuals, whereas in doing records you get nothing."

Jingles for products of every description — beers, sodas, banks, airlines, cars — made his work fascinating. He states, "That was what I loved about the studio: The challenge of playing something when you don't know what you're going to have to play. Because of my training, my reading was in good shape, so I could handle pretty much whatever they threw at me, and I enjoyed the challenge. But then after a while I felt myself losing my edge a little. I passed up all kinds of playing jobs, and that turned out to my detriment, because you lose that sense of experimentation, that sense of freedom when you're playing with people. So for studio work I created little devices to keep myself interested. Like one day I'd say, 'Okay, today I'm going to play everything fast.' [*Laughs.*] The next day I might play as simple as possible. So I'd give myself a framework with little goals to achieve, you see, to avoid getting bored."

Once he'd recovered from the more obvious injuries he had sustained, Jemmott began the long and difficult task of reschooling his muscles, training them to do what they'd once done with such ease, grace, and apparent effortlessness. For a while he drifted musically, not sure of where he wanted to take his instrument, even when he'd finished remastering it. "I'd done it all," he states proudly. "Productions, films, jingles, records, you name it. The desire wasn't great at that point to repeat any of those

"You start off here and just keep going. Never play the same thing twice. That's a no-no."

— there was nothing to gain from that. But around that time, Stanley Clarke was on the scene, and when I heard him in 1974 I said, 'Yeah, somebody's out there doing it. That's what I want to do.' Oddly enough, Paul Chambers and Stanley are both from Philadelphia. So Stanley inspired me to pursue a performing career. I figured it would take me maybe two years and I'd have it made [*laughs*]. I'd be out there, no problem, you know? It took me a long time to get my confidence back. I'd gone on some dates fresh out of my cast — phew, forget it. It just wasn't happening; the edge was totally off. It was very embarrassing, so I got gun-shy. That worked against me, too. People would call me, then they'd stop calling me," he explains without malice. "You see, you make work when people call you over and over again. If they call you once and you can't deliver . . . So I ended up making a bad name for myself." In fact, at one point, Jemmott actually changed his name to Rahsan Mfalme. "There were all these new people around, and I wanted to be a new person, too," he says wryly. "But that didn't really deal with the problems, either."

By 1976 Jemmott had regrouped, developed new playing techniques for himself, and come a long way back. Some advice from fellow bassist Richard Davis put him on a fruitful track: "He said to me, 'If you want to keep learning, you should start teaching. The best way to learn is to teach.' That was perfect. I had the desire — I really wanted to do something with my music again. And teaching taught me more than the studio ever did. It's a real exchange: I learn from what I have to teach, and the student gets something he couldn't get anywhere else. We study together." Jemmott still teaches, though he's broadened his approaches to it. He's authored the successful *Hot Licks* instruction tapes for the bass. He also joined forces with Jaco Pastorius on two projects, and is currently planning a program of regular instruction and a videotape instruction series.

In spite of his woodshedding and its payoff, though, Jemmott still found it difficult to reopen doors. "I had to do a lot of politicking, man, which was something I never had to do before. I had to learn. Used to be, I'd walk into a studio, do my thing, and walk out. I didn't meet anybody, I didn't *want* to meet anybody. I've always been shy and kept to myself. As a consequence, I didn't know anybody — that is, I didn't know who I knew. So I'd call people, but it was hard getting back in — very hard. In fact, in terms of studio work, you might say I've never really gotten back in."

Demoralizing as that was, it actually fit with Jemmott's new emphasis on performing. He put a band together called Souler Energy and played around New York, acting as bandleader for the first time in his career. It taught him a lot, but as he puts it now, "It wasn't really paying the rent. So, since 1976 I've taken on some kinds of work I used to turn down, like Broadway shows and house band gigs." He snorts, "Hell, I used to give those jobs away to people." But he did something he was quite happy with: A State Department tour with the Jimmy Owens Quartet and a European swing with the show *Ain't Misbehavin'*, based on pianist Fats Waller's music. Of that experience he says, "I was playing acoustic bass for the first time in 16 years, but I got back on it quick. It really let me know how badly I'd been hurt, because it was hard. But it made me stronger."

Jemmott also used his recovery period to broaden his own musical scope, and he began to write seriously for the first time. "Hell, people have told me they wrote whole tunes from one bar of one of my lines," he says, his voice mixing pride with a touch of loss. "So during the time I wasn't able to play, I started working with [arranger/songwriter] Don Covay. He taught me how to write, how to construct a song phrase-wise." So far, Jemmott has had limited success placing his material with other artists. He works in a number of different idioms, from movie music to disco, reflecting his broad musical background and tastes.

While he was retraining his muscles, Jemmott expanded his repertoire of techniques to include the innovations of the '70s. "I got into thumb-popping, harmonics, octaves, all that stuff," he says. "I've always been one to keep up with what's going on, and I've always admired other musicians who were able to do that. People want to hear certain sounds, and they have to be a part of your repertoire. I've always played around with harmonics, but I didn't really explore them until I heard Jaco. Anthony Jackson and Stanley Banks [bassist on albums by George Benson and Harvey Mason, among others] were big inspirations for me, too. You know, it's funny. The big bass players I listen to all listened to me. It's really strange

"Too many people overplay because they don't pay attention to the people they're supposed to be accompanying."

how things go around."

What Jemmott's devotees were hearing, aside from his undeniable proficiency and seemingly endless inventiveness, was his uncanny ability to listen for openings and subtle shifts of patterns, and wrap his rolling and stuttering bass lines around them without ever losing the groove. Jemmott never tries to dominate the sound of an ensemble. "You've got to listen first, and then play," he emphasizes time after time to his students. "Too many people overplay because they don't pay attention to the people they're supposed to be accompanying." Jemmott doesn't object to a bassist soloing, but his own emphasis remains the overall sound of the group and its music.

That same sense of perspective shapes his attitude toward his equipment. No collector, he sees his instrument as a tool rather than something valuable for its own sake. Until recently he used mostly Fenders, and he still has his Jazz Bass with an ESP neck and 21-fret rosewood fingerboard, which he prefers to maple. The electronics were rewired by Larry Brown to include treble and bass boosts and a preamp. But he's just recently had a bass made for him by Abe Rivera. Designed by Jemmott and Rivera, with electronics by Larry Brown, the new bass is a beauty. In fact, it's so impressive that Rivera has begun work on another similar one — this time for Jaco Pastorius.

Jemmott describes his new love: "It's a hollow-body, with the neck running through the entire instrument. The neck is made of bird's-eye maple and padauk, and the fingerboard stretches two full octaves. It's beautiful to the eye, beautiful to the touch. The controls are active and passive, and I can have the pickups in or out of phase. There's a volume control so I can do Strat-like volume effects. The pickups were supplied by Seymour Duncan, a specially wired set. We're going into the studio to finish fine-tuning it electronically with the mixing console. Because it's an acoustic instrument, it's a little bit harder to control feedback. So Larry Brown's going to take care of that. It's pretty much a natural instrument; I'm totally happy with it."

Jemmott plans to feed his signal into his Kybo speaker bottom, made by Transylvania Power Supply of Walnut Creek, California. It houses a 15" Altec Lansing speaker in a projection cabinet. "It delivers like a six-foot-tall tube setup, but it's only about the size of an Ampeg B-15," Jemmott explains. "With the

Fender 300B head, it projects to 90 feet before the sound disperses." Jemmott likes the Fender amp because it combines power with serviceability; he also prefers the crisper transistor sound to the warmer sound of tubes for today's music. "But the sound is really what you put in there," he hastens to add. "It's in your hands." Although he sometimes uses a phaser or an Electro-Harmonix Memory Man digital delay, he generally works without effects. His strings are La Bella Quarter-Rounds, which he finds wear well and are quite adaptable to his variety of sounds and techniques.

Although he has been through good times and bad, Jemmott claims it all makes a kind of sense to him now: "To do anything in life, you have to be suc-

"The sound is really what you put in there. It's in your hands."

cessful as a person first. If you develop yourself, it will come through your music. Don't make music your entire life. Let it be the expression of your life. That way, your music becomes richer, and you have something to say." He pauses, and then sums it all up. "Now you could say I've taken a dive. But I've gone down so I can really go up — that's what I feel." He mentions again his plan to put together an all-star big band, with himself and Jaco playing basses and such luminaries as the horn-playing Brecker Brothers and percussionist Ray Barretto. "In terms of numerology, this is supposed to be my year," he concludes optimistically. After years of paying dues, Jerry Jemmott sounds as if he's ready for it.

– VERDINE WHITE –

BY JIM ROBERTS – OCTOBER 1988

ANCIENT Egyptian mythology describes the phoenix as a beautiful bird that lived alone in the desert. Every 500 years it consumed itself in fire, and then rose from its own ashes to live again.

Not long after Earth, Wind & Fire was formed, the group chose the phoenix as their symbol. It appeared on their album covers and clothes, and — in a spectacular, laser-created image — flying above their concert stage. This year, the symbol took on new meaning for EWF. Five years after disbanding, seemingly for good, the group rose up and took the stage again.

The new EWF is a streamlined version of the old band. Synths and drum machines have replaced a half-dozen horn players and percussionists, but the EWF sound is still unmistakable: Maurice White and Philip Bailey trade vocals out front, the rhythms churn and cook, and Verdine White's powerful, fluid bass lines hold down the bottom.

The current Earth, Wind & Fire tour brings Verdine White back into the spotlight. The 37-year-old was too busy producing records to play on the band's comeback album *Touch The World* (leaving the bass parts in the capable hands of Nathan East), but he is gearing up for the next EWF album. In the meantime, he's trying to juggle his schedule to fit his own projects around everything that's coming up for the new EWF.

"I've stayed behind the scenes since the band's last tour," he explains. "I enjoy doing that. I've been doing a lot of producing. A couple of years ago, I had the opportunity of working with Level 42. They've got Mark King, who's an excellent bass player. That was a great experience. Before that, I produced Pockets, another band with a great bassist, Gary Grainger. Recently I've been working with bands from the Washington, D.C., area that play go-go music: Redds And The Boys, Little Bennie And The Masters. We've got some things in the can. There are a lot of good players on that scene, but they aren't well known yet.

"The record companies, I think, are a little afraid of that music. It's sort of an offspring of rap music, and a lot of the A&R [artists and repertoire] guys just don't know what to do with it. You see, things are different today than they were when I started my career. One of the things I had going for me was I had a chance to develop, album for album for album. Now you get your first album out and it has to be a hit — or else! Younger musicians don't have the time to develop, and that makes it difficult."

In tracing his own musical development, Verdine White gives a lot of credit to his family and the rich musical environment that surrounded him in Chicago. "My father was a doctor," says White, "but he also played alto sax. That's how he paid his way through medical school. He put on records all the time, a lot of jazz, a lot of Miles Davis. And as I was growing up, I heard many other things, too: Motown, Chess records, the Beatles. And, of course, my older brother Maurice was in the business, which helped a lot."

When he was 15, White began to study classical string bass with bassist Radi Lah of the Chicago Symphony Orchestra. "I got into that immediately," he recalls. "It was great. I studied from the classical technique books, and I also listened to some of the older jazz guys like Paul Chambers and Ron Carter — studied musicians. I was just concentrating on the instrument, the technique, and it was fun. Technique is good for you. It covers you through all kinds of musical changes. The better your technique, the more you can get across your axe, the more you can get through musical barriers, and the more you understand what other people are doing.

"At the same time I was taking classical technique with Radi Lah," continues White, "I was also studying with Louis Satterfield. He's a bass guitar player who did a lot of work for Chess Records in the '60s. Later on, he was our trombone player in [EWF's] Phoenix Horns. Satterfield used to tell me, 'What you do most, you do best,' and that was a valuable lesson. I advise people to learn the technique all the way through and through, because those with the best technique generally last the longest. Technique carries over, no matter what changes take place in music. Learn to listen to the other instruments; then apply what you hear to the bass — but always remember the purpose of the instrument in a band. You can forget that onstage. Remember that the bass player is there to hold the pocket."

White quickly picked up the fundamentals — "the bass was a natural instrument for me" — and began playing club gigs around Chicago while still a teenager. "As I got out," he recalls, "I had a chance to hear and meet a lot of other bass players. I listened a lot to Cleveland Eaton, who was with my brother Maurice in the Ramsey Lewis Trio. He was instrumental in my development. I also worked with another bass player from Chicago, Charles Clark. He was an avant-garde jazz player with the A.A.C.M. [Association for the Advancement of Creative Music]; he died young and never got any prominence. And, of course, I heard a lot of the Chess Records and the Motown tunes with James Jamerson."

In 1970 Verdine White got a call from his older brother Maurice. A couple of years earlier, Maurice had formed the Salty Peppers. The group released a single on Capitol Records, and then moved from Chicago to Los Angeles and changed their name to Earth, Wind & Fire. The band was starting to take off, and Maurice wanted his younger brother to be the new bass player.

Although most people think of Earth, Wind & Fire as an L.A. band, Verdine White points out that their original concept was rooted in the diverse music of Chicago. "Chicago is in the middle of the country," explains White, "so the band was really influenced by a lot of different things. There was so much going on in and around Chicago, from blues to avant-garde jazz. Look at all the great people who have come from Chicago: [keyboardist] Herbie Hancock, [singer] Chaka Khan, [drummer] Tony Williams, the group Chicago. And Michael Jackson's from Gary, Indiana, which is just outside Chicago. Earth, Wind & Fire really began as an offspring of that Chicago concept, but that sort of got lost in the shuffle because of the way the music changed."

Earth, Wind & Fire's emphasis on theater is a carryover from the early days in Chicago. Right from the start, their concerts have been total productions combining music with dance and special effects — including the "levitation" of Verdine White. (Look inside the album cover of *The Best of Earth, Wind & Fire, Volume 1*, and you'll see a picture of White, hanging sideways about 6' above the stage.)

"Coming from Chicago," says White, "we always thought of theater and music together. We'd grown up with the Afro-Arts Theater and things like that, and so we never separated them. Dealing with the visuals was never a problem for me. It was always part of my career. Even being up in the air — that was easy. I was just resting!"

From 1970 to 1983, Verdine toured and recorded steadily with Earth, Wind & Fire. The band racked up an impressive string of gold and platinum records, with such joyous, pop-soul hits as "Singasong," "Can't Hide Love," "Shining Star" [*The Best Of Earth, Wind & Fire, Volume 1*], "After The Love Is Gone" [*I Am*], and "I Wanna Be With You" [*Raise!*]. In concert after concert, they filled the biggest arenas around the world. Then Maurice White decided it was time to stop, take a look around, and work on other projects. After the release of *Electric Universe*, EWF announced its disbanding.

If you're not an EWF fan from the '70s, you may not have heard more than a song or two that popped

"Technique is good for you. It covers you through all kinds of musical changes."

up on the radio. Even so, it's hard to miss the way White's playing dominates the band's sound. Unlike many funk bassists who favor a sparse, percussive approach, Verdine is a melodic player. His lines are fluid and active, underpinning the tunes with the kind of rich counterpoint often heard in jazz or classical music. The band's arrangements are cleverly structured to make the most of White's lines. The horns are used for punctuation and emphasis, the guitars usually stick to rhythm, and the bass sounds *big* in the mix. There's lots of room for bass fills, and Verdine White makes the most of it.

Surprisingly, White is not a slap-and-pop player. Although he admires players such as Larry Graham, Louis Johnson, and Marcus Miller, he says he's never used that technique because "it never gave me an individual sound. These days, all the guys use the thumb, and you never know who it is. It all sounds the same. So I just play with the fingers."

White's right-hand technique is extremely efficient. He firmly anchors his thumb and keeps his index and middle fingers straight and low, so there's no wasted motion. He sometimes strays from strict finger alternation to play octaves (a favorite sound) much like a jazz guitarist — by plucking with his thumb and index finger. Fingering strong upstrokes, he also gets a bright popping sound on the *D* and *G* strings. Both techniques can be heard on "Shining Star" and several other EWF hits.

White's left-hand approach was shaped by his classical training. When he first began to play electric bass, he carried over the standard string bass fingering, where the ring finger is used to support the little finger in the lower positions. As he became accustomed to the electric, he realized that his hands were large enough to make the reaches comfortably with his little finger, and he soon switched to the one-finger-per-fret method. These days, he favors a relaxed left-hand grip that's much like a rock guitarist's. His thumb sometimes sneaks over the top of the neck, but when he's executing quick sixteenth-note runs, he maintains the strict classical position, with the thumb in the middle of the neck.

To keep up his chops, White still works on scales, explaining: "Scales are the key to understanding harmony and sound. Every scale is different, and it offers something different." Although his rhythmic feel is superb, he has never practiced with a metronome or

"These days, all the guys use the thumb, and you never know who it is. It all sounds the same."

drum box: "There was always enough rhythm in my head. When I was growing up, I always had drummers around. My father banged on tables, and my brothers Maurice and Freddie are both drummers."

With Earth, Wind & Fire, White co-wrote such tunes as "That's The Way Of The World" and "Fantasy" [both on *The Best Of Earth, Wind & Fire, Volume 1*]. He also began to get involved with production, learning a lot from watching different producers put together the EWF albums: "When we worked with Charles Stepney, it was a very structured situation. He was an arranger, and he would have all the charts laid out. Other guys were more raw; we would just play, and then build from there. And I had that classical background — having played in orchestras — and I had also played in clubs at night. I had the opportunity to see a variety of different techniques for putting music together, so I can apply all that in the studio."

White's first production work was for Pockets, a Baltimore funk and fusion group. Between 1978 and '81, they recorded three albums for Columbia and toured as the opening act for EWF. After that, Verdine worked with Afterbach, General Johnson, and Level 42. Although he's done sessions with the Emotions, singer Deniece Williams, and pianist Ramsey Lewis, among others, he doesn't consider himself a session player. "That's not really my thing," he says, "although working on sessions was a good way to learn more about production."

These days, White is looking to expand his role as producer. "I've done music for a long time," he says, "and I'd like to get into TV and movies, too. It's time for all of those to meet. When I was younger, I wanted to be the greatest bass player of all time. I think I've accomplished something in that area, and I've influenced a lot of people with my style. I'm happy I've had the freedom to play my style, and I haven't been restricted. Now I'd like to take that into other areas, as well."

Playing, recording, scouting talent, producing — according to Verdine White, they're all components of making it in the late '80s. "Now, we're not only *music* people, but we're *business* people, as well," he stresses. "That's the game we're in today. It's a positive thing, when it comes to making money. There's no use playing all your life and having nothing to show for it. Sometimes the emphasis on money thwarts the creativity a little bit, but as time goes on, things even out so there's more emphasis on creativity. You shouldn't have to play just to make a record company a lot of money. I believe younger musicians need more of a chance to develop over a period of time, like I did."

These days Verdine White is a Yamaha man. Onstage with Earth, Wind & Fire, he plays a 1979 Yamaha BB-2000 through Yamaha amps, effects, and speakers. "The Yamaha bass plays great and feels great," says White. "It's strong, and it works well with the synthesizer." The bass has EMG P-J pickups and a lever that drops the E string down to D. "I put that on myself," says White. "It's an idea that I copied from classical string basses."

White also has a Yamaha BB-5000 5-string bass, a new Yamaha BX-1, and his familiar white 1965 Fender Jazz Bass, which he still uses in EWF's live shows for "After The Love Has Gone." The stock pickups on all of his basses have been replaced with EMGs, which White praises for their bright, clear sound. He uses La Bella and Rotosound roundwound strings.

His onstage rack includes a Yamaha SPX90 II, PB-1 preamp, and P-2200 power amp. His speaker cabinets are a Yamaha S215 Mark 3 and S2115 Mark 2. White praises Yamaha for being very helpful in assisting him to find the right combination of equipment to fit in with the band's new, synthesized sound. He prefers to go direct in the studio, although he sometimes sets up a small Carvin amp as a monitor. While he occasionally uses effects, he says he's primarily concerned with getting a deep, full sound.

Reminiscing about all the different gear he has used over the years, Verdine notes that his equipment history almost recapitulates the evolution of the electric bass: "For many years, I used a Fender Telecaster Bass. Then I had a Precision, then a Jazz. The first amp I had was an Ampeg B-15 that I got when I was 16. I used that on a lot of record dates. Then, after I moved to L.A., I went to Acoustic amps. When I went to Europe, I used Marshalls; I really liked their highs. Later on, I had some things that were made especially for me, but the sound was getting a little bit outdated. So I decided to streamline and move into something new, and I got the Yamaha gear. It gives me the sound I need for controlling the band these days."

THIRTY BASSISTS:
A SELECTED DISCOGRAPHY

The following is a selected discography of the bassists profiled in this book. It is by no means exhaustive, but it does provide a good starting point for listening to these inspiring musicians.

Jeff Berlin
  Solo album: *Champion*, Passport Jazz.
  With Bruford (on Editions EG): *Feels Good To Me*; *One Of A Kind*; *Gradually Going Tornado*; *The Bruford Tapes*.

Tim Bogert
  With Vanilla Fudge (on Atco): *Vanilla Fudge*; *The Beat Goes On*; *Renaissance*; *Near The Beginning*; *Rock And Roll*.
  With Cactus (on Atco): *Cactus*; *One Way . . . Or Another*; *Restrictions*.
  With Beck, Bogert & Appice: *Beck, Bogert & Appice*, Epic.

Jack Bruce
  Solo albums (on Polydor): *Songs For A Tailor*; *Harmony Row*; *A Question Of Time*.
  With Cream (on Polydor): *Disraeli Gears*; *Wheels Of Fire*; *Live Cream*.

Stanley Clarke
  Solo albums (on Epic, except where noted): *School Days*; *Journey To Love*; *Stanley Clarke*; *If This Bass Could Only Talk*, Portrait/CBS.
  With Return To Forever: *The Romantic Warrior*, Columbia; *Hymn Of The Seventh Galaxy*, Polydor.

Bootsy Collins
  Solo albums: *What's Bootsy Doing?*, Columbia; *Jungle Bass*, Island.
  With Bootsy's Rubber Band (on Warner Bros.): *Stretchin' Out In Bootsy's Rubber Band*; *Bootsy? Player Of The Year*.
  With others: Funkadelic, *One Nation Under A Groove*, Warner Bros; Parliament, *The Clones Of Dr. Funkenstein*, Casablanca; James Brown, *Revolution Of The Mind*, Polydor.

Nathan East
  With Eric Clapton: *24 Nights*, Reprise; *Behind The Sun*, Warner/Duck.
  With others: Richard Marx, *Rush Street*, Capitol; Kenny Rogers, *Kenny Rogers' Greatest Hits*, United Artists; Philip Bailey, *Chinese Wall*, Columbia; the Jacksons, *Victory*, Epic; Don Henley, *Building The Perfect Beast*, Geffen; Jeff Lorber, *It's A Fact*, Arista.

John Entwistle
  Solo albums (on Decca): *Smash Your Head Against The Wall*; *Whistle Rhymes*.
  With The Who (on MCA): *Tommy*; *Live At Leeds*; *The Who Sing My Generation*; *Quadrophenia*; *Who's Next*.

Larry Graham
  With Sly And The Family Stone (on Epic): *Dance To The Music*; *Stand!*; *There's A Riot Goin' On*; *Greatest Hits*.
  With Graham Central Station (on Warner Bros.): *Release Yourself*; *Ain't No 'Bout A Doubt It*; *Graham Central Station*.

Stuart Hamm
  Solo albums (on Relativity): *Radio Free Albemuth*; *Kings Of Sleep*; *The Urge*.
  With Steve Vai (on Relativity): *Flex-Able*; *Leftovers*; *Passion And Warfare*.
  With Joe Satriani: *Flying In A Blue Dream*, Relativity.

Anthony Jackson
  With others: Al Di Meola, *Land Of The Midnight Sun*, Columbia; Eyewitness, *Eyewitness*, Antilles; Chick Corea, *The Leprechaun*, Polydor; Steely Dan, *Gaucho*, MCA; Chaka Khan, *What Cha Gonna Do For Me*, Warner Bros.

James Jamerson

With The Miracles (on Tamla): *The Fabulous Miracles*; *Miracles Onstage*; *Greatest Hits From The Beginning*.

With others: *Souvenir Album* (various Motown artists), Motown; Jr. Walker & The All Stars, *Shotgun*, Soul (dist. by Motown); *The Motown Story* (a collection including representative songs by almost every Motown artist recorded between 1959 and 1971), Motown; Martha And The Vandellas, *Heat Wave*, Gordy; Supremes, *More Hits By The Supremes*, Motown; Marvin Gaye, *Greatest Hits*, Tamla; Four Tops, *Second Album*, Motown; Robert Palmer, *Pressure Drop*, Island.

Jerry Jemmott

With B.B. King (on ABC): *Alive And Well*; *Completely Well*; *Indianola Mississippi Seeds*.

With others: Roberta Flack, *Killing Me Softly*, Atco; Herbie Mann, *Push Push*, Atlantic; King Curtis, *Live At Fillmore*, Atco.

Jimmy Johnson

With Allan Holdsworth (on Restless): *Metal Fatigue*; *Secrets*; *Sand*; *Atavachron*.

With Flim & The BB's (on DMP): *TriCycle*; *The Further Adventures Of Flim & The BB's*.

Percy Jones

Solo albums (on Hot Wire): *Cape Catastrophe*; *Propeller Music*.

With Brand X (on Charisma, except where noted): *Unorthodox Behaviour*; *Moroccan Roll*; *Do They Hurt?*; *Livestock*; *Product*; *Masques*; *Xcommunication*, Ozone.

Carol Kaye

With others: Joe Cocker, *With A Little Help From My Friends*, A&M; the Beach Boys, *Good Vibrations*, Reprise.

Geddy Lee

With Rush (on Mercury): *Moving Pictures*; *Permanent Waves*; *Grace Under Pressure*; *Signals*; *Archives*; *Exit Stage Left*.

Michael Manring

Solo albums (on Windham Hill): *Unusual Weather*; *Toward The Center Of The Night*; *Drastic Measures*.

Paul McCartney

Note: Paul McCartney played on every one of the Beatles albums, an extensive collection covering the period from approximately 1960 to 1970.

Solo albums (on Capitol): *Flowers In The Dirt*; *Ram*; *McCartney*; *All The Best*; *Venus And Mars*; *Band On The Run*.

With Wings (on Capitol): *Red Rose Speedway*; *Wings Greatest*; *Wild Life*; *Wings At The Speed Of Sound*.

Marcus Miller

Solo albums: *Suddenly*, Warner Bros.; *Marcus Miller*, Warner Bros.; *The Sun Don't Lie*.

With Miles Davis (on Columbia); *We Want Miles*; *The Man With The Horn*; *Siesta*; *Tutu*.

Monk Montgomery

With the Montgomery Brothers: *The Montgomery Brothers*, Fantasy; *The Groove Yard*, Riverside; *George Shearing And The Montgomery Brothers*, Jazzland.

With the Mastersounds: *Jazz Showcase*, United Artists; *Swinging With The Mastersounds*, Fantasy; *The Mastersounds With Wes Montgomery*, Liberty.

Joe Osborn

With others: the Carpenters, *The Singles*, A&M; Simon & Garfunkel, *Bridge Over Troubled Water*, Columbia; the Mamas & Papas, *16 Of Their Greatest Hits*, MCA.

Jaco Pastorius

Solo albums: *Jaco Pastorius*, Epic; *Word Of Mouth*, Warner Bros.; *Invitation*, Warner Bros.

With Weather Report (on Columbia): *Black Market*; *Heavy Weather*; *Mr. Gone*; *Night Passage*.

With Joni Mitchell: *Hejira*, Elektra/Asylum; *Mingus*, Asylum.

With others: Pat Metheny, *Bright Size Life*, ECM; Herbie Hancock, *Mr. Hands*, Columbia.

John Patitucci

Solo albums (on GRP): *John Patitucci*; *Sketchbook*; *On The Corner*.

With Chick Corea's Elektric Band (on GRP): *The Chick Corea Elektric Band*; *Light Years*; *Inside Out*.

Chuck Rainey

Solo album: *Chuck Rainey Coalition*, Cobblestone.

With others: Albert King, *Truckload Of Lovin'*, Utopia; Nils Lofgren, *Cry Tough*, A&M; Jimmy Witherspoon, *Spoonful*, Blue Note; John Handy, *Hard Work*, ABC; Sonny Rollins, *Nucleus*, Milestone; Steely Dan, *A Decade Of Steely Dan*, MCA.

Steve Rodby

With the Pat Metheny Group: *Still Life (Talking)*, Geffen; *First Circle*, ECM.

With Ross Traut: *Ross Traut*, Headfirst; *The Great Lawn*, Columbia; *The Duo Life*, Columbia.

Billy Sheehan

With David Lee Roth (on Warner Bros.): *Eat 'Em And Smile*, *Skyscraper*.

With Mr. Big (on Atlantic): *Mr. Big*; *Lean Into It*.

Chris Squire

Solo album: *Fish Out Of Water*, Atlantic.

With Yes (on Atlantic): *Fragile*; *Close To The Edge*; *The Yes Album*; *90125*.

Steve Swallow

Solo albums: *Carla*, XtraWatt (dist. by ECM); *Swallow*, XtraWatt; *That's The Way I Feel Now: A Tribute To Thelonious Monk*, A&M.

With others: Carla Bley, *Heavy Heart*, Watt; John Scofield, *Bar Talk*, Arista/Novus; Gary Burton, *Turn Of The Century*, Atlantic.

Verdine White

With Earth, Wind & Fire (on Columbia): *All 'N All*; *The Best Of Earth, Wind & Fire, Vol. 1*.

Bill Wyman

Note: Bill Wyman has played on every album in the extensive Rolling Stones catalog.

Solo albums: *Monkey Grip*, Rolling Stones Records; *Stone Alone*, Rolling Stones Records; *Bill Wyman*, A&M.